FROM
EMPIRE
TO
NATION

FROM

EMPIRE

TO

NATION

THE RISE TO SELF-ASSERTION OF
ASIAN AND AFRICAN PEOPLES

Rupert Emerson

HARVARD UNIVERSITY PRESS

Cambridge, Massachusetts

1960

Distributed in Great Britain by Oxford University Press, London

Publication of this book has been aided
by a grant from the Ford Foundation

Library of Congress Catalog Card Number 60–5883

Printed in the United States of America

TO
BILL AND NINA,
TISH AND RUPERT.

Preface

It is a hazardous enterprise to seek to squeeze between two covers peoples as diverse as those which are dealt with in this book. In the ordinary course of events I shy away from loose expressions such as "a country like India" or "a people like the Egyptians." Countries and peoples are unique and are not so easily lured into identity with each other save on limited and specific points. Yet these pages abound in large generalizations, including, I fear, some of the country-like-India variety.

I have thrown my scruples to the winds and joined in a search for uniformities on the grand scale. In justification I can plead only that I have made one unifying theme the central core of the book: the rise of nationalism among non-European peoples as a consequence of the imperial spread of Western European civilization over the face of the earth. With revolutionary dynamism that civilization has thrust elements of essential identity on peoples everywhere. The operation of similar forces throughout the world has tended to produce results in Asia, Africa, and elsewhere which are comparable not only among themselves but also with the effects those forces produced in the Western world in which they originated during the last few centuries. Great differences continue to exist because of the diversity of the original material on which the forces operated and because of the different times and circumstances in which they were brought to bear, but the global impact of the West has for the time being run common threads through the variegated social fabrics of mankind. The frontiers of Western control of the world have been pushed far back since 1945; at the same time the West — particularly if Communism be taken as an aberrant creed of Western origin — has scored an extraordinary triumph in that it is more than ever the model to which other countries look in their drive for development.

I have deliberately focused on the overseas expansion of Europe, on its aftermath in the rousing of the peoples on whom Europe impinged, and on the nature of the nationalism which is now coming to flower in almost every corner of the earth. Communist imperialism is dealt with only in passing, though others may see it as a far more legitimate topic than the anti-colonialism which receives so much attention here. I have no doubt of the importance of the forward surge of Communism, but I have even less doubt of the importance of the ending of the era of Western imperialism and the attainment by the peoples it overran of the ability to speak up on their own behalf.

I hope I do not need to add that although the colonial sins of others are from time to time examined in these pages I am amply aware that the United States is guilty of race discrimination on a massive and shocking scale.

My debt to former students is embarrassingly large. Over the years I have wantonly pilfered criticism, materials, and ideas from a number of student generations, without which I would be far poorer. To all of them I give my thanks.

Several friends and colleagues have read sections of the manuscript and have helped to improve it. Of these I shall single out only Karl W. Deutsch, then of M.I.T. and now of Yale, who has painstakingly read the bulk of it and offered invaluable suggestions as to how it might be made more adequate to its purpose. In particular he has characteristically urged quantification upon me as a means of building a solid foundation under speculations which otherwise float in air. For the most part I have failed him, but I hope that he may proceed to do what I have neglected.

Thomas J. Wilson, Director of the Harvard University Press, has gone over the manuscript with a care far beyond the call of duty.

The manuscript gradually assumed its present form through the devoted editorial and typing labors of Margaret Deems Cox, Elizabeth Jezierski, Mrs. Frank Carpenter, and Louise De Vel Muller.

It is a pleasure to express my gratitude for the generous assistance of the Guggenheim Foundation, a model among its fellows.

RUPERT EMERSON

Cambridge, Massachusetts
June 1959

CONTENTS

PART FOUR
SELF-DETERMINATION

PART FIVE
BY WAY OF CONCLUSION

PART ONE

SETTING THE STAGE

CHAPTER I

Introduction

Empires have fallen on evil days and nations have risen to take their place. The First World War left behind it the shattering of the great land empires of Europe, and the second brought to a climax the disintegration of overseas empire in Asia. Even though Africa remained temporarily a continent of colonialism, there was a final reversal of the tide of centuries which had swept the peoples of Europe into domination over most of the rest of the globe. The non-white peoples of the earth had declared, in terms which none could refute, that they were no longer prepared to accept the position of inferiority which lay at the heart of the imperialist system; and, in the West itself, the earlier firm belief in the acceptability and rightness of empire had been sapped beyond repair.

In 1917–18 the imperial principle, based on rule from above and heedless of the claims of nations, lost its major European strongholds and, in the peacemaking, formally surrendered to the right of peoples to decide their own destinies. Two unlike partners, Woodrow Wilson and Lenin, met at this point of national self-determination to give new life to the disparate doctrines which they had inherited from the nineteenth century. Germany, Austria-Hungary, Russia-in-Europe, and the Ottoman Empire — all gave way to a sorting out of the nations which, however much marred by compromise, expediency, and the hard facts of the case, meant the end of an old order and the beginning of a new. But the old order lingered on intact for the colonial empires. Self-determination, like the earlier principles of equality and the rights of man to which it bore its uncertain relation, had been proclaimed as a dogma of universal application, but in practice it was not intended by the Western allies to reach significantly beyond the confines of Europe or, even there, to penetrate into the territory of the victors. For the moment, a return to the imperially disciplined and Europe-centered world of 1914, despite Lenin's contrary views, seemed not wholly implausible, although it took no very discerning eye to see that the whole structure of imperialism was threatened by the "rising tide of color" in such ancient centers of civilization as China, India, and Egypt.

Far more global in its direct impact and in its implications than its predecessor, the Second World War made self-determination a living principle for the non-European world, opening the door to a full assertion of the nationalist claims which had been mounting in the interwar decades. The old game was played out: even by the time of the First World War the forward sweep of Western imperialism had already lost its momentum, and, in the years between the wars, the imperial powers could manage to hold on only by a series of concessions and rearguard battles. It was symbolic of the temper of the times that the Fascist attack on Ethiopia was generally recognized to be an anachronism even though neither the powers separately nor the League of Nations took more than halfhearted steps to block it. After 1945 imperialism of the old style was in full retreat, and the Charter of the United Nations, asserting the paramountcy of native interests, explicitly pointed the way to colonial emancipation as the goal. For Asia and the Middle East the continued existence of a few embattled European dependencies could not obscure the fact that colonialism was dead despite the fears of Asians that it might reassert itself in old or new guises. The reversal of the earlier situation is reflected in the fact that, where before it had been necessary to explain the aberrant independence of Siam and Afghanistan, it now became necessary to seek out the special circumstances which made comprehensible the continued colonial status of Hong Kong, Dutch New Guinea, and the more tranquil backwaters of North Borneo.

India's independence and the total removal of China from the Western sphere established a world in which the old signposts no longer served as useful guides, and had even become dangerously misleading. In the United Nations the emergence of the Asian-

African bloc gave notice that the former underdogs had become the highly vocal and watchful champions of the non-white peoples in general, and the colonial peoples in particular. That their zeal on behalf of non-self-governing territories strained the limits of the Charter was obviously of far less moment than that the newly freed peoples, often making common cause with the Soviet bloc, had resolved to liquidate colonialism. They have taken their destiny into their own hands and are insistent on playing an active and equal role in the affairs of the world. Thus, while the League — which might be regarded as a club of the European powers to which some outsiders were tolerantly admitted — had been generally unconcerned with the colonial problem, the more broadly based United Nations was constantly embroiled with it. Colonies had ceased to be the private preserve of their imperial owners. In a wider range, the era had passed when gunboats and marines could bring to heel recalcitrant peoples who failed to adjust their ways to meet the desires of traders and investors, missionaries and diplomats. Both the climate of world opinion and the balance of world forces had undergone a fundamental transformation as the failure of the Anglo-French attack on Egypt in 1956 dramatically demonstrated.

Much of Africa south of the Sahara remains colonial but immense changes are under way at a speed which would have seemed fantastic even a decade ago. The transformation of the Gold Coast into independent Ghana in 1957 opened an ever-widening gap in the walls of the last great continental stronghold of colonialism. In 1884 the Powers met at the Berlin Conference to lay down the ground rules for the partition of Africa. In December 1958, Ghana served as host to the All-African People's Conference which made the unification of Africa one of its central themes. Chairman Tom Mboya of Kenya proposed the slogan "Europeans, scram out of Africa" in explicit refutation of the European scramble for Africa which the Berlin Conference had formally inaugurated.

A great era of human history has come to a close — the era of Western domination over the rest of mankind. In many respects that era is too near to us, too much a part of our daily lives, whether we be of the West or of the East, to make possible the kind of objective and dispassionate evaluation which would be desirable. To undertake to be the historian of several hundred years hence or that always shrewd and penetrating visitor from Mars is a risky business. A plausible case can, however, be made for the proposition that the future will look back upon the overseas imperialism of recent centuries, less in terms of its sins of oppression, exploitation, and discrimination, than as the instrument by which the spiritual, scientific, and material revolution which began in Western Europe with the Renaissance was spread to the rest of the world.[1] To broaden this proposition as widely as does a recent analyst of British rule in India who contends that imperialism throughout the ages has been "the main process by which civilization has been diffused" [2] is to leap unduly far. The importance of more peaceful and egalitarian processes of cultural diffusion need not be minimized in order to identify the positive role which imperialism has played.

To assert that imperialism has served through the ages as a great diffuser of civilization is not to imply that every imperialism played the role of bringing a higher civilization to a people at a lower level. Imperialism, by definition, involves the domination of one people over another, of a stronger over a weaker community; yet it would be grossly improper to assume a universal identification of greater strength with loftier culture. Few today would back the optimistic claim of Walter Bagehot in the first flush of evolutionary doctrine, not only that the strongest nations tend to prevail over the others, but also that "in certain marked peculiarities the strongest tend to be the best," and his further, more elaborate, claim that:

> Conquest is the premium given by nature to those national characters which their national customs have made most fit to win in war, and in many most material respects those winning characters are really the best characters. The characters which do win in war are the characters which we should wish to win in war.[3]

The general superiority of Roman civilization to that of the bulk of the peoples whom Rome overran would not be open to much question, but Rome also overran Greece and was itself later overrun by the barbarians from the north, and the Mongol hordes imposed themselves on China. The diffusion of civilization through imperialism is by no means always a one-way affair. In the contemporary scene, Nazi imperialism would find few supporters as the vehicle for the advance of civilization.

In the case of the overseas imperialism of modern times, the peoples of Western Europe have carried with them the civilization of the revolution which they were experiencing, driven or inspired by the force of the revolution itself and increasingly endowed by it with the necessary greater strength. This is, of course, in no way to suggest that it was the deliberate intent of the builders of empire to fulfill the *mission civilisatrice* of which they occasionally boasted and by which their apologists justified their actions. Only in the rarest instances, if ever, do states or statesmen, embarking on imperial expansion, appear to have been swayed by the desire to do good for their fellow, but alien, man. Missionary zeal of one stamp or another has rarely been wholly absent, but the desire for power and profit, the rivalry of states and peoples, and perhaps even a sense of insecurity, have all been more constant factors in imperialism. The question of intent is, however, in the long run of less consequence than the actual impact of what was done. Even the resolution to hold back the peoples who were overrun by denying them access to the languages and instrumentalities of European civilization could do no more than delay the impact. It was only by staying firmly at home that the Europeans could fail to spread their new outlooks and techniques, and staying at home was the one thing which seemed quite impossible. The imperialist explicitly out for the profit, strategic advantage, or glory of his own people was likely to be as radical a transformer of the native society on which he impinged as the avowed missionary or modernizer. As one of the Soviet leaders phrased it, "Imperialism itself is the stimulator of revolutions." [4]

Certainly no claim is here advanced that imperialism was the ideal instrument for the spread of the civilization of Western Europe or that it fulfilled this mission with any particularly praiseworthy success. Its shortcomings are too notorious to require elaborate examination and include such blots on the human record as the slave trade, the decimation of Indian populations in the Americas, the disintegration of peoples in the South Pacific, or the atrocities of Leopold's Congo. The inadequacy of its achievement can be illustrated by a glance at the low estate of the underdeveloped three-quarters of mankind as the imperialist era draws to a close.

The skeptic may legitimately ask whether any other system of mass diffusion of civilization might have succeeded better, particularly if this system were conceived, not in ideal abstraction, but as set in conditions at least approaching those of the real world. Any number of conflicting lessons can be drawn from such great historical happenings as the spread of Chinese or Roman civilization, or of Buddhism, Christianity, or Islam. There remains, however, good reason to doubt that the non-European peoples could have been induced, without compulsion, to undertake in any comparable span of time a revolutionizing of their societies which involved abandonment of their established way of life. Similarly, it cannot be assumed that the peoples which embarked on imperialism would have been prepared to make the very substantial sacrifices necessary to an essentially altruistic program for the education and development of their less favored brethren. The warnings, issued in connection with the Mandates System, that the Mandatories should not be so strictly debarred from the possibility of profiting from their assignment as to discourage them from taking on the job, were not without an element of sound realism.

Even in our own enlightened day, the meagerness and spottiness of the efforts of the United Nations and of individual powers to carry out the much acclaimed task of promoting the development of underdeveloped peoples indicate some of the problems encountered.

Furthermore, it is questionable that we have enough knowledge about the immensely complex questions involved in cultural change to enable us to proceed in any planned and assured fashion. The current debate as to the most effective modes of securing advancement through technical assistance, capital investment, and other approaches, suggests that there are still great areas of controversy. In the colonial realm, the proffered solutions range all the way from the immediate and drastic remodeling of the traditional societies on modern industrialized lines — of which the Communists are the most vigorous advocates — to slow, gradual, and balanced advance within the framework of traditional institutions and concepts. For the French, and, in a different fashion, the British, the key point of attack is the elite which can serve as the link between the colonial power and the native mass; for the Belgians, it is the mass itself, or at least a substantial middle class, which must be raised as a whole without thrusting a Europeanized few above it. If no agreed formula can be found for dealing with the problems arising from the contact and interpenetration of civilizations, then something can be said for the accidents of imperialism which allowed a large range of varied experimentation.

At all events, there seems little utility in trying totally to reshape a great stretch of history which happened as it did, whether we like it or not, and which created the world in which we live. Of far greater significance is the effort to understand what went on, what heritage it has left us, and what lessons can be drawn from it. In these terms some part of the issue can be simply stated. In Western Europe a highly dynamic civilization developed which shortly began to overflow its borders and to flood the domains of many millions of peoples of different, and largely static, cultures. Problems of cultural adjustment and adaptation immediately arose. In the main, these were left to work themselves out as best they might, even though churchmen, statesmen, and others from time to time examined them with great seriousness. There is ample ground for condemnation of the governments of the imperial countries for their past failure to devote themselves to the social welfare and advancement of the alien communities overseas which they had come to dominate in a generally haphazard process of expansion. Such condemnation is idly divorced from historical reality, however, if it overlooks the fact that, until quite recently, these and other governments assumed no such responsibility for their own people at home. In addition, a substantial time lag usually separates the adoption of benevolent policies at home from their translation to overseas dependencies. Let it not be forgotten, on the first score, that slavery was outlawed in the United States less than a century ago.[5]

One basic element in the situation is that, by the nineteenth century, the power of the advanced European states was vastly greater than that of the other peoples with whom they came increasingly in contact, even where the latter had far larger numbers. At the outset, the English had gone to India as humble suppliants for trade and, at best, could hope for some measure of equality in power; two centuries later, they had achieved an organized strength which made it possible for them to overrun India by exploiting cleavages among the Indians themselves, to push China around at will, and to sweep aside such opposition as they encountered in Africa. This drastic imbalance of power in the nineteenth century found its perhaps inevitable expression in the imperialist system of European predominance in the world, taking, in some cases, the form of outright colonial rule and, in others, that of a looser control of the limits within which nominally independent states could act freely. The entire process appears to be far less the product of conscious human intent than of the working of forces of which men were only dimly aware. In sum, it may be said that the imperial peoples had both a dynamic drive and the power to make it effective, while the non-European peoples lacked the power to put up any sustained resistance.

It was an equally inevitable concomitant of the Western supremacy in power that the peoples who came under the sway of the white man should soon yearn to possess the secrets and the sources of his power for themselves. If only for the purpose of survival, it became necessary for any non-white people which sought to maintain its identity to achieve some mastery of the ideas and techniques, the institutions and instruments, which had enabled the imperial conquerors to take over the world. This sense of an otherwise impending doom led the Japanese to undertake their uniquely successful effort to pull themselves into the modern world by their own bootstraps, rather than to allow themselves to be pulled into it by alien force. In face of the inability of any of the non-European societies to produce a countervailing strength from within themselves, the alternatives were sharply drawn: either to seek out and adopt those things from which the white man derived his power or to accept a subordination to which there was no foreseeable end and which might involve disintegration as well.

In fact, the matter was only rarely reduced to these harsh and oversimple terms because, in addition to the drive for survival, there was an almost universal tendency within a newly rising leadership to accept the conquering Western civilization as superior and in itself desirable. If the first reaction of the peoples on whom the West imposed itself was generally a xenophobic defense of the existing order, the next phase was likely to be a swing in the direction of an uncritical self-humiliation and acceptance of alien superiority. The third phase, in the fashion of the Hegelian dialectic, was a nationalist synthesis in which there was an assertion or reassertion of a community with pride in itself and in its past but still looking, at least as far as its leaders were concerned, in the direction of Westernization and modernization. Those leaders were, almost without exception, men who had achieved substantial acquaintance with the West.

The most obvious element to be sought after by the non-European peoples was the duplication of the immense material advance which the West had made for the purposes of both peace and war. Increasingly this advance was seen to embrace, not only the new gadgets of all varieties which the West introduced, but also the scientific outlook from which they sprang, an outlook resting upon a revolutionary rationalism which undercut old ways of life and thought. The nineteenth-century efforts of the Ottoman Empire and of Mohammed Ali in Egypt to take over from the West only its military instruments and techniques were soon demonstrated to be futile. The new modes of transportation and communication, modern medicine, hygiene, and sanitation, and the achievement of higher standards of living through a basic reorganization of economic life, came to be adopted as goals which the non-European societies now set for themselves. Colonial governments came to be damned not so much because they had ruthlessly upset the old order of things — although they were damned for that too — as because they had so inadequately carried through the work of industrializing ancient societies and dragooning them into the modern world.

Education on Western lines for both the elite and the masses was eagerly sought. This education plus economic and other pressures brought a swing toward acceptance of individualism and a far greater measure of egalitarianism in social and political life. The Indian caste system was undermined by the conditions of factory work and of travel on train and bus, and the African chief became subject to the control of councils elected by commoners. There grew up a sense that the introduction of Western-style parliamentary democracy symbolized the attainment of political maturity — save for those who sought salvation in Moscow's brand of Westernization. Although a scattering few like Gandhi declined to acknowledge the West as a model, much the more usual reaction was to seek salvation by entering voluntarily into the new world, both spiritual and material, which had been opened up. All this is by no means to suggest that the traditional cultures were totally repudiated by Indians and Indonesians, Iraqi and Nigerians, but the non-European peoples in general, or at least the leading and vocal elements among them, have very largely acquiesced in the notion of the superiority of Western civilization which the white man so confidently held in the nineteenth century.

In one of its most recent expressions this acceptance of the West was strongly reflected in the first political manifesto to appear in the Belgian Congo. In 1956 a group of Congolese *évolués* called for a new nation in the Congo which would be a synthesis of "African character and temperament and the fundamental riches of Western civilization."

> A new civilization is being born from Belgium's civilizing action in the Congo. It will be our own civilization. The principal elements of Western civilization are penetrating ever more deeply into the Congo. There is primary education for the masses and an intellectual elite goes to the university. Science and modern technology are being mobilized against disease and want, and form the basis of a growing prosperity. The Christian religion teaches us the deeper meaning of life, the fundamental dignity of the human individual and the brotherhood of all men.
>
> But we have only gone halfway as yet. We want an all-round civilization. A growing number of Congolese wants to have more responsibility and initiative in the future. They want to incorporate in their national life other fundamental values of Western civilization: respect of the human individual and of his fundamental liberties, without racial distinction; the search for greater social justice; the right of peoples who have reached maturity to govern themselves; real democracy, based on the equality of all men, and the participation of the people in the government of the country.[6]

Imperialism spread to the world at large the ideas, techniques, and institutions which had emerged from many centuries of European history. By its direct impact, sometimes involving the migration overseas of large numbers of Europeans, as in the Americas, the older British Dominions, and North and South Africa, it established many of the forms and methods of the West abroad, inevitably disrupting in greater or less degree the native societies on which it encroached in the process. Upon those unprepared to accept a status of permanent inferiority — and, in the long run, none were prepared to remain inferior — imperialism forced a reconsideration of the entire foundations of their lives in order, by the adoption of the alien instruments of power, again to assert themselves.

Here let me linger briefly to glance at the inescapable, interminable, and necessarily inconclusive controversy as to whether the working of these forces represents Progress. Are the advanced peoples "advanced" in some universal sense, and is "development" a desirable thing? This controversy is inescapable because it cuts to the roots of human society and its goals; it is interminable and inconclusive because it revolves around values about which people and peoples will for all time differ.

The history of this controversy is marked by curious reversals. Setting out in the nineteenth century from the firm Victorian conviction that its new ways represented the true road to progress, Europe, in the twentieth century, began to lose faith in its own rightness and to doubt the justifiability of making its brand of progress the measure for the rest of the world. Buried in the remote past were such judgments as that of Macaulay in his famous minute of 1835 on Indian education that "a single shelf of a good European library was worth the whole native literature of India and Arabia." [7] At the same time that the West was questioning its faith in itself, the Asians and Africans were reversing the process by shifting away from their original rejection of the alien civilization which had been thrust upon them and were coming to a growing acceptance of it. After World War II, in the wave of devotion to the idea of development, as represented by the various national and international aid programs and the Communist insistence on industrialization, the two divergent views have met again in common acceptance of the desirability of Western-style change. But it would not be stretching the matter too far to suggest that if anyone now deserves criticism for seeking to overturn established cultures and supplant them with newfangled inventions, it is the leaders of the underdeveloped peoples and not the ethnocentric spokesmen for the West. To contend at the present time that the underdeveloped countries should remain undisturbed in their own cultures and not make the transition into the modern Western world would be to brand one's self as an old-style colonialist, striving to hold back the peoples who are beginning to come into their own. This proposition could easily be tested by observing the result of telling Mao Tse-tung, Nehru, Nasser, or Nkrumah that their countries should abandon modernization and industrialization and revert to their ancient patterns of life.

The case for identifying the modern West with progress can perhaps rest on this pragmatic ground, that the peoples most affected are themselves making such an identification, even though they often also want to hold on to as much as they can of their traditional culture. I will not try to argue here the case which can be made for the contention that what the West has contributed to the world has in it many elements which are both unique and a positive benefit to mankind. Respect for the individual and for the common man, the immense growth in power over nature and in the ability to organize men for their common purposes, the curtailment of disease and suffering and the extension of the span of life — these and many other similar things are not lightly to be dismissed. But it is evident that they must be weighed against the shattering of much of the intimate stability of social and family life, the hideous destruction brought by modern war, the misery of slums, and the totalitarian oppression of man by man. The best that can be said is that the West has discovered the potentiality of access to a richer life than was possible before. In many ways it has made appalling use of that potentiality. Always, in the background or foreground, stands the double question whether fallible man can determine with any assurance what constitutes the good life, and, if he can not, by what right he asserts that one mode of life should be substituted for another. Is the African village best left alone within its unbroken cake of custom, or should there be a frontal attack upon the superstition, ignorance, infant mortality, hunger, slavery, and tribal warfare which are the price it pays for its traditional existence? Let it be reckoned from the outset that progress does not come cheap. The villagers must pay a great price in being torn from their established orbits in order to achieve the boons which the civilization of the West can provide for them. Furthermore, the world of tranquilizers, hydrogen bombs, traffic jams, and supersalesmanship to which they are being introduced is still some leagues remote from paradise. Maurice Zinkin has put a part of the matter well in his comment that a Westerner who sees only the poverty and dirt of an Asian village tends to miss the point:

> He does not realise that he is looking at a community, most of whose people still today have the deepest of all satisfactions; they have a place in a community; in the East unlike the West a man knows where he stands with his neighbours. He may not like them or they him; they still have to accept him.[8]

These are, however, questions more fitted for the academic closet than for the real world. The forces of the West have been let loose, the cake of custom has almost everywhere already been broken, and the world appears to be moving along the path which the West has taken. No doubt the realistic issue is less whether people should travel or want to travel that path than whether it is in any fashion conceivable that the pressures which force them onto it can be checked. Ideas and instruments of incalculable power have been set in motion from a small starting-point in Western Europe. That their own momentum will lead them to sweep the earth seems far more probable than not. It is, perhaps, consoling that Asian and African leaders have generally expressed their desire to be swept along by them, although that desire is essentially irrelevant to what would at all events happen in due course. The process can be guided, delayed, or speeded up, but there is little reason to think it can be halted.

Of the mainsprings of mass action we have so far only the scantiest knowledge, despite centuries devoted to its study. We do not really know the causes of war or of imperialism, nor can we be wholly sure of the forces which, in recent decades, have brought the era of Western overseas imperialism to a close.

It is flattering to the ego of the Western world to ascribe the ending of imperialism to an advance in moral conscience which condemned domination and exploitation; it is equally flattering to the ego of the peoples coming out from under imperialism to attribute its ending to a combination of their new-found strength with their ability to persuade the world of the rightness of their cause. All these factors played their role, but there were others as well. On the Western side, in the course of the last half century or so, there have been fundamental changes in the climate of opinion. These have made Western peoples and governments more responsive to the claims of those under their domination and less ready to resort to the devices of imperialism. Although the rise of the masses to political participation in Western Europe and the United States had found them by no means uniformly hostile to the lure of imperialist slogans and adventure, the general effect of the spread of democracy and of liberal and socialist doctrines was to alert the public conscience to sins to which only a few had earlier paid heed. For the United States and Britain the Spanish-American and the Boer wars may be taken as marking the beginning of a moral and actual retreat from imperialism, at least in its cruder and more overt forms. The two World Wars worked strongly in the same direction. Some of the wartime denunciations of autocracy and Fascism inevitably rubbed off on imperialism, and the war-inspired enthusiasm for the themes of democracy, self-determination, human rights, and anti-racialism, although aimed in a different direction, were promptly put to anti-colonial use. The Russian Revolution added the flood of direct Communist attack on the imperialists and their colonial holdings. Moreover, the two World Wars weakened the sheer physical strength of the European imperial powers and considerably undermined both their political ability and their will to extend or even to hold their domains.

Another highly significant element is that imperialism has been drawing to a close precisely because it has been fulfilling the historic but inadvertent function of spreading abroad the dynamism inherent in the great Western revolution of modern times. No masterwork of synthesis was achieved under the aegis of imperialism, but enough was accomplished to spell the doom of imperialism itself. The peoples who were being driven into the modern world by alien masters had learned enough of a lesson to insist that, henceforward, they would themselves take control of their further advance into modernity. To sum the matter up in the briefest fashion: through global conquest the dominant Western powers worked to reshape the world in their own image and thus roused against themselves the forces of nationalisms which are both the bitterest enemies of imperialism and, perversely, its finest fruit.

The setting in motion of similar economic, social, and intellectual forces will tend to produce similar results, even across great
differences in time and place and in the peoples and cultures involved. More concretely, this means that the pattern of response
in Asia and Africa to the intrusion of the elements which have
characteristically shaped the contemporary West has tended to
repeat the original pattern developed in the West. In transmitting
to the rest of the world what it had evolved for itself, the West
loosed the same forces as those which had engineered its own transformation.

The new ideas, techniques, and instrumentalities which appeared in Western Europe had the revolutionary effect overseas as
well of prodding first the bourgeoisie and then the broader masses
into active social roles. As these classes rose from passive obscurity
to take their place on the stage of history, they repeated the earlier
European experience in turning to nationalism as one of the most
significant manifestations of their new power. Of African nationalism Thomas Hodgkin says that it is characteristically African but
still has definite resemblances to nationalisms elsewhere. He suggests that these resemblances seem more natural if "the rise of African nationalism is thought of as the final stage in a chain-reaction,
deriving its operative ideas originally from the French Revolution
— the doctrine of the Rights of Man interpreted as the Rights of
Nations." [9]

It is not the old, unreconstructed Indonesian sultans or Nigerian
chiefs, nor the unlettered and tradition-bound peasantry anywhere
who have effectively challenged the imperial powers, but the new-
style national leaders like Sun Yat-sen, Gandhi, and Nehru, Bourguiba, Azikiwe, and Nkrumah, who have drunk deeply of Western
education and Western lore. The first instinctive reaction of hostility to the alien intruder was, with rare exceptions, a futile effort
on the part of the old society to reject change. The Indian Mutiny,
the rising of the Mahdi in the Sudan, or the Boxer Rebellion represent essentially an old and anachronistic world. It was the turning
of the weapons — the ideas, the instruments, the institutions — of
the West against itself which swung the balance against imperial-

ism. The Indian National Congress, the Convention People's Party of the Gold Coast, and similar nationalist movements of a modern type were the ones which won independence.

Imperialism forged the tools with which its victims could pry it loose. In this sense it scored a spectacular success; but its success in diffusing Western civilization was markedly more limited. The peoples of the world are still far from having made even a significant approach to a single global level. There continues to be an immense imbalance of power and a gross disparity in standards of living and in working acquaintance with the concepts and techniques which have made the modern West what it is. The long-run trends may head toward a world-wide evening out of differences, but there is still a vast distance to go. At the moment, the gap between the developed and the underdeveloped peoples in material well-being and technological advance is still widening rather than narrowing.

The inadequacy of the way in which the task has been done is vividly illustrated within each of the underdeveloped countries by the disparity which exists between certain segments of their people in terms of acquaintance with the modern world. There are great variations from country to country and some characteristic differences between those which — like the Philippines and Ceylon — had a long and intensive experience of Western colonialism and those which — like Saudi Arabia and Afghanistan — had either no or very small contact with it. Yet something of a common pattern is discernible throughout. Everywhere only a relative handful of people has achieved any intimate familiarity with the West and its ways through education abroad in the imperial centers or in Western-established schools and universities. In India and Indonesia, in Tunisia and Ghana, it is this thin layer of a new, highly Westernized elite, for the most part concentrated in the urban centers, which has supplied the leadership for the nationalist movements and manned the governments which took over with the coming of independence. For the French dependencies, Bertrand de Jouvenel sees the main feature of the developing crises as

> a battle of ideals which takes place within the context of French thought and French political vocabulary. The main rebels against French rule in the French overseas territories are also the personali-

ties least foreign to France; they can be recognized as conscious replicas of Lafayette, Mirabeau or Robespierre. They are playing a role against France which is taken from a French script.[10]

The great base of the social pyramid, made up for the most part of the age-old peasantry, is far removed from these Westernized few who have become the heirs of the imperial powers. Poverty-stricken, illiterate, and effectively conscious of little beyond their immediate neighborhoods, the peasant masses have, to be sure, everywhere felt in some measure the impact of external forces and ideas and have come to some awareness of a new climate of expectations. Considerable numbers have traveled further in their direct experience of military service or labor for alien employers in agricultural enterprises, mines, factories, or government services. Yet, when all this has been taken into account and the mushrooming urban proletariats added in as well, the fact remains that the West has transmitted its essence to only a small upper crust while the people at large, inchoately touched by the new, have still not left the old. Nor is much of the new necessarily of any real concern to them: for the millions of villagers in Indonesia the party rivalries, cabinet overturns, and governmental crises of the capital are remote irrelevancies which barely intrude on the serious day-to-day concerns of life.

Such great internal cleavages obviously point to serious trouble ahead or, at least, to a long drawn out process of adjustment to a changing balance of forces. The inner dynamics of these societies, uncertainly edging their way into the modern world and yet reluctant to abandon their past, will be largely determined by the balance which is struck by the divergent elements developing within them. What manner of societies they will turn out to be and what role they will play are questions to which there can be no confident answers at present.

On a more material plane the same confused picture emerges. Roads, railways, and air networks, highly developed mines and agriculture, and rudiments of up-to-date machine industry have all been introduced, but they have not yet become an integral part of the lives of most of the people. Large-scale trade and commerce, banking and finance, and the upper levels of the internal distribution mechanisms tend to continue in the hands of the Europeans or other alien population groups, such as the Chinese in Southeast Asia or the Indians in East Africa. As direction and control rest largely with the aliens, profits are frequently drained off abroad. Unquestionably there has been a great increase in production and productive facilities, but the combination of this with the importation, however meager, of modern sanitation and medicine has brought about a surging upswing of population, as in India, Java, Egypt, and Puerto Rico, which has held living standards close to the age-old subsistence levels and threatens to devour all future advance. A superstructure of material modernity has been erected, usually directly under alien auspices, which interpenetrates the old society but has neither effectively merged with it nor taken it over. An inner self-sustaining momentum or development has appeared virtually nowhere except in Japan.

Imperialism scattered the revolutionary seeds of Western civilization in haphazard fashion over the surface of the globe and started them on the first phases of their growth. Its most important result, ironically enough, was to rouse against itself the nationalisms — and in some instances even to create the nations — which worked to make its continuance impossible. When imperialism began to draw abruptly to a close, its unintended tasks were only very partially completed. The world was still confronted with the necessity of dealing with many of the conditions and problems to which Western domination had furnished its own kind of solutions. Only the most naive or doctrinaire anti-imperialist could believe that merely by transforming colonies or quasi-colonies into independent sovereign states would it be possible to cut off the complex entanglements of the imperialist system without bequeathing a host of old and new problems to succeeding generations. Denunciation of imperialism in terms of its primary purpose of promoting the interests of the few advanced powers should not be allowed to obscure its role as a principal pillar of the world order of its day. The effective control of most of the rest of mankind by a small number of states, each acting in its own interest, has been a major social, political, and economic fact of modern times. Its drastic impairment forced a fundamental recasting of the structure of the world.

The principal beneficiaries of this recasting are the successor states to empire which have repudiated alien domination and taken their destinies back into their own hands. It is with these states, the nations which they represent, and the nationalisms which inspire them that this book is primarily concerned.

CHAPTER II

The Era of The Two World Wars

THE SELECTION OF PARTICULAR DATES to demarcate great historical processes may be justified primarily in terms of the convenience of the illusion that the seamless web can be tidily snipped off at certain intervals for study and analysis. Such global cataclysms as the World Wars of 1914–1918 and 1939–1945, however, not only hasten or retard existing trends, but also themselves set in motion forces which reach far beyond the ending of hostilities and shape the destinies of peoples only remotely, if at all, concerned in them. The colonial problem underwent so drastic a change in the thirty years from the beginning of the first of these wars to the ending of the second that it is difficult to discern even the dim outlines of the chaotic world of today in that still tranquil summer of 1914, only little removed from the age of Victoria. Whether or not it adds to the sum of human wisdom to categorize the wars as in any sense "imperialist wars," it would be difficult to overemphasize the influence which they had on the turn of imperialist events. As watersheds they divide an era irretrievably past from the uncertain future.

In 1914 the hegemony of Western Europe over most of the world was almost unquestioned, even though Japan and the United States had come to have ideas and dependencies of their own, and a great Russian empire stretched across Asia to the Pacific. Politically, economically, and culturally, it was a world which centered to a striking degree on the peoples of Europe and their offshoots overseas; they set its tone and served as the dynamic leaders of the international society. After 1945 Europe stood in the shadow of the two superpowers on its outer boundaries, and an Asian-African bloc was rising to assert the claims of the non-European peoples.

The decade and a half from the turn of the century to the outbreak of World War I were the last years in which a complacent colonialism could flourish as a part of what seemed the natural order of things. Even though liberal and socialist attacks on imperialism's basic assumptions were growing in volume and vigor, the belief in white supremacy was at its height. The open revelation of colonial abuses — of which the international demand for reforms in the Congo was the most notable result — was not seen as involving a repudiation of the colonial system itself. If it was coming to be recognized that a reconsideration of the methods of dealing with dependent peoples was in order, there was, as yet, no widespread sense that the white man's rule over alien races was necessarily reprehensible or peculiar. The racialism of the later nineteenth century, to which Darwinian concepts appeared to give a new scientific validity, lent theoretical and moral justification to the prevailing state of fact.

Nevertheless, by the First World War the old-style colonial venture had virtually run its course, although new dimensions of imperialism lay ahead with the continental expansion of Nazi Germany and the Soviet Union. The Spanish-American War had inaugurated a series of transfers of territory from one imperial system to another, but the only significant additions to the colonial domains from 1914 to 1945 were short-lived: Mussolini's shoddy and anachronistic seizure of Ethiopia and the Japanese drive on China and, later, Southeast Asia. By the middle of the century the frontiers of empire had receded far behind their points of greatest advance as the new nations rose to take over in imperialism's stead.

In 1914, although the Chinese Revolution of 1911, the turmoil caused by the partition of Bengal, and other ground swells were omens of what lay ahead, colonial nationalism was an almost unknown phenomenon. The not infrequent colonial rebellions, such as that of the Hereros against the Germans in Southwest Africa, were rather the dying struggles of the old tribal or traditional society than manifestations of the new nationalism. In 1945, few colonies had not been touched by it in some degree and for many it had come to be the dominant order of the day.

In contrast with the Second World War, the First involved colonial issues only slightly. Neither as direct causes of the war nor in the peace settlement which followed it were colonial problems of any great consequence. As far as the fighting was concerned, the limited spread of military operations produced a lesser impact on the colonial peoples than the calls made upon them, primarily by Britain and France, to furnish soldiers and workers. That many of the men who were thus torn from their native environment should have gone home ready to embrace new creeds and to seek a change in their status, if necessary by violence, was not surprising. A leading French colonial administrator has written: "The 175,000 soldiers, enrolled during the years 1914–18, dug the grave of the old Africa in the trenches of France and Flanders." [1]

If Ireland, a colonial problem *sui generis*, be left out of the reckoning, no colonial people seized the occasion of the war to rise in revolt or even to cause serious trouble.[2] Even India, so soon to be swept by political turmoil, took the war calmly and, under British management, made great contributions to the Allied cause. On the outbreak of war the pre-Gandhian Indian National Congress affirmed its devotion to the throne and its firm resolve to stand by the empire. In 1918 it congratulated Britain on the successful termination of a war fought "in the cause of Freedom, Justice, and Self-determination." [3] No more than a year or two later these resolutions of the Congress would have been incredible.

For the peacemakers of 1918–19 the only colonial issue which seriously presented itself concerned the German colonies and the Arab areas which the Allied statesmen had been so busily and often contradictorily dividing up in the course of the war. The Mandates System, invented to deal with these territories, is fair game for both idealist and cynic since it represented a new and enlightened approach to colonialism and was also a practical expedient for sharing the spoils of war among the victors without too grave a violation of nonannexation pledges. Taking the existing colonial system as a model, it imposed certain standards and restrictions on it and subjected the Mandatory Powers to a modest but unprecedented international supervision — which they, no doubt, assumed would be exercised primarily within the family. Aside from the Mandates the only explicit reference in the League Covenant to the colonies came in the catch-all Article 23 which included the undertaking of the members "to secure just treatment of the native inhabitants of territories under their control." This clause might have been utilized for a broad sweep of League activity, but very little was, in fact, built on its loose foundations. The one sphere in which the League and its neighbor, the International Labor Organization, busied themselves with general colonial affairs was in the attack upon slavery and forced labor — issues which, as the cases of Liberia and Ethiopia demonstrated, reached well beyond the colonial domain.

Nowhere in the period at the close of World War I is the slightness of the concern with the problems of overseas imperialism more evident than in the lack of reference to it in the entire debate over national self-determination. The ringing phrases in which Wilson and other Allied leaders proclaimed the right of self-determination had all the sound of universality, but for practical purposes that right and the corollary proposition of protection for national minorities were regarded as matters for application in Europe. The rest of the world barely entered in. Where Wilson himself stood in relation to colonial demands for freedom is somewhat obscure. At home he had earlier denied that the Filipinos had any right to liberty until the United States had brought them maturity and self-mastery, but late in his presidency he urged Philippine independence. In the Paris peace negotiations colonial issues, save for the Mandates System, played an insignificant role for him. Of the famous Fourteen Points only the fifth made any mention of the colonies, calling for a free and impartial adjustment of colonial claims, based upon the principle that "the interests of the populations concerned must have equal weight with the equitable claims of the government whose title is to be determined." It is symbolic of the times that the man who set out to make the world safe for democracy went no further than to suggest that the interests — not the national desires — of the colonial peoples should be lifted to an equality with the claims of their alien rulers.

Three days before the proclamation of the Fourteen Points, Lloyd George outbid Wilson by proposing that the peace conference, in dealing with the German colonies, should have "primary regard to the wishes and interests" of their native inhabitants, and that self-determination was as applicable to them as to Europe since their chiefs and councils could speak for them.

The promulgation of self-determination as one of the guiding principles of Allied policy came too early in the development of colonial nationalism to have its impact felt to the full immediately. Its inherently revolutionary implications, however, spread to every corner of the world. Linked with the whole body of ideas developed in the course of the war — the demand that autocracy give way to democracy, the emphasis on the rights of small nations, the insistence that peoples should not be bandied about like pawns in a game — the right of self-determination was one to which the colonial nationalist leaders, so soon to rally the masses behind them, could not fail to lay claim.

The principle that nations should freely determine their own destiny was presented to the world in 1917 not only by Woodrow Wilson, somewhat less than wholeheartedly endorsed by most other Allied leaders. It had behind it also the dramatic and persuasive backing of the Russian Revolution, repudiating Czarist imperialism and announcing the dawn of a new day of freedom for all peoples. While the Western Allies were understandably reluctant to see the principle carried seriously beyond Europe, the Bolsheviks not only made use of it at home but found it an ideal instrument for the confusion of their enemies and the incitement to revolutionary action of the imperialistically downtrodden. The formal transformation of the Russian Empire into an egalitarian multinational federation echoed far beyond the borders and gave new life and direction to the anti-imperialist forces. If the cause of independence for the nations of Asia could be even partially identified with the international Communist movement, an incalculably great step would have been taken toward ultimate triumph; and Lenin is reputed to have said that the road to the taking of the world lay through Asia.

For the longer haul the most significant effects of the war were in the realm of intangibles. In addition to the spread of the doctrines of democracy and self-determination — peculiarly revolutionary in the colonial setting — the profound cleavage in the ranks of the white rulers of the world was laid bare for all to see, and the spectacle of white man fighting white man, particularly where colonial troops were drawn in to redress the balance, held some obvious morals. The withdrawal of Communist Russia from the imperial white fraternity further emphasized the potentialities of European disunion. For the Western European powers the war involved serious losses in wealth, resources, and manpower which impaired their ability to flourish their imperial might with the old abandon. Most serious were the loss in prestige and the intrusion of gnawing doubts as to the supremacy and even the validity of Western civilization itself. The West's decline of faith in itself coincided with the East's growing confidence in its right and ability to assert its equal claims. If Spengler's philosophic speculations as to the decline of the West had a special relevance to the Germany of his day, they also expressed a widespread sense that the relations between the races of mankind which had been typical of the nineteenth century could not be expected to project themselves far into the future.

In the interwar decades the attack upon colonialism continually gathered momentum. On the entire frontier of the Western world, in the great sweep from Morocco through the Middle East and South Asia to China, the peoples were rising to rid themselves of imperial domination. The end of World War I was the signal for the effective beginning of the great upsurge of nationalism which reached its fruition after 1945. As Arnold J. Toynbee put it, it was a movement which was remarkably uniform in its two principal features: in its negative phase it consisted of a drive to throw off the ascendancy of the Western powers; in its positive phase it was an impulse "to adopt the military technique, the political institutions, the economic organization, and the spiritual culture of the West, but to adopt these by deliberate choice instead of being compelled to conform to them under pressure." [4]

In Morocco Abd-el-Krim challenged the Spanish and the French; in Egypt Saad Zaghlul Pasha led the nationalists against the British; and in Syria there was rebellion to throw off the French Mandatory rule. Turkey, Iran, and Afghanistan saw the rise of revolutionary leaders who attempted the forced-draft modernization of their countries in dictatorial guise. Of these, by far the most striking and successful was Mustafa Kemal who, discarding the anachronistic trappings of the Ottoman Empire, saved Turkey from defeat and humiliation, consolidated it as a national state, and started it on its modern path. At the furthest remove from Europe, the Chinese revolution gradually emerged from the tangled campaigns and alliances of the war lords, and the Kuomintang came to be the major embodiment of Chinese nationalism as Chiang Kai-shek beat back the ill-judged Communist bid for power.

In the colonial sphere the principal focus of attention was inevitably India which, despite its anomalous charter membership in the League, was much the greatest prize among the world's colonies. The demands of the Indian nationalists, coming increasingly under Gandhi's spell, went far beyond what the British were prepared to grant, and the Congress widened its base to become a mass movement capable of virtually paralyzing the government. In Asia, the Middle East, and Africa nationalist leaders and movements looked to Gandhi and the Congress for guidance and inspiration.

Of the major Asian dependencies, only the Philippines and Ceylon were granted constitutional reforms which roughly kept pace with nationalist demands — leaving aside Malaya where nationalism remained almost nonexistent prior to World War II. The most significant and unprecedented move was the creation of the Philippine Commonwealth in 1935 under a timetable which guaranteed full independence after a transitional decade of full domestic autonomy. In Burma, the Netherlands Indies, and Indochina the tentative imperial moves toward larger installments of self-government always lagged behind the mounting aspirations of the nationalists who were building their organizations and deepening their popular hold. Violent outbreaks occurred in all three colonies, sometimes under Communist leadership, but in none was the colonial government seriously threatened until the Japanese invasion swept all the established regimes away.

The effects of the depression intensified the nationalist and anti-imperialist trends which were already in swing. The crumbling of world demand for the raw materials and foodstuffs of the underdeveloped countries brought a drastic decline in private and public income which highlighted their precarious dependence on the industrial West. Charges of exploitation and discrimination found new substance in the tariffs and quotas devised by the imperial powers to bolster up their own shaky position. The contemporary argument as to the "have" and "have-not" countries was in some measure by-passed by taking it out on those which had least of all. For the purposes of stimulating political activism it was significant that the groups most directly affected in the underdeveloped areas were naturally those which were most closely geared to the world economy and hence most divorced from the traditional society. Those which lingered in the old-style subsistence economy suffered only minimal disturbance.

Another effect of the depression which fed into the nationalist stream arose from the necessity for both colonial governments and private enterprise to cut down on their expensive European staffs and economize by making greater use of local people. Although this did not open to the latter the upper posts of command, it did extend their access to middle bracket jobs and gave them a range of experience formerly closed to them.

On a Marxist line of analysis the depression might have been expected to produce a heightened imperialist drive, and this was indeed its effect for Germany, Italy, and Japan who aggressively seized the initiative. The Western imperial powers, however, clinging to the status quo, drifted toward a decline in the will to power, which produced a corresponding rise in the confidence of the peoples under their sway. Britain, France, and the United States, already well equipped with empire, were, at the most, concerned to hold on to what they had and by no means sure that they were prepared to do battle even for that. For them the depression brought rather a concentration on domestic problems than a resort to imperialism abroad, either to divert popular attention or to speed economic recovery. The most capitalist of the powers, the United States, undertook a striking turn away from at least the cruder forms of imperialism: far from using its great strength to spread its imperial wings, it not only moved to free the Philippines but put its Latin American relations on a basis of good neighborly equality.

In the interwar decades it was the frontier of the Western world from Morocco through to China which was most passionately aflame with nationalism. It was this same great belt which, in nearly all its parts, felt the most direct impact of World War II outside Europe itself. India, it is true, was neither a battleground nor, like Iran, taken over by occupying forces, but the war approached it closely and the political repercussions were immense. For Africa south of the Sahara total war demanded an extension in depth which brought the mobilization of many of Africa's peoples, resources, and strategic potentialities. The islands of the Pacific became major battlefields, and even the remote West Indies saw submarine warfare and the establishment of American bases.

The first great lesson of the war in the colonial realm, deriving from the shock of the Japanese tidal wave which swept over Southeast Asia after Pearl Harbor, was one of bitter disgust with colonialism. The morals seemed obvious: the sins of imperialism had been broadcast to all the world, the prestige of the white man had been wiped out, and colonialism was dead. The second great lesson, distilled more slowly from the experience of war, headed in precisely the opposite direction: total war made more valuable than ever before the possession of empires which offered strategic depth, indispensable resources, and refuge for the temporarily defeated or hard pressed. In the war's aftermath both lessons had their advocates, with the United States often uneasily in the middle, but it soon became apparent that anti-colonial sentiment had a global momentum behind it which made it irresistible.

What had complacently been assumed to be strongholds of empire, safe against external attack and internal upheaval — the fortress of Singapore was the outstanding symbol — turned out to be hollow shells of imperial might in the actual circumstances of a two-front war. Perhaps most shocking of all was the revelation that the colonial regimes had generated so slight a loyalty among the colonial peoples who were at best indifferent, at worst ready to welcome the Japanese invader as an ally against their alien rulers. Only among the Filipinos was there any widespread sense that the existing order was their own and worth fighting for, yet even here it was not difficult for the Japanese to find collaborators. That the Southeast Asians before long turned against the heavy-handed oppressiveness of the Japanese had no significant effect in endearing the former colonial authorities to the colonial peoples.

The net effect of the Japanese occupation in promoting nationalism and political self-reliance in Southeast Asia was very great. Most significantly of all, it hammered home the sense that revolutionary change was a working possibility within the grasp of man. The disruption of the colonial order, the shift to Japanese rule, and the final defeat of the new conquerors were ideally calculated to release all the new forces which had been gathering in the preceding decades.

The peoples of Southeast Asia made important gains in political and military experience during the war. The inability of the Japanese to fill all the positions from which the white men had vanished and their desire to conciliate nationalist sentiment opened to the peoples of the different countries governmental and economic posts from which they had previously been barred. In the military realm, the Japanese themselves trained substantial armies, large numbers of people fought in the resistance movements, and the Japanese defeat made quantities of arms available to the new national governments or other dissident groups. The Japanese squeezed what they could out of the occupied countries in the way of materials and manpower, but they also strove to convince the peoples of the substantive reality of the independence granted to the Philippines and Burma in 1943, held out as a promise to Indonesia, and later tolerated for the Vietnamese. As a Burmese government publication of the postwar period put it:

> Despite the great difficulties, despite the occasional Japanese intervention, Burma was able to show that she could keep up the prestige of the sovereign status she had won. From ashes and debris, the structure of freedom slowly rose and shone. The "independence" was therefore not all "sham," not all glitter — there was a substance in it, and the glitter, at least a part of it, was the reflection of real gold.[5]

In Indonesia and Indochina the interval between the Japanese surrender and the arrival of the "liberating" forces of the Allies, brief in retrospect but long in the opportunity it gave the nationalists, enabled the Indonesian Republic and Democratic Republic of Vietnam to consolidate governments and armies, the extent of whose sway shocked the Dutch and French as they sought to restore the colonial systems which the war had irrevocably swept away.

The great ground swell of anti-colonialism spread far beyond Southeast Asia. In India the Congress flatly repudiated Britain's right to thrust the country into war and in 1942 moved to its "Quit India" resolution, threatening a mass struggle on nonviolent lines. The British response was the outlawry of the Congress and mass imprisonment of Gandhi, Nehru, and many thousands of others among the Congress leaders. By curious irony it was the Communist party which became the most ardent champion of the British and of the war, a radical swing in the party line which cost it dearly in national standing for a number of years. From Morocco to Iran the war and the fighting forces penetrated in varying degrees, stimulating the drive toward an end of imperialist domination. For the duration of the war Africa south of the Sahara was generally peaceful, but after its close Madagascar rose in bloody revolt against the French, and lesser disturbances broke out in the Gold Coast and Nigeria which spurred the British on to colonial reform.

For the imperial powers of the West, including the United States, the colonial problem posed an interlocking and crucial series of dilemmas. Even more than the First World War, the Second emphasized the themes of freedom, democracy, and the fundamental rights of man — all of profound import to the dependent peoples — yet few championed the proposition that these themes should find any prompt and full-scale application in the colonies. In the West, self-determination no longer had the same look of providing an answer for the world's ills as in 1918. Even if one could assume sheer altruism on the part of the colonial powers, endless room was still left for disagreement as to the pace, nature, and direction of colonial advance. A vast and potentially disastrous gap divided the Western approach to the colonial problem from that of the colonial peoples themselves. What the colonial nationalist put forward as the most urgent necessities of self-determination and basic human rights, the West was likely to view tolerantly as a slate of proposals deserving serious study when occasion offered.

Substantial differences also divided the major allies among themselves. The anti-imperialist position of the Soviet Union requires no comment save that it was held in tight rein during the war and immediately thereafter when maximum collaboration with the imperial partners in the war was of greater consequence than freeing the colonial masses. The United States remained generally faithful to its traditional anti-colonialism. Inevitably this position led to friction with the British who also resented American criticism of their wartime treatment of India. The Prime Minister's attitude to American anti-colonialism and Roosevelt's interventions in British imperial affairs was expressed at a later date in good Churchillian phrase:

> In countries where there is only one race broad and lofty views are taken of the color question. Similarly, states which have no overseas colonies or possessions are capable of rising to moods of great elevation and detachment about the affairs of those who have.[6]

In the case of France the war's burdens and dislocations were intensified by the conflict between the Vichy regime and the Free France of de Gaulle which relied heavily on French territories overseas and, for a time, came to rest in North Africa. The General himself was imbued with a strong sense of French imperial destiny, but recognized the need for an overhauling of the old colonial system. For the French African territories south of the Sahara the distinctive turning point was the Brazzaville Conference of 1944 — attended, characteristically for those bygone days, by leading French officials but not by any Africans — which recommended basic reforms in many spheres. As for the challenge of colonial nationalism, however, the conference produced an uncompromising verdict, not to be overridden until de Gaulle again came to power in 1958:

> The aims of the work of civilization accomplished by France in its colonies exclude all idea of autonomy, all possibility of evolution outside the French bloc of the Empire; the eventual establishment, even in the distant future, of self-governments is to be dismissed.[7]

Inevitably the contradictions and ambivalences which had developed during the war in relation to colonialism projected themselves into the postwar period. The lesson that colonialism was dead was backed by the great central fact that the peoples of Asia, very shortly to be followed by the peoples of Africa as well, had been swept fully into the nationalist stream and passionately rejected colonial inferiority. But the other lesson of the importance of empire was also in evidence. In winning the war the imperial democracies of the West had come to a new appreciation of what their hold on overseas territories contributed to their security and well-being. In the San Francisco debates over the United Nations

Charter a British spokesman protested any thought of destroying the colonial empires on the ground that in the early stages of the war Britain had been saved from defeat only by the existence of the African colonies, the essential materials which they provided, and the route from the Middle East across the heart of Africa which they offered: "And if we had been defeated at that time very likely none of us would be sitting here today." [8]

A number of other factors dampened Allied enthusiasm for a drastic attack on the problems of colonialism. The psychological impact of defeat and occupation on France, the Netherlands, and Belgium undoubtedly played a role in strengthening their reluctance to abandon empire. Alien occupation, resistance movements, and the great war themes of freedom and democracy should perhaps have brought sympathy with the claims of dependent peoples, but in fact many in the imperial countries were swayed by the sense that national prestige demanded a defense of the imperial heritage — not to mention to obvious need of wartorn countries for raw materials and foodstuffs.

Neither of the two Allied superpowers which had embraced the anti-imperialist position was inclined at the war's end to swing into an all-out attack on colonialism. An immediate return by the U.S.S.R. to its standard onslaught on imperialism was presumably delayed by concentration on the immense tasks of home reconstruction and also by a recalculation as to where Communist advantage lay in the confused postwar situation. American anti-colonialism was tempered both by the need to maintain amicable relations with the allies and by the embarrassment arising from the covetous eyes with which the United States viewed some of the Pacific islands recently won from Japan at such terrific cost. The new American strategic frontier had moved virtually to the China coast. Okinawa became a major base, covered neither by annexation nor by Trusteeship. The Philippines, Formosa, Japan, and South Korea all became outposts of American power. As a British student of Chinese affairs put it:

> In actual terms of commitments America thus now became the heir of all the imperialists in the Far East; she took over Britain's sea power, Japan's empire and the leadership of the Western nations in China.[9]

Given the conflicting viewpoints among the Allies, the chapters of the United Nations Charter devoted to colonial matters necessarily represented a number of compromises, but in net effect they constituted a recognition that the colonial problem was now in the international public domain. The Trusteeship System, although its territorial range was even more limited than that of its predecessor, was an elaboration on the well-established foundations of the Mandates. The most striking innovation was the Declaration Regarding Non-Self-Governing Territories, embodied in Chapter XI, which for the first time gave the organized international community some access to the way in which the colonial powers were behaving and some title to debate their achievements and shortcomings. How wide the measure of access and how extensive the title to debate were questions to which no specific answers were given. To the colonial powers it was evident that as strict as possible a construction of the Chapter was in order, while the anticolonial bloc wanted the widest possible stretching of the loophole the Charter had opened.

In somewhat curious contrast to its absence from the League Covenant, the principle of self-determination made an explicit appearance in the Charter. What the principle meant as an operative part of an international constitutional instrument will be reserved for later examination. The Asians, at any rate, left no doubt as to what it meant to them as part of their living creed. Within the span of five years from the end of the war, India, Pakistan, Ceylon, Burma, the Philippines, Indonesia, Jordan, Syria, Lebanon, and Israel had all achieved their independence. In 1954, after a bitter war involving both Communism and French colonialism, they were followed by Cambodia, Laos, and a divided Vietnam; and in 1957 Malaya received its independence from Britain. China, save for the remnant of Formosa, withdrew from the West into an alliance with the Soviet Union. After much international bickering over the fate of the Italian colonies, Libya was made independent, Eritrea was joined with Ethiopia, and Somaliland, provisionally a Trust Territory, was promised independence in 1960. The Sudan, Morocco, and Tunisia were all removed from the control of their imperial superiors, and Egypt rid itself of the last vestiges of British dominance. In Africa south of the Sahara the beginning of the new era was marked by the transformation of the Gold Coast into independent Ghana, forcing a revision of all the timetables for African colonial advance. Ghana was joined by British Togoland, first of the African Trusteeships to be freed from tutelage, while French Togoland and the Cameroons reached their separate destinies soon after. Following de Gaulle's return to power in 1958 the French colonial empire in Africa made a further large step toward self-government, with Guinea the first territory to declare its independence. In the Caribbean, Puerto Rico and the Netherlands Antilles achieved new styles of self-government, the French West Indies were given the status of Departments of France, and the laboriously created Federation of the British West Indies approached independence within the Commonwealth.

Colonialism was on the way out far more speedily than had seemed at all possible. Only the old Czarist empire remained intact, undergoing the novel rhythms of Communist development, while the European satellites opened up a new dimension of empire.

CHAPTER III

The Rejection of Colonialism

Lord Lloyd, High Commissioner in Egypt from 1925 to 1929, reflected on his experiences there and elsewhere. From them he distilled a moral which was peculiarly unacceptable to the colonial peoples. With obtuse forthrightness he laid bare one central element of the imperial dilemma, which, within the confines of imperialist logic, had a certain plausible coherence of its own, but suffered from the singular defect of being alien to the desires of flesh-and-blood human beings.

He expressed — although we can perhaps be less sure that he shared — the prevailing doubts as to whether the gifts the West had to offer were blessings or curses, whether the political discontents of the West entitled it to regard as "pathetic" the placid contentment of other races.

We are no longer firm believers in the permanent value of what has so long been called progress; still less are we sure that the lines upon which our own development has run are the best lines for the development of other countries of a different stock. Law and order, internal peace and quietness, and impartial justice, these remain the only gifts about the advantages of which little argument would be heard. And if this is true, then there is really only one article of belief upon which we can confidently depend — that good administration is the first requirement to be fulfilled, and that all other questions are subordinate to it.[1]

The essential cause of the troubles of his day, as he saw it, was to be found in the conflict between those who stood by the old and tested ideal of benevolent administration, based on knowledge of the East and belief in the welfare of the masses, and those who gave priority to the silly slogan, the disastrous cry, of a Western schoolman's theory of self-determination. Independence, he contended, could not be counted on to promote the welfare of the colonial peoples. Furthermore, the masses neither understand nor want independence and the newfangled political machinery with which they are being endowed. It should not for a moment be imagined that they have genuine political aspirations, even though agitators inflame them by dwelling on their grievances. And again he reverts to his central positive theme:

> Good administration is their only desire and concern — and it is because we have allowed administration to be obscured by political issues that we have brought such heavy troubles upon the shoulders of all concerned. In these countries the real problem has been administrative, and we have chosen to regard it as political.[2]

This is an argument which has a measure of cold rationality about it and reveals the underpinning of a great segment of imperialist thinking. It contains, to be sure, no hint of the additional but not alternative doctrine that the purpose of colonial rule is to advance the administered masses to the point where they can take over for themselves. Such an addition would mar the stark symmetry of the proconsular pattern as seen not by Lord Lloyd alone but by others as well. This pattern rests essentially upon the two assumptions, familiar to aristocracies everywhere, that the backward masses, incapable of administering themselves and misgoverned by their own regimes, will receive a far better deal at the hands of their advanced overlords, and that they are primarily interested only in living their lives in peace and quiet with rising standards of welfare to be provided for them from above. The proper focus of colonial attention is the "real" people, the simple peasant mass, which gratefully accepts benevolent paternalism and which should be protected from the arousing of discontents since it has neither desire nor competence to play an active role in its own and the world's affairs. The occasional outbursts of political agitation reflect, not the demands of the "real" people, but only the self-interested machinations of an untrustworthy few who, caught in transition between two worlds, represent neither East nor West and seek to make capital of the academic yet dangerous theories of that earlier Man in the White House. It is not to these new pretenders to power that the guileless masses should look for sympathetic understanding, but to the disinterested imperial administrators.

Even though its day is past, this version of colonialism is by no means all myth. Unquestionably many colonial administrators and proconsuls have been prepared to give fullhearted devotion to their charges and, within the limits of the imperial creed, spent their best wisdom in the bewildering task of governing and reforming ancient societies which a changing world had rendered anachronistic. Unquestionably, likewise, the old regimes, such as Indian principalities or Malay sultanates, which the colonial authorities replaced or controlled, were often decadent, corrupt, oppressive, and little fitted to the inescapable assignment of adapting their people to the new order. There is much in the colonial record which can legitimately be taken as net gain. Where the colonial regimes achieved the minimum governmental function of establishing law and order and imposing internal peace, they often gave to the ordinary human being a degree of protection and security which had been the lot of none of his ancestors throughout history.

At least for the last century or so the rooting out of what were, in Western eyes, gross offences against human rights and decency has been generally accepted as one of the major responsibilities of colonial administrations. Western conceptions of the dignity and equality of man, slow enough to become living reality at home, moved ahead at a snail's pace in the lands under imperial control. Consciously or unconsciously, however, the Western administrator brought these conceptions with them in their mental baggage and in the institutions which they introduced. The barriers were not only in the bad will or the shortcomings of the Western rulers but also in the traditions and social structure of the peoples upon whom they had trust themselves. The boasted equality of Islam could not hide vast actual inequality; the caste system of Hinduism was explicitly based on a pattern of absolute superiority and inferiority; and slavery, in one or another guise, was an almost universal institution.[3]

In terms of political practicality the means to implement the desire of the colonial administrator to promote equality or check oppression and arbitrary exaction were likely to be meager at best. At home the conceptions of the philosophers had behind them the demands of increasingly powerful groups and classes for recognition as equal human beings. In the colonies, however, the administrators were an isolated and alien handful of men operating in the setting of an apathetic and often hostile social climate. To produce gold, coffee, or rubber or to build jails or roads is a far easier assignment than to transform the inner social structure of old and close-knit communities.

In another dimension lay the gnawing problem as to the right of the alien to cut into the fabric of the society whose destiny he had undertaken to control. Some things, such as cannibalism, Hindu widow-burning, or the cruder variants of slavery, constituted such outrageous violations of the fundamental Western code that they might, as particulars, properly be attacked; but to cut deeper raised an ethical issue of fundamental importance as well as a fear that the whole cloth might disintegrate. The administrator soon became aware that he was damned if he did and damned if he didn't: to undertake the reform of the society was wantonly to impose alien idiosyncrasies on a rounded and living culture, whereas to refrain was to protect the very backwardness which had justified intervention in the first place.

Colonialism at its extreme best brought no new heaven on earth nor did it produce any approximation of the advances which had been made in the metropolitan countries, but it undoubtedly worked to adapt the administrative structure of the societies on which it impinged to the requirements of the modern world. However adequate the indigenous political systems were to their traditional tasks, they were normally as inadequate to meet the new pressures as the governments of medieval Europe would have been. With occasional exceptions the dependent peoples have been given more rationalized and efficient administrations in the present century than they had known before. This was particularly true of the central colonial governments and of areas brought under direct Western rule. Even in territories, such as West Africa or Malaya, where the indirect rule so highly esteemed by the British maintained the position of traditional authorities, the trend was fairly constantly in the direction of curbing arbitrary personal power and regularizing the transaction of public business. The lowliest were raised somewhat in status, and the ever revolutionary doctrine of equality began its work. Institutionally the latter found expression in the movement toward equality before an objective and impartial law.

Even the wider ramifications of Lord Lloyd's exclusive plea for good administration are not wholly to be rejected out of hand. Whether one looks at Indonesia, Iraq, or Sierra Leone, it is evident that the gulf between the unlettered mass and the Westernized leaders who challenged the colonial systems renders suspect the claim of this latter elite to represent the people. Certainly from the standpoint of the conscientious colonial administrator — especially if his native bent led him neither to humility nor to the role of the teacher — it was a very painful thing to hand over the intricate machinery which he had laboriously built to people whom he did not trust or judge competent or representative. Benevolent paternalism no less than lust for power or profit can render the transition to independence exceedingly difficult.

An effective statement of the case against premature relinquishment of control to the Western-trained few was made by the Watson Commission in the Gold Coast in 1948. This statement, however, preceded by only a very short interval the decision to transfer to native hands so large a share of political power as to make self-government and independence inevitable next steps.

The moral justification for Britain remaining in the Gold Coast lies in this: out of a population of approximately four and a half million Africans, on a fair assessment, barely ten per cent is literate. We have no reason to suppose that power in the hands of a small literate minority would not tend to be used to exploit the illiterate majority in accordance with the universal pattern of what has happened elsewhere in the past throughout the world. His Majesty's Government therefore has a moral duty to remain until

a) the literate population has by experience reached a stage when selfish exploitation is no longer the dominant motive of political power or

b) the bulk of the population has advanced to such a stage of literacy and political experience as will enable it to protect itself from gross exploitation, and

c) some corresponding degree of cultural, political and eco-

nomic achievement has been attained by all three areas now part of
the Gold Coast.[4]

In an American version of the same doctrine, Secretary of War
Taft protested in a special report to President Roosevelt in 1908
that it was not enough for the United States to await the organization of a Philippine oligarchy or aristocracy which could take
over the government. It was his conviction that "we are the trustees
and guardians of the *whole Filipino people*, and peculiarly the
ignorant masses," who must be given sufficient education to know
their civil rights.[5]

More pungently and with different overtones Winston Churchill in 1931 condemned the Indian National Congress as possessing
neither the numbers, the strength, nor the virtue of the Indian
people:

> They merely represent those Indians who have acquired a veneer
> of Western civilization, and have read all those books about democ-
> racy which Europe is now beginning increasingly to discard. . . .
> To transfer that responsibility to this highly artificial and restricted
> oligarchy of Indian politicians . . . would be an act of cowardice,
> desertion and dishonor.[6]

A counterattack upon the nationalists as unrepresentative of
the people for whom they claim to speak is thus a standard feature
of the defense put forward by beleaguered colonial authorities,
who also contend that nationalist victory is likely to mean no
real advance toward meeting popular needs and aspirations. It can,
indeed, be argued that the achievement of independence does no
more by itself than to answer the demand for independence. "The
problems which really concern the welfare of the masses in Egypt,
or in India, or in Palestine," to draw upon Lord Lloyd again, are
to be answered by the uses which may be made of independence
and not by the mere throwing off of the alien yoke.

So much can be said for the kind of thesis for which Lord Lloyd
made himself the spokesman, but a good deal can be said on the
other side. In theoretical terms an attack might be made upon it
by raising the query as to whether it does not involve the dubious
conception of pure administration — pure in the sense of being
divorced from political decision and direction, which implies
divorce from any choice in values.[7] It may be that certain tech-

niques and standards of administration stand on their own feet in any time or clime. The broader and more hazardous issue concerns the purposes which administration serves. Even technical perfection in such matters as incorruptibility, efficiency, and justice can not serve long to justify an administration whose ends are not those of the people whom it governs. But the essential ethical justification of any colonial regime must be that it knows better than its wards what they need and should want.

Translated into concrete terms, the breaking point is the universally demonstrated unwillingness of peoples, as they come to an awareness of themselves in the modern world, to tolerate being run by aliens or to continue subordinate to a foreign state. It is this deeprooted perversity of man which makes an abstraction from reality necessary if the thesis of good administration as an acceptable end in itself is to be sustained. In a logic detached from the record of recent history there is no necessary reason why people should passionately prefer to be governed by what they regard as their own kind rather than to allow an efficient corps of alien administrators to manage their affairs for them. Yet nationalists the world over have revolted against alien domination and, in occasional bursts of frankness, have stated their case in such classic phrases as that they would rather be governed like hell by themselves than well by their imperial rulers.[8] Nkrumah's Convention People's Party in the Gold Coast took as its motto: "We prefer self-government with danger to servitude in tranquillity."

The simple truth is that, once a certain stage of development is passed, colonial peoples will not accept good government as a substitute for self-government. Their own version of what they want coincides with the answer given to Lord John Russell in 1854 when he suggested that if the Italians would only keep quiet Austria would be more humane and grant them more privileges than they could secure by insurrection. To this proposition Daniel Manin, defender of Venice, replied:

> We do not ask that Austria be humane and liberal in Italy — which, after all, would be impossible for her even if she desired; *we ask her to get out*. We have no concern with her humanity and her liberalism; we wish to be masters in our own house.[9]

In point of fact, good government, far from being a substitute for self-government, appears to be one of the prime keys to the emergence of clamorous political demands. It is not the most down-trodden who rise in their wrath, but those who have made a good start on the path of advance: "A population that rebels is a popu-lation that is looking up, that has begun to hope and to feel its strength." [10]

If one would devise an equation to serve as a guide to the cir-cumstances under which colonial nationalism is most likely to appear, two major variables would need to be taken into account.

In the first place, the greater the disruption of the old society under the impact of the intruding Western forces — assuming that that disruption takes the form of a development of modern enter-prise and administration and not merely the suppression of the native population — the speedier and more complete the assertion of nationalism is likely to be. Those countries which have experi-enced the largest measure of Westernizing change are the most restive under colonialism, and the elements of their population which have been most drastically divorced from the close-knit pattern of their traditional society are the most susceptible to the appeal of nationalism.

In the second place, the appearance of a Westernized elite is an indispensable part of the movement toward nationalism. It is this elite — the new intelligentsia and the professional men — which translates to the local scene the nationalist experience and ideology of the West and serves as the crystallizing center for the inchoate disaffections of the mass.

It would be pleasant to be able to conclude that colonial vice is punished and virtue rewarded in the sense that the sharp edge of nationalism might be blunted by economic advance, the intro-duction of freer and more democratic institutions, and a modern educational system. The evidence points strongly in the other direction. In fact, the record establishes that such measures only encourage nationalism and facilitate its spread, while less liberal and enlightened policies limit it and hold it down. This was a propo-sition of which Gladstone was well aware in relation to Cyprus when he warned that Greek sympathies would surely prevail.

and instead of earning, even by the benefits you may confer upon them . . . gratitude and attachment in the form of a disposition to continue in political connection with you, the more you improve their condition the quicker will be the development of this strong sentiment of nationality, and the more earnest the desire of the Greeks of Cyprus to be united with the free Greeks of the rest of the world.[11]

Paradoxical as it may seem, colonial nationalism is far less a response to oppression or neglect than to the widened horizons opened up by progressive colonial governments. The concurrent spread of nationalism and of free institutions in the Philippines can be cited as an obvious example. Equally striking is the contrast between developments in British and French West Africa and other African territories. The earlier appearance and wider sweep of nationalism in British India as compared with the Netherlands Indies is surely not unrelated to the greater freedom and political advance of the former.

The bitter nationalist struggle of the Koreans under Japanese rule indicates, however, that such freedoms and advances are not in all circumstances a necessary condition of nationalism, particularly where old-established peoples are involved. Within the limits of its ability to evade or overwhelm the colonial police power, nationalism will perhaps roll ahead as relentlessly toward its goals in a repressively dictatorial as in a liberal setting once it has gained momentum, but the evidence suggests that it is likely to come to birth at a substantially later stage and pick up speed more slowly.

If, on a hypothesis contrary to the one I have been presenting, low estate and gloomy prospects were the principal inspirers of nationalist agitation, the focal points of disturbance would presumably be the somewhat tattered remnants of the Spanish and Portuguese empires which now stand at the bottom of the developmental scale. The fact is, however, that to all outward appearance they remain politically quiescent and, aided by a more tolerant attitude toward the race question, are not seriously affected as yet by the backwash of agitation from neighboring territories. Lacking the pressures and tensions which arise from a drive for development, these colonies have held to a minimum all the conditions which promote nationalism: there has been little disruption of the native society in a modernizing direction, the new-style leader-

ship is for the most part lacking, and colonial policy has been un-
tinged by political liberalism.

Next in line, but for a very different set of reasons, would
be the Belgian Congo which has combined massive European economic development and impressive social welfare programs with
political authoritarianism and, until recently, a deliberate policy
of holding back the appearance of a Western-educated African
elite. The lack of nationalist activity can certainly not be regarded
as deriving from the undisturbed maintenance of the traditional
society. Primarily because of the demand of Western enterprises
for labor, nearly a quarter of the population lives outside the so-
called *milieux coutumiers* — the traditional tribal areas. There
has been a surging growth of urban centers: from 1938 to 1954
the urban population had risen from 8.33 per cent to 21.5 per cent
of the whole. Belgian policy secured the postponement of nationalism by preventing the emergence of a modern African leadership
and by denying political freedom and instrumentalities through
which the rising forces could express themselves. The outbreaks of
violence in Leopoldville and elsewhere in 1959, however, indicated
that the days of undisturbed paternalism were coming to an end.
Word of the riots in the Congo spread quickly across the border
into Angola.

It might be contended that the failure of nationalism to manifest
itself at an earlier stage in the Spanish, Portuguese, and Belgian
colonies is to be traced, not to other differences in colonial policy,
but to the success of the governments in repressing actual or potential troublemakers. Such a contention cannot be made to square
with the facts. Although the authorities in these colonies have been
ruthless enough in suppression and have from time to time found it
necessary to crush local "nativist" movements and revolts, often
stemming from aberrant religious sects like the Watchtower or
Kimbanguism, such movements lacked the authentic character of
Gold Coast or Nigerian nationalism and constituted no real threat
to the colonial regime.

Even giving full weight to what may be achieved through
repressive measures, the bulk of the local, more traditionally oriented disaffections and risings which all African colonial regimes
have put down at one time or another did not have the potentiality

of turning into modern nationalist movements without substantial changes in the societies from which they arose. Representing the old society rather than the new, such movements contain elements of protest on which later leaders may draw, but they are themselves only forerunners of the more serious revolutions which lie ahead. Educational, social, and economic advance is the precondition for the emergence of nationalist movements; their actual coming to birth and their further development can be greatly speeded by a climate of political freedom.

I have been suggesting that the demand for self-determination has characteristically developed in the colonies which have been pushed ahead rather than in those which have been held back. An added complication arises from the improvement in the general standards of colonial management in recent decades. If it were possible to establish a marked increase in oppression and exploitation, the ever-spreading recourse to nationalism could perhaps be explained. On the contrary, even if much of the talk about "a sacred trust of civilization" has ended in pious words rather than effective deeds, the turn for the better in colonial practice is striking. The counterpart of this turn is, of course, a speeded tempo of development with its consequent uprooting of people, increased urbanization, spread of wage employment, and creation of a proletariat as well as of a middle class.

Many of the more flagrant abuses of colonial rule have been either eliminated or ameliorated. The obligations undertaken in the United Nations Charter to move toward self-government, develop free political institutions, and promote well-being have been accepted by the colonial powers as part of the modern creed which they cannot publicly challenge and must give the appearance of implementing. The practice of other times which tolerated the slaughter of colonial peoples and legitimized their exploitation has vanished from the scene, to be replaced, if not by full recognition of the paramountcy of native interests, at least by the proclamation of a new formula of partnership from which both sides should profit.[12] A large gap often separates the brave words of the formula from the colonial realities. The claims of the white man continue to be accorded a far-reaching priority in colonial territories and most notably in areas where white settlement impinges on established native populations, as in Algeria, Kenya, or the Rhodesias, not to mention the most tragic and threatening example, South Africa. But, whatever the current sins of colonialism, it is absurd to deny, in the fashion of Moscow and its erstwhile Cominform, that there has been a very real and substantial change for the better.

During the past century the position of the workers and, more generally, of the lower social classes has been transformed in the advanced industrial countries of the West. Basically the same forces and factors which brought about this transformation have been at work in the colonies, although with a considerable time lag and diminished vigor. It is impossible in both instances to determine with any degree of precision how much of the credit should go to a more or less automatic evolution or rationalization of the social-economic system, how much to a rise of more liberal and humanitarian attitudes which consciously sought reforms, and how much to the pressures of the underdogs themselves.

The first of these categories, embracing enlightened self-interest or, in a broad sense, sound business practices, played a significant role, as was earlier the case in the turn against slavery and the slave trade. In the more recent period the inner rationale of modern economic life has worked upon both government and large-scale Western enterprise in the colonies in much the same way as at home, although in the colonies it has not had as powerful external support from the pressures of organized labor and an aroused public opinion. Instead of seeking the quick return which might be secured from methods which literally maimed and killed off the labor supply, Western enterprise moved somewhat hesitantly to the conclusion that the conservation of the labor force was a paying proposition. It arrived at the calculated conviction that less was to be gained from ruthless exploitation and compulsion than from dealing with the problems of the turnover and inefficiency of labor by meeting some of the more obvious grievances, improving health standards and the physical condition of the workers, and giving labor a slightly larger incentive to work. No better example of this trend exists than the Belgian Congo, of which Negley Farson said a number of years ago that "it is being developed by the latest big-business methods. The natives as a carefully conserved supply of black labor get the best housing and the best medical attention in Africa." [13] The increasingly complex processes and techniques of colonial enterprise made necessary the multiplication of skilled workers and clerical and supervisory personnel. Since these could be imported from home only at an excessive cost there was a clear incentive to encourage the training and education of local people.

As the new needs of Western economic interests coincided with changing conceptions of the proper role of government, which were similarly a belated translation to the colonial scene of Western ideas and practices, colonial governments underwent a rationalization of their own and broadened their range of activity. Education was expanded, and at least a modicum of social welfare programs was introduced, including health and sanitation services. To meet the basic requirements of the economy and of the government itself, transport and communication facilities were overhauled and brought up to date. It would be a misreading of the picture to see a complete identification of private Western enterprise and of government because, in fact, their outlooks and interests not infrequently diverged considerably. Colonial governments developed from the beginning a range of functions and concerns of their own — they were, after all, *governments* and not commercial companies. The colonial civil services liked to regard themselves as the protectors of the peoples they governed and not as the instruments of private economic interests. K. M. Panikkar, certainly no champion of colonialism, states this point vigorously in relation to India:

> An important characteristic of the Civil Service was its open refusal to be influenced by commercial and industrial interests in India. The classes from whom the Civil Services were recruited helped to form this idea. . . . There was thus no alliance between the Civil Service and big business and the British Indian bureaucracy was not interested in the exploitation of India. In fact it could legitimately be said that the services championed "their India," the India of the dumb masses, against British businessmen and capitalists, except where these had become powerful vested interests in rural areas, like tea plantations in Assam and indigo plantations in Bihar.[14]

Government and private enterprise were, however, living in the same world and were subject to similar pressures to bring colonial conditions of life up-to-date by the introduction of some of the newer conceptions and practices of the West.

On a variety of counts, including the independence which has recently come to so many hundreds of millions of colonial peoples, it is in order to assume that the present century brought a fairly steady advance in over-all colonial standards. But what these rising standards actually meant in terms of happiness and well-being would be far more difficult to estimate. For the ordinary human being the identifiable increments of advance were usually slight or even nonexistent. Only a fraction of the people were directly drawn into the new Western enterprises, and for most of them, at least in the earlier stages of the transition, the conditions of life and work were as grim and oppressive as they have characteristically been for the workers in societies moving into the industrial revolution. The bulk of the people continued their traditional peasant existence on much the old lines, but perhaps seriously squeezed by the growth in the population. In principle the operations of government extended equally to all; in practice they bit much more significantly into the pressing problems of urban centers and the environs of the new-style economic life than into those of the remoter rural areas and the traditional agricultural economy. The latter were only marginally and gradually affected by the impact of the West whereas the former underwent something approaching total disruption or reconstruction.

The curse of bigness was on the more recent improvements in colonial management, both economic and governmental, bringing with it the chilly atmosphere of impersonal efficiency and the remoteness of the upper managing personnel from the peoples whose destinies they so largely determined. The district officer who had lived close to his wards now motored or flew to the mounting paper work of a distant office. Rabindranath Tagore put it in the following fashion:

> We have seen in our country some brand of tinned food advertised as entirely made and packed without being touched by hand. This description applies to the governing of India, which is as little touched by the human hand as possible. The governors need not know our language, need not come into personal touch with us except as officials. . . . But we, who are governed, are not a mere abstraction. We on our side, are individuals with living sensibilities.[15]

The ordinary human being shared in few of the fruits of the increased productivity which came into existence under colonial auspices, and in some areas recent decades have seen a decline in living standards for the masses.[16] Despite mounting attacks upon them, many of the old evils lingered on. Among these were devices compelling entry into the labor market (often at great distances from home and involving the break-up of families), wage rates far below Western standards, and the curtailment of land available for native use through alienation for white settlement or other purposes. Improved agricultural methods, the extension of irrigation, and other developments increased agricultural yields in the native sector of the economy. The really outstanding gains in productivity, however, those which are usually reflected in the soaring figures of external trade, took place in the export industries to which Western capital and skills had been attracted, and from which the profits were largely drained off to alien investors. The type of economic development which normally held the center of attention was the production of raw materials which were then shipped to the West for processing and manufacture. Colonial industrialization, despite much conversation about it, was kept at a low and generally inconsequential level.

Another factor which has prevented improvement in living standards is the burst of population growth which has so frequently accompanied modern colonialism. On the strength of the experience of the South Sea Islands and a few other places lugubrious speculation arose some decades ago about the ruinous effect of the Western impact in decimating native populations; more recently there has been horrified acknowledgment of the fact that colonial and ex-colonial peoples are multiplying at a rate which, bringing Malthus very much to life, constantly threatens to outstrip the production of foodstuffs. It is, in its way, a flattering tribute to the successes of Western colonialism that its imposition of internal peace, its health and sanitation measures, and its immense advances in production, transportation, and distribution have made possible the skyrocketing of the populations of India and Indonesia, of Egypt and Puerto Rico. Statistics of population growth, however, are cold comfort to men and women whose daily lives reflect little of the gains of the new era and whose daily portion of rice or grain is as slim as ever.

Nonetheless, the tendency of colonial peoples to flock to their nationalist banners cannot be attributed to any general worsening of conditions. A more suggestive line of approach is that a painfully slow advance has been accompanied by growing consciousness that far higher standards exist for a privileged minority of the world's peoples and that an approximation of these standards is possible for others as well. The change in the level of expectations had no adequate counterpart in actual achievement. Furthermore, the colonial peoples were increasingly persuaded that for the realization of the newly perceived potentialities they must look, not to their present alien regimes, but to national governments which would drive ahead with the vigor of Ataturk's Turkey, Meiji Japan — and of Soviet Russia and Communist China.

It is relatively simple to assess material standards in terms of such substantial goods as food, clothing, and shelter. The accounting becomes more difficult when less tangible services such as those connected with health, education, and social welfare are added. It departs almost wholly from the range of the objectively calculable when the inquiry shifts to the realm of the human spirit and an assessment of the general sense of individual and social well-being. Yet it is this assessment which must be undertaken if there is to be any hope of understanding why passive acceptance of colonial subjection has been replaced by its impassioned rejection under the symbols of nationalism. The actual state of facts is likely to be of markedly less consequence in this dimension of inquiry than the state of mind in which those facts are approached. If the inquiry could legitimately be confined to the sphere of the relatively material and tangible, it would perhaps be possible to deal with the problems of colonialism within Lord Lloyd's formula of good administration. The peoples themselves, however, have risen to reverse his dictum and to insist that the "real problem" is not administrative but political.

To Lord Lloyd and other like-minded colonialists the gravest threat to the work on which they were engaged was that the masses, failing in their innocence of spirit to recognize where their true interest lay, would throw in their lot with the "agitators," who inflame them by dwelling upon their grievances, "utterly disregarding the fact that political changes would have no more re-

medial effect upon these discontents than the man in the moon." [17]
A few "agitators" could be dealt with by various means of suppression, but the situation of the colonial power became hopeless
as soon as a substantial segment of the general populace rallied to
their support.

It is markedly simpler to discern the factors which have led
the "agitators" themselves — or, in more acceptable terminology,
the new Westernized elite — to assert their claim to political
leadership than it is to present any watertight case which will explain why the masses chose to follow them.

For the elite, the primary element is that they are the ones
who have been most directly exposed to the Western world. Only
a very partial and superficial answer can be found by seeking to
shift the responsibility to third parties by laying major emphasis
on the influence of Wilsonian self-determination or Communist
anti-imperialism. Both of these doctrines depended very greatly
for their effectiveness on the existence of persons and groups ready
to make use of them. The proclamation of national self-determination as a part of the Western creed had as large an importance in
indicating to the growing body of attackers a weak spot in the
Western defenses of imperialism — an Achilles heel of bad conscience — as in directly stimulating dangerous thoughts.

The few in the colonies with a Western type of education were
well prepared to receive Wilsonian doctrines of democracy and
the right of people to govern themselves. Whether the immediate
sources were British or American, French or Dutch, Western education could hardly fail to transmit these ideas and ideals and to
sing the praises of past wars and revolutions for freedom. Colonial
educational systems have frequently been attacked, with evident
justice, for teaching the history of the metropolitan country or of
Europe rather than local history — the stock image is that of children of French Africa or Madagascar reciting "nos ancêtres les
Gaulois" — but it was from European history that the lessons of
the struggle for freedom could on the whole be most effectively
learned. The knowledge of Western languages opened up vast
bodies of literature teeming with seditious thoughts which the
young men who came upon them were not slow to apply to their
own problems. The effect was likely to be greatest for the tiny

minority which actually went to live in the West for study or other purposes, yet the seeds of revolution also took root in the larger group who received Western schooling in their home territory.

These young men and, more rarely, women were the ones who were most drastically shaken loose from the traditional institutions and patterns, and who acquired the most vivid sense of the contrast between that society and the vastly richer and more powerful Western world. As possessors of the knowledge and technique of the West they were the obvious claimants for the power exercised by the imperial authorities. At the same time they were the group most likely to be fully exposed to and most sensitively aware of race discrimination and the color bar. Conscious that they no longer fitted into the older society from which they had emerged, they found themselves rejected as equal partners by the dominant Westerners. While many were absorbed into the framework of colonial government and enterprise, they were denied access to the upper positions of responsibility, command, and wealth. Inevitably they felt the bitter frustration of inability to secure in their own societies positions which corresponded to their expectations and newly acquired knowledge and skills — a problem which found a close parallel in the grievance of the Soviet Union's minor nationalities.[18] Once the rising colonial elite had shaken off their awe of the almost magical mastery of power possessed by the alien rulers, they demanded that an end be put to the gross discrepancy between the ideals of freedom and equality which the West preached and the colonialism which it practised. The Christian doctrines spread by the missionaries who controlled so much of colonial education also squared badly with race discrimination and economic exploitation.

Save in the sense that Western-inspired changes in the economic structure underlay much of the disruption of the older societies, it is doubtful that the economic aspects were as significant as the political and social in turning the new colonial elites to nationalism. Although it could be argued that the turn in a political direction resulted from a calculation that political control was necessary to correct economic abuses, it is doubtful that this idea played more than a minor role. It is in no sense my contention that there were not ample grounds for hostility to the colonial economic systems, but only that they were not generally the original source from which the more basic hostility sprang. Once nationalism entered the picture most people would refuse to accept a higher standard of living bought at the price of alien rule, whereas the achievement of national ends would be held to outweigh economic deprivation. The more fundamental elements were the sense of inferiority inherent in colonialism, the indignation aroused by determination of status on racial grounds, and the gnawing consciousness of being a second-class citizen in one's own country.[19]

The Western-trained intelligentsia and professional men were usually joined by the rising indigenous entrepreneurs and businessmen, as in India or in West Africa where the women traders must be included as well. Aside from other inducements to enlist in the nationalist cause, the local businessman was likely to find, or at least to be persuaded that he had found, his way blocked by Western economic interests which, better equipped with capital and the techniques of modern trade and enterprise, could also draw upon the support of the imperial and colonial governments. I have suggested earlier that, although there was by no means an across-the-board identity of attitude and interest between colonial governments and Western business enterprises, the latter had easy access to government at all levels. The demands of home constituents for a favored entry to colonial markets and for adequate supplies of foodstuffs and raw materials at low prices were far from easy to resist. In addition, it was always easy to argue that, since it was a major responsibility of the colonial government to secure the development of its territory, encouragement should be given to white settlers or to experienced Western enterprises which could be expected to do a quicker and better job than the ill-qualified natives who might learn from seeing others do.

Even where the government gave no all-out support to the economic claims of its nationals or other Westerners, it was too much to hope that it would give to indigenous enterprises the kind of vigorous backing that was needed, particularly where they were in competition with metropolitan interests. No government will devote itself as abundantly to promoting the economic development of a dependent people as to caring for the interests of the home constituents to whom it is politically responsible. If the Irish famine of 1846–47 had taken place closer to the gates of West-minster, would the British response have been so slow and so meagre?

The desire of indigenous economic interests for more whole-hearted and extensive governmental support led them to make important financial contributions to the nationalist movements in India and some other countries, but they generally furnished no corresponding share of the leadership — again perhaps evidence of the priority of political over economic matters. This was peculiarly the case where "middle-class" economic functions were performed by aliens, such as the Chinese in Southeast Asia and the Indians in East Africa. As the effects of Western rule and economic penetration spread in ever-widening circles the nationalist elite was joined increasingly by the leaders of workers' and, more rarely and belatedly, peasant movements.

The factors which have been summarily described above were certainly of far less consequence for the people at large than for the newly rising elite. Indeed, the differences in education, outlook, and environment served — as the colonial authorities took pleasure in pointing out — to divide the Westernized few from the masses and to sow some measure of dissension between the two elements. A typical example is the friction which has accompanied the effort to bring within a single framework the new educated group and the chiefs of the traditional society whose status was maintained under indirect rule. Although the Western-trained nationalists normally put themselves forward as the only proper interpreters and guides of their people, no less a figure than Nehru has well expressed the spiritual difficulty of their position in a comment on his own ambivalence.

> Indeed, I often wonder if I represent any one at all, and I am inclined to think that I do not, though many have kindly and friendly feelings toward me. I have become a queer mixture of the East and the West, out of place everywhere, at home nowhere. Perhaps my thought and approach to life are more akin to what is called Western than Eastern, but India clings to me, as she does to all her children, in innumerable ways; and behind me lie, somewhere in the subconscious, racial memories of a hundred, or whatever the number may be, generations of Brahmans. I cannot get rid of either that past inheritance or my recent acquisitions. They are both part of me, and,

though they help me in both the East and the West, they also create in me a feeling of spiritual loneliness not only in public activities but in life itself. I am a stranger and alien in the West. I cannot be of it. But in my own country also, sometimes, I have an exile's feelings.[20]

Western encroachment was felt far more slowly and indirectly by the masses than by the new elite. Whereas the latter came, in varying degree, into frequent and intimate contact with the West — its people, ideas, and instrumentalities — the ordinary villager rarely laid eyes on a white man, had no knowledge of his language, and received any inkling of his ideas only at a second or third remove. He was presumably only dimly aware of a remote colonial government whose edicts were filtered down to him through several layers of European and native officials.

It is possible to emphasize either the unchanging character of the traditional society or the revolutions which have been introduced into it. The environment and pattern of life of the mass of the rural population has generally changed only gradually and almost imperceptibly; but the money economy, the new mobility of various types, the innovations introduced by government from above, and the resulting individualism — all worked to alter much of the substance of existence even though the continuance of the old forms gave an outward appearance of immutability. On the other hand, the basic traditional structure of village and tribe has often remained unimpaired to a surprising degree, bending itself to the storms of war and shifts in overlordship but weathering them as it has weathered similar storms throughout the ages. Thus, for example, despite the drift of the Indonesian central government toward political bankruptcy and disintegration, the ancient village structure remains largely intact and the villager lives much as he has always lived; as the tribal life of Africa similarly retains a vitality of its own.

The Western economy and institutions, as well as Western ideas, have loosed an immense process of adaptation and transition which has moved at very varying rates not only in different parts of the world but also in nearby parts of the same country. To seek to embrace the results in a few neat phrases is to pretend a simplicity and coherence far removed from the complex reality.

It is, however, obvious that in the degree to which the rural population was left to its own devices it escaped the direct impact of precisely those forces which were most significant for the new elites. Nationalism is essentially and in the first instance an urban phenomenon. In colonial countries it is typically in the cities, whose growth has been one of the most striking events of recent decades, that regular contact with the white man brings the vivid sense of contrast between his modes and standards of life and those of the native community. The almost universal poverty of the local people is inevitably compared with the wealth of the aliens who are generally a quite unrepresentative sample of the white society as it exists on its own home grounds. J. H. A. Logemann suggests that the problem is further aggravated by the fact that precapitalist society has little to contribute to capitalist activities in the cities except a large supply of unskilled labor:

> It is in the city, therefore, that the wide yawning gap between wealth and poverty is almost brutally exhibited in the way the living quarters of the rich and poor are in contrast. In Leopoldville, there are 1,300 whites per square kilometer, as against 15,000 Africans. The fact that in highly built up Brussels the density is 6,500 people per km² may give you some impression of the congestion indicated by the second figure.[21]

The people of the countryside have no immediate evidence either of the white man's vastly higher standard of living or of the fact that substantially all whites are provided with such services as education, sanitation, and medical facilities which most of the native population normally do without. Unless he feels the pressure of alien encroachment on his land or of demand for his labor, the peasant may wholly escape the thrust of racial discrimination which plays so large a role in the making of nationalists. Even where it does strike him, he may well shrug it off as merely a new variant of the status system to which he has been accustomed from time immemorial. Only those who are brought closely in touch with the West will be seriously tempted to measure themselves and their place in the world by Western standards.

The elements of the rural population most susceptible to the nationalist appeal are those which have been brought nearest to the superimposed Western society, through such channels as migration to the labor forces of mines and plantations or through military service, particularly abroad. A fertile recruiting ground for nationalist and other dissident political movements is created wherever heavy pressure of population on the land drives the peasant or tribesman in search of a living into the urban centers or to the European enterprises. Sullen resentment and sometimes open hostility reach their peak when the people of the country, confined to overcrowded and increasingly inadequate native reservations, as in Kenya, see land which they regard as rightfully their own taken over by the white man for his own use. The deep sense of grievance which such a situation arouses is little likely to be calmed by the white man's effort to argue the case in terms of his version of the legalities involved or to place the blame for poverty on the shortcomings of native agriculture.

CHAPTER IV

Colonial Policy and National Movements

Nations, like individuals, are products of heredity and environment, although in the case of nations heredity is to be sought not in the genes but in the social heritage which flows from generation to generation to give some national content to men's minds. What is significant in the environment enters into this heritage to change the direction of the national stream and to enrich or diminish it.

Over the centuries the national heritage of many peoples has been diverted into new channels by the colonial experience which they have undergone. Indeed, the creation of nations themselves is in some instances, as in the Philippines and Ghana, to be attributed primarily to the bringing together of diverse stocks under a single imperial roof. In this fashion inner unity has often been promoted by colonial rule, while at the same time the multiplicity of colonial systems has emphasized the diversities between peoples by forcing them into disparate colonial patterns. To the great original differences between the Indians, the Vietnamese, and the Indonesians, a new dimension of difference has been contributed by British, French, and Dutch supremacy. The Africans who live their lives under the particular conditions of the Belgian Congo are emerging with many differences from their neighbors in Portuguese Angola, British Northern Rhodesia, and French Equatorial Africa. Even within a single territory the use of divergent colonial policies, as in northern and southern Nigeria, produces different results for the peoples involved. Uncertain as the precise meaning of the term "national character" may be, it is beyond doubt that the character of the nations now coming into the world has been greatly influenced by the type of colonial regime to which they have been subjected. Nor is this peculiarly a contemporary phenomenon: the imprint which the Roman Empire left behind it is still far from having vanished, and the Moslem empire in India brought forth Pakistan long after its own demise.

The nature of the colonial setting and the contrasting colonial policies of the powers have played a significant role not only in the shaping of nations but also in the development of nationalism, influencing the speed with which nationalist movements have swung into action, their membership and structure, the demands they pose, and their tactics and strategy. In Asia and Africa nationalism is essentially the response of peoples to the impact of the West. Since in dependent territories the timing and intensity of that impact are controlled in large measure by the colonial regime, the importance of the latter as an agent in the creation of nationalism tends to be correspondingly great. Such matters as the type of economy the imperial power encourages, the goals it sets, the colonial institutions it establishes, the civil and political rights it extends to the people, the utilization of direct or indirect rule, and the strength or absence of alien settler communities are all of major consequence in determining the character of the political movements which arise to challenge the colonial overlords.

In the case of the three countries — Spain, Portugal, and Belgium — whose African domains have been the last to swing into political activism, the relationship between political quiescence and colonial policy seems easy to establish. For both Spain and Portugal, as I have suggested, the primary circumstances involved are the failure to move ahead to large-scale development along modern lines and the lack of free political institutions. The result is that there has been neither the shaking up of the old society and the emergence of a new-style leadership nor the creation of a climate congenial to the spread of ideas and the launching of political movements. The loss of the great Spanish and Portuguese empires in the Americas and elsewhere was brought about not by "natives" who had been goaded into nationalism but by overseas Spaniards or Portuguese, or their descendants of mixed blood. Only in the Philippines was the central issue a rising of the original people of the country against alien rule.

With the loss of Morocco the Spanish holdings have dwindled away almost to the vanishing point. The Portuguese overseas empire, however, embracing the two large African areas of Angola and Mozambique, is the third biggest in the world. Constitutionally all Portuguese territories are parts of a single state in which the overseas provinces have full formal equality with the European home base, even though sharp distinctions are drawn between the inhabitants of the state in terms of their cultural status. On joining the United Nations in 1955 Portugal firmly denied any obligation to report on non-self-governing territories under Article 73e of the Charter since the existence of such territories was incompatible with basic constitutional provisions. By all other criteria than the formal fiat of Lisbon, however, Portugal's African territories are quite as much dependent and non-self-governing as those of any other colonial power, and more so than most.

An over-all estimate of the conditions in Angola and Mozambique is necessarily a somewhat mixed one because of the combination of lack of development, of swift and harsh suppression of Africans who step out of line, and of acceptance on more or less equal terms of the few who through education and way of life are regarded as being assimilated into the Portuguese culture. A generally relaxed and unhurried atmosphere and the absence of a rigorous color bar — the usual statement is that there is a culture bar but not a color bar — point up a sharp contrast between these territories and the Union and the Rhodesias. On the other hand, the African who wants to make his way in the world may well move across the border, as hundreds of thousands have done, into the more highly developed neighboring British territories where greater opportunities for employment exist. Furthermore, charges continue to be heard that, despite legislation to the contrary and heated denials, the Portuguese continue to tolerate conditions approximating forced labor.

The Portuguese maintain that they have achieved a condition of interracial harmony which stands out in happy contrast to the embittered upheavals of other African colonies. Vigorously challenging this contention, a recent observer of the state of affairs in Mozambique claims that what is practised there "is simply one of the several varieties of *apartheid* which are to be found all over

Southern Africa." The assumption of the Negro's inferiority, he contends,

> coupled with the arbitrary beatings, the discriminatory wages, the forced labor, the curfews, the denial of freedom of movement, the unilateral contracts, the compulsory crop system, the separate and unequal educational system, and the subjection to arbitrary, personal justice on every hand, leave little room for the Portuguese or their well-wishers to maneuver.[1]

The Portuguese boast that they take fully into the fold those Africans, termed *assimilados*, who have demonstrated their abandonment of their own culture through the adoption of European civilization. Among other things, this system tends to remove from the African society and incorporate into the Portuguese precisely those persons who are likely to be the most dangerous troublemakers if they are left without access to the ruling group. It has, in consequence, presumably served to slow up the emergence of political activity, but its practical operation is not very far-reaching as far as numbers go. The Portuguese have been associated with their major African dependencies for upwards of half a millennium. In that time, according to the census of 1950, they have in Angola brought into the *assimilado* ranks 30,039 Africans of a total "uncivilized" population of over 4,000,000, while in Mozambique the corresponding figure was a mere 4,353 Africans of some 5,700,000 "uncivilized." Whether the period of Portuguese association with the two territories be taken for these purposes as 500 or 100 years, the time which would be necessary to achieve the purposes of assimilation, bringing the mass of Africans to equality with the Portuguese — and hence to a share in the trifling political rights which have been conceded to anyone — stretches out into infinity. As John Gunther put it, stressing the very limited educational facilities, "Of course the catch to the whole system is that it is difficult almost beyond conception for an African to qualify." [2] According to the 1950 census, 99 per cent of the African population of Mozambique was illiterate, and eight years later the territory was reported to have "exactly one African with a university degree." [3] The effort of the Portuguese government to add to the already substantial body of white settlers works not only to diminish the significance of the rise of the assimilated Africans but also to foreshadow the kind of trouble which a settler community always brings in its wake.

I have heard an African student in the United States comment that it is after all useless to hope that a country which is itself undemocratic and undeveloped should introduce democracy and development in its overseas dependencies.

In the case of Belgium and the Congo the situation is obviously a radically different one. Belgium itself ranks both among the leading democracies and among the major industrial economies of the world, and the Congo has moved to become an economic power in its own right through its intensive development as a producer and, in less degree, a processor of raw materials. With impressive results Belgian energies have been devoted to the building up of the economy of the Congo on modern lines. The magnitude of the change can be found in the previously mentioned fact that nearly a quarter of the African population were living outside their customary tribal areas by the end of 1956 — for the most part, as an official Belgian information booklet puts it, in "the 'centres extra-coutumiers' made up of conglomerations of uprooted masses grouped around the European establishments." Between the demand for labor for Western enterprises and the attraction of the cities, African manpower has been drawn away from the countryside to the point where both the traditional community life and native agriculture have been seriously endangered.

The massive economic advance of the Congo has been accompanied by a degree of attention to African social welfare which, however much it may fall short of European standards, can serve as a model for the rest of the continent, even though its costs were very largely met from the forced savings derived from the low wages paid the great bulk of the Congolese workers.[4] The concern with social welfare was not imposed from below by African pressures and demands but from above as a result of a mixture of humanitarianism, a desire to live down the shocking legacy of Leopold's Congo, and sound business practices which were particularly in order in a relatively underpopulated territory. The keynote of the Belgian attitude has been paternalism, normally untainted by any assumption that the African might be encouraged to step forward on his own.

Although no hard and fast color line has been drawn and the Congolese have been given an opportunity to rise to progressively higher levels of employment, the hierarchical separation between the races continues to be a pervasive reality. It is typical that cities should have grown on the principle of a clear division between the European and the African quarters. Shunning the avowal of a strictly racial basis for their policies, the Belgians have with full candor expressed their belief in the "civilizing mission of the West" and in the rightness of European supremacy.[5]

In the political sphere the Belgians have prided themselves on their empirical approach. For the first two or three decades after Belgium took over the Congo it was possible to concentrate almost wholly on economic development and the introduction of some basic elements of social welfare. No serious attention needed to be paid to a political future in which an unchallenged paternal white rule appeared to stretch unbrokenly into the future. As time went by, however, a well-elaborated body of doctrine was evolved which must now be adapted to situations undreamed of a few years ago.

The heart of this doctrine was the conviction that Belgium's responsibility was to bring as much of the Congolese mass as possible into the modern world and not to rest content, as Britain and France were accused of doing, with the production of a thin upper crust of Western-educated leaders into whose oligarchical hands the country could be delivered. The Belgian authorities have insisted upon the need to create a strong Congolese middle class as an essential underpinning for democracy and as a potential check upon the African elite which might at some point take over. Until the mass and the middle class were prepared for their new roles, political rights were to be denied to everybody. "Everybody" decidedly included the growing body of Europeans resident or settled in the Congo — in 1956 the white population amounted to 107,413 persons — even though the latter were inclined to doubt that their claims to a share in power should be put on all fours with those of the Africans. In principle all power flowed from Belgium. The official philosophy found expression in Governor General Pétillon's statement in 1954 that Belgium could not envisage delegating powers of decision to African councils as long as the political education of the Congolese was incomplete. To hand over the controls of the Congo to a European minority, he added, "would be tantamount to renouncing forever the Belgo-Congolese community" which was being formulated as the ultimate goal.[6]

At least until 1959 the Belgian authorities retained the initiative: they could still call the tune for the Congo and determine the time at which it would be played. The political calm which reigned was to be attributed not to the suppression of clamorous nationalist demands for freedom — although the authorities stood ready to suppress — but to the substantial nonexistence of such demands. The disturbers of the peace have in the past been leaders of aberrant and messianic religious sects rather than nationalists seeking the political overthrow of the regime. The intimate relation of these movements to colonial policies and institutions was persuasively stated by Basil Davidson, who saw them as part of the price Belgium has had to pay for its refusal to undertake political advance:

It cannot be an accident that these "dissident religions," these strange Biblical forms of subversion should be peaceful in territories, such as the Gold Coast or the French Sudan, where Africans have a legitimate political outlet, and the reverse of peaceful in the Belgian Congo, where Africans have none. There are close analogies in Kenya and South Africa. Wherever Africans are balked in every means of political advance, they tend to take their own way out.[7]

One of the key elements is that Belgium, by withholding access to higher education, has succeeded in the past in preventing the rise of a Western-trained elite which would formulate "national" grievances and give leadership to the new forces. The few Africans who rose to higher levels of education from the mission schools were frequently drawn into the priesthood and hence diverted from the political scene. With 1,282,645 children out of a total population of nearly 13,000,000 reported as being in the Congo's schools in 1956, the groundwork is evidently being laid for a new social and political order. Even more significant for the immediate political future is the recent opening of two universities in the Congo and the education abroad of the first trickle of Congolese allowed to go to Europe and the United States.

In the Congo as in most of the rest of Africa the future has come surging in with a rush. What looked as if it could be entrusted to the patient work of generations to come must now be telescoped within a decade or two at the best. Developments within the Congo have combined with happenings elsewhere in Africa — the independence of Ghana and other states, the transformation of French Africa, the African conferences held in Accra — to render all earlier programs and timetables hopelessly inadequate.

Despite the lack of pressure from below, a few Belgian authorities had already begun by about 1950 to take serious cognizance of the new situation which was in the making. The first significant outcropping of Congolese nationalism was the unprecedented political manifesto issued in July 1956.[8] Its generally mild and unhurried tone, contemplating a thirty-year plan for emancipation, indicated that the pressures were still not very intense, but for the first time the Congolese had spoken up for themselves in modern terms. As in the case of a number of other African political movements which in their early stages have adapted themselves closely to the policies and institutional opportunities offered by the colonial government,[9] the manifesto accepted the idea of a Belgo-Congolese community as the goal to be sought. This broader community was, however, not to be a direct growth from the Belgian-dominated colonial situation but was to follow the independence of the Congo which would freely negotiate the terms of its collaboration with Belgium.

The assumption of indefinite continuation of colonial paternalism has given way to official acknowledgement of the need to move forward toward a community based on partnership between the races. Partnership has come to be a blessed word in more than one African country — blessed at least for Europeans — but what the Africans in their millions will make of it remains wholly obscure. In 1956 Governor General Pétillon asserted that "Two ethnic groups of different civilizations are animated by the same will: to form together a single people" [10] — a cheering conclusion but not one on which the Congolese people have ever been consulted or expressed themselves. Nor, for that matter, can one be wholly sure that the Belgians in the Congo will gracefully yield the supremacy they have so far enjoyed. One Congolese has said of the Europeans in the colony that "they live as far away from us as if they inhabited the planet Sirius," and most of them have known the African only as a servant or in some other inferior role.

The ponderous caution of the Belgians was reflected in their first application of democratic procedures in the Congo when in 1957 elections were held on a sharply limited basis for municipal councilors. The trifling share in power which was transferred was less significant than the bare fact that Europeans and Africans jointly participated in the vote.

The bloody and destructive riots which broke out in Leopoldville early in 1959, following the All-African People's Conference in Accra, came as a profound shock to the Belgians and hastened the process of political advance. Only a few days after the outbreak of the riots the Belgian government issued a declaration which announced the intention to "organize a democracy in the Congo which will be capable of exercising the prerogatives of sovereignty and of deciding upon its independence." [11] In the future, it was announced, political institutions at all levels must draw their authority and legitimacy from universal suffrage, and a program was elaborated for the establishment of a series of elected and appointed councils to which real power would be given. At the end of the road the Congo and Belgium are to decide freely on the maintenance of a partnership between the two countries. All traces of racial discrimination are to disappear in the Congo, but in the unspecified interval before independence Belgium reasserted her "responsibilities toward all the inhabitants of the Congo" and the need to maintain a sound administration under Belgian control. The Belgian authorities have been forced to undertake a drastic recalculation of their position. It remains to be seen whether their revised program goes far enough and fast enough to meet the demands which will increasingly be made upon them.

Belgian colonial policy can be summed up with precision because it concerns only the Congo and adjoining Ruanda-Urundi. Any effort to generalize in similar fashion about French and British colonialism is immediately rendered suspect by the multiplicity and diversity of the territories involved. Furthermore, each power has adopted several different approaches to meet particular circumstances, as illustrated by the contrast between the way the British have behaved in the Rhodesias and in West Africa.

The stock phrases used to differentiate British and French policy have their utility even though they exaggerate the degree of divergence between the two. By native inclination the French have always tended to find the true inspiration for their colonial activities in the doctrine of assimilation. As far back as 1792 a revolutionary decree declared that "all men, without distinction of color, domiciled in the French colonies are French citizens and enjoy all the rights assured by the Constitution." From time to time they have temporarily swung away from assimilation and distinguished individuals have renounced it as unfeasible or undesirable. This has not prevented a constant drift back to the basic proposition that the ideal of the French colonial vocation is to bring less fortunate peoples within the fold of the French culture and a single all-embracing France. This fundamental French appreciation of the nature of the colonial problem is clearly distinguished from that of the British whose tendency is to assume that peoples are properly distinct and separate. The contrast between the two policies, however, cannot be said to lie in the degree to which the Westernized elements are brought within the cultural heritage of the metropolitan power. Although it may contradict the abstract logic of the case, the British colonial elites which emerge from Oxford and Cambridge or from the colonial educational systems are no less indoctrinated in British ways of life and thought than are the French-produced elites in French ways.

The roots of the difference in the two positions are to be sought in the British conviction that there are many breeds of men, each destined to develop along its own lines and the contrary French belief in the ultimate oneness of mankind. It has fitted the French genius in the past to assume that the people of their colonies could become Frenchmen and to aim at their integration into the homogeneous society of a single Greater France revolving about Paris. The British, on the other hand, work toward the creation of a looser Commonwealth made up of diverse and independent peoples. Save in the special case of the Irish — an example which did not encourage repetition, although it has been proposed for Malta — the British have consistently rejected the French practice of bringing representatives of the colonial peoples into the imperial parliament. The British lean toward a large devolution of power to the colonies themselves (or to the officials in them) which are regarded as constituting distinct and unique entities, while the French system has been based on far greater centralization in Paris.

The French in the colonies are likely to find themselves most at home with the *évolués*, the British with the simple and "unspoiled" peasant, villager, or tribesman. Perhaps it can be hazarded that the French, more rationalist-universalist in outlook, find it natural that their colonial wards should aspire to be Frenchmen, while the British, culturally pluralistic and seeing their pattern of life as something peculiar to themselves, almost resent the thought that another people might enter into it, and, indeed, have the gravest doubt that it can really be done. To the British, a man who has so far departed from his own is a natural object of suspicion; to the French, he is a man who has seen the light. I have heard an Algerian quote Krishna Menon as saying that the British called the Indians many names but at least never called them British.

French spokesmen have contended that France must inevitably carry its own principles of freedom and democracy with it into its overseas territories, and so in a sense it must, but it has been laggard in endowing these territories with free political institutions. In a characteristic reversal of British practice, until very recently France has only grudgingly conceded any real share in the management of their own affairs to its dependent peoples, although the Fourth Republic made elaborate provision for their representation in the central governing institutions in Paris. The equitableness but not the principle of this representation was impaired by the heavy overweighting given to France itself as against the dependent empire and to Europeans as against the indigenous peoples. The most striking lapse was the grant of equal representation in the French National Assembly to European and Moslem Algerians despite the fact that the Europeans were outnumbered by nine to one.

France has traditionally set itself distinctive assimilationist goals in its colonial policy, but has it achieved equally distinctive results? French culture has penetrated deeply wherever France has ruled, although perhaps no more so than the culture of other colonial powers such as Britain and Spain. In the political sphere if the assimilationist doctrine worked fully France could hope to be spared the impact of colonial nationalism because the new elites would merge into the widening French society and not demand national separateness. For much of the French colonial empire the answer is already in. The peoples of former French Indochina, Tunisia, Morocco, and Guinea, and presumably Algeria as well, have rejected identification with France. Peoples which have evolved high and intricate cultures of their own and are aware of a history stretching back to an immemorial past are unlikely to accept assimilation to an alien culture which has imposed itself from outside. For peoples at the level of those of tropical Africa the outcome is perhaps less certain. Even here it is unreasonable to look for more in the way of political assimilation than nationalism sufficiently tempered by French indoctrination to enable the emerging African communities to live at peace in some form of association with France.

Two themes stand out in a favorite French version of the issue. One is that since nationalism is outmoded in a world of interdependence the pursuit of national sovereignty has become a futile and dangerous anachronism. The other seeks to enable dependent peoples to bypass the stage of nationalism through laying stress upon the freedom which is brought to all their individual members. As Premier Guy Mollet put it in a speech in New York in 1957:

> In Algeria, as in Black Africa, France intends to ensure the complete liberation of the peoples for whom she is responsible — in other words, the individual liberation of each man and each woman, their economic and social liberation by freeing them from poverty, their political liberation by putting them in a position where they can freely express their opinions.[12]

This is in many ways an admirable and attractive doctrine. The fatal flaw is that, with the rarest of exceptions, the dependent peoples are not content to receive their freedom merely as individuals but are insistent upon the liberation of their nations as collective bodies.

The African need perform no great feat of memory to establish that until the end of World War II forced labor and the *indigénat* (a special and prejudicial penal system for Africans) were in force, that French citizenship was limited to a handful, that there was virtually no representation either in Paris or locally, and that, in brief, the ordinary African was a "native," very largely at the disposal of the French administrator and employer. Cultural and social assimilation was for practical purposes restricted to a small elite. Economic assimilation went far in relation to markets and investment but carried no implication that standards of living and social services should rise to the level of those in France. Even when the postwar reforms were introduced, there remained the racial discrimination of the *petit blanc* in the colony, the continued harassment by the old-style employer or official, and the manipulation of supposedly democratic political processes to produce the results called for from above. On these scores and a variety of others, including bitter colonial warfare in Indochina and Algeria, it is easy to see why the peoples of the French territories overseas should be wary of seeking their liberty, equality and fraternity within the French community rather than as national entities which would come to some sort of terms with France.

It is, however, true that African leaders within the French orbit have sometimes been extravagantly responsive to the lead given them by France, although the drift in recent years has been in the other direction. Thus Blaise Diagne, African deputy from Senegal, proclaimed in 1922 that "We, French blacks, want to remain French, France having given us every liberty and mingling us without reservation with her own European children." [13]

Even as late as 1957 when this strand of thought had already largely lost its appeal, it was firmly echoed in the rhetorical question posed in the United Nations by Félix Houphouet-Boigny, Ivory Coast leader, member of the French Cabinet, and head of the major French African party, the *Rassemblement Démocratique Africain*:

> Is there a single country in the world which would offer to an African of my color, race, and stage of civilization, the liberty, equality, and fraternity we can find in the French community? [14]

To the *mystique* of national independence, which he dismissed as negative and antiquated, Houphouet opposed the interdependence of nations which he portrayed as the imperative of this century. Meeting with Kwame Nkrumah in Abidjan shortly after Ghana had achieved independence, he rejected for "Africans of French culture" the solution which Nkrumah had won for the

Gold Coast, seeking instead "a community of peoples, equal and fraternal." [15]

One other key personage, who is more in the current vein, may be singled out: Léopold Sedar Senghor, a dominant figure in Senegal, a French poet of distinction, and also a member of French Cabinets. With Houphouet, Senghor saw nationalism as too narrow a creed for the twentieth century, but he expressed a greater sense of Africa's distinctive cultural heritage, of the necessity of taking into central account the *Négritude* — a favorite term with him — which is Africa's essence.[16] Looking to federalism for salvation, he insisted that a federal union could have real meaning only if each of the partners to it was strong and antonomous, and he therefore demanded the maintenance and strengthening of the two federations of African territories, French West and Equatorial Africa, as a prior condition for the Franco-African community. In 1956 and after, he denounced the French authorities for Balkanizing French Africa by undermining the federations through the grant of a large installment of self-government to their twelve constituent territories.

Continued association of some sort between France and its African territories still commands favor as the 1958 decision of all except Guinea to adhere to de Gaulle's new Community demonstrated, but the persistent trend in the postwar years has been toward an assertion of the unique personality of Africa — a personality which must find expression in its own and not in French terms. The subordinate partnership implied by the abortive French Union of the Fourth Republic has given way to a claim for Franco-African equality. The price for African participation in an association with France is constantly on the rise.

The new temper was expressed by one of the leaders of the *Rassemblement Démocratique Africain* at its Bamako convention in September 1957, when he laid down the condition: "We accept marriage with the metropole only if the right of divorce is reserved." [17]

The trend makes itself felt in many ways. Where political parties and trade unions were a few years ago affiliated with French parties and unions, they are now for the most part independent bodies with a solely African base. Where membership in the National Assembly and even more in the government in Paris had previously been a matter of prestige for the political leader, it is now of more dubious value because of the implication that he is tied to French policy instead of being free to pursue African interests. Houphouet retained his leadership of the R.D.A. at Bamako but the younger and more radical Sékou Touré of French Guinea appeared to have a larger influence in the shaping of a policy which challenged France more sharply than Houphouet, firmly established in Paris, found to his taste. The orientation toward Paris is declining, the inward concentration on Africa is growing. A significant step in that direction was taken early in 1958 when the major French African parties, meeting (be it noted) in Paris to consider merging into a single party, asserted their claim to a right of independence even though their immediate goal was stated to be the creation of a federal republic including France and other overseas territories.

The political transformation which French Africa has undergone in the last years is staggering in its scope and speed. Three major landmarks can be singled out. First came the striking innovations of the 1946 constitution which embodied much of the changed outlook derived from the war years and led on to further reforms in the succeeding decade. The next big jump ahead, clearing the way for decentralization and self-government, was the adoption of the law of June 23, 1956, the so-called *loi cadre* which strengthened the overseas legislatures and moved toward the principle of responsible cabinets. It also created everywhere a single electoral college based on universal suffrage, thus depriving the locally established Europeans of the privileged position which they had retained in some territories. Granted by France well before African pressures became irresistible, this piece of legislation implied the abandonment of both assimilation and the time-honored concept of the Republic, one and indivisible. For practical purposes the key issue now was not whether self-government was on the way but how fast it would come. In the Trust Territories of Togoland and the Cameroons independence was promised for the immediate future.

The third great step was that taken by de Gaulle in 1958 after his resumption of power as a result of the Algerian crisis. No longer was France to adhere to the rigid pronouncement of the Brazzaville conference, called under the General's auspices in 1944, that self-government outside the French orbit was inconceivable for the overseas territories. Only for Algeria itself did this doctrine survive. For the rest, in a move which appeared to rouse little excitement in France, de Gaulle in effect proclaimed that any overseas territory which at any time wanted to declare its independence was free to do so. In the constitutional referendum of September 1958, which amounted overseas to a plebiscite on independence or adherence to France, all the territories save Guinea voted "yes" for the maintenance of the French tie. In most instances the vote was so nearly unanimous as to raise unhappy memories of the plebiscites held in totalitarian regimes. The "yes" vote in the Ivory Coast, Upper Volta, and Middle Congo came to 99 per cent, in Ubangi-Shari to 98 per cent, in the Sudan and Senegal to 97 per cent, and in Mauretania to 94 per cent. On the other side of the fence, in Guinea where Sékou Touré — having earlier told de Gaulle that "We prefer poverty in freedom to riches in slavery" — threw his full weight against the French connection, the "no" vote amounted to 95 per cent. Only in Niger, Chad, and Madagascar did as many as a fifth of the voters stand out against the majority. Most extraordinary of all, in Algeria where some 80 per cent of the registered voters participated, 3,589,876, or 96.7 per cent of those voting, voted "yes"; in the Algerian case, however, independence was not an alternative in the plebiscite.[18]

The constitution of the Fifth Republic set off in its preamble from acceptance of "the free determination of peoples" and moved on to lay down the ground rules for a Community in which France and the overseas territories choosing to accept it would be the member states. After the plebiscite, in which Guinea had declared itself independent, all the French territories south of the Sahara with the exception of Somaliland declared themselves republics endowed with the far-reaching self-government assumed by the constitution. Then began the exploration of the functioning of the new Community and its joint institutions for the control of foreign policy, defense, common economic affairs, and other matters entrusted to it.

De Gaulle has conceded what probably no other French leader

would have dared to concede. Essentially he must have gambled on the proposition that if the peoples ruled by France were given freedom to go their way they would prefer to remain associated with France, as the British territories other than Ireland and Burma have chosen to remain in the Commonwealth.

To achieve a working Community, however, France will have to abandon traditions and attitudes which have deep roots and somehow reconcile itself to the possibility of a non-white majority in federal institutions dealing with such vital matters as military affairs and foreign policy. The universal sweep elsewhere of the demand for self-determination establishes a strong presumption that French Africa will follow the standard pattern in insisting upon equality and independence, however ready it may be to maintain ties of some sort with France. Assimilation is progressively losing its force as it spreads out over the mass. A small group of individuals may be assimilated — the first generation or two of *évolués* who prize their role as intellectuals raised up out of the native mass — but once some not precisely definable barrier of numbers has been passed, new forces come into play which bring qualitative as well as quantitative change. The more the people at large come to be involved, the greater is the probability that African nations and not France will take the center of the stage.

It was Senghor who asserted that the "yes" vote was not an acceptance of the colonial regime but a "yes" for African independence in a rediscovered unity:

> The Community is for us only a gateway and a means . . . to prepare us for independence in the style of the British dependent territories. Beyond nominal independence — which is easy to obtain — it is real independence that we want to achieve.[19]

The French acceptance of a right of separation for their dependencies was delayed until de Gaulle almost casually announced it in the course of his African tour in 1958; the equivalent British step was taken significantly earlier. Since 1945 it has been the British practice to hasten toward the ultimate goal of independence rather than to linger in search of definitive proofs of economic and political maturity. The doctrine still remains that self-government should be accorded those who are fitted for it, but the criteria of fitness have been drastically tailored to meet new circumstances, as have the assumptions as to how best to promote the imperial interest. Only in the white settler territories is there serious difficulty: just as the independence which de Gaulle conceded to Black Africa did not extend to Algeria, so Britain's policies stumbled and halted when they came to Kenya and the Rhodesias.

To date the British have salvaged far more from the disintegration of empire than have the French or the Dutch, and a large part of the reason for their success lies in their sage decision to work with rather than against the forces which their imperial presence aided in bringing into being. The British, once they have decided to break with colonialism, have shown their ability also to rise above the prejudices of race and color which have always plagued their relations with their subject peoples. Over a century ago Lord Durham in his report on Canada rendered the pungent verdict that

> It is not anywhere a virtue of the English race to look with complacency on any manners, customs or laws which appear strange to them; accustomed to form a high estimate of their own superiority, they take no pains to conceal from others their contempt and intolerance of their usages.[20]

The British club which excluded the natives of the country was a notorious symbol of the way the British acted overseas. With the passing of colonial rule these attitudes appear to have vanished as well. Departing from their dependencies before they were pushed out, the British have been welcomed back as friends and associates.

With the possible exception of the United States, Britain has consistently gone further than any other power in endowing its dependent peoples with political institutions which had the makings of self-government in them. Despite the long list of imperial abuses and acts of oppression, the measure of freedom of speech, press, and assembly which was customarily granted in British colonies put to shame many independent countries. In consequence, it is the British territories which have consistently produced the most vigorous and mature nationalist movements. Sir Frederick D. (later Lord) Lugard was by no means alone in his boast that this was encompassed within the British intention:

> If there is unrest and a desire for independence, as in India and

Egypt, it is because we have taught the people the value of liberty and freedom, which for centuries these peoples had not known. Their very discontent is a measure of their progress.[21]

To cite India as the most striking example is to risk being charged with overlooking the bitterly repressive measures in which the British engaged in the last decades before the grant of independence. Even when these have been taken fully into account, and the question of the color bar added for good measure, a vitally important array of facts remains for consideration. These include such things as the large number of Indians who secured a Western education, the flourishing of an Indian press which spent much of its time building up the national cause, the existence of great political organizations such as the Congress and the Moslem League, and the creation at various levels of councils and administrative bodies in which Indians increasingly took the lead. Indian nationalism derived less from the defects of British rule than from its positive accomplishments. It is significant that the nationalist movement centered in British India proper and not in the princely states which generally lagged behind in adaptation to the modern world. Unanswerable as the charge may be that what the British did prior to 1945 was too little and too late, it was still in many ways a model of political advance as compared with most other colonial regimes, and the democratic stability of India after independence was a tribute to the British as well as to the statesmanship of Nehru and his associates. Britain's mode of leaving India made it possible to remember some of the best of the long relationship and to forget some of the worst.[22]

Often accused of resorting to the imperial device of dividing in order to rule, the British have more recently been taking active steps to bring nations into existence in their colonial territories where no nations existed before. The most interesting case of this rare phenomenon — the effort of a colonial power to forge the instruments to which it can turn over its responsibilities — was that of Malaya,[23] but the same sort of program could be found in the African territories. In the West Indies the pressure toward federation came rather from London than from the islands themselves. The determination to speed the surrender of power made possible a degree of collaboration with nationalist leaders which was ruled out by earlier attitudes: Nkrumah was brought from prison to head the new-style government of the Gold Coast. Indeed, the limit of collaboration comes to be set not by the fear of consorting with those who are subverting empire, but by the fear that through consorting with them too much and too openly their standing as intransigent nationalists will be compromised. For the proper nationalist an at least ritual denunciation of the imperialists is essential, even though he may be working on intimate terms with the men whom he is denouncing.[24]

As independence was approached or achieved, a number of nationalist leaders have expressed their gratitude to Britain for starting their countries on the way, in strange contrast to the customary onslaughts on colonialism. Ghana's Prime Minister Nkrumah paid tribute to Britain's "wise leadership and guidance" and was encouraged that Britain could still be counted on as a "great and ever-abiding friend." When the Eastern Region of Nigeria was granted self-government, Prime Minister Azikiwe similarly extolled the "gallant heroes" who had braved the tropical climate to contribute to Nigeria's progress.[25]

Any sense that the colonial millennium has come is dissipated, however, when one turns to dependencies in which white settlers constitute a dominant elemant. Here British traditions begin to cross each other and tangle matters up. Who shall exercise self-determination and what are the obligations of imperial tutelage? The American Revolution, as well as the evolution of the older dominions, might be taken as establishing the right of the free-born Englishman overseas to govern both himself and the original inhabitants of the lands he has taken over — a point to which the French make unkind reference when the American anti-colonial tradition is cited as justifying support of the Algerians rather than the French *colons*. It was regarded as a triumph of liberalism when Britain in 1909 relaxed its imperial control over the South African colonies and established the Union in which the white minority had full supremacy over the African majority, and when in 1923 the whites of Southern Rhodesia were granted self-government.

The other side of the medal was vigorously represented in the British White Paper of 1923 which set so high a standard that it has only rarely been reached:

Primarily, Kenya is an African territory and His Majesty's Government think it necessary definitely to record their considered opinion that the interests of the African natives must be paramount, and that if, and when, these interests and the interests of the immigrant races should conflict, the former should prevail. . . . In the administration of Kenya, His Majesty's Government regard themselves as exercising a trust on behalf of the African population, and they are unable to share or delegate this trust, the object of which may be defined as the protection and advancement of the native races.[26]

The whittling away of this ideal was not very long delayed. In 1931 a Joint Committee of both Houses of Parliament undertook a restatement, accepted as British policy, in which native paramountcy was defined to mean no more than that the interests of the overwhelming majority should not be subordinated to those of a minority of a different race. In its most recent incarnation the magic word is no longer paramountcy but partnership, with the European minority as senior partner. The creation of the Central African Federation in 1953, over vehement African protest, was a demonstration that for working purposes predominance rested with the white man. In Kenya the balance has been held somewhat more even under the moderately watchful eye of the Colonial Office — although note should be made of the comment of a former Governor in relation to a particular settler-African issue: "But Downing Street, as always when faced by determined settler resistance, capitulated." [27] The Lennox-Boyd constitution of 1957 for Kenya contained ingenious devices to ensure that the 6,000,000 Africans should not secure an undue advantage over the 60,000 Europeans.

African and other experience, including that of the Indians in the Americas, does not justify any easy conclusion that white settlers are a very useful element in promoting the advancement of the peoples among whom they live. On the contrary, despite the fact that the white settler areas have made by far the greatest economic advance, it is more plausible to see white settlement as delaying African advance rather than stimulating it. Like the rest of mankind, the settlers are inevitably concerned with their own interests, which include the maintenance of white supremacy and the continuance of a supply of cheap and amenable labor. Holding the leading positions of all kinds, they have little incentive to push the Africans ahead as rivals. The white man's dominance has unquestionably contributed to the relative backwardness of the Africans in East and Central Africa as contrasted with West Africa in such spheres as education, the professions, and economic and political life. In 1951 it was asserted that "after half a century of European rule in East and Central Africa, not a single African has yet been appointed to a major post in the civil service there." [28] Three years later one of the elected African members of the Central African Parliament protested that "Intelligent African leadership hardly develops in a state where the relationship between the European and the African is one of master and servant, superior and inferior." [29] The Africans of Central Africa and Kenya have in consequence felt that they would do better under Colonial Office protection than by exposing themselves to local European rule. In a petition to Queen Elizabeth asking continued British control, some chiefs and others of Nyasaland identified federation with dominance by European settlers and warned that

> the African has seen how that political dominance has operated in the Union of South Africa and in Southern Rhodesia to the detriment of the Africans, and he knows by experience what to expect if the European settlers' political domination is extended to Nyasaland.[30]

Nyasaland's riots of 1959 carried the protest a violent step further.

Not only Africans are wary of European settlers and the effect they may have. Chester Bowles reports that when he asked the Governor General of the Congo what it would take to bring the Congo under Communist rule, the answer was "One hundred thousand white settlers." Another Belgian official, asked what he would do if he were Governor of Kenya, replied that he would buy the land and move the settlers out, even if it required all the NATO armies: "If the settlers are allowed to keep control, they will bring all of Africa tumbling down about our ears." [31]

Concrete samples of the problems involved can be found in a number of territories. In the Trust Territory of Tanganyika the issues were elaborately canvassed in the report of the United Nations Visiting Mission of 1954 and in the comments and debates elicited by that report. The population imbalance made this a peculiarly striking case of a multi-racial society since the country contained some 20,000 Europeans (of whom fewer than 3,000 were regarded as permanently settled) and 84,000 Asians as against 8,000,000 Africans. At the time of the Mission's visit, the nonofficial side of the Legislative Council reflected parity between Europeans and non-Europeans, with seven Europeans, four Africans, and three Asians. In 1955 the parity principle was to be recognized in a different guise through the acceptance of the racial groups as equal political entities, each entitled to nine unofficial seats. As the Visiting Mission pointed out, this type of representation did not reflect the greatly disparate numbers of the racial communities "but their relative state of economic and social advancement and their influence in public affairs." An official majority was also maintained, presumably in part because, as the Mission commented, the term "multi-racial society" was an optimistic misnomer covering the fact that there were actually three essentially separate societies. In his appearance before the Trusteeship Council, Julius K. Nyerere, representing the leading political party, the Tanganyika African National Union, stated that TANU had accepted the principle of parity of representation on the understanding that it was a transitional stage toward a more democratic form of representation with African majorities, leading on to full self-government. Denying that his party had ever advocated that Tanganyika should be governed by Africans alone, he insisted that non-Africans should feel at home in the country, but that all the rights and duties of Tanganyikan citizens should be shared on the basis of individual, not collective, equality. The Mission similarly contended that "a self-governing or independent Tanganyika will inevitably be a state primarily African in character with a government mainly in African hands." [32] One may wonder how much at home a few thousand European voters would feel in an electorate dominated by several million Africans.

One colonial territory which stands out in almost full uniqueness is Puerto Rico, whose more than two million people have been prepared to forego — or to sublimate — their nationalism and to accept an unprecedented status within the political system of the United States. Whether because of honest persuasion that they form a part of the American community or because of a calculation of advantage, the Puerto Ricans as a whole have abstained from the vehemence of nationalist agitation. In accepting their Commonwealth status in 1952 they did not by any means abandon their separate existence as a Spanish-speaking people shaped by their own distinctive heritage, but they recognized that a substantial part of that heritage was now linked with the United States. The role which they elected to play was far closer to statehood in the American union than to independence. Their outstanding leader, Luis Muñoz Marín, has spoken of Puerto Rico achieving its independence within the independence of the United States, and of his coming to awareness that love of the homeland and independence were two conflicting ideas, the latter "a mortal enemy of the people." What he said of his countrymen can be said of few elsewhere:

> I learned that among the simple people the nationalist concept does not exist, because in its place there is a deep understanding of freedom. I learned that in their wisdom they prefer — if they have to choose — one who governs respectfully from a distance to one who governs despotically from nearby.[33]

The experience of the other major American territory acquired at the same time was a very different one. In contrast to American uncertainty as to the proper destiny of Puerto Rico, there was from the outset the assumption that the Philippines would be accorded independence at the end of a period of tutelage. The Filipinos on their side rarely wavered from their devotion to their national cause and to independence as the goal: the party which spoke for the most and quickest independence could normally be counted on to win the election. But, presumably because of early encouragement from America, Filipino nationalism has been compatible with a large measure of friendship for the United States: the efforts of political candidates to win favor through a parade of anti-Americanism has not proved rewarding. For the period of American rule, however, the Filipino attitude was close to what Kwame Nkrumah describes as the motto and policy of the Gold Coast's Convention People's Party: "We prefer self-government with danger to servitude in tranquillity" and "Seek ye first the political kingdom and all things else shall be added unto you." [34]

Many elements have entered into the massing of the anti-colonial forces. Not all of these elements can be laid out with scientific accuracy because they in good part lie in the realm of the intangibles rather than the tangibles of the colonial relationship; nor is it easy at this close distance to be at all sure of the proper verdict on colonialism.

A verdict of an unusually balanced variety has been attempted by Herbert Lüthy, who rightly emphasized that the dependent peoples demand more and not less Europeanization. It was Lüthy's conclusion that

> *Europe's colonization of the world was neither a chain of crimes nor a chain of beneficence; it was the birth of the modern world itself;* not one of the former colonial peoples remembers it with gratitude, for it was an alien rule, but none wishes to turn the clock back, and that is colonialism's historical justification.[35]

Both of the aspects here brought out — rejection and acceptance — need to be kept in mind in looking back on Europe's conquest of the world and in assessing the future of a world out from under Europe's control.

Man as a social animal needs a community with which he can identify himself and to which he intimately belongs. In compensation for the older close-knit communities whose survival they threatened, the colonial governments could offer at best such admirable but glacial matters as law and order, impartial justice, and good administration. A colonial government might, in ideal abstraction, be a paragon of honesty, justice, efficiency, and benevolence, but as one of the well-known colonial officials of our times has put it:

> Its fabulous powers did not derive from any popular consent; it was neither for the people, nor by the people, nor of the people. Its deliberations and its aims were a deep mystery; its plans were hatched in seclusion; its hand struck out of the blue.[36]

A far deeper emotional appeal lay in the concept of the nation which the rising leadership brought back from its study of the West. Here was a creed which could serve as the crystallizing center for the growing unrest. It offered not only a new community to unite societies in process of atomization, but also a program of action in which the people themselves were to be the principal actors.

Nationalism looms up as the greatest single resultant of the colonial era, yet on closer view many aspects of it turn out to be highly problematical. The nations and nationalisms which the imperial powers have had so large a responsibility for bringing into existence are still very much in the making. The outer boundaries of the nations are in some instances undetermined and their effective membership is amorphous, while the directions their nationalisms will take are variable and uncertain. Any effort to specify the common denominators of spirit and value which are shared by the Western-educated leaders in the urban capital, the unemployed half-educated, the disinherited proletariat of the African or Asian cities, and the illiterate peasants of field and village is likely to end as well as to start in florid generalities. While it would be wholly unrealistic not to recognize that this national indeterminateness and inner pluralism attaches to nations everywhere, in the older nations — more homogeneous products of a gradual evolution — the disparities are at least less glaringly evident and intense. But at this stage it becomes necessary to turn to an exploration of the known and unknown terrain surrounding the idea of nation and nationalism, and the ways in which it has worked in the modern world.

PART TWO

THE ANATOMY OF THE NATION

CHAPTER V

The Nature of the Nation

ONE OF THE CENTRAL FEATURES of the great revolution of our times which has brought the modern world into being is that the peoples of mankind in successive stages have been swept into a vivid and sometimes all-consuming sense of their existence as nations — or at least of their desire to create nations where none existed before. That the peoples of Asia and now, somewhat hesitantly and often in embryonic fashion, the peoples of Africa are flowering out into luxuriant nationalisms of their own may be taken as a sure sign that the revolution has come their way. The new ideas and forces which have radiated out from their starting point in Western Europe have loosed the bonds of custom and tradition in the rest of the world as they did earlier in Europe itself. Ever-widening circles of people have been roused to a new social and political consciousness, a dynamic awareness of the possibility of change and progress, and an activism of which one of the central manifestations is national self-assertion.

Nationalism is so much with us, plays so large a role in shaping the setting of our daily lives, that it is often taken as a simple matter about which we know more or less as much as we need to know. In fact we do know a great deal about it, but what we do not know or have taken for granted without adequate evidence adds up to an impressive body of ignorance and uncertainty which is all the more dismaying because of the frequent failure to face up to the limitations of our knowledge. It is a far more complex and elusive matter than it is usually given credit for being. Many of the points at which our knowledge breaks down are fundamental to an understanding of nationalism and hence to an ability to deal with the problems which it raises. To indicate three vital areas of doubt or ignorance I suggest that we do not know with any certainty the answers to such questions as what nations are and how they are shaped, why nationalism should have come into being at the time and under the circumstances which it did, and whether its destiny is, as has often been assumed, to supersede itself by the merging of nations into a broader internationalism or to feed upon itself until it turns into some form of nationalist totalitarianism. I lay no claim to the possession of the magic hat from which the answers to these questions and their like may be pulled, but I am sure that they deserve to be asked and searchingly examined. Furthermore, I am sure that many of the answers and assumptions with which we have been at least moderately content in the past are the product rather of a sleight of hand which deceives the eye than of the truer magic of pressing inconvenient questions as far as they will go. To add to the confusion, there can be little doubt that once nationalism has established itself as the fashionable creed of the times its name and symbols are utilized to cloak movements not in fact based on nations, although nations may in due course emerge from them.

To start at what is at least one of the beginnings, there is no real agreement as to what a nation is. No one has succeeded in devising a definition which is watertight in the sense that, without opening up a number of leaky "ifs" and "buts," it enumerates the constituent elements of the nations we know in such fashion as to distinguish them satisfactorily from other types of communities in which men have intensely lived their lives through the ages. By rule of thumb we can usually count on knowing a nation when we see one, but if we face up to the limitations of our knowledge it must be recognized that all too frequently the determination that a nation exists can effectively be made only after the fact when the nation has emerged full-blown and leaves little reasonable doubt that it is there and must be reckoned with. We acknowledge the existence of a Turkish and a Filipino nation without doubt; with some hesitation we can perhaps accept a Burmese and a Ceylonese nation; but is there such a thing as a Ugandan or a Malayan nation? A large margin of error attends any venture into the realms either of prediction in relation to nations still in the making or of efforts satisfactorily to explain why and how mature and established nations came to take on the particular contours which they now possess.[1]

A thorny problem is disposed of far too easily if it be assumed, as it often implicitly is, that each nation is a preordained entity which, like Sleeping Beauty, needs only the appropriate kiss to bring it to vibrant life — and perhaps even that it was willfully put to sleep by some evil genius. For Mazzini, a nationalist prophet of wide influence, it is bad governments which have distorted the natural divisions of the peoples ordained by God, who "divided Humanity into distinct groups upon the face of our globe, and thus planted the seeds of nations."[2] The experience of the new nations and those still struggling to be born highlights this problem because their frequently indeterminate and in some sense accidental structure draws attention to the arbitrary elements in the formation of other nations whose present firm existence lends their past a fictitious air of inevitability. After the fact each nation may come to have the look of a God-given entity, but while it is in the stage of growing pains the divine intent is likely to be obscure. Although it is no doubt too much to ask of the ardent nationalist that he should recognize that the nation in whose cause he is wholly absorbed might have been other than it is, the objective observer should seek to penetrate further into the mysteries.

In part the difficulty has arisen from the fact that the first nations to make themselves evident in the modern world embraced peoples who had already achieved a large measure of internal unity and were not significantly plagued by minority problems arising from the presence of distinctive ethnic groups. Through the continuing spread of the same forces which had brought it into existence and no doubt aided by some element of imitation, the type of community which had gradually established itself over the centuries in England, France, and a few neighboring Western European countries became the dominant pattern for other peoples whose development had followed very different lines. As nationalism began to spread, the complexities embedded within it, which the special circumstances of its Western European origins tended to conceal, thrust themselves more and more insistently to the fore. But even for the oldest and most fixed of nations, such as France, the further back the inquiry is pressed the less inevitable does it appear that this particular France should have emerged from the long course of history,[3] and it is not difficult to conjure up other kingdoms, built perhaps on feudal foundations, which might have divided its unity or joined parts of other neighboring peoples with it. Across the Channel an English nation may for the sake of argument be taken as given, even though it is itself an amalgam of tribes and conquerors. Yet the English nation has curiously merged, without total loss of its identity, into a greater British nation which includes Scots, Welsh, and even some Irish within it, while the Irish as a whole have remained recalcitrantly outside. By the time the national era came to flower, however, the national configuration of France and Britain had achieved a coherent mold which aroused expectations of similar national coherence elsewhere only rarely susceptible of fulfillment in radically different circumstances.

Of the more recently created nations the most striking and extraordinary case is that of Pakistan where a nation which almost no one had foreseen and few could credit in advance as even a possibility came into being virtually overnight through its own assertion (or that of a small number of leaders) that a nation existed which had not been there yesterday morning. By the accepted criteria of nationhood it was obvious that there was in fact no such thing as a Pakistani nation: three or four decades ago even the present Pakistanis or their immediate predecessors did not conceive themselves as a nation except occasionally perhaps in some metaphorical sense. Yet once the assertion of nationhood was made and accepted as a living reality by the people concerned, the fact that it confounded the theorists was a matter of singularly little relevance. The case of Pakistan came close to sustaining the theory that a nation is whatever can get away with establishing its claim to being one; and if East Pakistan were now to break off into a separate national existence it would be idle to seek to deny its claims on theoretical grounds. Similarly if India were to break up into several nations on the European pattern, perhaps on a linguistic basis, the emerging entities would surely be accepted as nations as the South would have been if it had won the Civil War, dividing the United States in two.

Wherever the inquiry is carried, much the same confusion and uncertainty emerge. In the Arab world states have been erected which appear to carry with them the implication of being based upon or of shaping nations, but a wider sense of Arab unity also exists which is clearly of a national order, while several Arab states contain peoples whose tribal consciousness has not yet been superseded. Morocco and Tunisia have some measure of national coherence; Algeria is plagued by its million or more European settlers; and Libya has barely a glimmering of national identity. As one moves southward in Africa the problems multiply, in part because the colonial boundaries arbitrarily imposed in the course of partition cut across ethnic lines, taking no heed of the problem of future nations, and in part also because the older tribal patterns are only gradually breaking down. Everywhere in Africa, including the independent states of Ethiopia and Liberia, the Sudan and Ghana, the sense of national existence is hesitant and precarious, and the outlines of the presumptive African nations are often still dim. A continuing study of the processes by which they shape themselves in the years ahead may add significantly to the understanding of one of the important and perplexing phenomena of our time.

The two most significant elements in the rise of nationalism as the modern world intrudes upon different countries are the disintegration of the older forms of society and communal life and the emergence of the bourgeoisie and the "common man." For reasons which remain only partially explained, the interaction of these elements produces a vigorous sense of national identity which shortly translates itself into political action. In many instances (e.g., England, France, Spain, Poland, Japan, China) nations or consolidated peoples already existed which were roused to a new type of consciousness, while in others (e.g., virtually all of Africa south of the Sahara) the basic foundations for national communities still remained to be achieved *after* the nationalists had been called into action.

There seems little doubt that if the inquiry is pressed far enough back the European and African situations might in a sense be held to be substantially similar since even the best established European nations were also at some point a congeries of stocks and tribes. In the classic European examples, however, many centuries had been devoted to the processes of unification carried on by conquest, centralizing monarchies, the church, and other agencies which worked to mold the peoples into common patterns. In Africa the processes of unification began for the most part only a short number of decades ago when the colonial regimes made their first moves toward the imposition of unity upon disparate and often hostile tribes.

A significant point of difference is that earlier the welding together of peoples took place before the general populace had been aroused to any consciousness of its rights and powers. The rise of both the bourgeoisie and the masses as well as the demand for democratic participation followed centuries of nation-building, while in the newly independent African states and in the French and some of the British colonies national unity must be pursued among people endowed with the vote and constitutional rights and organized in parties and unions. The most significant element, however, is that where the nationalist in Europe and some other parts of the world could appeal to a reasonably clearly delimited people already in part aware of its identity through long experience of some share in a common destiny, normally including a common language, the African nationalist still has before him almost the entire task of creating the nations in whose name he professes to speak. On the European model he claims to express the grievances and aspirations of a people but in most instances it is open to the gravest doubt that such a people as yet exists. He advances a plea for self-government, but the nature and composition of that self still remain to be determined. Particularly in British and French territories in Africa the colonial system has fostered the emergence of a layer of persons, always thin but varying in dimensions, who bear the characteristic features and attitudes of the nationalist as he has in successive stages developed everywhere and whose demands are couched in the familiar nationalist terminology of the age. Even more than elsewhere, however, the nationalism which they represent is characterized by its negative elements, by the passionate anti-colonialism which is the starting point of their endeavors. The inescapable logic of their position forces them to speak for peoples which are not yet nations in being but only nations in hope.

Is it to be taken as a difference in degree or in kind that there was a French people, a Greek people, a Japanese people, and at least an approximation of a Chinese people who required only to be brought to an active and popular consciousness of their national identity whereas no real trace of such an historical community of language, custom, and tradition can be found in Nigeria, Kenya, or the Congo? Does the vast diversity of the peoples who go to make up India render their nationalism something of a different order from that which knits together the Germans or the Italians? In virtually all colonial countries there is vehement rejection of alien imperial rule, but the existence of this hostility is by itself far from establishing the fact that it is being expressed by a nation which has achieved any real measure of coherence and integration. It would appear that there are nationalists where there are still no nations — Machiavelli in the concluding chapter of *The Prince* pleaded for an Italian nation which was to come to no awareness of itself for four centuries. Even at that later time Massimo d'Azeglio commented: "We have made Italy, now we must make Italians!" [4]

WHAT IS THE NATION?

The nation is a community of people who feel that they belong together in the double sense that they share deeply significant elements of a common heritage and that they have a common destiny for the future. In the contemporary world the nation is for great portions of mankind the community with which men most intensely and most unconditionally identify themselves, even to the extent of being prepared to lay down their lives for it, however deeply they may differ among themselves on other issues. The full extent of the nation's claims found rich expression in Abba Eban's assertion to the General Assembly in 1955 of Israel's right

> to apply the elementary principle that those who enter Israel's gates shall be men and women the central passion of whose lives shall be devotion to Israel's flag, loyalty to Israel's independence, zeal for Israel's welfare and security, and a readiness to defend her against all assaults from near or far.[5]

The nation is today the largest community which, when the chips are down, effectively commands men's loyalty, overriding the claims both of the lesser communities within it and those which cut across it or potentially enfold it within a still greater society, reaching ultimately to mankind as a whole. In this sense the nation can be called a "terminal community" with the implication that it is for present purposes the effective end of the road for man as a social animal, the end point of working solidarity between men. "In our world, it is still as citizen of a national state that one is oppressed or liberated; willy nilly, one lives the destiny of one's nation." [6] Within it there is the assumption of peaceful settlement of disagreement, based on the supreme value of national unity, whereas in conflict between it and other communities there is an assumption of the possibility of violence.

Since the state is in modern times the most significant form of organization of men and embodies the greatest concentration of power, it is inevitable that there should have been, and should still be, a great and revolutionary struggle to secure a coincidence between state and nation. The nation seeks to take over the state as the political instrument through which it can protect and assert itself. Less than a century ago Lord Acton could lay down the dictum that "A state may in course of time produce a nationality; but that a nationality should constitute a state is contrary to the nature of modern civilization"; [7] but the nation has in fact become the body which legitimizes the state. As in earlier times the state achieved legitimacy through, say, its monarch or its religion, it is now legitimate if it is the embodiment and expression of a nation. Where the state is based on any principle other than the national one, as is by definition the case in any imperial system, its foundations are immediately suspect in a nationalist age. Once the people of such a state have come to a consciousness of national identity, the presumption is that the state will shortly be swept away, to be replaced by another cleaving as closely as possible to the national foundations. Where the peoples of several nations are seriously intermingled, as they are at so many points on the face of the globe, discord and trouble are the almost inevitable result.

However great its present importance, it is evident that the nation is only one of the many forms of community in which men have intensely lived their lives through the ages. Conceivably, rare individuals have existed who represented the isolated atoms from which the theorists of the social contract constructed their systems, but all ordinary men have been intimate members of close-knit social groups of different dimensions and structures. There have been, and there still are, many types of communities, and still other variants will appear in the future. Among those which have held predominance in the past and have played much the same role as the nation there may be singled out the family, the tribe, the city-state, and the body of adherents of a religious creed. All of these, without vanishing from the scene, have bit by bit and often after harsh struggle yielded pride of place to the nation in the sense that for constantly growing numbers of men the claims of the nation have come to be accepted as taking priority over claims coming from any other source. This is obviously not to say that for all men and under all circumstances, even in societies most solidly and indisputably saturated by the sense of national identity, loyalty to the nation will in fact override all competing loyalties. Family, tribe, locality, religion, conscience, economic interest, and a host of other appeals may at any given time and place prevail over national allegiance for particular individuals or groups. But it is the characteristic feature of the national era that for most men the national allegiance takes precedence over all other claims which may be made upon them when they are con-fronted by alternative choices of allegiance, as most strikingly in time of war. Nor is it adequate to point to the supreme coercive power of the state as the decisive factor; the supremacy of that coercive power itself rests upon the fact that men in the mass acknowledge the legitimacy of the demands which the national state makes upon them and accept the nation as the community which makes the nearest approach to embracing all aspects of their lives.

Despite its triumphal sweep in the course of the last century and a half the primacy of the nation is by no means unchallenged. The challenges come not only from the older forms of community, generally more local and narrower in extent, which frequently continue to lead a vigorous life of their own, but also from newer variants which seek to supplant, or at the least to supplement, the nation by broader unities. At the furthest reach a small number of people believe themselves to have outgrown the parochial bonds of nationalism and to have achieved a full sense of cosmopolitan identification with all of mankind. It may be that they represent the future kingdom of heaven, but their present influence on the conduct of the world's affairs is negligible. Much greater political importance attaches to the movements which seek to draw upon and to create a sense of regional identification, subordinating the nations involved to a wider but still far from global loyalty. Of these the most significant is the effort to achieve a united Western Europe, capitalizing on the centuries-old sense that Europe, despite its wars and cleavages, has a distinctive unity of tradition, culture, and outlook. If, under the spur of the conflicting Soviet and American pressures, greater progress toward a realization of this unity has been made in Western Europe in recent years than at any previous time, the gap between the actual hold of the nations and the ideal of a united Europe is still great. Whatever the future may produce, it is a striking fact that in virtually no instance have nations which achieved independent statehood in modern times voluntarily merged themselves into a large entity which took over their sovereign rights or any substantial portion thereof. For all the talk of European unity the European nations have generally continued to deal with each other at arm's length, although Benelux and Scandinavian cooperation have made real headway. In the Americas the search for Pan-American solidarity, for Hispanic American brotherhood, or even for a federation of Central American peoples has brought forth only the most meager results. Unions of states in the Arab world, spurred by Nasser's initiative, must be taken in part as movement toward the acknowledged goal of Arab national unity.

In terms of its current impact the challenge to the hold of the nation which has had by far the greatest effect is that of the Communists who, at least in theory, give their first allegiance to the class community of the workers of the world, which will, through the irresistible operations of the Marxian dialectic, bring about the transition to the ultimate and global classless society. For the Communist the nation is properly no more than a human frailty, always suspect in its bourgeois implications, which must be humored until such time as the people come to comprehend their true need and destiny — even though the Communists, where it serves their need,

put themselves forward as the true patriots, champion self-determination, and have made highly effective use of the nationalisms
which they profess to deplore. In the Communist language patriotism is often as admirable as nationalism is despicable. As a working reality the primary loyalty of the Communist must go, not to
his nation, but to Moscow as the heart and brain of the fatherland
of the world proletariat, unless it be that Peking has now intruded
itself as an alternative focal point of loyalty. Within their own domain of the Soviet bloc the Communists have imposed a unity
which claims to have moved beyond nationalism, but Hungary
showed that nationalism lives fiercely on.

For purposes of scientific accuracy it would be both pleasant
and convenient to have reliable criteria by means of which to
distinguish the national community from other types of community, but such criteria have not as yet been evolved. We can distinguish the Athenian or Florentine city from the Greek or Italian
nation both in terms of the sheer number of people involved and
— to beg several vital questions — because the nation seeks, as the
city did not, to embrace all those who form an ethnic whole; but
the concept of what, for national purposes, forms an ethnic whole
drifts off into shocking looseness.

On the score of size it is a generally plausible assumption that
the nation involves societies of substantial magnitude, but since
nations range from a million or so people to hundreds of millions
nothing approaching precision is possible. At what point would
it be possible to say that a city which reaches out to embrace some
of its surrounding countryside or hinterland was clearly and irrevocably to be denied the title of nation? There are throughout the
world tiny tribes and groupings of peoples, including a number of
little island dependencies, which can by no stretch of the imagina-
tion be transmuted into general acceptance as nations, but when
one turns to such relatively large tribal units as, say, the Baganda
or the Kikuyu, it is difficult to deny them the possibility of nationhood even though the probabilities are against them. If they were
to assert their claim to separate national identity and in particular
if they were to achieve separate statehood, could a claim be maintained against them that they lacked some essentials of the nation?

In the direction of greater rather than lesser magnitude it is also patently the fact that a number of other variants of community exist or are emerging, which reach beyond the nation and are compounded of similar ingredients. The nation is a community of people who feel that they belong together, but in many instances the elements of which that feeling is the resultant, such as language, culture, and common historical experience, spill over far beyond the national borders, carrying with them a less intense but still significant sense of kinship. Of such ingredients, mixed together in different qualities and quantities, are made the various "pan" movements which have from time to time sought to bring related peoples within a common frame. I have already mentioned the ambivalences in Africa south of the Sahara as well as those of the Arabs who hesitate uncertainly between the states into which they are now divided and the great Arab community which at its extreme reaches from the Arabian Sea to the Atlantic frontiers of Morocco, and even beyond these limits stretch the still wider horizons of Islam. Asia does not appear to have many ties which link together peoples who are divided on the basis of ancient and exclusive cultures. Although there have been many assertions of Asian solidarity, occasionally held to derive from Asian spirituality as opposed to the materialism of the West, this claim to "Asianism" had more substantive meaning when there was common hostility to the white imperialist than when the divergent national interests of independent states both absorb attention and emphasize intra-Asian rivalries and conflicts.[8] The chances seem greater that China, India, Pakistan, or Indonesia might break down into smaller units based on language, regional attachments, or some other formula than that any existing or foreseeable sense of common identity would bring about voluntary mergers among them or with any of the neighboring states. Although some bonds of cultural and religious affiliation, such as those of Islam or Buddhism, reach across national frontiers, no evidence indicates that they are likely to serve as foundations for communities rivaling the strength and appeal of the existing nations. A much expanded union of the Thai people might conceivably come into existence, and many links of race and culture connect the Malay peoples of Indonesia and Malaya, reaching more tenuously into the Philippines. Like the marginal border areas of uncertain allegiance which can be found at many points, these are, however, fringe cases which barely touch the vast Asian mass. A Communist take-over would be more likely to impose unity, or at least close coordination, than any other cause which is now discernible.

For the full richness of ties which crisscross national frontiers it is necessary to turn to the Western world which has produced them in bewildering profusion. Europe has for all the centuries since Rome had a lingering sense of unity, and within it there are interpenetrations of race, language, and culture, as of the Germanic, Slav, and Latin peoples. Beyond its borders Europeans have overflowed in a torrent into all parts of the world, and particularly into the temperate zones which they have taken over and made their own. Even though these migrants took pleasure in shaking the dust of the old continent off their feet they could very rarely, if ever, fail to carry with them a greater or less degree of attachment to the communities in which they originated. Newer nations, primarily or predominantly European in composition, have come into being in the Americas and Australasia, and more hazardously in Africa, which, however various the nature and intensity of the ties, are linked to the mother countries and the peoples from whom they derived by elements not different in kind from those which go into the making of nations. Of their separate and distinct nationhood there can be no question, but equally there can be no question that their lives are colored, socially, culturally, and politically, by the attachments which descend to them from an often distant heritage.

Of these attachments the most extraordinary are those which bind together the British Commonwealth — become even more extraordinary since the voluntary adherence to it of India, Pakistan, Ceylon, Malaya, and Ghana — which successfully eludes all precise description but for all that is a living entity of real consequence in the world. The United States stands outside the Commonwealth. Its alignment with Britain, Canada, Australia, and New Zealand is, however, certainly not wholly to be explained in terms of a *Realpolitik* of economics, strategy, and political calculation. As also in the case of Latin America the same forces are operative here as those which have served to knit the national communities, and it is evident that in a diluted fashion some of the same political consequences flow from them.

The moral of the tale is that the nation is only one variant, though currently a centrally important one, on a social pattern which takes on many guises, flowing virtually indistinguishably from one into another. It has, to be sure, certain distinctive elements but they are none of them unique to the nation, and the combinations in which they appear defy orderly analysis.

ELEMENTS OF NATIONHOOD

The simplest statement that can be made about a nation is that it is a body of people who feel that they are a nation; and it may be that when all the fine-spun analysis is concluded this will be the ultimate statement as well. To advance beyond it, it is necessary to attempt to take the nation apart and to isolate for separate examination the forces and elements which appear to have been the most influential in bringing about the sense of common identity which lies at its roots, the sense of the existence of a singularly important national "we" which is distinguished from all others who make up an alien "they." This is necessarily an overly mechanical process, for nationalism, like other profound emotions such as love and hate, is more than the sum of the parts which are susceptible of cold and rational analysis.

These forces and elements are the common coin of all the writers and theorists who have sought to reduce the mystery of the nation to comprehensible terms, but the work which has been done on them has still not produced very satisfactory results. The myth of the nation has come to have so immense a hold upon us that it is difficult to see how arbitrary and precarious have been some of the stages by which it has been shaped. The general tendency, understandable enough for the nationalists, has been to lay primary emphasis on the factors which have worked toward unification without recognizing their often ambivalent nature and without giving adequate attention to those which have headed in different directions. To grasp the problem in all its complexity it is essential both to pose the alternatives of the might-have-beens which failed to appear and to take into account not only the forces and elements which seem clearly to be nation-forming but also those which work to other purposes. Examined with a skeptical eye, factors which are confidently advanced as the basic cement and building blocks of the nation not infrequently dissolve into perplexing insubstantiality or lend themselves equally well to structures other than those which have actually emerged.

As the classic European models tended to set the pattern which other rising peoples followed in their explosive demand for national unity and independence, so the theoretical approaches to the concepts of nation and nationalism have been dominated by the European experience, even though this European-derived framework fitted the facts in much of the rest of the world in only indifferent fashion at the best. It was not that all of the European experience was of a single piece. There was in fact much diversity in it which had already introduced more than enough complexity. The German and Italian nations were in important respects very different creatures from those of France and Britain, and eastern and southeastern Europe added a number of new variants, but with some discreet evasion of aberrant cases they lent themselves to reasonably adequate generalization. The peoples of Asia and Africa, stemming from totally diverse roots, brought with them an array of further complexities which were often singularly ill-adapted to the old formulas, as Arnold Toynbee has repeatedly emphasized in his *Study of History*. The conventionally accepted definitions and approaches tended to become less and less applicable as the phenomenon of nationalism widened out to embrace the entire globe.

The ideal model of the nation toward which the European precedents pointed, even though no such nation ever existed in total purity, is a single people, traditionally fixed on a well-defined territory, speaking the same language and preferably a language all its own, possessing a distinctive culture, and shaped to a common mold by many generations of shared historical experience. That the Europeans themselves deviated often from this ideal model needs no more in the way of substantiation than the mention of Switzerland or Belgium, the intermingling of peoples in the Balkans, or the claims and counterclaims to territories which two or more peoples regard as traditionally their own. If this ideal model was peculiarly applicable to the original examples of England and France, it was not wholly a caricature of a number of other European peoples, but it was frequently far out of line for peoples outside the European orbit. Japan perhaps most closely paralleled the European model, while several others, including the presently divided Korea and Vietnam, could be picked out as reasonable approximations of it. The native bent of many countries leads them in quite different directions. China is a controversial case of approximation; India presents great linguistic and other diversity and only somewhat dubious elements of past unity; Afghanistan, Iran, and Ethiopia have not overcome the divisive character of their tribal foundations; and colonial Africa has barely begun the process of integrating its potential national communities. Yet the model of the nation toward which these peoples and countries strive is that which came to the fore under the unique conditions of the Europe of the last century and earlier.

The model was of course impressive not only because it was derived from the original and pace-setting European nations, but also because it posited a type of social and political base which had obvious merits and strengths. A people profoundly united in language, culture, and tradition and possessing a territory not seriously encumbered by alien intrusion might perhaps be accused of a drab national conformity but could certainly be expected to work together in political harness more effectively and to survive domestic and international crises with greater unity than one not so endowed. Where the social-political reality departed fundamentally from the ideal, as it unmistakably did in much of the world, something had to give way, either in at least partial abandonment of the ideal or in a hazardous effort to fit the recalcitrant living reality within the limits of a blueprint designed to fit quite different circumstances.

In the many definitions of the nation which have been attempted four elements which insistently recur as essential to the creation of a sense of common destiny are territory, language, a common historical tradition, and the intricate interconnections of state and nation. Others which have appeared with somewhat less regularity and whose relevance for this purpose is more dubious are race, religion, and a common economic system.

CHAPTER VI

People, Territory, and State

THE NATION is not only a community of brethren imbued with
a sense of common destiny. It is also a community which, in contrast to others such as family, caste, or religious body, is characteristically associated with a particular territory to which it lays
claim as the traditional national homeland. The emotional and intellectual tie in the minds of men is buttressed by a location in
space which anchors the nation with permanence on the face of the
earth. When the nation achieves its full self-realization in the form
of a sovereign state this double base of spirit and soil emerges
in a perplexing and often dangerous contradiction which lies embedded at the heart of the national concept.

In accord with the fundamentals of the political structure of
the modern world the state asserts jurisdiction over all persons
within its borders, but the nation on which it is based and from
which it derives its legitimacy is likely neither to be wholly confined within the state frontiers nor to have its state domain all to
itself, unencumbered by other peoples. The national principle and
the state principle, despite the close ties which have grown up
between them in modern times, are far from being identical and
not infrequently come into dramatic conflict with each other. The
existence in almost all corners of the earth of explosive minority
issues and in others of troublesome irredenta is the political expression of this disparity.

Of the close relation between the nation and the national territory with which it identifies itself there can be no serious doubt.[1]
No single theme recurs more constantly in national anthems, songs,

legends, and symbolism than the reference to the peculiar virtues, beauty, and excellence of the lands and waters with which each nation has happily been endowed. It is a part of the mythology of the nation that the defense of the national territory is a first charge upon men's loyalties, even though it is difficult to discern the psychological mechanism by which the individual takes as his national own a vast expanse of which he can normally have had only the slightest personal experience. Is the answer to be found in some curious transmutation of his natural attachment to the locality in which he passed his childhood, or of the peasant's love for his land, to the far larger area embraced by the nation? This is the explanation which is most often given or at least uncritically assumed, but an immense gap separates the direct experience of a familiar neighborhood from the learned acceptance of an unseen and in some measure arbitrarily defined country. The affinity between the two is by no means self-evident.

The case of the Jews has sometimes been cited in contravention of the principle that the nation is bound to a particular territory, but it is a singularly ill-chosen one. Whatever the propriety of regarding the Jews as a nation at all times in their history rather than as a religious community, they stand out as a people for their devoted attachment to the land of their fathers. Throughout the centuries of the Diaspora the Jews through their religious ceremonies and by other means fervently maintained the symbolism of identification with the country from which they had been driven in the far-off past; and no other corner of the earth's surface could meet the need they, or at least many among them, felt to return to their own. As the Zionist saw it in the more recent phase, what was involved was not the acquisition of a new Jewish homeland, but the long-delayed reëntry of a people into its national heritage. This historic right was in his eyes in no significant degree impaired by the occupation of the homeland of Israel for many centuries by the Arabs.

The people of Israel present a striking illustration of the intimacy of the relation between nation and territory. The other principal religious group which has turned itself into a nation in the recent past comes much closer to casting doubt on the proposition that the territorial element is a necessary constituent part of the concept of the nation. In the always troublesome case of Pakistan there is no good reason to assume any traditional identification of a Pakistani nation still in the making with even an approximation of the divided lands which came to it, although Moslems felt a special attachment to certain areas such as Sind in which they had long predominated. The Northwest of India was the point at which Islam entered and first consolidated its hold and which the Moslems might best regard as their traditional base, but both Hindu and Moslem had an old-established awareness of the Indian subcontinent as a whole to which each in his different fashion might lay claim in its entirety. The Moslem conquest had, at least in principle, extended to the entire area. The boundary lines which were drawn in 1947 corresponded to no established territorial division between the great creeds but only to the need to bring together in the new state the areas in which Moslems predominated. On each side of the lines many millions of people were left who might more properly have been on the other side, and of these, millions fled in an appalling mass migration.

It may well be that the really significant question is not whether the Pakistanis are to be regarded as a unique sample of a nation not rooted in a traditional territory but whether they should rather be seen as a religious community, located within the boundaries of India, which, in the modern vein, sought to be transformed into a nation. It is, of course, of crucial importance that the religion they professed was Islam which is not merely a body of religious beliefs set beside a separate secular existence but an all-embracing way of life, lending itself to the creation of a distinct people. The Indian National Congress took the essentially territorial position that all established inhabitants of India constituted the Indian nation, whereas the Moslem League asserted the personal communal basis of the nation they claimed to represent. Sir Muhammad Iqbal, one of the principal forerunners of the drive for Pakistan, explicitly repudiated the Western concept of the nation as a territorially defined country, holding the latter incompatible with both Islam in general and the special position of Islam in India.[2] Yet the concrete political aims of the Indian Moslems necessarily included a fixed territory as the earthly foundation for the state.

Wherever the nation remains a destination in prospect rather than an achieved reality, as is the case where tribal or other pre-national allegiances predominate, the territorial principle is also necessarily of somewhat dubious applicability. It is difficult to see how a claim to a national territory can be maintained where there are as yet no nations, no consolidated peoples. In the nationally inchoate Africa south of the Sahara, the pooling of tribal lands to form a new national territory, has been peculiarly delayed by the slowness in moving beyond tribalism. Certainly, also, it should be remarked that the typical nationalists in Asia and Africa as elsewhere have been those most divorced from their traditional roots — the urbanized and Westernized — and hence those most remote from old-established association with the land.

One cannot go beyond some such loose statement as that a nation is identified with a "reasonably well-defined" territory. In typical contrast to the formal organization of the modern state whose boundaries must be firm and fixed, even though at any given moment there may be disputes as to frontiers, the territory of the nation is characteristically less sharply defined. In every instance the main body of the national homeland is well established, at least in the minds of those who lay claim to it, but the vagrant impulses of peoples have often led to confusion at the extremities where the demographic frontiers have become inextricably intermingled. Of such situations the most familiar and notorious are probably those of eastern and southeastern Europe on which the spotlight of Wilsonian self-determination, and later of the League's minority protection system, came to be focused with particular intensity: the intermixture of Germans, Slavs of varying attachments, and other peoples; the claims of Poland and Hungary on the basis of past greatness to territories far beyond the present reach of the Polish and Magyar peoples; and the extraordinary crazy quilt of the Balkans.[3] Now trapped within the overwhelming embrace of Soviet satellitism, the nationalist controversies of this part of the world have largely vanished from public view. Titoism, the Hungarian revolution, and Poland's response to the new freedom which followed Stalin's death all indicate, however, that the old nationalisms, temporarily suppressed, are ready to break out again whenever the Communist hold is relaxed, although in somewhat altered form because of the large-scale population exchanges which have been undertaken.

It is by no means only in the Balkans and eastern Europe that such confusion of nations and territories is found. Everywhere peoples have been on the move. At many places they have become tangled with each other to the point where self-determination ceases to have clear rights and wrongs — except for the partisans of either side — and the solutions which emerge are those imposed by the nation which comes out on top. Such confusions of peoples lead to a wide array of potential or actual border disputes. As new states emerge into independence these are sure to be multiplied, as witness Pakistan's difficulties with India over Kashmir and with Afghanistan over Pushtoonistan, Burma's controversy with China, and the impending problem of determining sensible frontiers for an independent Somalia. In Palestine the conflict went far beyond the range of a border question because the entire territory was in dispute, and Malaya could conceivably have the tragic makings of another Palestine. Occasionally there are surviving remnants of peoples, such as the Kurds and Armenians, whose traditional territories cut across the boundaries of present states. In addition to the problems brought by European settlers, Chinese and Indians have migrated overseas in large numbers, the Chinese particularly to Southeast Asia, the Indians to Burma, Ceylon, Malaya, and eastern and southern Africa, laying the foundations for claims which might prove explosive as India and China grow in strength.

Although it is always a potential source of trouble, the existence of different ethnic groups within the same state becomes a chronically acute danger only when the people begin to have a burning awareness of national identity and demand a share in political power. When that stage is reached, new elements of revolutionary dimensions are introduced. The concept of the modern national state tends to exclude both the complex interlinking of separate communities, best exemplified by the millet system of the Ottoman Empire under which each major religious community managed its own affairs, and a feudal type of structure with a diverse hierarchy of loyalties and jurisdictions. The device of extraterritoriality is also unacceptable, having been repudiated as an imperialist instrument. Particularly in Europe the centuries preceding the nationalist age saw the development of the centralizing monarchical system which built the state on the territorial principle in the sense that all people encompassed within the boundaries of the state became subject to the sovereign rule of the king regardless of their perhaps divergent ethnic ties. When the national forces began to well up within the old forms the conception of the territorial state was taken over intact with the result that a double criterion, made up of two disparate elements, was established. Although the state sets a single political authority over all its people, the nation in whose name and for whose purpose the state has been created rarely includes all those within the territorial orbit of the state, nor are all the members of the nation embraced within the state. The more fluid communities of the nations evade in both directions the rigid geographic bounds of the state. Thus there are Arabs in the explicitly Jewish state of Israel and there are Jews who are not within it.

Maurice Zinkin has contended that, whereas the old Asian loyalties were religious, caste, or racial in character, "the new loyalties follow territorial boundaries . . . Asia, like Europe, has discovered that modern Governments can only function when all are citizens, and all citizens are of equal value." [4] This proposition obviously contains some sound truth, but it covers only part of the story and in particular fails to take into account that the modern governments which have been instituted rest upon a nationalism which has a rationale and driving force of its own. In a nationalist age, even when all are citizens, all citizens are by no means of equal value. The Chinese in Thailand or Indonesia or the Jew in Arab states well know the barriers which may divide the citizen of the state from the nation which gives the state its modern meaning. Is the Christian or Hindu in a Moslem nation in fact to be accepted as a citizen of equal value?

Even for Europe itself the proposition which Mr. Zinkin advances is most effectively applicable to the ideal model derived from such cases as those of England and France where so-called "political nations" could take over already formed states. Where "cultural nations" came to assert their claims, particularly in ethnically mixed areas, the presumption that the nation-state embraced all of and only one single homogeneous people was speedily seen to be a much more dubious matter. To give an example which played a fatal role: when Czechoslovakia was established — explicitly as the political expression of the Czechoslovak nation — the Czech national territory was defined in terms of the traditional lands of the Bohemian crown, but among the old-established occupants of those lands was the mass of the Sudeten Germans. It was all too painfully apparent that loyalties did not in fact follow territorial boundaries and that the formal equality of citizens was a facade behind which much in the way of national inequality held sway although the Czechs stood high in their observance of obligations to minorities. The state in theory extends its benefits and protection equally to all its citizens or subjects and all equally participate in it, but the inherent personal-community element of the nation works to limit full partnership in the state to those who can establish their national acceptability.

As a modest if not wholly practicable adjustment to these problems, Otto Bauer and Karl Renner put forward the conception of the organized personal and nonterritorial national community in Central Europe around the turn of the century. This was the proposal for national-cultural autonomy, functioning within the general framework of a supranational state, which was so bitterly attacked by Lenin and other leading Bolshevik spokesmen. In 1958 it reappeared in British proposals for a settlement of the Cyprus conflict. In this plan for Cypriote partnership, which was carried over in modified form into the final settlement of early 1959, the Greek and Turkish communities were each to have a separate House of Representatives endowed with final legislative authority over its own communal affairs, while a central council, drawn in part from these bodies, would deal on a territorial basis with noncommunal matters and internal security.[5]

In tragic contrast to this humane approach to the problem must be set the tendency, all too often put into practice in our times, to legitimize the idea that where territory and nation fail to coincide, the national territory embraced within the state may, and perhaps should, be cleared either by the mass expulsion of the minority group or by its flight to safer refuge before the axe falls.

It is to Hitler and the Nazis that we are indebted for the full development of the appalling potentialities of the national concept, in both its personal and its territorial aspects, although it must be acknowledged that they had substantial precedents to draw on in the expulsions and exchanges of population after World War I. Under the spell of the Nazi racial doctrines Germany moved to ruthless implementation of the dogma that only the proper German was a member of the nation, entitled to an equal share in the state. Applied against the Jews to the point of extermination, this racist-nationalism was turned as well against other peoples such as the Slavs, and even against those racially acceptable Germans whose opinions and affiliations made their Germanism suspect in the eyes of the ruling clique. The Nazis likewise developed the fullest application of the idea that all persons whose origins were in the German community continued to be members of the *Volk* whatever their present residence and citizenship. The evil seeds hidden within the national concept which nineteenth-century liberalism had so confidently accepted now lay exposed for all to see.

The translation of nationalism to non-European peoples has brought no lessening of the contradictions which it harbors. The plural society is a characteristic phenomenon of great stretches of the world: the "crazy quilt of the Balkans" is generally more typical than the model nations of England and France. Even the disappearance of colonialism in its various guises would remove only a fraction of the plurality. Indeed, the transition from colonial status to independence will probably serve to aggravate rather than to alleviate the problem. The colonial governments have often played a role akin to that of the monarchies which developed the centralized territorial state in Europe. They constituted the state authority which ruled over all persons within the colonial boundaries, and, in principle, stood with equal neutrality above the several ethnic groups which might be present there, save for the normally favored position of the white (or Japanese) settler or entrepreneur. It is when claims to self-determination are asserted on behalf of the people themselves that the issue of the definition of the "self" comes inescapably to the fore. In Burma, Ceylon, Indonesia, and pre-partition India the contradiction between the nation as a territorial entity and as a community of the like-minded or racially akin has thrust itself forward as soon as the people came to political self-assertion or achieved independence. In Malaya, however, despite the stirring up of racial discontents by the Japanese occupation and the war and postwar ferment, the Malays, Chinese, and Indians have to a surprising degree overcome their differences and managed the first phases of independence under the single banner of the Alliance. It appears inevitable that Africa's further advance should be punctuated by a series of contests between tribal groups, each newly aware of its communal identity, such as those which marked the transition of Nigeria and the Gold Coast to independence and lay behind the bloody riots in Brazzaville in February 1959.

The other and more important side of the story is that all nations have been built up over the centuries through the gradual coalescence of distinct peoples into larger communities with a relatively high level of social and cultural integration. Through conquest, peaceful penetration, and the mere fact of long-extended living together, disparate peoples have become assimilated to each other to a point where original differences have vanished or have been submerged in a broader national unity. At some early stage in their evolution, peoples seem far more malleable than at a later time when they have taken on a national imprint of greater fixity.

While no grounds can be found for any assertion that the historical processes have come to an end with the present national units as the ultimate communities, it seems that once the formative phase has been ended and the national imprint given, that imprint offers a profound resistance to further change of the same order. Bulgarians, Chinese, or Egyptians are the resultant of the mixture of many peoples and cultures, but once they have passed some stage in their development, not to be pinpointed with precision, which has turned them into Bulgarians, Chinese, and Egyptians, they are no longer equally susceptible to the further operation of similar forces.

A possible objection to this proposition might be that one of the elements involved is a fundamental disparity in time scales. That is, the first part of the proposition deals with vast stretches of time whereas in the second part the time scale has been reduced to a very limited and finite period. If the second part is stretched far enough into the future, my proposition vanishes in the sense that new and presently unforeseeable transformations will surely take place. Nonetheless, I still believe that the proposition contains significant validity for an analysis of the contemporary scene and the future with which we can calculate.

One marginal correction which needs to be made concerns not the great bulk of the people who stay at home, but the relatively few who migrate. The fixity of the national imprint certainly attaches to the settled mass within the national frontier and not equally to the migrant individual or family. Nowhere is this more evident than in the Americas whose several nations are so unmistakably the product of the fusion of immigrants from many lands, but even here the melting pot has often worked slowly and hesitantly. Both city and countryside demonstrate that where individuals and families of the same ethnic stock have settled compactly together the process of assimilation has been long delayed. On the whole, however, it has been carried through with amazing success. Indeed, the success has been so great and so familiar as to make it difficult for Americans to comprehend that the typical European or Asian national minority is a very different kind of animal. Rumanians in the mass are not tempted to turn into Hungarians, nor Jews into Arabs, nor Tunisians into Frenchmen. Individuals may shed one nation for another, although the mature migrant can never completely rid himself of the deep psychic attachment to his original people. Nations as a whole are more resolutely set in their ways.

Many doctrinal disputes divide those who have attempted to explore the nature of the nation and its making, but there is a wide measure of agreement that nations differ so greatly from each other in their make-up and historical antecedents that no single set of factors can serve as more than a useful check list. Of the many and complex forces which have entered into the shaping of the nations one which may be singled out as having distinctive importance is the role of the state. Stretching the matter to its furthest limits Rudolf Rocker went so far as to say, in terms similar to those of Lord Acton: "The nation is not the cause, but the result, of the State. It is the State which creates the nation, not the nation the State." [6] For the sake of achieving a single and coherent theory it might be very nice if this were true, but the historical evidence indicates clearly that it cannot be sustained in any such across-the-board fashion. Another more acceptable version of the same proposition is that of Ortega y Gasset who suggested in relation to Europe that "every linguistic unity which embraces a territory of any extent is almost sure to be a precipitate of some previous political unification. The State has always been the great dragoman." [7]

Over and over again, if the inquiry is pressed back in time, it will be found that there was a state structure, or at least a political system approximating a state, which coincided to a striking degree with the modern nation in terms of territory and people. The nation is in a very large number of instances a deposit which has been left behind by the state — although this evades the query as to whether the state itself was perhaps the product of prior ethnic unity. Where the state has survived for many generations reasonably intact within an approximation of the same frontiers, as is the case with France, England (though here Great Britain becomes more problematical), Ireland, Spain, Portugal, Egypt, China, Japan, and certain others, the argument is so obvious as to need no elaboration. In such cases the territory claimed as the national homeland is substantially identical with that enclosed within the boundaries of the state. Poland, Hungary, Bohemia, and Bulgaria may serve as good examples of states which vanished from the historical scene for longer or shorter periods of time but left behind them firmly established national precipitates.

These and similar examples indicate a coincidence which is too striking to be ignored, but, as with so many other aspects of the analysis of nationalism, a certain amount of legerdemain is necessary. While it is possible and plausible to single out those periods in history during which, say, the Hungarian and the Bohemian people were given a national mold by a state which had, prospectively, a "national" base, these peoples were at other considerable periods of their history incorporated in quite differently oriented state structures. For one phase of it, if Poland be taken as an example, a glance at an historical atlas establishes that the Polish state extended to vastly different expanses of territory in the course of its long existence. Coming at the problem from another angle, the peoples of eastern and central Europe and the Balkans have over the centuries lived their lives in a number of different state and imperial systems. An arbitrary trimming of the facts to fit the theory inevitably attaches to any effort to single out some one era of their political experience as the determinative one while others are ignored or minimized. Yet the fact remains that in many instances communal identity appears related to an identifiable prior state structure.

Once the European peoples had acquired their national mold in the relatively remote reaches of time, that mold tended to stick with them. Neither the Hapsburg nor the Ottoman Empire was able to erase or basically to modify the deep communal attachments which had been shaped in the past. By the time the national era came to full flower in the nineteenth century those underlying attachments were so fixed that the main bodies of the peoples to whom a national appeal might be successfully addressed were fairly clearly delimited. The nations which came forward at that time to assert their claims were evidently not chance assemblages of miscellaneous individuals but coherent ethnic entities which might — and did — pretend to an ancient and honorable lineage. It was not possible to appeal to the Czechs in terms which were meaningful to the Hungarians, nor to the Greeks in terms which were meaningful to the Bulgarians.

The two most impressive cases of nations for which no honest argument as to prior political unification can be put forward are the classic samples of nation-state integration in nineteenth-century Europe — Germany and Italy. In neither instance is it possible to isolate any substantial period of time during which it might be contended that a people was being welded together through the process of common subjection to a single political authority. For Italy the imperial grandeur of Rome was unquestionably a source of political inspiration, but Rome in the sweep of its expansion never lingered significantly within the confines of an Italy marked out by the Alps and the sea, nor was there any later period in the course of which even an approximation of the present Italy was under a common rule. For the shaping of the German nation it is even more difficult to discover any phase in its history which would serve to justify a contention that it was the product of an earlier state. Friedrich Meinecke, in laying the groundwork for his study of German unification, suggested a basic distinction between cultural nations, formed by such elements as common speech, literature, and religion, and state nations, formed through the working of common political institutions.[8] On this basis, Germany and Italy are clearly to be counted in the ranks of the cultural nations; but Meinecke proceeds to comment on the greater frequency of the cases in which political influences and interests determine the emergence of a common speech and literature.

Outside Europe the role of the state as the molder of nations is at least as great as within it and perhaps even greater.[9] Certainly in the Americas the importance of the state in setting the boundaries within which nations were to appear has been immense. Here there can be no question of ancient communities being called to a sense of national existence at some late stage in their development, except as communal ties were included in the spiritual baggage of those who migrated across the seas. Although no perfect correlation can be worked out, in Latin America the boundaries of the states whose peoples came to a sense of national identity tend to show a high degree of coincidence with the provincial jurisdictions marked out by imperial Spain and the other ruling powers.[10] The boundaries of these colonial jurisdictions frequently followed lines in some measure imposed by geographical features, as most strikingly in the case of the Andean frontier between Argentina and Chile, but the role which even the most salient geographic elements play is often a highly equivocal one. The Mississippi and the Rockies are integral parts of the United States, the Amazon is embraced within Brazil, and the Rhine does not form the boundary between Germany and France. There is an all too human tendency to work on the basis of an *ex post facto* reasoning which plays up as proof of a geopolitical determinism cases where barriers such as mountain chains or rivers have demarcated nations and states, but ignore both similar barriers which do not divide peoples and frontiers which seem geographically arbitrary.

In North America, even when the presence of the French Canadians is taken into account, the national separation between Canada and the United States is to be attributed primarily to the fact that through a series of historical accidents two distinct states came into existence which worked upon their peoples in different fashions and brought into being two distinctive national communities. The sweep of the boundary line from the Great Lakes to the Pacific makes it clear that here no predetermined national territories existed and that only somewhat arbitrary political decisions demarcated the two peoples. If the dice of political fortune had rolled in some other fashion the whole of Canada might have been included within a single North American nation, however indigestible the French might have proved, and some very different drawing of the boundaries might have produced equally consolidated nations. In the Caribbean Britain's difficulties in achieving a federation of its West Indian territories were accentuated by the fact that they were for the most part islands but derived even more from their old established separate political status. The nations which have emerged in America, both North and South, owe their existence peculiarly to the operation of political forces. The independent states which have come into being have worked not only to intensify but also to create the feeling of national separateness and identity.

Nowhere is the significance of the state in its capacity as nation-maker more inescapably evident than in the colonial sphere. In some instances, such as those of the Burmese and the Vietnamese, the peoples who have recently claimed nationhood had achieved a vigorous earlier communal identity, despite the annoying presence of minorities. In other instances, such as those of the Philippines and Indonesia, the lines drawn on the map by the imperial power were the determining element in establishing the boundaries within which peoples have developed national awareness. The common government was a major instrument in pressing diversity into a common mold.

The way in which the existence of a single political authority works to knit together the people over whom it rules is easy enough to lay out in general terms, including the special consequences which flow from alien rule of the colonial variety. Subjection to a common government immediately operates to impose some elements of a common destiny on the people embraced within the political boundaries and to mark off the territory from neighboring countries, facilitating personnal intercourse within and erecting barriers to easy intercourse with peoples outside. The growth of a single network of communications is encouraged. The public educational system is based upon a common body of ideas, principles, and materials. In all probability a single common language of administration is utilized at least by the central government, and that language is likely to become the language of education at one or another level. For the country as a whole a common body of law and a common administrative system reflect something of a single political philosophy, although the effective impact of unity of law and administration may dwindle off to a vanishing point under indirect rule. The consolidation of a political system is an almost indispensable pre-condition for the building of an integrated economy. More broadly, if less tangibly, the government reflects a common cultural pattern brought to bear on all the people within its domain.

Of the limits within which these forces of consolidation are effectively operative two are perhaps particularly worth taking into account, especially within a colonial context. One concerns the nature, strength, and stage of development of the peoples concerned, and the other the type of policies adopted by the colonial power.

On the first score, it is evident that the human material involved sharply limits the effect of the forces set in motion by the achievement of political unification. Integration is far more likely to occur where peoples have an original similarity than where they are divided by large-scale disparities in such basic elements as race, culture, religion, and language. Thus the closely related indigenous communities of the Indonesian archipelago lent themselves to an approximation of a general national pattern when they were brought under a single roof by Dutch rule, while the Chinese in Indonesia presented almost insuperable barriers to any comparable assimilation. To cite again the familiar cases of Malaya and Palestine, one may doubt that any government, whatever its policies, would have been able to bring about a national consolidation of the Malays, Chinese, and Indians in the one case and the Arabs and Jews in the other. In such instances the bonds of prior communal attachment were too deeply rooted and the differences between the peoples too profound to allow the state to play its role as the great dragoman. Similarly in Africa, through the superimposition of a colonial government, a group of African tribes may achieve a sense of national identity into which Europeans and Indians living under the same government are highly unlikely to be drawn.

In addition to mere difference, both qualitative and quantitative distinctions enter in. The presumption in favor of integration becomes greater if the people to be integrated accept the culture of those to whom they might be assimilated as being at a higher level than their own, and the presumption declines to the extent that they look down upon the other as inferior. The working of the American melting pot was eased by the frequent readiness of the immigrant to accept assimilation to "Americanism" as desirable. The European in Africa, on the other hand, or the Chinese in Malaya looked down upon the people to whose country he had come and regarded acceptance of their culture as a descent in the scales. Where one side has a great overbalance in numbers, as in the different African multi-racial societies, the vast majority cannot be expected to make a speedy or complete transition even to a culture accepted as higher. The more highly developed peoples are likely to have passed through the formative stage in their evolution and to be no longer readily susceptible to remolding. In particular, Islam appears to set a stamp upon peoples which is immensely resistant.

As for the bearing of colonial policy, in the past it could be taken for granted that there would be a lack of zeal on the part of the imperial power to achieve the national welding together of peoples over whom it ruled. What emerged in the way of national unity was an accidental by-product rather than an intended result. Even in the present changed imperial climate, where nation-building has found some acceptance as a proper colonial goal, colonial administrators cannot take on the tasks which only a national government can assume. The persons who head the administration and determine its policies are by definition alien; their values and outlooks are foreign to the peoples ruled; and the potentially national symbols and traditions cannot be drawn upon effectively. Where a national government encourages the development of a rounded national economy, colonial governments have typically developed colonial economies — the *pacte coloniale* of the French — directed toward the export of raw materials and foodstuffs in exchange for the manufactures of the mother country. Lines of transport and communication, which in other circumstances aim at knitting the country together, tend to flow from inside the dependency outward to serve the purposes of the alien government, investors, and traders. In one unique fashion, however, the colonial government serves the national cause: in the hostility to itself which it generates it pulls together the heterogeneous segments of the people under its sway.

Any colonial system which builds on ethnic diversity as one of its fundamental elements is sure to impede the processes of national integration. Whatever the virtues of indirect rule, one of its effects is undisputably to hold peoples apart rather than to bring them together. While direct rule will not necessarily produce a merger of disparate ethnic groups, the acceptance as the base of the colonial structure of traditional societies, each equipped with its own body of law and custom and its own native authorities, is to emphasize diversity rather than to encourage homogeneity. In West Africa the French policy of direct rule appears to have subordinated tribal differences to a greater extent than the indirect rule which has until recently dominated British practice. The difficulties which the British have encountered in promoting the development of Uganda as a unitary state derive in considerable part from their earlier acceptance of Buganda and other African polities as the building blocks with which they worked. There is no occasion to accept as valid across the board the customary contention of the nationalist that indirect rule, whether in its Lugardian African form or in such devices as the princely states of India, reflects the evil intent of the imperialist to divide and rule, but the nationalist has good reason to view such practices with dismay.

The same kind of results flow from other systems which take as their starting point the racial or other diversity of the peoples concerned. At the extreme, the South African doctrine of *apartheid* explicitly rejects any conception of building a single national community out of the peoples to whom the state's authority extends. At a lesser level obstacles to nation building are intruded wherever communalism comes to official recognition, as in the systems of election and representation in India prior to independence, in Ceylon at one stage, and in East Africa. A still different variant was the plural society of Malaya where, within the carefully preserved framework of the Malay Sultanates, the several racial communities lived largely separate lives with a varying political and legal status and with different school systems and languages. At the other end of the scale, assimilationist policies on the traditional French pattern may be as suspect to the nationalist as indirect rule or accepted pluralism since the assimilationist goal is the merger of colonial peoples into a nation of which the core is the mother country.

The effect of colonial governments in bringing about a consolidation of nations is obviously great, but our experience is too short and the variables too extensive to make any definitive assessment possible. That a certain outcome of colonialism can be observed in India or the Philippines is scant reason for assuming that the same will happen in the Congo, Madagascar, or New Guinea. Nor can it be assumed that, because a political movement of colonial protest takes on the fashionable coloration of nationalism and, achieving success, establishes an independent state, the nation on which it claims to base itself is in fact a viable community.

In the *Communist Manifesto* Marx laid it down that

though not in substance, yet in form, the struggle of the proletariat with the bourgeoisie is at first a national struggle. The proletariat of each country must, of course, first of all settle matters with its own bourgeoisie.[11]

On the same line of argument, in the normal course of events a colonial people seeking independence must settle matters in the first instance with its own colonial government, and the mere fact of common battle against a common enemy carries with it some impetus to unity. Particularly in Africa the survival of that unity beyond victory is obviously problematical.

Summary examination of the relation between colonialism and emergent nations in a few concrete cases may throw light on the subject. One case which is peculiarly complex and perennially absorbing is that of India. Here was a vast subcontinent, a Europe in itself, characterized by a diversity of languages, religions, and patterns of life, which had still achieved through the centuries some feeling, however loose and ill-defined, that all the diversities had their place in a single whole. This amorphous spiritual identity had found virtually no expression in political unity. The characteristic political condition was a shifting array of states and principalities, of conquests and alliances, which enabled the British to utilize Indians in the conquest of the country and lent color to the trite comment that India was only a geographical expression. Whether India would have moved toward consolidation or disintegration if the British had not taken over is a question which can have no answer.

Whatever the might-have-beens, the effect of British rule in promoting a working sense of Indian unity was of vital importance. The maintenance of law and order, administrative unity, the introduction of a common body of social and political concepts and values, the appearance of English as a *lingua franca*, and fiscal and economic integration all served to link together the heterogeneous elements which made up the Indian society; as did the common national struggle against British rule. At least for the newly rising leaders who created and took over the headship of the nationalist movement the fact of a common British background seems almost as important as the fact of the common Indian heritage.[12] When India achieved its independence, the British trained and educated element dominated the scene — British trained and educated even though many of them had spent much of their lives in British jails — and the Indian Civil Service, one of the most strikingly successful products of the British connection, carried on the administration through the first difficult years.

Here Britain scored a success which cannot be written off as being wholly in the realms of irony, for many among the British saw a united, viable, and independent India as the true goal of the imperial connection. But if this was in fact the goal, an immense defeat was also involved in that the last turn of the wheel brought not unity but partition. For those who accept the often repeated Indian charge that it was the deliberate British policy to divide and rule which created Hindu-Moslem communalism in its ugliest political aspects, this will appear not as a defeat but as the inevitable reaping of what had been evilly sown. It is at all events an irrefutable demonstration, confirmed also by Ireland's partition, that a single political system does not necessarily bring national unification in its train. Whether the emphasis be placed on the Machiavellian intrigues of the British, on the irreconcilable original cleavage between Hindu and Moslem finding new expression under changed conditions, or on more ephemeral and accidental elements such as the character of Gandhi or the role and ambitions of Jinnah, the fact remains that from one British India there emerged two independent states.

Two markedly less controversial cases are those of the Philip-

pines and Indonesia. In each of these instances, even when it is
acknowledged that the human material involved was already so
fashioned as to ease integration, the preëminent importance of the
colonial regimes in determining national contours seems beyond
question. The scattered lands inhabited by the peoples of Malay
stock, including therein the Philippines, the entire Indonesian
archipelago, and such parts of the Malay Peninsula as were primarily Malay were not so laid out by nature or originally so settled
by man as to make any one political partition of them more self-
evident than another. The existing frontiers are, as far as both geography and ethnology are concerned, essentially arbitrary and reflect the limits of the colonial spheres carved out in the conflict of
imperialisms. These frontiers have worked to shape not only separate political units but also distinctive peoples, each asserting its
national indentity. Perhaps the most striking feature is the Cathol-
icism of the Philippines which stands in sharp contrast to the predominantly Moslem character of Indonesia, but this is only one
facet of the differentiation in language and education, political
experience and outlook, social structure, and economic orientation
which has evolved as the result of subordination of two different
colonial systems. President Quezon acknowledged the debt of the
Philippines to Spain for laying the foundations of national unity
through religion and education, and to the United States as well as
Spain for so molding the national character as to fit the Filipinos
for independence.[13]

The integrating impact of the colonial regimes has unquestionably separated the people on one side of the frontier from those
on the other, but it has not had an equal effect in producing internal
unity. This is particularly true in Indonesia where national solidarity has been gravely challenged and where for such communities as the Moluccans and the Achinese, serious doubt exists as to
whether the sense of attachment to an Indonesian nation overrides
more local loyalties. Original ethnic cleavages were emphasized by
significant elements of Dutch policy, including the use of indirect
rule, the differential treatment of certain areas, and the very late
incorporation of some peoples within the Dutch system. Achin
was not conquered until the last years of the nineteenth century
and West New Guinea was barely touched before World War II.

In one of the wilder flights of nationalist fancy, attributing to divine providence what has all the outward look of being peculiarly the work of man, President Sukarno of Indonesia suggested that God Almighty created the map of the world in such fashion that even a child can tell that the British Isles are one entity — which might surprise the President's nationalist counterparts in Ireland — and that a child can see that the Indonesian Archipelago is a single entity stretching between the Pacific and the Indian Oceans and the Asian and Australian continents, from the north tip of Sumatra to Papua; [14] whence derives the Indonesian slogan "from Sabang to Merauke." It would take a child gifted with magnificent political prescience to discern from a map devoid of political boundaries that New Guinea was divided in the middle, that Indonesia was separated from the Philippines and Malaya, and that North Borneo was in British hands.

The claim of the Indonesians has been specifically to the territories which were ruled by the Dutch, and they have so far neither sought to reach out beyond them to expand their domain to include Portuguese Timor, British Borneo, or Australian New Guinea, nor have they been prepared to tolerate any diminution to those territories. The latter point has come up most clearly in the controversy over West Irian (Dutch New Guinea) where the Indonesian case has explicitly rested upon the fact that this was an integral part of the old Netherlands Indies. The Dutch countercontention that the people of New Guinea are ethnically distinct from those of the rest of Indonesia is held to be of far less importance than that the Republic of Indonesia is the heir to the undivided empire of the Dutch. The Indonesian nation is defined by the Netherlands imperial boundaries, as, in a curious parallel, the Soviet domain has been primarily defined by those of the Tsars.

For other Asian territories the effect of the era of colonialism was less marked both because the duration of colonial rule was briefer and because the ethnic identity of the peoples had already been well-established by prior political unification or other elements in their long history. Since Korea, for example, has an ancient lineage of independent existence under its own rulers, Japanese domination served less as a unifying force than as a stimulant to national awareness and political action. In Indochina much the same was true for the Vietnamese and Cambodians both of which peoples look back to long centuries of separate, if checkered, existence. The French colonial regime took these differences explicitly into account in the federal structure which it erected. Where it went beyond them in its tripartite division of Vietnam it did not succeed in breaking up the unity of the Vietnamese people, although the latter were destined to undergo a new partition at the end of the French era. Burma similarly had a distinct heritage of its own: however low its estate at the time of the successive British conquests, Burma was a going concern which the British took over and did not create.[15] The effect of British rule was indeed rather to emphasize ethnic divisions than to weld together the minority peoples and the Burmese proper.

No brief summary of the long and intricate history of the Arab world could hope to disentangle the forces which have shaped its states and peoples. The Arabs themselves have not sorted out the communities to which they belong and arranged them in hierarchical order:

> In the Arab world one could — and probably still can — find a Druse nationalism operating within a Lebanese nationalism, a Greater Syrian nationalism, and a Pan-Arab nationalism.[16]

Prior to their joining forces in the United Arab Republic, both Syria and Egypt stated in their constitutions that they formed a part of the Arab nation, and the Proclamation of the Republic held it to be a preliminary step towards the realization of complete Arab unity. For a full-scale analysis it would be necessary to evaluate the whole record of Arab experience, including such matters as the tribal, sectarian, and other divisions, the effects of Ottoman rule, the machinations of the European powers, and the role of Islam and of the Arab language and culture. Egypt owes far less to its decades of British control than to its ancient heritage centered on the Nile Valley; Saudi Arabia clearly attaches to the older Arab past, while Jordan, which constituted a national entity neither before nor after the acquisition of its share of Palestine and the Palestinian Arabs, owes its existence primarily to the British desire to have a line of access from the Mediterranean to the oil fields lying further east.

Without attempting to attach preëminent importance to the recent phase as against the illimitable stretches of the past, it is evident that the present political constellation derives in very considerable part from the partition imposed by the powers after the First World War. In its brief life the Mandates System produced the same effects as other variants of colonialism. Charles Issawi has summed up the results in the following fashion:

> Each country, absorbed in its own struggle against a specific foreign government, tended to isolate itself from the others. In each, different foreign traditions and methods began to implant themselves — French in Syria and Lebanon, British in Iraq and Palestine, Italian in Libya, Spanish in Morocco. Education in foreign schools and universities produced very different values, prejudices, and ways of thought. Not least important, in each country dynastic, political and administrative vested interests arose, whose position stood to suffer from a merger of their country in a bigger whole.[17]

If the inquiry as to the relation of states to nations is carried into Africa south of the Sahara, an even more hazardous terrain is opened up than in the Arab world. For the Arabs reasonably fixed landmarks of history and affiliation stand out among the ambiguities of the present situation. In relation to the Africans such landmarks are much less evident and have a less direct bearing on the problems of nation-building. The pre-colonial history of Africa had its quota of internal wars, conquests, and empires, but their effect in integrating large masses of people into broader and potentially national communities was far more limited than elsewhere.[18] The tribes, varying greatly in size and inner cohesion, have been, and in large measure remain, the typical social and cultural units of sub-Saharan Africa.

As to what even the immediate future may hold in the way of unification and division of African peoples, a glance into any one crystal ball is as good as another. For the moment, however, Africa is the continent par excellence to sustain the thesis that colonial governments may be the major instruments in shaping nations, by amalgamating tribes into larger communities. Political demands are inevitably directed to the colonial authorities, and, since national self-determination is what the contemporary world expects, anti-colonial movements are automatically assigned to the familiar rubric of nationalism and are assumed to be serving as the agents of nations.

Since most African countries are the product of recent political accidents and have neither a tradition of common origin nor a common outlook on the future, Lord Hailey has asserted that the term "nationalism," describing a readily recognizable force in Europe, is difficult to apply in the different conditions of Africa. In its stead he suggests the use of the term "Africanism," covering both the negative aspects of anti-colonialism and the constructive phases of a drive to express "the characteristic spirit of Africa as interpreted by the modern African," but not embracing the implication of a political movement for pan-African unity.[19]

Lord Hailey rightly contends that the African people have in the past missed the dynamic influence of the concept of territorial nationalism. Yet the current drift has unquestionably been toward a territorial nationalism which takes the existing colonies as setting the frame of political reference. It might be argued that in Africa the territorial foundation has come to be of peculiar importance, not because of any traditional association between the colonial territory and the people, but because the putative nations, lacking ancient roots, are defined solely in terms of colonial frontiers. The cases on which we can generalize as to the relations between colonies and African nations are, however, still so few in number, so limited in time, and so uncertain in their bearing as to make any generalization immediately suspect. Nowhere can we have any assurance that a process of definitive political crystallization has set in. It is, indeed, nearer the truth to deny that any solid and coherent nations exist as yet in Africa south of the Sahara than to claim that each of the political jurisdictions has shaped a nation within its ethnically arbitrary frontiers. Even among the whites of South Africa the Afrikaner has not been prepared to accept absorption into a single South African nation with his British-descended countrymen. Liberia, the oldest of the African states except Ethiopia, remains divided between the Africans of the hinterland and the descendants of the settlers from America despite recent efforts to bring the two together.

If the Gold Coast established a symbolic link with the past through the invocation of the name of Ghana, Nigeria has no thread of history to which it can attach itself except the British rule which belatedly pulled its diverse peoples together. In 1920, deriding the embryonic political aspirations of the National Congress of British West Africa, Governor Sir Hugh Clifford found the notion of a West African nation as absurd as that of a European nation, "at all events until the arrival of the Millennium," and put forward the counter-proposition that each of the major Nigerian tribes constituted a nation in itself.[20] A quarter of a century later a Nigerian who was shortly to become one of his country's major political leaders came to much the same conclusion:

> Nigeria is not a nation. It is a mere political expression. There are no "Nigerians" in the same sense that there are "English," "Welsh," or "French." [21]

His plea to the British to abandon the folly of trying to develop Nigeria into a unitary state was translated into the actuality of a federal constitution. The approach to Nigerian independence brought an increasing demand for recognition of the ethnic diversity of the country through the creation of more regions than the three into which Nigeria was already divided, but this demand was officially rejected in the aptly named "Report of the Commission appointed to enquire into the fears of Minorities and the means of allaying them." [22] Even in the smaller and more homogeneous Gold Coast a plea was made, particularly in Ashanti, for a federal instead of a unitary constitution as the British withdrawal came near, and it has been a major preoccupation of Nkrumah to ward off the forces which have threatened disintegration.

In the neighboring territories of Togoland and the Cameroons the relatively brief period of German rule superimposed on the original multiplicity of tribes a sense of political unity which still lingers on in some quarters. According to Thomas Hodgkin, Ruben Um Nyobe, General Secretary of the *Union des Populations du Cameroun*, reported in 1952 that "Chrétiennement parlant, tout le monde reconnaîtra que Dieu a créé un seul Cameroun," to which Mr. Hodgkin appended the remark:

> If God did in fact create a single Cameroons, then the Prussian State — as Hegel thought — must have been acting as the divine agent. For the movement for Cameroons unification has as its aim the

recreation of the Cameroons State within its pre-1911 German frontiers.[23]

The African countries which have been mentioned are among those which have experienced the largest measure of political advance. Elsewhere in sub-Saharan Africa the process of community-building of a modern political variety has been even more delayed and unclear in its outlines. The colonial governments have perhaps been shaping nations, but whether in fact nations will emerge, and what particular nations they will be, are matters which lie beyond anyone's present ken.

The uncertainties of the situation can be illustrated on every side. The independence of Guinea, for example, suddenly asserted in the 1958 referendum on the De Gaulle constitution, carried no necessary implication that its people constituted a nation. The terms of reckoning were again changed by the hasty decision to form a union between Guinea and Ghana, which, following the model of the development of the United States from the thirteen original colonies, was seen as the nucleus for a union of West African states. This was the first step in realization of Nkrumah's repeated insistence that Ghana's independence was only a stepping-stone on the way to Pan-African freedom and unity, and was also a key move in the rivalry between Nkrumah and Nasser for leadership in the new Africa.

Many other plans have made their appearance. A resolution adopted by the All-African People's Conference in December 1958, denounced colonial frontiers dividing peoples of the same stock, endorsed Pan-Africanism, and called for the ultimate creation of a commonwealth of Free African States. The creation of groupings of independent states governed by Africans, such as North and West African federations, was recommended as a means to this goal which would begin the process of subordinating linguistic, religious, and cultural divisions as well as national sovereignty to "the over-riding demands of Pan-African Unity." [24] Following the dismantling of French West and Equatorial Africa, the French territories in Africa have engaged in negotiations looking toward the formation of "primary" federations which would then join in "secondary" federations with France; and some proposals link British territories with each other or with their French neighbors. Among other schemes based on tribal affiliations, one would carve a new state out of parts of former French Equatorial Africa, the Belgian Congo, and Angola, and a second would create a greater Somalia to embrace not only the colonial Somalilands but also parts of Ethiopia and Kenya.

The one constant factor is that Africa is caught up in a ferment of change whose end is far from being in sight. Tribes, colonies, federations, Pan-Africa — all are actively entered in the race to determine the political form in which the much-heralded African Personality will clothe itself.

CHAPTER VII

Language

I T HAS BEEN WELL SAID THAT "Mankind instinctively takes language as the badge of nationality." [1] Although a number of exceptions spring to mind, the immediate presumption is that a man whose native language is French, German, or Italian is a Frenchman, German, or Italian. The ideal model of the nation, derived from Western Europe, rested in considerable part upon the belief that each nation is a separate linguistic entity. In Europe this idea had a substantial measure of coincidence with reality, but the Swiss and Belgian nations notoriously cut across the principle, and the English, Spanish, Portuguese, French, and German languages all reached in greater or less degree well beyond the national frontiers. The coincidence with reality tended to dwindle off as the drive toward the ordering of mankind on a national basis spread to the world at large. The effort, as Toynbee put it, to find "the criterion of Nationality in the shibboleth of Language" [2] is unavailing for great segments of the globe. Japan, Turkey, Thailand, more dubiously China and the Arab countries, and some fortunate others were endowed with a single language of their own, but the more common pattern was that of linguistic diversity. Where under the aegis of colonialism, as in much of Latin America, Africa, and Southern Asia, plural societies had come into being, some confusion of languages was an inevitable result. Malaya with its medley of tongues serves as one example; South Africa with its dichotomy of Afrikaans and English superimposed on the native African languages, plus the languages brought from India, is another of a different order.

The concept of a "language" is itself an imprecise one, by no means standing above the nationalist and political battles.[3] German is a language and Dutch is a language, whereas other local variants of German spoken in Germany linger at the lower level of dialects. The linguistic diversity of France has been swallowed up within a single nation, but each of the separate national units of Scandinavia is equipped with a language of its own. The Slavic languages of eastern and southern Europe are in general parceled out to peoples who have established their national identity, although the multiplicity of dialects might have lent itself to quite different classification. In the European setting, the successful assertion of the claim to nationhood established the presumption of a claim to a distinct national language, and absorption into a larger national entity worked to downgrade the local vernacular. The existence of a national state tended in a number of ways, as through its control of the educational system, both to bring uniformity to the national language and to differentiate it from its neighbors.

In view of its distinguished European ancestry the idea of a single national language may reasonably be supposed to carry with it both prestige and very real and substantial advantages. Whether those advantages outweigh the pains of seeking to secure national linguistic uniformity where the original state of affairs is linguistic multiplicity, is an issue requiring special examination in each particular case. The merits of linguistic uniformity are so obvious as barely to need statement. Leaving aside the fascinating if unanswerable query as to the extent of which each particular language both mirrors and fashions unique patterns of thought and thus reflects and molds a distinctive national soul, it is evident that language is the primary instrument of social communication. Those who speak the same language have an immense common bond, which also reaches back to a common store of social memories; those who do not, have a gulf of silence between them which can only be bridged by some third intermediary. Where there is linguistic diversity, schools, press, radio, speeches, literature must all employ the different languages, making it far more difficult to bring the same influences to bear on all the people and creating the likelihood that the linguistic communities will look to different sets of leaders. Certainly there is no need to dwell on the practical difficulties of organizing the modern state on a multilingual basis when one takes into account the problems of parliaments and civil services, of courts and legal systems, political parties and military forces. The existence of distinct language communities is a constant and often dangerous challenge to the all-embracing unity which is the national goal. At the start of the Commonwealth period President Quezon saw the development of a national language in the Philippines as essential in order to provide the unifying influence hitherto exercised by alien rulers.

If Carlton Hayes overstated his case in remarking that "until the French Revolution no attempt had been made by any government to force its citizens or subjects to use a particular national language," [4] a striking coincidence can still be found between the emphasis on language and the emergence of the nation as the community which legitimizes the state. What lay behind the eruption of the language issue was, of course, the emergence of the middle class and then of the broader masses of the people, familiar only with the vernacular languages but given a social and geographic mobility which overrode local dialects. As the people at large achieved literacy and came to political consciousness, the linguistic communities to which they belonged took on a new cultural and political importance. As a random European example, the emergence of the ordinary man into larger consequence in Belgium brought an increasing demand for the Flemish language. Throughout Asia and Africa the stirring of new forces has similarly brought language questions to the fore.

It was one of the aims of the French Revolution to impose a central national language on all the people of France. Since that time, wherever a diversity of languages was involved, the language issue became a major concern to every nation as it came to claim its place in the sun. Language controversies have everywhere been a central feature of the minority problem. Not without reason national minorities have felt that if they could preserve their language much of the battle for survival was won, while the majority has been persuaded that if its own language could be brought to acceptance the backbone of resistance was close to being broken.

The drive toward the achievement of linguistic uniformity has not been a matter of universal occurrence. The counter-proposition that a plurality of languages should not only be tolerated but even encouraged has received its most elaborate endorsement by the Communists, although for them the issue does not concern the multilingual nation — a conception they repudiate — but the multinational and hence multilingual state. The latter has been accepted both as a general principle and as a matter of policy in the countries under Communist rule, including both the new China and the Yugoslavia of Tito. That deviations have taken place in the application of the policy and that the Russian language has been accorded an increasing priority within the Soviet Union and to a lesser degree in the satellites does not impair the theoretical vigor of the basic Communist position. In the Soviet linguistic controversy of 1950 the importance and autonomy of language were strongly emphasized. Stalin himself intervened to establish by oracular pronouncement that national languages were neither a class matter nor to be relegated to the Marxist category of the superstructure but were a form of national culture serving both bourgeoisie and proletariat. The autonomous base of national languages was thus authoritatively established, even though Stalin also foresaw the ultimate triumph, through singularly mechanical processes, of one world language when Communism, taking over the world, had healed all cleavages among men. But the Communists should not be allowed to establish any claim to unique credit for their acceptance of linguistic pluralism, all the less since it is their explicit aim not to build nation-states but to establish multinational societies which should in time embrace the globe. Non-Communist states have moved with success in the same direction, and in several instances antedated the Communist experiment. Switzerland and Belgium have already been mentioned; Canada and South Africa have acknowledged a duality of languages; and occasional other countries, such as Czechoslovakia in the interwar decades, have handled the linguistic aspects of their minority problem with tolerant discretion.

By far the more common pattern, however, has been and is the urgent insistence on the single national language as one of the central cores of the national being. Nationalist movements have with regularity been accompanied by a flurry of philological activity. As the Communists found the Russians to be the inventors and discoverers of all good things, so the nationalist must seek to derive his language solely from its own native roots without the intrusion of terms and constructions which have an alien flavor. Of the many cases in which an effort has been made to cast out the alien root and branch and bring back the native tongue, perhaps the most striking as well as the least successful was the drive of the Irish nationalists to substitute an almost vanished Gaelic for the living English which the Irish people had in fact adopted as their own.

All the colonial peoples have been brought into the modern world under the aegis of an imperialism which superimposed a European language on the native tongue. This imperial language served three principal purposes which have an obvious bearing on the effort to secure national cultural identity. It was the language of instruction at least for higher education, it was the instrument through which intercourse of all varieties could be maintained with the advanced European and European-descended peoples, and it was frequently the *lingua franca* within each of the several nations and between them, as witness the central role of English at the Bandung Asian-African Conference of 1955.[5] The imperial languages were, of course, tied to the prestige system of the whites since the white man, with the partial exception of missionary and scholar, generally learned the local languages only as an act of grace or better to rule or trade with the subordinate peoples, whereas it was assumed that the natives who wanted to advance must rise to the level of the foreign language. The Japanese adopted the same attitude in Korea and Formosa, and particularly in Korea ruthlessly pressed Japanese as the one accepted language.

With the advent of independence troublesome questions arise as to the place to be accorded to the superimposed alien language which often continues to be the local *lingua franca* and the language of the dominant elite as well as the primary means of access to the West. National prestige demands that the national language take priority, and for poor and largely illiterate countries great practical problems are involved in educating any considerable number of people in one or more European languages. It is both proper and inevitable that the extension of education on a mass scale should normally be conducted in the language of the people concerned. Declaring that English could not continue to occupy the place of a state language, an Indian government commission on universities stated the matter in these terms:

> Use of English as such divides the people into two nations, the few who govern and the many who are governed, the one unable to talk the language of the other and mutually uncomprehending. This is a negation of democracy.[6]

Nonetheless it remains the fact that the major European tongues remain languages of international importance as media of general communication and as the main repositories at present of scientific and technical knowledge and advance. That this situation is already undergoing gradual change and may at some future point reverse itself does not furnish any easy answer to the dilemma now confronting the nationalist heirs of imperialism. Too sharp and drastic a turn to the national language could carry with it the severe penalty of loss of contact with the advanced world just at the time of the most extensive drive to achieve equality with the West by drawing on its learning and technique.

This question as to the future role of the Western languages in Asia and Africa is likely to prove less significant than the more basic issues which in some countries surround the question of the national language itself. Where there is such a language, in the sense that the great bulk of the population speaks some approximation of a common tongue, the difficulties of moving toward a single linguistic pattern may still be considerable, but the general direction is reasonably clear. In China, for example, the existence of one standard written language, whatever the burdens of its ideographic script, provides a base from which it has been possible to set off in replacing by a single common language the regional diversity of spoken dialects. Very substantial difficulties are involved in so standardizing and adapting Chinese as to make it an effective instrument for mass education on a national scale, bridging the cleavage between the learned elite and the mass, but a solid foundation was laid down in an immemorial past. Less bound to ancient tradition than their predecessors, the Communists have attacked the problem with vigor, including exploration of a possible shift to a phonetic alphabet, in order to secure greater efficiency and economy and to reach the masses better for purposes of indoctrination.[7]

Something of the same kind of problem exists in the Arab world where both dialectical differences and divergences between classical Arabic and the written and spoken vernacular force a new look at the linguistic problem to meet contemporary needs.

In the extraordinary national reshaping of Turkey under Ataturk, an ingenious cover and stimulant for linguistic adaptation was found in the theory of the Sun language which, bolstering national pride, eased the pains of making Turkish a more useful modern instrument. Turkish, according to this theory, became the mother language of all existing tongues, and "therefore any foreign term may be 're-adopted' provided that it be given a Turkish assonance." [8] Alien loan words and international technical terms could thus be incorporated in the language without jarring anyone's sensibilities. Furthermore, Ataturk enforced almost over night an amazingly successful shift from the Arabic to the Latin script and alphabet, modified to meet Turkish needs. Only the substitution of a Turkish translation for the traditional Arab prayers, which seemed too drastic a breach with Islam, ran into serious opposition.

It is where even an approximation of a single language is lacking that the most dangerous situations are created once the nationalist urge has taken hold. The most profoundly perplexing problems are presented in India whose vast and heterogeneous people scatter far and wide on the linguistic map, but India's linguistic multiplicity is shared in some degree by other Asian countries, such as Pakistan, Ceylon, Indonesia, and the Philippines, and by all of Africa south of the Sahara.

In the realm of theory the most radical means of dealing with the multilingual nation was that of Stalin who settled the matter in 1913 by a stroke of the pen which denied that there could be any such thing. Although he was prepared to concede that different nations might speak the same language, he ruled with arbitrary finality that one of the characteristic features which distinguishes nation from state is that "a national community is inconceivable without a common language. . . . There is no nation which at one and the same time speaks several languages." [9] This doctrine survives up to the present day and is applied in unlikely places. In 1957 a Soviet Africanist stated that if people speak different languages they cannot communicate with each other and "they are naturally incapable of forming a nation." [10] However sound this may be as Communist doctrine, it is not a position which could be expected to sit well with Indians or Pakistanis, Filipinos or Nigerians, whose nations are thus cavalierly brushed aside as nonexistent.

Even though the multilingual societies of South Asia and other parts of the world may rebel against the Stalinist dictum, they have not been content with their linguistic pluralism. The universal tendency has been to seek to move closer to the classic European model through the adoption of a single national language. Thus India has established Hindi as the official language, the Philippines Tagalog, and Indonesia the *Bahasa Indonesia* — but it need scarcely be added that a long leap separates inscription on the statute books from general acquiescence. An unusually successful venture was the adoption of Hebrew as the national language of Israel. According to Prime Minister David Ben Gurion,

> Only a hundred years ago there was not a single Jew in the world whose mother tongue was Hebrew; today it is the spoken language of hundreds of thousands.[11]

In territorially divided Pakistan the first swing toward Urdu as the national language, on the basis of its strength in West Pakistan, gave way to the vigorous demand of East Pakistan, breaking with the Moslem League and starting rumors of an incipient separatism, that Bengali be given recognition as an official language. Simultaneously the Constituent Assembly in 1954 opened the door to the possibility of according similar recognition to other local languages. The Constitution of Pakistan, adopted in 1956, provided that the official languages should be Urdu and Bengali, with English accepted for official use for twenty years, but here, as in India and even more strikingly in the Philippines, English retains a strong hold which may extend itself beyond its allotted periods. Malaya, seeking to lay hands on anything which might work toward national unity, has tossed uneasily between Malay, Chinese, and English, each of which plus some Indian languages, has played a role in the pluralistic educational system. With the coming of independence Malay has been adopted as the national language but with ample provision for the use of English and other languages. In Ceylon the demand of the Sinhalese that their language be accorded exclusive national status played a central role in the 1956 election and has led to serious clashes with the Tamils who make up a third of the population.

The linguistic problems which have plagued India justify more extended examination as an extreme sample of what other peoples face. On the linguistic score India is a nation singularly divided within itself. Nehru, guided by his optimistic and abiding faith in Indian unity, could assert that "India, as everyone who looks around him can see, has singularly few languages considering its vast size, and these are intimately related to each other." [12] But many who looked around them were persuaded that in fact the most striking feature was the number of large linguistic regions which in greater or less degree worked to impair the sense of national identity.

We need not here seek to disentangle the controversies which have existed over the precise number of Indian languages and the ways in which they may best be classified. There are certainly a dozen or more major languages, some quite unrelated to others, each of which is spoken by over a million people and which together embrace the great bulk of the population. To these must be added twenty-four tribal languages or dialects each spoken by 100,000 people or more, 720 Indian languages or dialects each spoken by under 100,000 people, and sixty-three non-Indian languages, among which English is far in the lead with 171,742 persons whose mother tongue it is.[13] By far the greatest linguistic gap, and the one of largest political importance, intrudes itself between the languages of the North, including Hindi, derived from or strongly influenced by Sanskrit, and those of the South, such as Tamil or Telegu, which belong to the radically divergent Dravidian group.

Given the far-reaching implications of language issues and the close ties between language and sense of community, this linguistic diversity inevitably had political repercussions. Stalin was on sound ground in warning the students of the University of the Peoples of the East in 1925 that while India was spoken of as a single whole there could be little doubt that "in the event of a revolutionary upheaval in India many hitherto unknown nationalities, each with its own language and its own distinctive culture, will emerge on the scene." [14] The inherent complexity of the situation was aggravated by a gap which developed between the administrative geography of the Indian National Congress and the provinces making up British India. As the Congress became a mass organization in the 1920's it reorganized its internal structure, under Gandhi's auspices, to coincide with the major linguistic regions, but it was unsuccessful in its demand that the government undertake a similar recasting of political boundaries to bring the provinces into line with the language communities. In addition, the Congress, which leaned strongly to Hindi as the future national language, was also pledged to the protection of the culture, language, and script of the minorities and linguistic areas. Nehru, although he saw Hindi as already almost a national language, insisted that if education was to spread and the people roused to political consciousness, the vernaculars must serve as the point of departure.[15]

In power in a free India the Congress was notably less happy about the prospect of reconstructing the country on a linguistic basis than when it sought mass support for the overthrow of the British. It took small consolation from the fact that its earlier theme of linguistic provinces was now taken up by the Communists who have varied their formulation of the issue according to shifts in the party line, but have on occasion gone as far as to propose a right of secession for the linguistic "nationalities."

In dealing with the problem the government has had to take into account popular and political pressures for reshaping the states on linguistic lines and at the same time to guard against too great encouragement for separatist forces. A country which has just suffered one partition on religious grounds is loath to risk the creation of new separatisms based on politically consolidated linguistic communities. After independence a postponement of action was achieved in part through the time-honored device of referring the matter to committees and commissions. These bodies, as well as leading political spokesmen, were inclined to look with a skeptical eye on the Congress's former position although the principle itself was not repudiated. Insisting that Indian unity and security must take priority over the satisfaction of linguistic demands, the Linguistic Provinces Commission, appointed by the Constituent Assembly in 1948, emphasized the nature of the dangers. It reported that it saw all the nation-building work of the Congress

> face to face with centuries-old India of narrow loyalties, petty jealousies and ignorant prejudices engaged in mortal conflict, and we were simply horrified to see how thin was the ice upon which we were skating. Some of the ablest men in the country came before us and confidently and emphatically stated that language in this country stood for and represented culture, race, history, individuality, and finally a sub-nation.[16]

In hesitant fulfillment of Congress pledges the government created the first linguistic state, Andhra, in 1953, after riots and demonstrations had broken out following the death by fasting of one of the Andhra leaders. (The Gandhian tactic of fasting as a mode of political pressure was, incidentally, not properly appreciated when it was turned against a Congress-dominated government.) To gain time and perspective Nehru later in the year appointed the States Re-organization Commission whose report, issued in 1955, sought a balance between the advantages flowing from federal units based on linguistically homogeneous peoples and the particularism and discrimination likely to be fostered by such units. Like its predecessor, this Commission pointed out that linguistic loyalties had deep roots in Indian history, and found that culture-based regionalism, centering on language communities, represented values more easily intelligible to the average Indian than did Indian nationalism. The latter, the Commission contended, "must acquire a deeper content before it becomes ideologically adequate to withstand the gravitational pull of the traditional narrower loyalties." [17]

In 1955 and 1956 the government struggled with the problem of working out a viable scheme of reorganization on the basis of this report. Although troubles broke out in the Punjab, where the claims of the Sikhs were at stake, in Bengal and Bihar, and elsewhere, the gravest difficulties arose in connection with the disposition of the city of Bombay to which backers of the two proposed linguistic states of Maharashtra and Gujerat both laid claim on historical and ethnic grounds.[18] After months of violent agitation and bloodshed the dispute was ultimately resolved by the abandonment in this instance of the linguistic state principle and the creation of a huge state of Bombay embracing both the linguistic states as well as the city. Here, as in other areas, the linguistic-political issues were complicated by economic considerations since the Maharashtrians, who furnish the bulk of Bombay's labor force, protest that they are exploited by the Gujerati who own many of the mills and shops. The bitterly disputed process of reordering India's political units came to an end with the reduction in the number of states to fourteen, or half their previous number, plus six centrally administered territories. Of the fourteen states the bulk represented consolidated linguistic communities, but both Bombay and the Punjab were deliberately established on a multilingual basis. Whether or not the issue has been laid to rest remains to be seen, but its implications are potentially explosive.

The importance which India attributes to the language question is further attested by the frequency of reference to it in the constitution. Part XVI of that instrument, wholly devoted to language problems, specifies that "the official language of the Union shall be Hindi in Devanagari script," but for fifteen years from the adoption of the constitution English is accepted for official purposes and Parliament may extend its use further. As part of a repeated constitutional assertion of the principle of nondiscrimination, the fundamental rights of citizens include the provision that any group having a distinct language, script, or culture of its own shall have the right to conserve it, and the state legislatures may utilize the local languages of the area concerned.

For educational purposes a tripartite structure has been evolved which has its parallel in other countries confronted by similar problems. Accepting the view that children can learn most effectively through the medium of their mother tongue, the schools start with the local language. Hindi is taken up at the next remove, and English and other foreign languages are taught to the more advanced students. The maintenance of the vital link with the mother tongue is wise, but it is sure to have significant cultural and political results which are still only partially foreseeable. As hitherto passive elements of the society rise in social and economic consequence and achieve literacy in their local languages, the effect may well be to foster a sense of provincial identity which will not necessarily mesh neatly into an India-wide national consciousness. It is characteristic of India's language communities that they form large and solid blocks which lend themselves easily to political manipulation. Furthermore, one student of India's linguistic problems has pointed out that at least in its early stages the interregional migration of India's peoples to urban centers has not uprooted old regional and social ties:

> At close quarters the friction only intensifies between rival enclaves of industrial labor in India's multilingual industrial melting pots. Wherever they go, India's linguistic minorities gravitate to "ghettoes" where the mother tongue and marriage practices of the home region remain inviolate.[19]

What will be the effects on Indian democracy of the distinction between the upper elements of the society which move in circles where learning Hindi and English is relatively easy and important, and the mass of the less educated who will not have moved beyond the local language and its cultural horizons? The probability is strong that leaders will increasingly emerge whose stature is essentially limited to their linguistic community with its political-emotional potentialities and whose claim to power may undercut the appeal of those who act at the national level. But though the risks of discord and separatism are undoubtedly real, the likelihood is that the deeper wisdom lies with those who are prepared to recognize and build upon diversity rather than with those who seek to crush it out and march with direct ruthlessness toward national uniformity.

It is the constitutionally prescribed dream that Hindi, enriched by the assimilation of ingredients from other Indian languages, should develop "as a medium of expression for all the elements of the composite culture of India," replacing English as the *lingua franca*. The realization of this dream within the fifteen years set for it, or even in the further future, is a matter widely viewed with skepticism. Particularly in the Dravidian setting of the south, the languages which are to be subordinated will yield priority to Hindi, if at all, only after what is sure to be embittered battle. Here the continuation of English as the all-Indian language would be more acceptable to many than the acknowledgement of the supremacy of Hindi. Dravidian India has already brought into existence cultural and political bodies which demand drastic remedies for the alleged Brahmin imperialism of the north. It is not necessary to follow Stalin in the implied denial of India's nationhood, but it would be idle to pretend that a nation whose unity embraces as wide and deep a range of internal cleavages as that of India is not exposed to danger.

As nations come into being in Africa south of the Sahara they are likely to be plagued with language problems as acute as those with which India and some other Asian countries are struggling. The differences between these two parts of the world are great, but so are the similarities. The most striking difference, reflecting the lower stage of development of African civilizations, is that the African languages had not achieved a written form prior to the appearance of the Europeans. The basic similarity, for the present purpose, is that generally speaking, as in the case of India, potentially national areas embrace several different languages. The troubles which lie ahead are magnified by the fact that although there are large African linguistic families, such as Bantu, the actual spoken language or dialects for the most part embrace relatively small numbers of people, thus making all the more difficult the discovery and establishment of a single national language. In some parts of the continent local languages have secured adoption as the *lingua franca*, as for example, Swahili on the east coast and further afield. It should, however, also be noted that in Kenya — a Swahili territory — some twenty vernaculars are in use for primary education, and in next-door Uganda the effort to introduce Swahili as a link to the rest of East Africa was defeated by the Kabaka who defended the right of his people to their native Luganda.

The fragmentation of African languages and the nature of the problem which flows from it can be seen from a glance at some of the material presented by Lord Hailey in his review of the languages in use in some African territories.[20] The people of Northern Rhodesia speak some forty different languages of which five principal ones are given official recognition. In northern Nigeria Hausa is predominant although a number of other languages are spoken; in southern Nigeria, Yoruba is strong in the Western Region, but in the rest of the south a great variety of languages is found with no common tongue in some coastal areas except pidgin English.

In connection with mass literacy campaigns in Nigeria, extensive publication has been carried on in Hausa, Tiv, Yoruba, Ibo, and Efik, but these are far from exhausting the languages which are actually spoken. In the southern part of Ghana, the four main languages are Twi, Fante, Ga, and Ewe, which are further subdivided by dialects. French West African languages are generally stated to number over 126. The Belgian Congo has four principal languages used for communication between Europeans and Africans, four other languages are widely used in primary education, and three more are used in certain localities.

The political difficulties of a people burdened with many languages are illustrated in the account of an electioneering meeting in the Nigerian village of Oyubia, where Oron is the local tongue.[21] On this occasion, the Prime Minister of the Eastern Region, who reportedly speaks Efik, Ibo, Yoruba and Hausa, but not Oron, spoke in Ibo. The candidate himself spoke in Oron, while two other speeches were in Efik and two were in English.

Given the current insistence on the desirability of using the vernacular as the language of instruction, particularly in the earlier school years — a matter which Unesco regards as axiomatic and which has the authority of a UN General Assembly resolution behind it [22] — the attainment in African countries of the nationalist slogan of "one country, one people, one language" will at best be long delayed. Even more than in Asia the temptation to draw upon a European language as the common language in many countries will be great.[23] The Gold Coast, shortly prior to independence, moved to substitute English for the vernaculars in education, and the All-African People's Conference of 1958, while it also urged African states to encourage the teaching of African languages, held that English should be taught in the secondary schools of French-speaking territories and vice versa in order to promote African intercourse on a continental scale. Such a turn toward European languages is necessarily at the cost of pride in a purely African language heritage, involving a mass shift into a wholly alien tongue. Instead, the future may conceivably see an expansion of the more widely spoken African languages, such as Swahili, and the adoption in particular countries of one or more of the local languages for the purposes of education and administration.

No easy moral can be drawn in the linguistic sphere other than that there is a gross lack of coincidence between language and nation in many quarters of the earth. Where substantial linguistic diversity exists the effort to enforce the use of what is adopted as the national language can be carried through only at an immense human cost, if at all, and the disruptive effect of a frontal attack upon an entrenched language may prove ruinous. Where the national, or possibly a European, language comes in only as a secondary supplement to the basic vernacular the situation is obviously eased. Educational authorities contend that a child starting his education in the vernacular will move more easily into a second language than if he is forced into it at the outset.

The problem takes on quite new dimensions as education comes to have a mass basis, requiring an extention of school systems far beyond their present limits. Where only a relative handful of Asians and Africans were securing more than the rudiments of education, instruction in an alien language for this small elite was comparatively simple. It becomes a monumental task when the aim is to bring entire populations to effective literacy; and the turn toward the vernacular in multilingual societies will inevitably emphasize rather than blunt ethnic diversity. In this situation something must give way, and it will presumably be the classical European assumption that each nation is, or should be, endowed with a language of its own. That a viable state can be built on other foundations is well established by a number of significant examples of a national variety as well as by the explicitly multinational Soviet Union.

The most spectacular development which presumably lies ahead is not directly related to language at all but is intimately bound to the spread of literacy or, more broadly, of education. In the earlier European setting the rise of nationalism and of popular political and economic movements was intimately related to the expansion of secular education in the national vernacular, mobilizing new elements of society to active participation and to self-consciousness. The similar mushrooming of education which is now taking place in so many Asian and African countries is bound to be associated with similar basic changes in the existing cultural, economic, and political balance. As the hold of the monarchs and aristocrats and then of the upper bourgeoisie was successfully challenged in Europe, so the dominant elites of the non-European countries will be increasingly challenged as their peasant and working masses emerge from timeless obscurity. The fact that these elites have been the formulators and heroes of the national movements will not save them from replacement as new generations rise with new attitudes and aspirations. The seeds sown with literacy are likely to sprout up in such fashion as to overshadow those who now have their heads in the sun.

CHAPTER VIII

Culture and Religion

THE ESSENCE OF A NATION," said Renan, "is that all the individuals have many things in common, and also that all have forgotten a good many things." [1] If, with Alsace-Lorraine fresh in mind, he added to this the celebrated phrase that the existence of a nation is "un plébiscite de tous les jours," it is still the fact that this is a plebiscite whose results have been in very large measure predetermined, not only from day to day but even from generation to generation, by both the myth and the reality of a common heritage from the past. A people comes gradually to a sense of its unique and distinct identity through that long living together which brings about the learning of common patterns of life and thought. A nation is shaped through the experience of elements of a common historical destiny, but Renan's wise inclusion of the things that must be forgotten is a constant reminder that history has worked in no single and uniform fashion. The most coherent and united of nations still has a troubled record behind it which contradicts unity almost as much as it affirms it: the diverse and the divisive are quite as real as the jointly shared. If Western Europe were now to achieve unity the kind of remembering and forgetting its people would have to undertake would be of the same order as that which makes the essence of a nation. What is cherished in the national myth may not only be shot through with inspired fiction but must also inevitably be a somewhat arbitrary selection from the multiplicity and perversity of the age-old record.

The notion of a single national culture, shaping the community and embracing all its people, is an admirable one whose principal shortcoming is its remoteness from historical fact. In an ideal state of affairs the entire body of the nation would over the generations have grown up within the common culture and thus been made ready to be roused to national consciousness when the appropriate circumstances came along. In actual fact, the people who come to form a nation have frequently been divided on religious lines, almost always on regional lines, and surely on class lines. Until a very late stage the national culture, and indeed the nation itself, are for all practical purposes the property of a small upper crust of the society, while the mass of the people, normally limited to far more parochial horizons, shares in both culture and nation only on the fringes. Certainly it is in order to view with a skeptical eye the claim that the nation as a whole can look back to a common store of ancestors, memories, and experiences. Challenging the usual assumptions as to the working of history, Boyd C. Shafer has contended that for most contemporary European peoples a common group history is almost wholly fictional if it is pressed back much beyond the nineteenth century: "The belief is real; the actuality never existed." [2]

Although the illiterate peasantry, and perhaps even the disinherited rabble of the cities, had a folk culture of its own, a great gap separated that culture from the one being evolved by the aristocracy and upper bourgeoisie with pretensions of being or becoming the national culture. The creation of nations is in some part a process of absorbing local folk societies into a larger whole. In this process each local community which is absorbed no doubt influences the final outcome, but the major influence is on the side of the aristocracy and the urban elite whose language and culture generally set the national standard, at least until such time as the rising masses begin to transform what they have at last inherited.

As with other elements contributing to the solidarity of the nation, such as a common language or an integrated economy, the emergence of a common culture is likely to be almost as much a resultant of the achievement of national identity as a creative cause of it. Without question the nation requires a substantial degree of preëxistent unity, of actual commonness of historical experience, among the people who compose it; it cannot be put together out of heterogeneous agglomerations of peoples who have made no progress toward a common pattern. Yet it is also true that many unassimilated groups are sure to linger within the general confines of the nation, particularly in the early phases of the growth of national consciousness. Once a nationalist movement has come into being and much more decisively when a national state takes over, the instrumentalities of the state and the pressure for national unity are themselves immensely powerful influences working toward the assimilation of divergent strands to what comes to be accepted as the national norm, although the effect may also be to consolidate the opposition of unassimilable minorities.

On the European stage the class differences prior to the nineteenth century were so great that often no national linkage was acknowledged across the class lines, as religious differences have at other times and places overridden national ties. Mme de Stael spoke of the French nobility as finding its compatriots among the nobles of all countries rather than among its fellow citizens in France; and the Abbé Siéyès was prepared to exclude the aristocracy from *his* French nation, which was made up of the third estate. The caste and class lines which have separated the Asian aristocracies from the mass of the people have been quite as real as those of Europe. The point at issue has frequently become a matter of vital political consequence: who represents the nation when national decisions must be taken? The heirs of the traditional society or those who speak for the new order? The aristocracy, the middle class, the peasantry, the urban proletariat, or the one charismatic leader who embodies the national ethos in his own person? The inherent difficulties become far greater where there exists a cultural gap of the kind characteristic of the non-Western countries in which an increasingly important segment of the society seeks to give a Western cast to the development of its country.

This is an issue which every people has faced: the nation derives its distinctive character from its past, from the history and circumstances which have peculiarly shaped it, but it is likely to be a condition of survival that the nation adopt from others the things which make them strong and give them an advantage in one or another sphere. The speeding up of the pace of change as a result of discovery and invention has made the issue constantly more insistent. Must the national heritage be sacrificed in order that the nation may live? The problem has been a lesser one in the Western

European societies in which the modern world of rationalism, science, and industry originated, although it was not negligible even there. The transition in France, for example, from the artist-artisan traditions to the machine age was a very painful process. Far more critical situations arise in the rest of the world where the new is an alien intrusion, opening a dangerous gap between the masses and the rising elite. For the most part the latter swing in the Westernizing direction, but some turn back to reassertion of the past and perhaps to a faith in the illiterate masses in whom a deep primitive goodness is discovered: the Slavophils as against the Westernizers in nineteenth-century Russia, the traditionalists as against the innovators in Japan after the Meiji Restoration, Gandhi and the Gandhians as against the modernizers in India. The dilemma is a real and tragic one. Nehru has borne witness that while the rising middle classes were heading toward the modern world represented by the West, at the same time:

> they wanted some cultural roots to cling on to, something that would give them assurance of their own worth, something that would reduce the sense of frustration and humiliation that foreign conquest and rule had produced. In every country with a growing nationalism there is this search apart from religion, this tendency to go back to the past.[3]

The problem is peculiarly acute for all the peoples who have had a sense of inferiority thrust upon them through being the underdogs of imperialism. For the restoration of their self-respect it is essential that their own cultures and histories be restored to a place of honor. It is, however, also essential that they demonstrate their ability to compete with their former overlords in the modern world — and the nationalists are precisely the men who look to a speedy overhauling of their societies on Western lines. Here is a fertile source of internal conflicts and contradictions. The search for a solid and accepted base of their own is of immense importance for peoples whose religions and ways of life have been openly disparaged as backward, superstitious, and corrupt.[4] Gravest of all is this search on the part of the Negroes who have not only felt the scorn for their traditional societies but have also had the crowning indignity of slavery inflicted upon them.

An ironic twist is furnished by the fact that the history, tradition, and culture to which Asians and African might return are in large part discoveries and resurrections undertaken by the Europeans. The past which had in many instances vanished from sight has been restored by the labors of white archeologists, anthropologists, historians, and students of languages. It was the French scientists accompanying Napoleon on his invasion of Egypt who began to open the door to Egypt's antiquity, and other Europeans read the Rosetta Stone. American Protestant missionaries in Syria in the nineteenth century played an important role in the revival of classical Arabic and Arabic literature. India's past was brought back to human ken primarily by British investigators, and Frenchmen rediscovered and restored Angkor Wat. The relatively slight relics of African civilizations have likewise been brought to light and placed in their historical periods by white men who have also tracked down the story of such earlier African empires as Ghana.

The positive content of nationalism is always a difficult matter to identify with any precision. A national culture is as elusive a matter to pin down as national character has proved to be. It forms no consistent and rounded whole but is made up of many strands, haphazardly assembled, some of which are incompatible with others. Only totalitarian dictatorship can arbitrarily determine that certain elements are nationally acceptable while others are ruled out as un-national. When the amorphous character of all nationalisms has been thus acknowledged, however, the fact remains that colonial nationalism has tended to be peculiarly negative: derived largely from the colonial experience, its major emphasis has been its anti-colonialism, postponing till some later time the argument as to what it positively stands for in addition to ridding itself of imperial control. This negativism is most notably in evidence where the unity and coherence of the nation are most in doubt, and where the cultural background is least highly evolved.

Recognition of the inadequacy of a nationalism so insecurely based has speedily brought the African nationalists, like their Asian counterparts, to seek out some solider foundation and greater glory on which to rest their case than mere opposition to their colonial rulers. The problems which have arisen as they have set off on this quest have been manifold. The African past is one dominated by tribalism; to return to tradition by that route is to undercut the nations which are the present goal. Or, alternatively, since the nations themselves are arbitrary constructious with only the shallowest of roots, the turn may be in the direction of a pan-Africanism.[5] In addition, the new breath of life which brought nationalism with it has been felt primarily in the great urban centers, sometimes wholly new creations, which have served as the focal points for Western trade, administration, and influence. These cities and the new African generation which has grown up in them are only tenuously attached to the old traditional life, and look to a very different kind of society from that which has been characteristic through the preceding ages.

Swinging full circle in reaction against the customary low view of Africa's culture and achievements, some of the rising African intellectuals have embarked on a reëvaluation which occasionally produces startling results. Gone are the shamefaced apology for the land from which they sprung and the homage often paid to the superiority of the West by their fathers. Instead, the new men assert, with Senghor, their faith in *Négritude* and their pride in the ancestry which they are discovering and embellishing for themselves, even though they must draw heavily on materials furnished them by white researchers. The exaltation of the African Personality is a key weapon in the battle against acceptance of inferiority.

In a moderate version of the new trend, Dr. K. Onwuka Dike contended that such seemingly abstract considerations as culture and history are as important as more material ones in building a nation, and found them fundamental to the problem of self-government:

> If the African has no past heritage, and no future except by imitation of European ways at a pace which the European thinks safe, then the Gold Coast is destined to fail. But if the instinctive belief of the African in his traditions is justified, the ultimate emergence of West African states as independent modern states cannot be doubted. . . . Every nation builds its future on its past; so the African must not only instinctively have faith in his own existence, but must also satisfy himself by scientific inquiry that it exists.[6]

F. Oladipo Onipede followed the same trail in his estimate of

African nationalism as moving in increasingly African channels, forcing the younger nationalists to formulate their appeals and programs in language intelligible to the masses rather than to the new middle class or to the Western world in which the latter was trained:

> One immediate implication of this fact is that *African symbols and institutions have begun to be given priority and preference over the ideas and language of Western liberalism.* Nor is this a surface phenomenon; it represents a deep-going trend of enormous importance for the future of African nationalism.[7]

A further conclusion which Onipede drew was that the chiefs, the natural rulers, would gain in political power and social prestige. On one hand, the nationalists would find it necessary to solicit their support, and, on the other, the chiefs would win popular acclaim as the defenders of the traditional values against the disruptive effects of the drive toward modernization and industrialization of the Westernized elite.

Such efforts to recapture for Africans a sense that they have an honorable place in the world are inevitable. As in the case of many other peoples, however, the momentum gained in the initial reaction from slavery and being looked upon as a low breed of mankind has carried beyond any plausible limits. Thus Cheikh Anta Diop has written a large book whose central purpose is to establish that it is not white men to whom we owe civilization but Negroes. In his reconstruction of the past, the great authors of antiquity have with surprising exactness instructed us concerning one basic fact, the race to which the Egyptians belonged:

> All inform us that the Egyptians were Negroes, like the Ethiopians and the other Africans; that Egypt has civilized the world.[8]

The evidence of the Ancients against the idea that Egyptians were white is so overwhelming, as Diop saw it, that the white man has had to distort it, ignoring some passages, translating "black" as "brown" in others, and destroying thousands of mummies which betrayed the true state of affairs. It has been the utilitarian purpose of the theories promulgated by the Europeans to establish that the Negroes have never created anything of value and have therefore no proper claim to national aspirations of their own.

The reality of history, as Diop portrayed it, was that the original Ghana came to the fore in the interior of the continent at the moment of the decline of Egypt and Carthage, as in the West empires were born with the fall of Rome. In recent centuries Africa has lagged behind; it is now high time for it to catch up and make its own contribution. But it can do so only if it is transformed into a federation of independent African states, covering the entire continent from the Mediterranean to the Cape, from the Atlantic to the Indian Ocean.

To this version of Africa's past and future another African writer, Dika Akwa, adds further laurels in demonstrating that virtually all mankind's achievements are to be traced to Negro sources. As Georges Balandier summarizes Akwa's elaborations on the theme, Moses and Buddha become Egyptian Negroes, Christianity derives from a Sudanese people, and such European philosophers as Nietzsche, Bergson, Marx, and the existentialists reflect the philosophy of the Bantus. On such lines as these, Balandier comments, the young African intellectuals are using their learning as an instrument of racial combat, as Soviet science was placed at the service of all the proletariats: not content with putting Negro culture on the same level as the greatest civilizations, these African champions "give it priority and proclaim it as carrying all the others in its bosom." [9] Racialism has come to a new life, not necessarily more attractive than that which it had before.

Even though one or another version of *Négritude* has an inevitable appeal, many African leaders recognize that if Africa is to make its place in the world it must reconcile itself to such abandonment of its traditional life as is necessary to make the transition to modernity possible. In December 1958, the All-African People's Conference at Accra attacked tribalism and religious separatism as evil practices which blocked African liberation, political evolution, and unity, and resolved that traditional institutions which have "clearly shown their reactionary character and their sordid support for colonialism" should be condemned. [10] Others demand a far more radical breach with the past, seeking the prompt transformation of Africa into a modern society on the Western model. Thus, George Padmore, West Indian, ex-Communist, advisor to Nkrumah on African affairs, and advocate of pan-Africanism, sets modern nationhood and parliamentary democracy as the goal. He holds the colonial powers responsible for perpetuating tribalism because they blocked industrialism which was the only force capable of liberating Africans from their traditions and prejudices. Seeing a cataclysm as necessary to free the traditional African way of life from its own decay, he looks to the newly emancipated and detribalized younger generation of Africans to bring about the required regeneration under the stimulus of Western political ideas and technocracy.[11]

The creation in Africa of reasonably stable national cultures is a task which remains almost wholly to be accomplished. In their different fashions the colonial powers have set revolutionary forces in motion, but they have not created national cultures, nor would it have been possible for any alien regime to do so. The ill-assorted fragments which must be combined to form future African cultures are largely assembled; the work of putting them together waits upon free African peoples. The undermining of the old African societies is moving ahead at full speed. Urbanization, new employments, changed family and tribal relations, the importance of money and education, new freedoms and new discontents are at work to bring about a still unrecognizable synthesis of the Africa of the past and the West which has so deeply penetrated it.[12] The tribal Africans of the bush have often been far more disturbed in their way of life than is superficially evident, and the Westernized often retain attachments to tribe and tradition which make no overt appearance in Western circles. The traditional African culture to which some romantics and rebels would return is almost sure to be one seen through sophisticated eyes and perhaps one largely interpreted for them by Western students. And the Africans of the cities have come into a Westernization which in its present incarnation involves mixing the superstitions of Africa with the worst of the West — alcohol, prostitution, violence, and the grim poverty of the slums.

The colonialism of democracies can produce perverse results. In a well-directed sally against white racialism, Peter Abrahams has put forward the proposition that Africans have in some circumstances proved themselves more dependable champions of Western culture than have the Europeans. Pointing his finger directly at Malan's government in the Union, he exposed the dilemma plaguing white men wherever the settler problem has become acute: "they must either reject the moral and ethical bases of Western culture or else give up their positions of power and privilege." Since they decline the latter course, finding it easier to abandon ethics than privilege, it is "the black leaders of the African National Congress" who defend the fundamental assumptions of the West in their demand for democracy.[13]

RELIGION

One of the major components of any culture is religion, but, despite its evident importance, the bearing of religion on the shaping of nations and nationalism is erratic and diverse. The lessons which were drawn from the classical experience of nineteenth-century Europe must be recanvassed as nationalism sweeps out to embrace the whole wide world. From this earlier phase the conclusion seemed warranted that the rise of nationalism coincided with a decline in the hold of religion.[14] The wars of religion gave way to the wars of the nations; religious toleration accompanied the spread of nationalism; and it became more important that a man was a Frenchman or German than that he was Catholic or Protestant. In none of the Western European countries, save perhaps Ireland, did religion appear to be of central significance for the formation of nation and state in the nineteenth century.

As nationalism moved into eastern and southeastern Europe and on into Asia the religious issue pressed more clearly to the fore again. Only in two instances, Pakistan and Israel, was religion the heart and essence of the national existence, but in many, religion lent a driving force to the nation which it would not otherwise have had. How different would Arab nationalism have been without Islam? In many political controversies religion came to the aid of other aspects of national differentiation, as, for example, in Cyprus, where the Orthodox Church served as a rallying point for the Greek Cypriote nationalists.

Wherever the imperial West intruded, the Christianity of the white man, whether or not he lived up to its precepts, marked him off from the people among whom he came and emphasized their own religion. When religion had as intense a hold and informed all of life, as did Islam or Hinduism, it was inconceivable that nations should emerge without being profoundly influenced by religious issues. If the advent of modernism in all its guises, including nationalism, tended to weaken the grip of religion, the other side of the coin was that, given the disparity in religion between ruler and ruled in the colonies, religion was inevitably drawn upon as a vital rallying point for nationalism by those who sought to preserve or refashion a sense of separate identity for their community. Thus, in Indonesia incipient nationalism found one of its first expressions in the association of Sarekat Islam, and in Burma in the Young Men's Buddhist Association.

Although religion looms larger in relation to the newer nationalisms than it did in those of last century's Western Europe, the fact remains that only an arbitrary line of coincidence links religion and nation. No sweeping generalizations can be made about the role of religion among Asian and African peoples. Japan has developed it as a nation-building force; in China its national role has been relatively negligible. Burma prides itself on its Buddhist background, and is working out a curious amalgam of Buddhism and socialism. Among Islamic peoples, Turkey under Ataturk turned its official back on the religion of the country, Pakistan found the reason for its being in Islam, and Indonesia is hesitant whether it should follow Pakistan in becoming an Islamic state or India in secularism. In Black Africa the native religions have been much less of a focal point for nationalism than in Asia, but separatist Christian churches, foreshadowing later nationalisms, have often cropped up.

Contact between nationalism and religion takes place on many fronts and in many forms. The rise of nationalism, as Hans Kohn has pointed out,[15] is likely to be preceded by a revival and reformulation of basic religious principles and outlooks. In Europe the period of the Reformation marked this phase of development. India in the nineteenth century, challenged by the tightening hold of Christian Britain on the country, undertook several revivals and purifications of Hinduism. India's Moslems, slower to respond to the new forces, followed after the Hindus in similar movements. For Islam in general and Arabia in particular, an outstanding event whose influence is still felt was the emergence in the eighteenth century of the Wahhabi movement with its stern insistence on a return to the original purity of the faith. In the period of Western imperialist expansion of the latter part of the nineteenth century, the intellectual and religious reawakening of Islam was greatly spurred by such leading figures as Jamal al-Din al-Afghani and Muhammed Abduh, who urged the need of adaptation to the modern world, restored a sense of victories still to be achieved, and pressed for political revival within a pan-Islamic framework.

The programs advocated by such movements and reformers vary immensely, stretching between the two poles of reaffirmation of established creeds and deliberate revolution to adapt the traditional religion to contemporary pressures. One course which is frequently followed, exemplified by the Wahhabi movement and Gandhi, is a demand for a return to the original faith, scraping off the corruptions and abuses accumulated in the intervening centuries. An advantage of such a procedure, involving the reinterpretation of documents and legends often ambiguous in meaning, is that substantial latitude is left to the reformer in shaping the future outlines of the creed. Surprisingly enough, the advocates of a return to origins not infrequently discover at the end of their researches what they set out to find — a bridge by which they and their coreligionists may easily and consistently move into the modern world without abandoning the faith of their fathers. Occasionally this results in the discovery that all of modernity, including inventions of recent date, was either available or clearly foreshadowed in ancient times. One political outcropping of such a refurbishing of the past is the contention that democracy was the form of government of Islam in its early classical days.

Another point of contact between religion and nationalism is the appearance of religious sects of protest and politico-religious movements of a messianic variety where the time is not yet ripe for full-blown nationalism or where political activity is barred by the colonial authorities. Thomas Hodgkin sees the essential point of the separatist church in Africa as being to make possible reconstruction of African communities under African leadership and thus to express opposition to European authority on the spiritual plane since its expression on other planes is barred. However primitive a phase in the development of nationalism this may be, he holds that:

> at least the prophets have awakened men's minds to the fact that change can occur; and the ablest of them, like their European prototypes, have shown themselves wholly capable of producing a myth, a literature and an organization.[16]

As the vast Indian subcontinent can be drawn upon to illustrate almost every aspect of nationalism, so in the religious sphere its experience is uniquely rich and varied. To a very great extent the past of India must be sought in its religions. The tragic dilemma was sharply sketched by B. R. Ambedkar, leader of the Untouchables, who wistfully remarked that India's prospects might be better if the Hindus and Moslems could perform the impossible task of forgetting their past:

> Their past is embedded in their religion, and for each to give up its past is to give up its religion. To hope for this is to hope in vain.[17]

As Stalin denied that a nation could be linguistically divided, so Khrushchev, then still traveling in the company of Bulganin, in a speech in Kashmir in December 1955, indicated that religious passions had been deliberately stirred up by the imperialists; he laid down the dictum that "religious beliefs have never been the main question in setting up a state." [18] This is a firm and forthright statement, eminently satisfactory to Khrushchev's Indian hosts, but its historical accuracy is open to gravest question.

To find the opposing case stated with fighting vigor, one need only turn to some Hindu and Moslem spokesmen who, happily, represent extremes of no wide appeal. Thus Sri Madhav Sadashiv Golwalker, leader of a militant Hindu organization, wrote that "Hindustan is the land of the Hindus and is the terra firma for the Hindu nation alone to flourish upon . . ."; while all those who fall outside the Hindu nation can have no place in national life unless they completely merge themselves in the National Race.[19] On the Moslem side, F. K. Khan Durrani in a book on Pakistan reminded his coreligionists that India was a geographic unity every inch of whose soil was purchased with the blood of their fathers: "India, the whole of it, is therefore our heritage and it must be reconquered for Islam." [20]

The origin of Pakistan as a state founded on religion is beyond question, and even for India something of a religious case can be made. In brief the argument would run that the Indian nationalism which was shaping in the latter part of the nineteenth century and which led into the Congress was explicitly Hindu in character; that the Hindu opposition to the partition of Bengal was a major element in the development; that Gandhi, whether or not he acknowledged it, was irretrievably and profoundly Hindu; [21] and that the Congress itself, despite the sprinkling of Moslems in its membership, was basically a Hindu organization. Two Hindu critics of the course of Indian nationalism, whose positions were otherwise far removed from each other, might be cited in support of such a view. Nirad C. Chaudhuri, in a revealing autobiography which also reported on the cleavage between Hindu and Moslem in the ordinary life of India, saw Gandhi as bringing the masses into the nationalist movement: "At last in India the Masses and the Man had become one." But the results, as he appraised them, were on the whole undesirable: "In the end Gandhism in politics and in practice came to stand for very little else but a congealed mass of atavistic aspirations and prejudices." [22]

A. R. Desai came to much the same conclusion although he blamed foreign rule for causing even the intellectuals to reject not only the alien rulers but also the culture which the aliens brought with them. In consequence the nationalist was led to invoke obscurantist and mystical parts of the nation's traditional culture, thus obstructing the growth of national unity. On such grounds Desai protested in quaint phrase: "Politics becomes tainted with religion, and is mystified." [23]

Thus, a case can be made for the proposition that the Indian National Congress was Hindu and that post-partition India is Hindu, but in neither instance is it a case which carries all the way. The Moslem League was precisely a *Moslem* league and Pakistan was fought for explicitly to create a Moslem state, whereas the Congress always included Moslems, sometimes even in its highest offices, and the India which took over in 1947 was established explicitly as a secular state. It is a striking and symbolic fact that for many years India's Minister of Education should have been a Moslem, Maulana Abul Kalam Azad, a close friend of Nehru's.

If the Indian position on Kashmir has fallen short of the high standards Indian spokesmen insist on for the rest of the world, it is beyond doubt that a considerable part of India's stand has been dictated by its secular claims. To concede that a territory's political destiny must be fixed by the religion of its inhabitants is to undermine a central tenet of India's official political beliefs. The loss of Kashmir, it is held, would be likely to strengthen reactionary Hindu forces.

For Nehru the denial of religion as the foundation of the modern nation and state is almost as fixed a position as for Khrushchev. In the years of the struggle for independence he repeated time and again his conviction that to make political life center about religion was a reversion to medievalism, that the two-nation theory was absurd, and that the real roots of the Hindu-Moslem conflict were to be traced to a clash of classes and vested interests. But Gandhi was assassinated by a Hindu for lack of adequate devotion to the faith, and the organ of a right-wing Hindu association has descended to the accusation that Nehru "would make a better Prime Minister of Pakistan than of Hindustan." [24]

Pakistan itself furnishes the most dramatic contemporary example of the ability of a religious community to establish itself as a political entity. Whether or not the Pakistanis constituted a nation at the time they achieved independence or had become one more than a decade later is a matter open to the gravest doubt. The difficulties which confronted them were exposed with full frankness in 1956 by a Moslem member of their Constituent Assembly, who set off from the underlying fact that it was a country uniquely divided into two wings, separated by a distance of more than a thousand miles:

> These two wings differ in all matters, excepting two things, namely, that they have a common religion, barring a section of the people in East Pakistan, and that we achieved our independence by a common struggle. . . . all other factors, viz. the language, the tradition, the culture, the costume, the custom, the dietary, the calendar, the standard time, practically everything is different. There is, in fact, nothing common in the two wings, particularly in respect of those which are the *sine qua non* to form a nation.[25]

It does not take a very long memory to recognize that these

terms are almost absurdly close to those in which Jinnah and others laid out the differences which separated the Moslem from the Hindu nation, adding, of course, the difference in religion as the crucial item.

Too much has been written of the Moslem League, Jinnah, and the origins of Pakistan to make it necessary to elaborate on those themes here. Two things emerge clearly from this oft-told story. One is that the sole overt ground for the creation of Pakistan was to rescue Moslems from Hindu domination and to enable them to live in a properly constituted Islamic society. The second is that this was a movement fostered and directed, not by the religious leaders and the devout of Moslem India, but by the same Westernized middle class elements — the professional men and the intelligentsia — as those which guided other nationalist movements. Jinnah himself was an outstanding example of such a man, and certainly not one marked by deep religious concerns. Although, once Pakistan had been secured, the religious leaders swung in to transform it into an instrument for the achievement of Islam's purposes, they abstained from or opposed the drive for a separate Pakistan. The heart of their objection was that Islam and nationalism were diametrically opposite to each other in spirit and aims. As one of their principal figures expressed it, Islam was not divided by nationality, race, country, or class, and had as its ultimate goal a world-state free of prejudice:

> when nationalism enters the heart and mind of a Muslim from one direction, Islam leaves them from another direction. Any Muslim who has pledged himself to the devil of nationalism has been divorced by the angels of Islam.[26]

The outlines of one among the many conflicts which have divided Pakistan were thus well established before the state came into existence. The religious leaders objected to its creation and later wanted to equip it with Islamic institutions for Islamic purposes, even though the precise nature of those institutions and purposes was often in dispute. The political leaders fought for a Moslem state to be carved out of India, but were strongly disinclined to have it emerge in a purely religious guise as a theocracy. They were aware both of world opinion and of the difficulty of finding an acceptable place in such a state for the Hindus and other minorities.

A constitution was ultimately adopted in 1956 which established the Islamic Republic of Pakistan wherein the Moslems might "order their lives in accordance with the teachings and requirements of Islam, as set out in the Holy Quran and Sunnah," but with freedom for the minorities to practice their religion and develop their culture. The presidency was reserved for Moslems, but this was the only office so circumscribed. Among the most difficult issues confronted by the constitution-makers were the extent of the legislative power of the state — had not all necessary legislation been divinely laid down in the remote past? — and the relation of legislation to revealed holy writ. Both issues were settled or evaded by constitutional provisions which left wide latitude for future maneuver. The first was dealt with by the opening declaration of the preamble that sovereignty over the entire universe belongs to Allah alone, and that the people of Pakistan can exercise authority only within the limits prescribed by Him. The second was embraced in the "Islamic Provisions" of Part XII, which affirmed that no law should be enacted which is repugnant to the Injunctions of Islam as laid down in the Koran and Sunnah; but the enforcement of this provision was left uncertain and was not entrusted to the learned in Islamic law, as had been sought on the religious side. The making of a constitution for Israel has been impeded by similar difficulties concerning the role of divinely established law. For both Pakistan and Israel one vital question which remains unanswered is whether a non-Moslem or a non-Jew can in fact be a full and equal member of a nation whose primary definition is couched in religious terms.

In 1958 General Mohammed Ayub Khan, ascending to supreme power in Pakistan, abolished the constitution which had been so laboriously put together. Among the urgent issues confronting him was the creation of a nation as the firm underpinning of the state, a task still to be accomplished even though Jinnah and his associates had optimistically asserted the existence of the nation two or three decades earlier.

In the rest of the Moslem world as well as in Pakistan, Islam and nationalism have had grave difficulties in coming to terms with

each other. The alienation of the urban, Western-oriented nationalist from the traditional society and its religion is one familiar facet
of the problem. Secular politics and the secular state sit more easily
with the former than do religious controversy and a theocratically
organized state. But the people at large have lived over the centuries
in their religious communities, and no religion affirms more vigorously than Islam that it represents a total way of life, having no
acquaintance with Christianity's separation of church and state.

Another facet concerns the relations between peoples of different religion within nation and state where religion remains the
central bond of community. On the improbable assumption that
the nation is one homogeneous religious fraternity, no need exists
to worry about divergencies in membership between religion and
nation; in all other circumstances the two may dangerously cut
across each other. Secular territorial states based on nations were
able to take over in the Middle East only at the cost of cutting
away from the traditional organization of social and political life
around the religious community. Religious affiliation has been in
process of giving way to affiliation with nations held together by
many other ties than that of religion — but how to identify the
elements which went to shape the nations remained obscure.
Among them, surely, religion itself inescapably figured as one of
the most signifiant ingredients. Egypt was able to become a full-
fledged nation only when it departed enough from Islam to take
the Copts and other religious minorities into the fold, and the same
was true in their different circumstances for Syria and Lebanon.
Yet the circle always tends to turn back on itself, since for any
Arab people Islam is one of the most vital centers of its heritage.
Here another dimension enters: to conceive of Arab nationalism
or, even worse, of the nationalism of particular Arab states, is immediately to depart from the universal religious community of
Islam.

The contrast between the old Middle East and the new was
brought to life in the autobiography of Edward Atiyah, a Syrian
Christian born in Lebanon, then a part of Syria. In his opening
pages he described how every influence worked against national
unity and in favor of identification with Islam or one of the
Christian sects, "all fanatical or, at the mildest, regarding one an-

other with aversion." To complicate matters, each religious community had an alien power — the Ottoman Empire, Britain, France, Russia, etc. — to support it and it was with these powers, and never with a Syrian nation, that each community identified itself. Atiyah testified that no attachment to the soil of Syria, no idea that Syria was the natural home of Syrians, crossed his mind:

> If ever there was a country in which every conceivable influence, divine and mundane, physical and moral, inherent and extraneous, militated against national unity and the formation of a patriotic sentiment, that country was Syria before 1914.[27]

Atiyah recapitulated much of the history of his people as he traced the path which led to nationalism. At the outset, devoted attachment to Britain as the source of all that was good, noble, and progressive. Then a bitter turning away when Britain failed to accept as equals the "natives" who gave it their devotion, and from this turning away there developed an identification with his "own" people of different religion. At the end some measure of reconciliation and abandonment of bitterness, involving recognition that the future must contain elements drawn from what Britain can contribute as well as what is derived from the nation itself. Is it prophetic that in the latter part of the book the Soviet Union is praised as seeming to provide the only satisfactory compromise between the local cultural claims of nationhood and the world's need for integration?

Nationalism has cut across such practical political universality as Islam might boast. Even among the Arabs, held together by language, culture, and history as well as by religion, feuds have broken out which have divided state from state, all too often with the encouragement of the European powers, and, more recently, of the United States. At the other end of the Islamic world, Indonesia has joined with India and other countries of diverse religion rather than with its religious brethren. Perhaps most striking of all, Pakistan, created for Islamic purposes and enjoined by its Constitution to strengthen the bonds of unity among Moslem countries, has met little success in its efforts to build up international Moslem solidarity. More particularly, it has been in an almost constant state of friction with its closest Moslem neighbor, Afghanistan, which has seen fit to collaborate, in the classic style of diplomacy, with Pakistan's other neighbor and antagonist, India. No rush of Moslem states to the support of Pakistan has been noticeable in the Kashmir controversy. Pan-Islam is not completely to be disregarded, but national considerations seem habitually to outweigh the injunctions of religious solidarity.

In the more domestic sphere Wilfred Cantwell Smith has come to the conclusion that even where the leaders have imposed a generally Western pattern on nationalist movements, "The driving force of nationalism has become more and more religious, the more the movement has penetrated the masses." [28] In addition, he contends that wherever nationalism has been adopted in the Moslem world, it has been a Moslem nationalism, neither transcending the bounds of Islam nor embracing non-Moslems as equal members of the national community, except perhaps in Indonesia. As he sees it, the modern Moslem world has accepted only those aspects of nationalism which contribute to the rehabilitation of Islamic society and are compatible with the central precepts of Islam.

It is Smith's general and persuasive thesis that the peoples of Islam have found their weakness and subordination in the last centuries incompatible with the basic tenets of Islam which not only promised power and greatness but once furnished them in abundance. After its long decline Islam is now again waking to a sense of its claims and potentialities and is reaching out to reëstablish itself in the world. Nationalism is one of the instruments, adapted from the West, through which that reëstablishment is taking place.

In this confrontation of universes, what survives of Islam and what of secular nationalism? The influence of Islam is undoubtedly immense, and it is plausible to think that it should grow as the masses, closer to their religious roots than are the Westernized elites, come to play a larger social and political role. As the spread of social mobilization has enhanced the importance of vernacular languages, so it might be assumed to increase the religious component in nationalism. Yet, it is doubtful how much the historical record sustains this view. Only rarely can a clear case be made for the proposition that nationalism has become more Islamic in content as it has penetrated the masses. To take only the Arab world, religion appears to have its strongest hold in the old-style and traditional countries, as Saudi Arabia or Yemen, where nationalism has the least popular hold. Elsewhere the drift has been secular, political, national in character, not religious. If Egypt may be taken as an example, there was indeed a swing toward the Moslem Brotherhood, particularly around the time of World War II and thereafter when disgust with the political parties and general disenchantment with the West were widespread. But the political action which was taken was the work of Naguib, Nasser, and company, and, in the upshot, it was the Brotherhood which was suppressed in 1954. The series of political upheavals which have shaken Syria in recent years and the Iraq overturn of July 1958, are likewise not the product of religious forces, nor is it possible to see them as filled with a popular Islamic content. Nasser may be hailed as the second Saladin by the Arabs, uniting them, overthrowing their enemies, and restoring their national pride, but "Nasserism" is only incidentally religious.

Nationalism is itself perhaps a waning force in the contemporary world, reluctantly yielding its place to other forms of community, but in the interim its normal course is to subvert the autonomy of religion and to add the religious emotions and affiliations of the people to its own wherever possible. At an earlier time in Europe, as in a different fashion in Islam, common ecclesiastical institutions and beliefs helped to establish a broad cultural consensus. Within the state the independent church, or the presence of several churches, acted in the Western world as a safeguard against oppression. Now the Christian sects and, more broadly, religions everywhere have been so largely absorbed into the nation that the religious leaders bless its arms and pray for the destruction of its enemies. The universal in religion has been driven to bow to the tribal gods of nations.

CHAPTER IX

Economics

Economic forces are involved in the development of nations and nationalism in a bewildering variety of ways. Such forces loom peculiarly large — perhaps even deceptively large — in an imperialist setting where the drive for material gain has been so strong on one side and the resentment against exploitation so bitter on the other. Yet, whatever else nations may be, they are not inherently consolidated economic entities nor the resultant of economic processes.

Although economic elements in many respects have been of central importance in rousing national consciousness, they have played only an incidental role in the shaping of the nations themselves. The correct formula must be a double-barreled and paradoxical one: nationalism has been immensely influenced by the working of economic forces, including the paramount importance of economic change in establishing the conditions under which it has come to birth, but the national communities upon which it bases itself are not themselves economic creations and cannot be explained in economic terms. What has typically happened is not that an economically coherent society, becoming aware of its national existence, has reached out to become a national state, but rather the reverse process by which a nation has sought statehood in order to impose a measure of economic unity upon itself through political means.

Early in the nineteenth century Friedrich List, speaking on behalf of underdeveloped Germany, attacked "Adam Smith and Company" precisely for failing to recognize that *political* economy required the use of state power for the purpose of building a system of national economy. The invisible hand upon which laissez faire relied was accused of leading to cosmopolitanism and of strengthening the strong at the expense of the weak. A national economy was not to be achieved through the working of natural forces, but only at the price of that state intervention which the classical economists decried. To cite a current Middle Eastern example: much has been heard of the demand for Arab national unity, but the last thing of which the Arabs of Syria and Jordan, of Saudi Arabia and Egypt, could be accused is that they now form a coherent economic bloc. They seek political unity in order to be able, among other things, to cut back on alien encroachment and to construct their own economic unity. For them as for others political action is needed to tame the economy and bring it under national control.

Given the basic materialist assumptions of Marx and his followers it is natural that they should be the most vigorous and consistent defenders of the thesis that economics furnishes the essential clue to an understanding of nations and nationalism. The three principal phases of the Marxist formulation are that nations are economic entities, that the national era is intimately linked to the emergence of capitalism, and that the bourgeoisie and proletariat are irretrievably opposed in their respective commitments to nationalism and internationalism. Despite a growing concern with the problems it presents, Marx and the Marxists have never been able to establish a wholly easy relation with nationalism: nations have about them an irreducible originality and a power of survival which makes them awkward and unruly misfits within the Marxist framework. They cannot be subordinated to the class struggle nor readily dissolved into the dialectic, and neither workers nor bourgeoisie can be counted on to act as they are supposed to. The more closely the Marxist theses on nationalism are analyzed, the more apparent it becomes that they rest primarily on arbitrary assertion and have little firm footing in the scientific pretensions of Marxism.

Since Marx paid little attention to the national question in his more systematic treatises, his views must be sought either in the *Communist Manifesto* or in his correspondence and lesser writings. At no point did he try his hand at a full presentation of his position, and much of what he had to say was related to particular political situations. This gap was filled in Russia at a later stage.

In 1913 Lenin wrote to Maxim Gorky that "We have a fine Georgian here," who was at work on all the Austrian and other data on nationalism.[1] In the same year Stalin produced an elaborate essay on "Marxism and the National Question" which has served the Communists as a central reference point ever since. In its opening pages he defined the nation as an historically evolved cultural community based on the familiar components of language, territory, and psychological make-up. To these he added "community of economic life, economic cohesion," without which there could be no nation. Using his own Georgia to illustrate his point, he asserted that it became a nation only in the latter half of the nineteenth century when the fall of serfdom, the development of means of communication, and the rise of capitalism bound the country together by shattering the economic self-sufficiency of the principalities and instituting a division of labor between them.[2]

One essential aspect of the link to capitalism is here clearly established: the dynamic new economic life appears as the agent to sweep away feudalism, break down local attachments, and clear the ground for the broader national community. By opening wider economic horizons and promoting social mobilization, capitalism makes possible the attainment of a single national language and culture. Many Marxist writers carried the analysis forward another large step, and into more dubious ground, by insisting that capitalism, in addition to creating the conditions for national unity, had a still more intimate link with the nation. Thus Lenin saw "the profoundest economic factors" driving toward the creation of the national state as "the typical, normal state for the capitalist period," in which the requirements of a modern capitalism could best be met.[3]

The justification for this position Lenin found in the need of the bourgeoisie to capture their home market and to have politically united territories in which people spoke the same language. As with Stalin, so for Lenin the significance of language as a central feature of the national community was very great since he saw it as the most important means of human intercourse and one of the most important conditions of free commercial intercourse on a scale commensurate with modern capitalism, making possible a close connection between the market and every proprietor, buyer, and seller. It remained unexplained why socialist societies should not find community of language equally useful and hence be equally attracted to the nation, unless it be that socialists have some peculiar gift enabling them to eliminate the linguistic diversity which overpowers capitalists.

Marxism thus came to the point of identifying capitalism with the nation in the dual sense that capitalism for the first time promotes a real national unity and that the nation furnishes it the milieu in which it can best flourish. The bourgeoisie is identified as the national class par excellence, unable to lift its sights beyond its national privileges and advantages.

The more bluntly this phase of Marxist doctrine is stated, the more apparent it becomes that it leads into a morass of confusions and uncertainties. Capitalism is bound up with the nation, yet as early as the *Communist Manifesto* Marx and Engels were proclaiming that the revolutionary role of the bourgeoisie had been to establish the world market and to give a cosmopolitan character to production and consumption in every country:

> National differences and antagonisms between peoples are daily more and more vanishing, owing to the development of the bourgeoisie, to freedom of commerce, to the world-market, to uniformity in the mode of production and in the conditions of life corresponding thereto.[4]

The bourgeoisie, according to the *Manifesto*, was creating a world in its own image; and yet here too the puzzling contradictions appear. In centralizing production and concentrating property control the bourgeoisie has broken down provincial interests and governments, lumping them together in one nation with one government, one code of laws, and one national class interest. Despite the cosmopolitan character of its production, which by all good Marxist principles should be the determining influence, the bourgeoisie was far from having achieved global unity within itself. In wholly unmotivated fashion it was involved, as Marx saw it, in battle at all times with the bourgeoisie of foreign countries. Similarly, the "struggle of the proletariat with the bourgeoisie is at first a national struggle," in form though not in substance.

The net effect is that an economic system which knows no

necessary political or geographic boundaries and is constantly battering down all Chinese walls, as the *Manifesto* put it, is at the same time curiously confined within national limits and managed by a class unable to supersede its national prejudices. Here is a contradiction which has habitually plagued Marxist theorists, and must continue to plague them because it has no answer within their system.

The conception that a nation is a community marked by any natural economic cohesion apart from that brought it by political unity and local intercourse among neighbors does not square with the facts. States such as China, Japan, England, or France which had long been under a single government inevitably developed some measure of economic identity, but even for them the great bulk of economic life was on the scale of local self-sufficiency or the market town rather than of the state as a whole. In the old-established kingdom of France it was necessary for the revolutionaries of 1789 to make the sweeping away of internal barriers to trade and movement one of their major concerns. Where political unity was lacking, economic unity was likely to be nonexistent. The north of Italy, for example, had a trade pattern and way of economic life almost totally different from those of the south, and the institution of a *Zollverein* was necessary to start the consolidation of the German economy.

Pressing this line of argument to its extreme limits Walter Sulzbach has emphasized that economic and national considerations are of a totally different order. Deep cleavages of economic interest divide the bourgeoisie of any one country, and economic dealings with non-nationals across the frontiers may be far more advantageous than business conducted at home. If economic systems had been left free to develop according to their own lights, the resulting economic communities would have borne only a quite accidental relationship to the existing nations:

> Tariffs do not protect the German or the French 'national economy,' but they first create it, because if there were no tariffs and no similar inconveniences at the frontiers, then scarcely any difference would exist between internal and external trade.[5]

The same kind of analysis holds true for dependent territories and other imperial offshoots, whose economies have notoriously been molded to make them fit the needs and preconceptions of the metropolitan countries. At least theoretically discarded elsewhere, the principles of mercantilism held on in the colonial sphere, making the colonies suppliers of raw materials and consumers of the manufactures of the mother country. Much of China, in similar fashion, was parceled out in concessions intended to promote the economic advantage of the Powers. As colonial production was oriented toward the imperial centers, so the communication networks were concentrated on facilitating the flow of goods from the interior to the coastal ports and not on linking the different parts of the country together. The building of a rounded national economy, based on an internal division of labor and vigorous economic interchange within the colony, was not accepted as part of the imperial responsibility. The best that could be hoped for in the way of national economic unity was the appearance in small territories such as Malaya, the West Indies, or Iraq, of an economy centering on a single commodity like rubber, sugar, or oil.

Even more in colonial and quasi-colonial areas than elsewhere one of the prime goals of the nationalists has been to secure control of the political machinery in order to escape economic bondage and to start the rounding out of a national economy.[6] The other side of the coin, of course, is that it is of the essence of the colonial situation that the nationalists are largely a product of the economic and other activities of the imperial power and that in a number of instances such economic unity as exists is also derived from the same imperial source, as, for example, in virtually all the African territories.

No better fortune attends the second Marxist proposition that the nation is in some fashion ideally suited to capitalism's needs. One of the striking features of nations, already commented on, is their identification over long periods of time with substantially the same territory. With minor modifications the territory of the French and German or the Persian and Egyptian nations has stayed constant for many centuries, yet economic systems have changed drastically. How is one to explain that a French or a Hungarian nation which took shape in the Middle Ages should have the proper spatial attributes for the capitalism of the nineteenth and twentieth centuries?

In the nineteenth century, by ignoring some inconvenient items, it was possible to believe that national states were keeping pace with economic change. The relatively large territories of Britain and France set the model of achieved nationhood, and the dynamic national development which overshadowed all others was the unification of Germany and of Italy. Disregarding such small peoples as those of Greece, Scandinavia, and the Low Countries, it was possible to conclude that the essence of the national movement was the construction of big states which met the expanding needs of the industrial revolution. This was the view of Marx and Engels who wasted no sympathy on small peoples and looked toward the consolidation of the larger nations, as did Friedrich List and many others.

Nationally united Germany and Italy were obviously better fitted for capitalism than were their component states and provinces, but only in the most rough and ready sense could one say that they furnished any necessarily appropriate sphere for capitalism, unless capitalism and the linguistic community have some peculiar affinity for each other. Furthermore, it is evident that the German, Italian, and other national communities which were roused to consciousness in the nineteenth century had been shaped, not by the forces of capitalism, but by the events and the ethnic and economic circumstances of many centuries past.

Even more troublesome was the fact that in the twentieth century the typical development of the principle of nationality was not the amalgamation of feudal pygmies into national giants, but the breaking down of larger empires into their smaller component parts. The Wilsonian self-determination which followed the First World War gave political expression to a number of small peoples, and the national movements following World War II have primarily involved the disintegration of the large-scale economic space of overseas empire. In terms of the economics of the industrial age or of capitalism as described by Marx in 1848 or by his followers a century later, what sense can be made of the shattering of the Austro-Hungarian Empire into its successor states or the emergence as nations of the Philippines, Burma, Korea, or Ghana? The height of economic absurdity is reached with the carving out of Pakistan and Israel.[7]

The Marxist escape from the dilemma created by the indenti-
fication of capitalism with the nation has been by way of the theory
of imperialism, which found its definitive formulation in Lenin's
Imperialism, the Highest Stage of Capitalism. Boiled down to its
essence, the argument was that capitalism could not survive within
the cramped limits of the nation-state and must overflow by occupying other territories, thus giving rise to imperialism and imperialist war. The same vexing question, however, remained without a satisfactory answer. The inadequacy of the nation-state as
the territorial base for capitalism was now fully recognized, and
yet capitalism continued to be inextricably entangled with it. The
bourgeoisie had been able to overcome the feudal and other divisions within nations and establish capitalist operations at the higher
national level: why must it now turn to imperialism and be unable
to unite the nations and secure a still wider economic space at the
regional (say, European) or even at the global level? The answer
could not be that the bourgeoisie was trapped within the political
structures of the existing states and could not create new and more
commodious ones, because that was precisely what it had done in
Germany, Italy, and elsewhere. Nonetheless, the dogma of the
national limitation of the bourgeoisie and of capitalism held fast.
Lenin derided the "renegade Kautsky" for proposing that an in-
ternationalization of capital might be under way, leading to a
single world monopoly. He conceded that in pure abstraction
there might be a trend toward such an ultra-imperialism, but asserted that in the real world it added up to no more than ultra-
nonsense.

As Nikolai Bukharin portrayed the process, the concentration
and centralization of capital were key phenomena of capitalist
development, turning the national economy into "one gigantic
combined trust . . . a state capitalist trust." But here, for reasons
which remained unexplored, concentration and centralization came
to an end:

> Competition reaches the highest, the last conceivable state of develop-
> ment. It is now the competition of state capitalist trusts in the world
> market.[8]

The original identification of capitalism and the nation, resting on no more solid Marxist base than the utility of a common language, was thus perpetuated into the future until such time as the rival national imperialisms, warring with each other, cleared the way for Communism to take over.

The bourgeoisie was mired down beyond recall in its national attachments. The proletariat, on the other hand, stood above such parochialism and represented not only its class interest but the global interest of mankind as well. Why the bourgeoisie should not be able to transcend nationalism with its evils of war and oppression and why the proletariat was destined to rise above it to peace and good will were mysteries which never received any effective scrutiny. Judging from the conditions of his time, Marx, to be sure, had maintained that the workers were stripped of every trace of national character and had no country; but history has taken a different turn. In the circumstances of a later day Otto Bauer found that capitalism for the first time brought all the people into the nation. Challenging the accepted Marxist position, he went on to contend that socialism, because it fully opened to the masses their heritage in the national culture, history, and language, would produce a growing differentiation of nations rather than an evening out of differences.[9]

On the other side, substantial numbers of the bourgeoisie declared themselves disgusted with nationalism, and some, following the lead of Marx and Engels, moved over to become leaders of the Communist movement in Asia and Africa as well as in Europe and the Americas. The Marxists were, however, more nearly justified in predicting the continued national allegiance of the bourgeoisie than in supposing that the workers would shed their national parochialism and take the world as their sphere.

A more acceptable version of the relations between economic forces and nations begins to appear if Marxist insistence on the unique centrality of economics is abandoned. Leaving other factors aside, two processes — the economic and the political — are going on simultaneously and continually influencing each other.

A major point of strength for the Marxist doctrine, although the latter has no exclusive claim to it, is insistence on the intimate tie between the growth of nationalism and of capitalism or, better, of the modern industrial society. There is much truth in Lenin's dictum that, the world over, "the period of the final victory of capitalism over feudalism has been linked up with national movements." [10] Nationalism everywhere, as has already been seen, is a response to the breaking up of the older traditional societies under a variety of pressures among which those arising from the kind of economic change characteristic of the contemporary world are of central importance. The opening up of the industrial era and its extension overseas through the channels of trade and imperialism produced the social setting in which certain categories of people came to vivid awareness of their national identity.

This vital link with the economic realm does not, however, establish the nation as an economic phenomenon nor as having any necessary affinity for any particular economic system, be it capitalist, socialist, or something else. What has actually happened is that economic change has contributed immensely to the rousing to life, and in due course to political action, of a community, the nation, in whose shaping economic elements had played a negligible role. What Lionel Robbins had to say of states as economic entities is equally relevant for nations if items such as language and tribe or clan are added:

> one and all have this common characteristic, that as units for the organization of production they have no relation to anything which is relevant to this purpose. They have been determined by wars, royal marriages, accidental geographic discovery, and the haggling of politicians at conference tables — by almost anything, in short, but consideration of their suitability for the administration of economic resources.[11]

With the spread of national awareness the nation moved either to take over the state, as in France in the Revolution and in the present century in China and the colonies, or to create its own state, as in the United States, Germany, Pakistan, and Israel. The nation-states, old or new, found their control over their own people and territory increasingly endangered by the welling up of the new economic life which spilled over all the economically arbitrary frontiers. It seemed evident on the face of it that national solidarity would be enhanced by economic unity, impaired by the lack of it. To the desire of farmers, manufacturers, and workers to protect their home markets for themselves was added the desire of patriots and the national authorities, both civil and military, to remove the nation from the hazards of exposure to the play of alien forces. In sum, the political instrumentalities of the nations were called into action to create and to strengthen a national economy which would safeguard the integrity of state and nation.

The native tendency of capitalism or of any other version of a dynamic industrial economy is indefinite expansion, establishing its centers of production at the most advantageous points and drawing its raw materials from, and distributing its produce in, the most advantageous markets. Observers in the nineteenth century — Marx and Engels in their fashion as well as the classical economists — were agreed in predicting that the economic system which was transforming society was international or, better, cosmopolitan in character. In its actual development, however, capitalism was deprived of much of its freedom of action because it got caught in the meshes of the national states, some vast and some tiny, which imposed arbitrary political controls on its further extension. In contrast to the *Communist Manifesto's* assumption of a single and uniform global sweep, the new economic system in fact followed the later "law of uneven development," appearing in different states at different times and under different auspices. In each state it grew under the special conditions prevailing there and was given a special form by political manipulation. For all the peoples — the Germans, the Japanese, the Indians, the Africans — to whom the industrial revolution came at a second or third remove, the role of the state in introducing and shaping the new economy was of particular importance. The result has been that foreign trade, expected to overshadow domestic economic activity, has failed to follow its nineteenth-century upward curve and in the twentieth century has declined in relative importance. Up to the present time, at least, neither socialism nor communism has shown greater ability than capitalism to make itself a working international system. The socialization of the nation and the nationalization of socialism to which E. H. Carr called attention have been salient facts of the present era. For planning and other purposes socialist societies have relied heavily on the power and machinery of the state, and the Soviet Union has been singularly self-contained in the development of its economy.

The factors which determine the spatial extent of an economic system are not to be found within the system itself, but far more in the social and political communities with which men feel themselves identified. The easy way out for capitalism, socialism, or communism is to work within the existing nation-state structure, but if the men in charge of any one of them come to the firm conviction that a new dispensation is in order, they can make their system function within any geographical area, be it regional, continental, or global. If socialism turns out to develop on an international or cosmopolitan basis, it will not be because of its necessities as an economic system, but because of the social and political convictions of those who guide its destinies. Similarly, capitalism has no necessary association with racial or national oppression, nor socialism with racial and national brotherhood.

As a point of transition to other aspects of the bearing of economics, one further Marxist difficulty with the nation might be mentioned. It has been pointed out by Bertrand Russell that:

> The rivalry between nations is just as much an economic conflict as the class war, and at least as important in modern politics; yet, according to Marx, all politics are controlled by the conflict of classes.[12]

Two contradictory means of dealing with the issue posed here were open to the Marxists and both have been utilized. The more orthodox approach was to see the workers lured by the capitalists into acceptance of a common national interest which was in reality nonexistent, thus producing national solidarity against other nations. In this version the nation served the capitalists as a handy device to keep their domestic class enemies happy. The other approach was one which Marxism, as represented by Lenin and others, has rather sidled up to than openly embraced. This is the doctrine that the class war has as a result of imperialism translated itself into international conflict. The internal split between classes has lost its significance as the world has developed its two camps of the rich bourgeois nations on one side and the poor proletarian nations on the other. To make too much of this interpretation is obviously to undercut Marxism's basic class theories, but it has its close relation to the realities of recent decades and is also a useful means of establishing an identity of interest between the communists and the rising peoples of Asia and Africa.

Of the multitude of other relationships between economic forces and nationalism, only a few of special relevance to the emergence of the non-European nations can be dealt with here.

Imperial economic systems worked in a variety of ways to stimulate the nationalism of the peoples on whom they impinged. In the ordinary course of events they did not create national economies overseas in the sense of encouraging a full-scale division of labor and internal diversification of products and markets. They did foster some consciousness of unity by generating a common resentment of subjection to alien economic domination. A sense of being exploited and victimized was associated with the penetration of an underdeveloped area by an advanced Western economy. On the consequent hostilities and frustrations every possible change was rung by the propagandists.

The typical line of development in the economics of empire was the building of a plural economy which in its simplest form consisted of a modern Western-style sector, producing almost exclusively for export, superimposed on an old-style native subsistence economy. In its more complex versions the plural economy added another intermediate layer or two, as in Southeast Asia where the Chinese occupied a middle position, serving as a link between the other two levels of the economy. Although it had many variants in practice, the classic model of a colonial economy was managed by a few well-to-do white men at the top — buttressed by a small number of white functionaries, policemen, and soldiers — while the work force was drawn from the indigenous mass at the bottom. The fact that a handful of local people were always associated with the white upper crust in one fashion or another, as sultans, rajahs, or chiefs, or as business or professional men, did not change the general accuracy or symmetry of the picture.

This was the plural society of which J. S. Furnivall has been the principal herald. Held together only by the cash nexus and dominated, as he saw it, by economic forces, of which a process of natural selection through survival of the cheapest was a major one, this society had neither a common social purpose nor moral restraints on the drive for economic gain.[18] The lack of a social purpose and will derived from the fact that the different sections of the society lived side by side, but separately, within a single political unit, with a division of labor along racial lines. Applying this conception to Burma, from which he took his starting point, Furnivall saw it as a country in which the four main peoples — Europeans, Indians, Chinese, and Burmans — had in common only the economic motive, the desire for material advantage. The interests of all save the Burmans could be summed up as capitalist since they sought the promotion of commerce and industry and had come to Burma for the central purpose of making a better living than they could get at home. For the Burmans, however, it was their own country which was involved. The result was to make the main political issue a conflict between the nationalism of the Burmans and the capitalism of the other peoples, who were joined together in a loose alliance. To reknit the social fabric and to create a social will which would impose checks on the ruthlessness of the economic man was the primary function of nationalism.

In a starker version of the plural society Chester Bowles has remarked that to the mass of Africans who live in poverty:

> the political economic equation becomes a simple one: the white man rules, the black man obeys. Therefore, the white man is rich while the black man is poor. A more ominous revolutionary situation is difficult to imagine.[14]

Within such a society both economic and political tensions and conflicts are heightened by the coincidence of race and class. The relation of the non-white worker to the alien white boss parallels the relation of the non-white subject to the alien white ruler. Either relationship is difficult enough to deal with, and the combination of the two embitters both. Although this situation is characteristic of overseas colonial areas, it is likely to be found in any area which contains a national minority. Thus Otto Bauer pointed out that in the Hapsburg Empire the ruling class was made up of Germans who tended toward a monopoly of wealth and education, while the Czech and Slovene masses, in their own home territories, made up the working and peasant population. In these circumstances the national and the social questions were merged into one: "National hate is transformed into class hate."[15]

Poverty and backwardness are not only the universal lot of the non-white peoples as contrasted with the ruling whites; they are also often portrayed as the direct consequence of the alien rule which has deliberately denied colonial peoples the progress they would otherwise have made. In cold historic fact a better case can probably be made for the reverse proposition that poverty was the cause of colonialism. In most instances the door was opened to the imposition of imperial control by the original poverty of the people and their failure to keep pace with the scientific and material advance of the West. This interpretation has far less appeal than the other, however, to those engaged in the drive for freedom. Thus, President Ngo Dinh Diem of Vietnam informed the Congress of the United States on May 7, 1957, of "the growing awareness of the colonial peoples that the origin of their poverty has been the systematic withholding of technical development." [16]

One last item may be added in identifying some of the economic elements which have entered into the making of Asian and African nationalism. The cause — indeed, one might almost say, the nature — of imperialism and colonialism is held to be capitalism. If the source of this belief was Lenin's theory of imperialism, it has by now become so widespread and deep-rooted that it normally passes as an axiomatic truth which needs no sponsor or justification. Roeslan Abdulgani, Secretary-General of the Indonesian Ministry of Foreign Affairs, gave it typical expression:

> In our experience colonialism is the child of capitalism. In its inevitable wake colonialism brought us national disunity and poverty of a degree which has probably never been known in the West. . . . The development, physical and mental, of our people has been stunted by colonialism. . . . Therefore, for us, socialism is an essential ingredient of nationalism. [17]

Here almost all phases of the reigning doctrine are wrapped up in one package, including the charge that colonialism is the cause not only of poverty but also of the disruption of a national unity which Indonesia in fact never had. Since nationalism is thus necessarily an enemy of capitalism, as was also suggested by Furnivall in his appraisal of Burma, the way of economic and political salvation must lie through some alternative to capitalism, such as socialism. Two additions which are implicit in it can be made to Abdulgani's characterization of colonialism as derived from capitalism: capitalism is the economic system of the West; and so long as alien capitalism remains implanted in any country the latter cannot be regarded as safely out from under the shadow of imperialism.

The validity of the identification of imperialism or colonialism with capitalism is open to the most serious challenge, but the destruction of the theory on the best of intellectual grounds is highly unlikely to have any significant effect on those who accept it as a statement of the obvious realities. The colonialism which the peoples overseas have experienced is closely bound up with capitalism, and their experience coincides with what their leaders tell them has been going on. It is a short step from here to the conclusion that freedom can come only with the elimination of capitalism.

The political acceptability of such a conclusion, which comes to be an integral part of the nationalist creed, is magnified by the fact that so few among the colonial people achieve any real stake in the superimposed capitalist order. As the headquarters of the colonial government are located in a remote capital, so the principal owners and main offices of colonial enterprises are to be found in Europe or America. Top management and professional skill come from abroad, and many of the functions which the national middle class performs in other countries are taken care of in the metropolitan center or at the point from which the foreign investment originates. The designers and makers of machinery, the staff planners and the financial controllers, and the manufacturers of the secondary products remain at home. The physical labor of the plantation, mine, and processing plant is the essential contribution of the people of the country who are thus easily persuadable that they can only gain from the overturn of the existing scheme of things.

The continued fear of the West and the repeated denunciations of colonialism arise primarily, of course, from the simple fact that the West conquered or otherwise took over most of the rest of the world and imposed its colonial rule on much of it. That the West may still be a source of danger, despite its avowed renunciation of its imperial past, is made to seem even more probable by the survival of capitalism from which the earlier evils were reputed to flow. In similar fashion, the pressure for nationalization of alien concerns and the hostility or ambivalence toward capital investment from the West is to be traced in part to the assumption that, wherever foreign capitalism manages to intrude or hold on, a renewed colonialism may not be far behind. This is a conviction which may also, unhappily, cut across the provision of foreign aid for purposes of development.

The beginning and the end of this chapter may be brought together by pointing out that both imperialism and the overseas nationalisms which it prodded into being have used their national political power for the purpose of imposing upon economic forces the directions and contours which have been governmentally determined to be desirable. The imperial countries spread their tentacles abroad to bring other territories and peoples within their economic domain and make them supplementary to the imperial design. In their turn, the rising Asian and African nations have established as a first priority the economic independence and modernization of their countries, perhaps even including the steel mill which they are always accused of setting their hearts on. Given the lack of private capital and entrepreneurial experience and initiative, the objective needs of their situations are buttressed by the general antagonism of capitalism. Regardless of the dismay of bitter-end American supporters of private enterprise, it is inevitable that the state should play a very large role in promoting development. The new governments are carrying on in the tradition well-established by earlier inhabitants of the industrial era in shaping national economies for nationalist ends. And, in "proletarian countries," where race and class so largely coincide, the labor unions are vital parts of the political process and of the nationalist movements, serving to ensure that the workers will have a national orientation.

The newcomers to the industrial era in some ways face the same problems and must use the same instrumentalities as those who preceded them, but in other ways their difficulties are far greater. The growing pains of the West as it came into the modern period were eased by the existence of a great expanse of open frontiers, as in the Americas, and, more broadly, of a world all the rest of which was composed of noncompetitive preindustrial space into which the Western economies could overflow. Since the Asian and African countries, plus the Americas, were precisely the ones into which the West expanded, they now have neither open frontiers nor noncompetitive economic space available to them. Instead they are confronted by highly experienced industrial giants on one side and by an array of similar aspirants to economic modernity on the other. Even all-out recourse to the power of the state — itself often a shaky and unreliable instrument — and to the driving force of nationalism will not make the task ahead an easy one.

CHAPTER X

The West and Non-Western Nationalism

NATIONALISM WHEREVER IT manifests itself is in essence a response to the forces which in recent centuries have revolutionized the West and have penetrated in successive waves to the farthest corners of the earth. Despite vast differences in time, place, and setting, characteristic threads of circumstance and development bring a measure of common identity to all emergent nationalisms. One can trace also significant elements of a common chronology, to be reckoned not by the calendar but in relation to the changes taking place within each society as it comes within the orbit of the expanding Western revolution. National awareness and nationalist agitation have regularly followed close on the heels of the intrusion of modernity.

The matter may be approached from many angles. The rise of nationalism may be ascribed to the spread of the ideas which have marked the growth of the modern world or more particularly to such economic aspects as the introduction of a money economy or the coming of age of the machine. It may be linked to the idea of progress and to the substitution of dynamic change for acquiescence in the existing order, or to such special factors as the growth of urbanism of which one feature in the colonies is a closer contact with the white man and his ways. Nationalism is a product of the breach with the old order of which a part is the disruption of traditional communities and their ties of kinship and custom. In the dramatic version of this negative aspect which Robert Montagne has presented, the modern state blindly and inadvertently destroys tribes, chieftainships, theocratic fiefs, and the patriarchal family:

Finally the inhabitants of the new state cease to belong to these traditional, coherent and ordered societies, every one of which had its part to play in the collective life. They become grains of dust driven in the wind of circumstance. Their mass, ever growing but discrete, congregates around the modern towns created by the West. The proletariat appears in the towns of Egypt, on the coasts of Africa, whenever modern economic effort creates new possibilities of work outside the customary bounds. In these overcrowded neighborhoods, where patriarchal discipline disappears so rapidly, Africa and the East are in decomposition; they are dying of a gigantic moral disaster, before the West has succeeded in building the order which it has designed.[1]

Leaving aside the dubious closing proposition that the West had in its pocket any design of an order for Asia and Africa, positive aspects of the Western imperial sweep must also be recognized. Not all was destruction. The atomization of the traditional societies in the teeming urban centers was often met, as in West African cities, by the spontaneous generation of a host of associations of all kinds, based on geographical, tribal, occupational, or other ties. Another counterpart of destruction was the mobilization of different strata of people into a greater or less degree of participation in the new world which was being pressed upon them. From this mobilization and from the ideas and instrumentalities which the West brought the countries it overran, there emerged the nationalism which was to be the rallying cry of the rising generations. For those whose traditional communities were crumbling or had vanished the nation offered a new community on the grand scale in which they could again find a social identity and in whose service they could regain dignity and purpose as they struggled to get rid of the alien overlords.

Despite all the learned speculation which has been devoted to the question, disagreement continues as to where and when nationalism got under way. Its starting points are surely to be located in space in Western Europe and in time in the checkered transition from medievalism to its unmistakable flowering in the nineteenth century. The French Revolution has with good reason been widely accepted as the conventional watershed marking the turn to the age of nationalism, but a number of nationalist phases and elements can be found far earlier. In England, for example, the era between Henry VIII and the Glorious Revolution produced fundamental changes, marking the transition toward a modern national as contrasted with a medieval feudal society. During this period, even though the Industrial Revolution still lay ahead, the English economy broke loose from its old moorings, the middle class began to establish its claims, and a strong sense of the existence of the English nation reached far into the people.[2]

It was, however, not until the French Revolution had explicitly challenged all the foundations of the older Europe that nationalism really came into its own. Weaving into its fabric many strands derived from the past, nationalism was now driven forward by the revolutionary force both of the great slogan, *Liberté, Egalité, Fraternité*, and of the new industrialism. For the first time the idea that the nation has a natural right of its own and that it is the nation which legitimizes the state began to be put forward in the nineteenth century as a proposition of universal validity. Where before it was taken as no more than a happy coincidence that in some instances the state rested upon the congenial foundation of a single homogeneous people, as in England, France, and Spain, such a merger of state and nation now came to be the goal toward which all eyes were increasingly turned. In the new dispensation the nation which did not have its own state was seen as missing its destiny, and the state which embraced either more or less than a nation was an anachronism.

The French Revolution presented the challenge — to be ignored by others at their peril — of a state which was no longer the king but the people, and thrust across the face of Europe the power of a nation in arms. Even when Napoleon in a sense became France, it was no longer the France of Louis XIV but of the French nation. Across the Atlantic the peoples of the Americas were likewise sorting themselves out on national lines and asserting their national claims, although in the case of the United States the Declaration of Independence and other formulations of the American case were, in good eighteenth-century fashion, couched in terms of the natural rights of individuals (and of Englishmen) and not in the next century's terms of the rights of nations.

The highway to the future was already clearly marked out, even though neither the American nor the French Revolution nor the appearance of the nineteenth century produced a universal sweep into nationalism or even a prompt general acceptance of it within Europe itself. In the aftermath of the Napoleonic Wars the ruling elements among the victorious powers struggled to hold nationalism in check, or to pretend to ignore its existence, as one of the more dangerous manifestations of the revolutionary devil which had just been exorcised. It was well recognized that the national principle was itself a revolutionary one, intimately bound up with the democratic aspirations of the masses for whom the troublesome bourgeoisie appeared as self-appointed spokesmen.

In addition to their desire to safeguard positions of power and privilege, the statesmen gathered at the Congress of Vienna sought to restore a stable Europe, unimperiled by the new legitimacy of the nation. Where nation and state already coincided, as in Britain and France, the threat was primarily the domestic one of the bourgeois-democratic drive (with the specter of the mob in the background) against anachronistic rank and privilege; elsewhere the threat cut to the roots of the international system since a wholesale redrawing of the political map was inescapable if the nations were to take over. The ability of the guiding spirits at Vienna to impose their will and to reconstruct Europe with only scant regard for the national principle must be attributed in considerable part to the fact that in eastern and southern Europe the ground was not yet adequately prepared for nationalism. Greece, remembering ancient glories, rose to seek its freedom and there were other nationalist stirrings, but Germany and Italy were both several decades removed from the full flowering of national fervor and other European countries were generally even further away. Leading German spokesmen, for example, were quite prepared to accept a Germany loosely composed of a number of small states placed in some part under the protection of the greater European powers.

Suggestive parallels can be found between the situation in Europe at the close of the Napoleonic Wars and that in Asia and Africa a century later. At the earlier time, although Western Europe was already largely parceled out on a national basis, the application of the idea of nationality could still be denied to most of the rest of Europe. In the corresponding World War I settlement, the statesmen at Versailles were confronted by a Europe in which the peoples had already risen to determine themselves. The universal proclamation of the doctrine of self-determination notwithstanding, however, the problems of Asian nationalism could for the most part still be passed by in silence. The Japanese were nominally equal partners in the peacemaking, although Wilson brushed off their demand for racial equality, but even in the Washington Conference of 1921–22 China remained essentially a passive object for the solicitude of the powers, not unlike Germany in 1815. At Versailles many importunate spokesmen pleaded for the Asian and Middle Eastern peoples, as at Vienna others pleaded for European national causes. In both instances they could be largely ignored for the moment because the societies they claimed to represent had not yet moved over the threshold into full-fledged nationalism.

The attitudes of the conservative leaders in Europe after the Napoleonic Wars were closely akin to those of their counterparts who in the first decades of the twentieth century sought to hold together the increasingly unstable overseas empires or to maintain imperial prestige and outposts in China and other quasi-colonial countries. The issue was not only the maintenance of favored positions, but also the protection of the established order against revolutionary clamor which threatened to undermine all its foundations. There is a striking similarity in the two periods in the views that were widely held as to the relative capabilities of the populace at large as compared with their properly ordained superiors. In each instance other arguments for the status quo were effectively buttressed by the strong paternalistic sense that, in the earlier nineteenth-century Europe, the aristocracy and upper elements of the bourgeoisie, and, in twentieth-century Asia and Africa, the imperial powers and colonial administrators, knew better than did the people themselves what was really in the popular interest. The white man's burden of imperialism had its intimate counterpart in the earlier nineteenth-century belief that the people, when anyone bothered to concern himself with them, were an ignorant and helpless mass requiring enlightened guidance. That guidance might, like the harsher phases of imperialism, have its unpalatable aspects, as in the practical deductions drawn from the iron laws of economics, but consolation was sought in both instances in the thought that the people were being led in the direction of their own good, whether or not they recognized it. To contend that the people should speak for themselves was to propose a dangerous heresy which, in addition to being against the nature of things, could only result in a worsening of their lot. And, perhaps the most surprising feature of all, for a considerable time in both periods the people on the whole humbly acquiesced in their own inferiority, passively accepting the established patterns of status as men have generally accepted them through the ages.

With the coming of the era of nationalism, precisely this unquestioning acceptance of the hierarchical ordering of society as a fact of nature beyond the will of man to change gave way as the new forces swung into operation. In the early decades of both centuries those interested in preserving the status quo identified in substantially the same fashion the persons and groups who needed the most careful watching as irresponsible agitators challenging the stability of society. If Metternich may be taken as a shrewd and not unrepresentative spokesman for views that prevailed widely in the first half of the nineteenth century, an impressive coincidence links those whom he and the later imperialists condemned as threats to the established order. As the colonial administrator esteemed the unspoiled and trusting native, so Metternich was persuaded of the natural goodness and trustworthiness of *the true people* — whom Metternich himself italicized. These latter, desiring only a strong authority over them to enable them to enjoy the fruits of their labor in peace, were good but also childish and in need of constant protection against the demagogues who betrayed their real interests. The essential enemy, in the eyes of the Viennese statesman, was the spirit of presumption, deriving from the whole train of developments since the Renaissance and Reformation. This had produced the presumptuous man who sought to make himself the measure of all things and embraced "the idea — absurd in itself — of the emancipation of the peoples," although his real goal was an anarchic freeing of all individuals. It was, as Metternich saw it, principally the middle classes, placed between the kings and the peoples, which succumbed to this moral gangrene, while the great mass of the people, too busy with their daily work, offered no hold for the disease.

Of the categories of Western European troublemakers whom Metternich specially singled out in his "Profession de Foi Politique" for Tsar Alexander in 1820, perhaps only the men of money, whom he described as cosmopolitans putting their profits ahead of all other concerns, would not figure prominently in a list of twentieth-century Asian and African nationalists. For the rest the listing fits with precision: the salaried employees of the state, the men of letters, the lawyers, the individuals in charge of public education. A year earlier, writing to Gentz, Metternich had somewhat surprisingly played down the role of the students as revolutionaries, although he saw a whole generation of revolutionaries being produced by the universities unless the evil was checked, but he continued to lay emphasis on the professors and intellectuals and even more upon the dangerously practical lawyers who were always meddling in other people's property.[3] The one point at which Metternich's appraisal of the presumptuous in the Europe of his day needs basic correction to bring it in line with contemporary Asia and Africa is in connection with the great development of the Communist movement, complexly cutting across and intertwining with nationalism. Otherwise, given a few unessential changes and additions, where might one turn for a better inventory of the major nationalist disturbers of imperialism's peace and tranquillity?

From its early European beginnings nationalism throughout the world has derived its first formulation and drive from the middle class elements which are so evidently a creation of the ferment of Western modernity. Arnold Toynbee has, indeed, suggested that the word "modern" in "modern Western civilization" can be translated as "middle-class," and that the ability of alien recipients of modern Western culture to make it their own may be tested by their capacity to enter the middle class Western way of life.[4] As nationalism progresses, the middle class elements are increasingly joined, in Asia and Africa as in Europe, by other layers of society as these are in their turn divorced from their traditional communal roots and mobilized into the new era: the lower white collar and clerical groups, the urban workers in shops and factories, and the growing proletariat of mines and modern agricultural enterprises. As compared with the Western European model the tempo of the development of nationalism in Asia and Africa is usually speeded up, but the general sequence is the same.

Paradoxically, the one place where the nationalists are characteristically not found is in those parts of the society which are most obviously representative of the heritage of the past, although these must furnish much of the claim to national distinctiveness. In Asia and Africa it is the disruptive force of the alien imperial encroachment which has brought new communities to birth out of the old societies, and the prime movers have been the people who represent rather the new than the old. The elements of society which can probably be taken as the most authentic heirs of the "national" culture and tradition are the rural peasantry, who everywhere constitute the great mass of the population, and such of the old aristocracy as have been able to hold on. These elements have, however, contributed neither the leadership nor the active rank and file partisans of Asian and African nationalism.

As far as the peasantry is concerned this is, of course, not to say either that no fringe segments of it have been drawn actively into the nationalist movements or that, as nationalism has progressed and established itself, the peasantry has not come to accept it. But in general the rural masses have been indifferent to the new currents or, at the best and belatedly, passive adherents to the nationalist creed.[5] The typical peasant movement or revolt is likely to be little concerned with the issues which most stir the nationalists. More frequently it is a protest against local grievances that are felt to be intolerable or an effort to maintain the customary way of life against alien encroachments. From time to time and place to place the nationalists, and the Communists as well, have been able to make highly effective use of peasant grievances and upheavals for their own ends, but with no necessary implication, even taking into account the peasant-based strategy of the Chinese Communists, that the peasant actors were themselves significantly imbued with either nationalism or Communism. Except where the special circumstances inciting to peasant revolt happened also to be present, the typical focal points of nationalist agitation have been urban centers.[6]

Of the old aristocracy or elite it may similarly be said that the more it maintained its traditional position and culture, with the tacit or explicit blessing of the colonial regime, the less it was able or willing to play a role in the developing nationalisms. In many instances, of course, persons stemming from families high in the traditional social scale — Nehru's Kashmiri Brahmin descent is an obvious case in point — took leading parts in nationalist movements, but these are uniformly men who had been exposed to a Western type of education and experience. Their numbers can be explained in part by the fact that the upper elements of any society are likely to be those wealthy enough to travel and study abroad.

In principle the nationalists were all men who had become familiar with the West in one or another fashion, but not all those who had had even full-scale exposure to the West were nationalists. Considerable numbers of the Western-educated were drawn into the civil service and were thus at least partially neutralized. For the few who belonged to the upper crust and whose privileged position depended to a substantial degree on the maintenance of the social-political balance established by colonialism, Western education might merely serve to tie them more closely to the ruling aliens. In the 1920's and 1930's the son of an Indian Rajah, returning to India from Oxford or Cambridge, was unlikely to desert his comfortable life to become a disciple of Gandhi; although there would always be some who would do so, moved by patriotism or indignation, eccentricity or the search for adventure. The men who turned to political action were more frequently those who were in some degree disinherited or whose place was on the fringes of the upper crust rather than solidly within it, such as the lower samurai who figured so importantly in the transition of Japan into the modern world.

It is not the Indian princes, Malay Sultans, or African chiefs who have typically taken the lead in the nationalism of their countries. The quarrel between the native ruler and his entourage, often sustained by the colonial administration, and the newly rising Westernized middle class elements has become a commonplace of the literature dealing with colonial problems. When E. M. Forster served in the court of Dewas Senior in India in 1921, he reported: "There is no anti-English feeling. It is Gandhi whom they dread and hate." [7] Even where, as in Morocco and Uganda, traditional rulers have become symbols of nationalist aspirations, the formulation and driving force of nationalism has rested in the main with the new middle class schooled in the West. Furthermore, the position which the upper class Western-trained elite attained in the new type of political activity appeared to derive more from their personal abilities and from their mastery of the ideas and techniques of the West than from their inherited traditional status, although the latter might also contribute to their prestige. Certainly their nationalist associates were likely to be men drawn from the lower ranks of society who had been able to rise through missionary or other education or to amass wealth from the new types of enterprise.

Of the Indian nationalist movement Nehru has said that "the backbone and leadership were always supplied by the middle classes," even though the direct action struggles were based on the masses and especially the peasantry. Finding the middle class an inchoate group, too much tied up with property and at the top allied with British imperialism, he still asserted that "paradoxically, it is only from the middle class intellectuals that revolutionary leadership comes." [8]

Any sample of the leading figures in the nationalist movements would demonstrate the immense preponderance of men who went through the processes of Western education and who may decently be assigned to the middle class.

Sun Yat-sen was a doctor who secured his lower education in Hawaii and his higher medical training in Hong Kong. Gandhi and Jinnah were British-educated lawyers, and Nehru was an Oxford man. In the Philippines Quezon and Osmena were both lawyers with extensive experience of the West. Luang Pradit in Thailand was a Paris-trained lawyer and Pibul Songgram studied military affairs in France. Among the Vietnamese, Ho Chi Minh lived long abroad in France, the Soviet Union, and other parts of the world, and Ngo Dinh Diem, a Catholic, graduated from the French civil service school at Hanoi and also lived abroad for many years. The assassinated Burmese leader, Aung San, was a product of Rangoon University and a law student; Ba Maw studied at Cambridge and obtained a French law degree; U Nu studied at the University of Rangoon, turned writer, and — a somewhat odd occupation for a devout Buddhist statesman — translated Dale Carnegie's *How to Win Friends and Influence People* into Burmese. In Indonesia, Sukarno was an engineer by training, Mohammad Hatta a university student in Holland, and Sutan Sjahrir a Dutch-trained intellectual and writer with an intimate acquaintance with the Western world and its thought. Ceylon's S.W.R.D. Bandaranaike was an Oxford-educated barrister. Among West Indian leaders Luis Muñoz Marín of Puerto Rico attended Georgetown University in Washington, D. C., while Eric Williams of Trinidad, Norman Manley of Jamaica, and Sir Grantley Herbert Adams of Barbados, first Prime Minister of the West Indian Federation, were all Oxford men. The latter two were also British-trained lawyers.

If one turns to Africa the situation is the same. Habib Bourguiba of Tunisia is a Paris-trained lawyer, married to a French woman. Both Nnamdi Azikiwe of Nigeria and Kwame Nkrumah of Ghana studied at Lincoln University and elsewhere in the United States. Obafemi Awolowo, Premier of Nigeria's Western Region, studied in England and became a barrister. Among other leaders in Ghana, Kojo Botsio took his B.A. at Oxford, J. B. Danquah was a lawyer and holder of a doctorate from Cambridge, while K. A. Busia secured his Ph.D. from Oxford. In French West Africa Léopold Senghor, a product of the Sorbonne, is a Parisian intellectual and poet of distinction, while Félix Houphouet-Boigny was trained in medicine. Sékou Touré, who took Guinea out of the French Union, had only a limited formal education, partially in French schools in Guinea, but has traveled in both Western and Eastern Europe. In Kenya, Jomo Kenyatta studied extensively in both London and Moscow, and Tom Mboya spent a year at Oxford; Julius Nyerere, head of the Tanganyika African National Union, is a product of Edinburgh University.

Such a listing as this, representing an arbitrary selection of a few key figures, covers only a fraction of the names which might be brought forward. In West Africa, for example, it ignores completely the impressive list of those who have secured their training at such institutions as Achimota College or the University College at Ibadan. It should, however, serve to establish beyond a shadow of doubt that the revolution against imperialism has been carried on primarily under the leadership of Asians and Africans in whose intellectual formation the West itself had a very large share.[9]

The strength of the West was something to be studied and copied, and a major component of that strength was the existence of integrated nations. For Asians and Africans who underwent a Western type of education at home or abroad, this lesson was sharply emphasized by the body of doctrine which was thrust upon them. Since it was an age of nationalism in the West the achievement and maintenance of national unity and independence were central themes of the literature, history, and political tradition to which they were exposed. The praise of freedom and equality, and of the patriots who fought for national honor and integrity were basic assumptions of their new intellectual milieu. The writings of Rousseau, Burke, Fichte, and Mazzini, or their intellectual descendants became familiar to them and exercised among them the influence which they had first exercised in the West itself. They came to an acquaintance with the great figures of American independence, with Cavour, Garibaldi, and Bismarck, and with the new doctrines of social Darwinism, not to mention the later nationalist vehemence of Hitler and Mussolini. The academic fare which was laid before them and the climate of ideas and expectations in which they came to live formulated for them their own grievances and aspirations and pointed the paths they might follow. Though the differences were great — as, for example, between Catholic missionary schooling in French Africa, the Sorbonne, the London School of Economics, Oxford, and Lincoln University in Pennsylvania — common elements of the Western tradition still pointed in the same direction. In the more recent phase a variant strand of Western thought and political action has made its impact through the revolutionary doctrines of Marx, Lenin, Stalin, and their followers.

To stress the Western origins of nationalism is not, of course, to deny that the interactions of the Asian nationalists on each other and the stimulus given to one country by a neighbor were of great importance; but even here the original spark was derived from Europe and was passed on through an Asian or African intermediary, suffering, perhaps, some sea change on the way. As the nationalist spark moved eastward and southward in Europe, with each country in some measure influencing the developments in others as they caught fire, so in the rest of the world the interactions of peoples have been a significant element.

The rise of Japan gave new hope to Asia and set a model which might be followed elsewhere. Sun Yat-sen pointed to the fact that the new Japan, transformed into a first-class power and victor over a great European state, had caught up with Europe and given inspiration to the rest of Asia: "We once thought that we could not do what the Europeans could do; and we see now that Japan has learned from Europe and that, if we follow Japan, we, too, will be learning from the West as Japan did." [10] But it is obvious from Sun's words that it is Europe which is the true and original model, and he was not averse to drawing directly on it and later on Communist Russia which gave him both economic guidance and the political technique of the centralized one-party state. Particularly for the Vietnamese, so much more influenced by China than the rest of Southeast Asia, Sun himself, the Kuomintang, and later the Chinese Communists became sources of nationalist and organizational inspiration; and Sukarno has paid tribute to the teaching of Sun for its contribution to the growth of Indonesian nationalism. Throughout Southeast Asia the nationalism of the Chinese immigrants has had a very real influence both through their example and even more through the strong local reactions to the political activism inspired in them by China's revolutions.

Almost everywhere, and most notably perhaps in Indonesia in the interwar decades, Gandhi and the Indian National Congress were models to be studied and followed with respect; but nowhere can the nationalism of Asia be traced to Europe with greater assurance than in India whose leaders were so profoundly affected by their British association. Indian independence has brought no lessening of Indian influence but rather an increase of it. Itself now freed from colonialism, India has felt the call to aid in breaking colonial chains elsewhere, particularly in Africa. Through many channels Nehru and other Indian spokesmen have expressed their devotion to the cause of African freedom; the Indian radio speaks directly to Africa; and considerable numbers of African students have been encouraged to come to Indian universities. In the inter-Asian gatherings, in which India has played a leading role, the collaboration of the new nations to put an end to colonialism and to promote the right of self-determination has been a central theme.

With the exception of Gandhi, Nehru, and Sun Yat-sen, no single non-European individual has rivaled the influence of Ataturk, whose name has still not lost its magic. His was an uncompromising and sharply conceived nationalism which successfully challenged the European powers, united a dispirited and defeated people, and set in motion a drastic program of secular modernization. Particularly in the Islamic belt from Afghanistan to Morocco, although his fame and achievements were widely known as far afield as China, Ataturk's Westernizing reconstruction of Turkey on an explicitly national base set a pattern which many others have tried to imitate but which none has as yet effectively surpassed.

Within the Arab world it is presumably Egypt, both as an intellectual center and in terms of its own political experience and activity, which has had the largest influence in shaping nationalist movements and ideologies, although it was not until World War II that Egypt identified itself with the Arabs. Itself balanced uncertainly between the old and the new, Egypt has been able to play two roles which, sometimes blending harmoniously and sometimes clashing, reflect the inevitable Arab ambiguities. As the first of the Moslem countries to loosen its bonds to the Ottoman Empire and to come within the Western orbit, it served as a major center from which the new trends derived from Europe could radiate. At the same time that it was drawing on the French and British models it strengthened its position as a focal point for the reformulation of Islamic doctrines, most notably through the ancient university of Al Azhar, and for a regathering of the forces of Islam for both defensive and offensive operations. With the formation of the Arab League in 1945 and the location of its headquarters in Cairo, a new political instrument was created through which the Egyptians could spread their influence. The most dramatic phase of Egyptian leadership came, however, with the rise to power of Gamal Abdel Nasser after the curt dismissal of Farouk in 1952. Hailed as the new Saladin, Nasser won wide popular acceptance as the embodiment of the dual revolution against Western imperialism and against the anachronistic domestic forces of privilege and exploitation.

In Africa south of the Sahara the familiar processes of interaction are now repeating themselves. If Nigeria and the Gold Coast drew primarily on British and American sources, they have moved ahead to stimulate each other and to establish patterns and goals to which African eyes increasingly turn, focusing a reconsideration of fundamental policies by imperial authorities elsewhere. The mere fact that African peoples can achieve such advances is by itself of vast importance to others still in earlier stages of the colonial cycle.

The West has involuntarily contributed to this interaction of Asian and African peoples by attracting the potential leaders of the non-European world to its great metropolitan and academic centers. In Paris, Berlin, and Moscow, in London, Oxford, and Cambridge, and in American cities and universities the students and the intellectually and politically conscious from all the countries entering the modern world have gathered together and come to know each other, thus reversing the process of divorce from neighboring areas which is a usual consequence of imperial regimes. As in the nineteenth century the students, political leaders, and conspirators of Europe used London and Paris as the cosmopolitan headquarters in which they might establish contact and shape the revolutionary movements of that day, so in the twentieth century the colonial and quasi-colonial peoples have drawn upon these centers for the same purposes. Beyond the processes of formal education the ever-growing body of students learned of the Western world at first hand, were exposed to Communist and other indoctrination, and experienced both the intoxicating freedom and equality which the West offered and the racial discrimination, particularly in the United States, which sharpened their sense of national grievance and of solidarity against the imperialists.

Nor was the effect of this marshaling of forces abroad one which cut across only colonial and international frontiers. In many instances it also speeded the development of a sense of national identity for people coming from the same territory who had been separated from each other by internal barriers of many kinds. Indians of different castes and from different regions of the subcontinent were thrown together and became aware of the bonds which linked them to each other and distinguished them from their British colleagues. West Africans in England brought into being the important West African Students Union as well as groupings which reflected more local and traditional elements. The political parties of Indonesia in some part had their birth in the activities of Indonesian students in Holland and were carried back to the islands from abroad by Hatta, Sjahrir, and their associates. For considerable segments of the Middle East, Paris was a focal point of inspiration and agitation. What Ch.-André Julien has written of Paris is equally true of many other educational and political centers:

> It is not only in the shadow of the great mosque of Tunis but on the terraces of the cafes of the Latin Quarter that the symbiosis between the Mohammedan students of North Africa was effected. Paris, even more than Tunis, was the crucible where the nationalisms of the Maghreb were fused.[11]

In the new dispensation of independent Asian and African states the importance of the European capitals and universities as central world meeting points for the colonial and quasi-colonial peoples has somewhat declined or at least been supplemented by meeting points within the new states themselves. Asian-African solidarity was impressively displayed at Bandung in 1955, and again, with a strong leaning in the Communist direction, at the conference of 1957 in Cairo which has served as host to other Asian-African conferences as well. Accra has been the meeting place for African states and organizations, and is the seat of the permanent secretariat of the All-African People's Conference of 1958.

I have been contending that the leading nationalists have been drawn from those elements of the non-European societies which had the closest contact with the West and were therefore able to challenge it in its own terms. Nationalism in Asia and Africa has characteristically represented a drive toward modernization, constituting rather a breach with the past than its preservation or restoration. Western Europe has been the seedbed of the dynamic forces which have been at work revolutionizing mankind in the last centuries and its imperial spread overseas set the present chain of events in motion. The nationalisms which have emerged are neither a spontaneous and self-generating movement among the Asian and African peoples nor merely an effort on their part to get rid of the alien intruder. Far more they are an assertion of their rediscovered or newly created individuality, already sharply influenced by the imperial impact, and an effort to adapt themselves to the new forces.

It is necessary to distinguish between the early instinctively defensive reactions, in which xenophobia played a considerable part, and the later nationalisms whose aims, structure, and leadership reflect the new trends. In the case of India an illuminating example is furnished by the contrast between the Indian Mutiny of 1857 and the nationalist activities, centering around the Congress, of the period after World War I. The pre-nationalist nature of the Mutiny has been well brought out by Nehru:

> Essentially it was a feudal outburst, headed by feudal chiefs and other followers and aided by the widespread antiforeign sentiment. As such, inevitably it looked up to the relic of the Moghul dynasty, still sitting in the Delhi palace, but feeble and old and powerless. . . . There was hardly any national and underlying sentiment among the leaders, and a mere antiforeign feeling coupled with a desire to maintain their feudal privileges, was a poor substitute for this. . . . Nationalism of the modern type was yet to come; India had still to go through much sorrow and travail before she learned the lesson which would give her real freedom. Not by fighting for a lost cause, the feudal order, would freedom come.[12]

Three quarters of a century later, a similar example might be found in the Burma Rebellion of 1931, led by the ex-monk Saya San who claimed to be the destined King of Burma and asserted the possession of magical powers to protect himself and his followers. In its leadership as in the course it took, this expression of popular discontents and grievances, aggravated by the great depression, followed traditional Burmese patterns, drew little from Western models, and did not enlist the support of the educated Burmans. The application of Western ideas and techniques was to be the contribution of the new group of Burmese nationalists, the Thakins, then in process of gathering their forces. One Burman sees the Thakins as:

the boys who had taken the disastrous result of Saya San's rebellion of 1930 seriously. They had left their colleges to go to the masses and teach them better ways of gaining independence than throwing away the lives of young Burmans fruitlessly. They believed that Burma was what she was because she had not kept pace with the West, and that she would never become "somebody" in this world by just living in the glories of her past. To keep abreast with the ever-moving West the Burmans must take long strides, and this could be done only with the help of books. So they adopted the slogan, "Write books, translate books and do it by the hundreds." They were out to educate the masses and stuff them with western ideas and ideals.[13]

In China, where the issue was complicated by the necessity of carrying on a two-front struggle against the alien Manchu dynasty as well as against the Western intruders, both the Taiping and the Boxer Rebellions resemble the Indian Mutiny in the sense of belonging rather to the old than to the new world. The earlier rebellion, despite its curious Christian trappings, was essentially a peasant movement which lacked any clear-cut political doctrine and suffered from inadequacies of political organization. The Boxer rising was the last great upsurge of the older China, seeking at once to dispose of the Manchus and to give expression to the xenophobic abhorrence of the ever-widening European penetration. The shock of the Japanese victory over China in 1895 gave the impulse which was needed to incite Chinese nationalism and to compel a basic reconsideration of the possibility of maintaining intact the traditional Chinese society, but the Boxers still represented far more a reaction against the alien forces than an adaptation to them. With Sun Yat-sen and his immediate intellectual predecessors China moved into an unmistakably nationalist phase.

In seeking to apply the same type of analysis to the development of nationalism in Africa south of the Sahara one must guard against the danger of being deceived by outward appearances and labels and of obscuring reality through adherence to inapplicable general categories derived from quite different situations. The course of African events, however, has in the main followed the same pattern as that evolved elsewhere, even though in the African case the brevity of the effective colonial contact, the less highly developed cultures, and the considerable areas of white settlement confuse the picture.[14] Full-fledged nationalist movements were for a brief time limited to West Africa. They are now spreading to the rest of the continent at an almost incredible speed. With the appearance of a Western-educated intelligentsia and professional class, the inchoate compulsion to shake off the disturbing alien presence is transformed into a popularly based political movement seeking development on Western lines. There is sound truth in the comment of W. W. Macmillan that "the ferment in Africa today springs basically from the sometimes passionate effort of so many of its people to escape from their old life." [15]

In the large, nationalism in Asia and Africa, as in at least its initial phases in Europe and America, is a forward-looking and not a reactionary force, a spur to revolution and not a bulwark of the status quo. It is an inevitable concomitant of the rise of nationalism that an attempt should be made to glorify a real or mythical national heritage, presumably both to bolster collective self-esteem and to justify the claim to separate existence; but few among the nationalists have had their eyes upon a restoration of an Asian or African past rather than on the creation of a Western future. After the first instinctively defensive and xenophobic reaction has exhausted itself, the effort to reëstablish the old order has been replaced by a deliberate attempt to shape the society on the model of the Western intruders. Although the nationalists have often proclaimed the optimistic but unreliable slogan that the best of the old should be wedded to the best of the new, they have on the whole appeared unconcerned to preserve more of the ancient heritage than seemed compatible with a Western-style rebuilding of their societies. Or, to put it in more meaningful terms, where the old gets in the way of, say, a five-year plan, urban and rural development projects, the creation of modern armed forces, or the institution of Western political forms and controls, it is the old which must give way to make room for the new. The symbols of unity and the title to distinctive greatness may be sought in the past, but the present substance of action and desire is the transition to the modern world.[16]

Of the outstanding nationalist leaders it is really only Gandhi, with his unique mixture of the modern West and traditional India, who has pressed for a rejection in principle of characteristic elements of the West in terms of a reassertion of older and more in-digenous values. This aspect of Gandhi's life and teaching has been carried on and distorted by right-wing Hindu groups, such as the Hindu Mahasaba. It is more properly reflected in the demand for concentration on the villages rather than on industrial develop-ment, in the Community Projects, and in the Bhoodan land gift movement of Vinoba Bhave; but it is the Westernism of Nehru which has set the official tone for independent India. In China Chiang Kai-shek preached something of a return to Confucianism and to the traditions of the older Chinese society, although he also saw the need to study Western civilization to make China strong; but the Communists who preached a strident and radical modern-ism drove him to Formosa. While one can find everywhere religious and other groups and movements which look backward rather than forward, such as those represented in Indonesia by Darul Islam, in Egypt by the Moslem Brotherhood, and in tropical Africa by unreconstructed chiefs of the old school, these are not the ones which have taken over command as the imperial controls gave way. Only in a few countries, such as Afghanistan, Saudi Arabia, and Ethiopia, which had evaded colonial subjection or had no more than a passing experience of it, has nationalism tended to be more largely identified with traditional structures and values.

Far from seeking a return to the past the bulk of the nationalists have concentrated rather on bringing to their countries the dy-namism, the Faustian drive, of the modern West. That there must be a certain ambivalence in their attitude lies at the heart of the paradox which envelops them. They are attacking the West and repudiate Western supremacy; yet it is the instruments and out-looks of the West which they would have their people master in order to substantiate their claim to an equal and independent place.

Having come to intimate acquaintance with the West, the nationalist leaders found peculiarly humiliating their rejection as equals by the Westerners who had taken over their countries. From a Javanese prison cell to which he was consigned by the Dutch after his return from Holland, the distinguished Indonesian leader, Sjahrir, wrote of the isolation in his own country of the Western-trained intellectual. Few among his own people, Sjahrir declared, had similar interests, and the path into the European community in Java was firmly blocked:

> For us that is as far away as Europe itself; indeed further away, because Europe can be reached by ship and plane, but the social barrier, the race division in the colonial society, is a great deal harder to bridge over.[17]

Nehru emphasized a different and more threatening aspect since it involved acceptance by the Indians themselves of the stigma of inferiority:

> We developed the mentality of a good country-house servant. Sometimes we were treated to a rare honor — we were given a cup of tea in the drawing room. The height of our ambition was to become respectable and to be promoted individually to the upper regions. Greater than any victory of arms or diplomacy was this psychological triumph of the British in India.[18]

In such situations the reaction might have been to shun everything Western, to refuse to try to cross the social barrier or gain admission to the drawing room. On the contrary, the turn was in fact toward an intensification of the drive to rival the West on its own terms and thus to demonstrate — if need be, to enforce — the equality which the West denied.

This modernizing drive of the nationalists, the heirs of the colonial regimes and of imperial predominance, is not one which could be expected to take over without encountering serious opposition. Even the new elites themselves are inevitably torn by spiritual discords. They cannot help but seek to reintegrate themselves in their national traditions at the same time that they seek to revolutionize their societies into Western modernity. In varying degree everywhere they are bound to be challenged by the representatives of the old order. The new Westernized elements still constitute only a thin upper crust, superimposed on societies the great mass of whose people have achieved only a meager acquaintance with the world into which their present leaders would take them. The latter have perhaps established themselves in the urban centers, but the great sweep of the countrysides is still only dimly aware of what is at stake. The rising nations of Asia and Africa are communities all too evidently headed in several directions at once, built on a national unity which often has in it more of diversity than of oneness. In the first round of succession the nationalists of the Western school have taken power to themselves and won the allegiance of their people against the encroachments of the alien imperialism. It is not self-evident that they will be able both to maintain their power and to hold firm to their purpose as imperialism recedes and as other aspirants to power challenge their leadership.

PART THREE

NATIONALISM AND DEMOCRACY

CHAPTER XI

Nationalism and Democracy: Background and Foreground

NATIONALISM HAS in its time been variously acclaimed as an integral and necessary part of democracy and denounced as the open gateway to autocracy and dictatorship. In fact, to assign it any particular political coloration is presumably impossible since it has been associated in one or another time and country with almost every conceivable political regime and attitude. Even though an impressive case can be made for the proposition that any true nationalism contains a strong strain of fundamentally democratic elements, there are many ardent and unmistakable nationalisms in which democracy is either virtually nonexistent or is no more than a façade of outward conformity with current political fashions. Where the general constellation of forces has been such as to promote democracy, as most notably in Western Europe and the countries which it has settled overseas, nationalism has maintained a predominantly democratic cast; where the underpinnings of democracy have been weak, as in much of the rest of the world, nationalism has betrayed the democratic promise which the nineteenth-century liberal saw in it and has become an instrument of the established ruling groups or of totalitarianism. Everywhere it is the champion of self-government in the sense of national as opposed to alien rule, but it is only accidentally self-government in the sense of rule by the many as opposed to rule by the few. Reduced to its bare bones, nationalism is no more than the assertion of a particular "we" arrayed against the "they" of the rest of mankind, by itself giving no clue as to how the "we" may choose to manage its own affairs.

The themes of nationalism and democracy cross and recross each other at so many vital points that it is essential to seek some understanding of their intricate interrelations. In some instances nationalism and democracy have been so intimately associated with each other as to be almost indistinguishable; in a number of others, for example the colonies of the Western powers, the nationalist movements have regarded themselves as the bearers of a democratic structure of state and society; but there remain a substantial number of important cases, among which Japan would head the list, in which democracy was at the best an afterthought. Furthermore, one strand of logical development inherent in nationalism, happily more frequently recessive than dominant, leads directly down the path of totalitarianism. The issue to be explored is whether any general principles can be discerned which suggest the circumstances under which nationalism does or does not take the democratic path.

At a time when nationalism in the West has often drifted in reactionary or militarist directions and when the most dangerous and abhorrent elements in it have so recently been arrogantly paraded by the Fascists and Nazis, it may appear paradoxical, or even outrageous folly, to suggest the existence of an essential bond between nationalism and democracy; yet both in idea and in actual historical development this bond has been of central importance. Hans Kohn has put the matter in the extreme form of saying that "nationalism is inconceivable without the ideas of popular sovereignty preceding — without a complete revision of the position of ruler and ruled, of classes and castes." [1] On the face of the historical record no statement as uncompromisingly sweeping as this can be sustained . . . and yet it has more than a germ of fundamental truth.

Once full-fledged nationalism has appeared, a transformation of deep and lasting importance in the relations of people, rulers, and state tends to occur. Even in the Fascist variants the role which the people play is sharply distinguished from their role in the earlier type of dictatorship or monarchy, as witness the efforts of Fuehrer and Duce to carry the masses with them, to give the appearance of popular consultation through plebiscitary techniques, and to spread the tentacles of the Party down into every cranny of the society. This, certainly, is not democracy, and yet it is equally certainly a perverse offshoot from democratic roots, a post-democratic phenomenon. The Leader and the Party put themselves forward as emanations of the popular will, as a truer distillation of the national *volonté générale* than the people themselves can produce.

To reduce the question to its most basic terms, the argument linking democracy and nationalism would run something as follows. Nationalism is peculiarly a product of the distinctive forces which have gone into the shaping of the modern world. Those forces are inherently and inevitably "democratic" in the sense that they mobilize formerly submerged elements and classes of society into new social roles, eat away at traditional relationships, and work toward the building of a new great society into which, in principle, all men are actively drawn. Obviously what is involved here is by no means necessarily a democratic constitutional structure nor even an immediate approximation of a society striving toward egalitarianism, although both of these are likely to be present at least as active aspirations. Far more, it is the general conception, derived from the changing social scene, that the people, the mass of ordinary human beings, are of consequence, that they are achieving a sense both of their own worth and of their right and ability to do something about it, and that the leaders must speak in their name. The national era comes to be an era of mass communications and mass production, inescapably headed toward mass politics.

The heart of the argument is the proposition that the rise of nationalism is normally associated with deep-running social ferment and change which disrupt the old order of society and speed the processes of social mobilization. On this basis nationalism is seen as one of the major manifestations of what Karl Mannheim has spoken of as "the fundamental democratization of society," the stirring "into action of those classes who formerly played a passive part in political life." [2] As the peoples begin to come of age and to a new consciousness of themselves, they demand a new place in a society in process of transformation. One of the characteristic forms which this demand has taken is insistence upon the centrality of the national community and upon the latter's right to make the state the sovereign organ of its identity and will. The people, after all, compose the nation, and it is thus not beyond the bounds of reason to suggest that the revolutionary importance of the fact that the social-political community which has come to occupy the center of the contemporary stage — taking over the state in its own name and establishing a new criterion of legitimacy — should, therefore, be defined in terms of the people. In the new dispensation the state could no longer be seen as made up of the ruler and those who happened to be his subjects, but became in principle the emanation and instrument of the nation. The forward thrust of the bourgeoisie in Europe and, in due course, of the masses, had its close overseas parallel in the awakening of colonial peoples, in roughly similar circumstances and similarly under middle class leadership, to the struggle against their alien masters.[3]

At the next remove it might be contended that the only true nationalism is one which has deep popular roots. "Genuinely nationalist movements," Harold Lasswell has written, "are not to be confused with separatist demands which may be made in nationalistic vocabularies but with which the masses are not identified. A ruling elite may buttress its own demands by adopting a nationalistic phraseology, although the community remains aloof, which was true of some of the secessions from the Spanish and Turkish empires." [4] Those who would give full credence to the democratic thesis are tempted to settle the troublesome problem of nondemocratic nationalisms in this abrupt fashion, and possibly something can be made of it; but the easy course of cutting Gordian knots with the paper sword of definitions is one to be resisted. There is an element of obvious absurdity in any scheme of analysis whose premises lead on to a denial that nationalism existed in, say, Japan at one or another period since the Meiji Restoration or in Iran in the twentieth century. However demonstrable it may be that democracy in all or some of its aspects was missing from these countries, and that nationalism preceded rather than followed social-economic change, common sense will not permit the ruling out of what all the world has regarded as nationalism. But, even though the common term of nationalism be applied across the board, it remains necessary to distinguish between different types of nationalisms and to examine their very diverse relationship to democratic assumptions and practices.

That the national and democratic principles were for many purposes to be regarded as opposite sides of the same coin was a commonplace in much of the political thinking of nineteenth-century Europe, although quite a few commentators stood out against such an interpretation and a number of contemporary developments belied it. As it was a part of the basic beliefs of the liberal publicists and statesmen of the period that democracy was on the march and that the people must come to a constantly growing share in power, so was it also an article of faith that mankind was divinely or naturally divided into nations and that these nations set the territorial and demographic boundaries within which democracy would operate. Increasingly it was taken for granted that if men were set free to choose for themselves, they would organize their societies on national lines. Woodrow Wilson, as the heir of nineteenth-century liberalism, made national self-determination an integral part of his democratic remedy for the world's ills. "By 1918 nationalism and democracy were generally taken as synonymous in the thought of the Western nations. The nation-state was regarded as the political expression of the democratic will of the people."[5] In the tortuous United Nations debates on human rights the presumption has from time to time been vigorously asserted that national self-determination is the starting point and indispensable condition of all the other rights and freedoms associated with a democratic society.[6]

This thrusting of the nation into a central position in relation to the concept of democracy meant a striking and significant innovation when contrasted with the democratically inclined political thought of preceding centuries. Where the latter, as most notably in the variants on the theme of the social contract, had appeared to assume that any chance assemblage of men might lay the foundations of a state, the nineteenth century moved to the conclusion that a viable state and particularly a viable democracy required the firmer foundation of an already existing community of sentiment, culture, and tradition. The social contract theorists may have implicitly taken for granted that the rational beings who were contractually establishing political obligations and institutions would have a prior bond among them; but, if they so believed, they for the most part signally failed to say so. Though Montesquieu had earlier pointed to the role of environment, only with Rousseau, in this school, are the elements of emotion, custom, and social milieu brought significantly into the picture, leading on through romanticism to the national age. For the dominant rationalism and individualism of the seventeenth and eighteenth centuries, the nineteenth century tended to substitute a Burkean return to history and a sociological approach which stressed the traditionally shaped communities of men. To the natural rights of individuals were added the natural rights of nations.

By the middle of the nineteenth century the new outlook had consolidated its hold to the point where its basic propositions could be asserted almost as truisms. It would be difficult to find anywhere a calmer statement of the issue, assuming as self-evident matters which are in fact open to grave dispute, than that of John Stuart Mill in his *Representative Government*.[7] Setting off from his definition of a nationality as a portion of mankind united among themselves by common sympathies, desiring to be under the same government and a government by themselves, he continued on to affirm that where such a national sentiment existed in any force there was a prima facie case for the establishment of a separate national state. This proposition he linked to fundamental democratic conceptions by suggesting that it "is merely saying that the question of government ought to be decided by the governed." While this statement may appear to be a commonplace expression of the democratic creed, he added to it the truly surprising assertion that: "One hardly knows what any division of the human race should be free to do if not to determine with which of the various collective bodies of human beings they choose to associate themselves"; whereas in fact it is far more plausible to contend that this is one of the last, most difficult, and most precarious of the freedoms to which human beings may lay claim. It deserves notice that the book in which this tranquil judgment appeared was published in 1861, at the start of four years of warfare in which the South sought to assert its right to associate with itself and not with the North in the United States.

For Mill, as for many other thinkers of his own day and since, the relation between democracy and the national principle went well beyond the proposition that if peoples were left free to choose they would sort themselves out on national lines and that they should be given an opportunity to do so. The claim was frequently made that democracy required a national setting, or at least that it flourished best where the people concerned were knit together by emotional and traditional bonds. As Mill put it, "it is in general a necessary condition of free institutions that the boundaries of governments should coincide in the main with those of nationalities." Such institutions he saw as being "next to impossible in a country made up of different nationalities," because of the lack of a united public opinion, of common sources of information, and of leaders having the confidence of an undivided public. Pointing to the Hapsburg Monarchy he emphasized the danger to liberty in a multinational state in which the rulers could play off the antipathies of one element in the population against another and could rule "with the iron rod of conquerors" through the instrumentality of an army lacking both national attachment and sympathy with the people.

Here there was, perhaps, a far too easy transition from the accepted principle of the rights and freedoms of individuals to the rights and freedoms of nations with little awareness that the insatiable appetite of the latter might come to consume the former. That the transition was confidently made by Mill and many others of his day and later is beyond dispute. The English social philosopher, L. T. Hobhouse, summed the matter up some decades later in his confident claim that "national and personal freedom are growths of the same root, and their historical connection rests on no accident, but on ultimate identity of idea." [8]

In its youthful exuberance nationalism has at least the appearance of being a movement of liberation which embraces all other good things, including the freeing of the individual to pursue his own destiny in the democratic company of his fellow citizens. Only as nationalism progresses does it become evident that the claims of the individual may be subordinated to the drive for national unity and independence and that liberal democracy may give way to an authoritarianism in which the actual and diverse wills of the people of the nation are replaced by a leader or an elite supposed in some mystical fashion to express the national ethos. The French Revolution itself drifted into the hands of

Napoleon; a number of thinkers, such as Bonald and De Maistre, stressed the conservative and traditionalist aspects, finding the nation embodied in its aristocracy rather than in the newly rising elements; in Germany Bismarck, and not the liberals of 1848, accomplished national unification; and in southeastern Europe the achievement of the national goals, under whatever auspices, took priority over the implementation of liberal ideals. Despite these and many other nondemocratic manifestations of nationalism, including its turn in militarist and imperialist directions, faith in the identification of nationalism and democracy remained widespread until Fascism, Nazism, and the shortcomings of Wilsonian self-determination made inescapable the doubts which Lord Acton and others had expressed. The young nationalisms of Asia and Africa are still disinclined to take such doubts significantly into account.

On the historical record two items may be cited as buttressing the democratic thesis. One concerns the regularity with which the loosing of the forces of the Western revolution has served as a stimulant to national sentiment, and the other, the fact that democracy in the modern world has appeared to flourish at its best in a national setting.

Wherever the characteristically modern processes of social mobilization, of fundamental democratization, have been set in motion they have with a striking degree of consistency operated on men to heighten or to create a sense of identification with national communities.[9] To whatever corner of the world one may turn, whether it be Europe or America, Asia or Africa, a central fact of modern times is that the encroachment of the new upon the earlier patterns of society has brought peoples to an increasingly vivid consciousness of their national distinctiveness (even though the nations concerned may still be in process of creation) and urged them on to nationalist self-assertion. Later developments have worked both to sustain the assumptions of Marx and Engels as to the national attachments of the bourgeoisie and to override their contrary assumptions as to the essentially unnational character of the proletariat. The masses no less than the classes have been drawn into the national stream once the modern ferment has been introduced.

On the second score, whether it be because the nation furnishes that "common understanding and sense of belonging together" without which "successful democracy is not really possible," [10] or for other reasons, the record shows that democracy in the modern world has worked best within the nation-state. If the existence of an opposition as an integral part of the governmental system may be accepted as a touchstone of political democracy, then one may suggest that an overriding sense of national unity has been a key element in transforming it into a *loyal* opposition. The rise of democracy as a political phenomenon has coincided too closely with the emergence of nations as conscious entities to allow of an explanation in terms of random chance. This is not to say either that all emergent nations have taken the democratic path or that some other form of social cement may not be discoverable to serve as a substitute for the social solidarity of the nation. What does appear evident is that the reason of man, on which the social contract theorists had generally placed primary reliance, needed to be supplemented by some other bond of unity, and it was nationality which came to the aid of rationality. Perhaps the next turn of events will see the emergence of larger supranational entities, as, for example, in a unification of Western Europe. To date, however, democratic institutions have not moved significantly beyond the national level.

The experience of the modern world suggests that national unity has been a necessary condition for democracy, but that it is far from being a sufficient one. The classic Western European models indicate that democracy has been at its best where history has shaped homogeneous peoples who managed to dispose at a relatively early stage of some of the more urgent issues of national identity. Contrasting the fortunate position of Britain with that of other European countries, R. H. S. Crossman has written:

> British democracy evolved within the firm framework of national unity, and British Liberals could demand freedom without any fear of disrupting the nation into nationalistic minorities. . . . They could speculatively atomize English society precisely because it was *not* atomistic, but a community inspired by the deepest of common feelings — patriotism.[11]

In Britain national unity was already solidly established by the time the nineteenth century presented a host of new economic and social challenges. In less happily situated countries the emphasis was a very different one. The experience of Eastern Europe and the Balkans indicates that democracy has not fared well in a multinational setting or when the drive for national unity and independence came at a late stage and took precedence over the issues of social, economic, and political reform which were simultaneously beginning to crowd in on peoples whose national destinies were still unresolved.

No simple and straight-line theory of cause and effect, however, can hope to embrace the actual historical diversity. The pitfalls into which one may all too easily stumble can be illustrated, for example, by the failure of old-established Spain and Portugal, both reasonably well-consolidated nations, to develop on democratic lines and by the contrary situation of an ethnically divided Czechoslovakia which achieved national statehood only late in the day and yet was certainly to be counted among the successful democracies. It must also be said immediately that the characteristic forces of the modern world, with the concomitant rise of the middle class, had penetrated deeply into at least the Bohemian portion of Czechoslovakia whereas they had impinged only lightly and in passing on the countries of the Iberian Peninsula.

To the positive proposition that democracy has taken firm root and flourished best in consolidated nations can be added the obverse contention that democratic institutions have shown little or no ability to cope with the problems of the multinational state. One can, indeed, argue that where deep-running ethnic diversity exists the introduction of democratic institutions is likely to have the effect of intensifying national distinctions and antagonisms since such institutions work to force a reconsideration of the definition of the "we" into whose hands power is passing. In the European setting two obvious instances are the dissolution of the Hapsburg Monarchy into its component nationalities and the failure of the British parliamentary system to meet the needs of militantly nationalist Irishmen. In Asia the splitting off of Pakistan from India is the most striking example.

Such generalizations would carry a firmer ring of conviction if, as with every generalization about nationalism, there were not so many borderline cases and exceptions. Democracy has indeed flourished where national unity established the emotional framework of basic consent within which political disagreement could be tolerated. Yet, among the small number of European or European-descended nations clearly to be counted in the democratic camp, a surprising number deviate markedly from the classic model of across-the-board national homogeneity. One need only suggest the familiar examples of Belgium, Switzerland, and Canada, each divided in language and culture. The British nation embraces English, Welsh, Scotch, and some Irish. The United States and, in varying degree, other "overseas" democracies settled primarily by Europeans, have been melting pots for peoples of many tongues, creeds, and races. In these instances it is certainly not stretching the known facts to surmise that the existence of democratic institutions aided in the process of welding national unity from original diversity.

The problems involved in the relations between nationalism and democracy are adequately complex if they are examined solely within the confines of Europe. They take on a different magnitude and emphasis as they are pursued into the vast areas of Asia and Africa. In many of the newly rising Asian and African countries a good case can be made for the proposition that the association between nationalism and democracy has been as intimate and the democratic character of the nationalist movements as unmistakable as in the earlier Western European models. Particularly countries with a considerable European colonial experience, such as India, Burma, Indonesia, the Philippines, and Ghana, took a full-scale and immediate leap into democratic institutions not only in constitutional structure but also in the extension of the franchise on a universal basis. However problematical their political future may be, the record shows clearly that the nationalist movements saw themselves also as the champions of democracy.

On the other side of the fence, in a number of countries, such as Japan, Thailand, Iran, Ethiopia, and various of the Arab states, not to mention many Latin American examples, nationalism has had no more than a bowing acquaintance with democracy in any of its forms. In most instances, to be sure, a *pro forma* compliance with the mode of the day has been made through the adoption of constitutions of a nominally democratic variety. The working reality, however, has been the exercise of power by a small clique of insiders who have often not even bothered themselves seriously to take cover behind their constitutional façade, although postwar Japan may be taking its democracy more to heart.

If there is validity in the general proposition that the rise of nationalism is to be seen essentially as a phase of the expanding Western revolution, then it seems plausible to look for at least part of the explanation of the difference between democratic and nondemocratic nationalisms in the diverse circumstances under which that revolution has developed or been transmitted. This revolution has by now penetrated in varying degree to every corner of the earth, and every people has been forced to make some sort of response to the challenge which it imposed. The nature of the response is conditioned by the way in which the challenge was presented as well as by the character of the society undertaking the response.

One line of analysis which appears worthy of exploration is to draw a distinction between nationalisms which are original or primary in character, and those which are imitative or secondary and which, through their customary failure to draw in the broader masses of the nation, may properly be regarded as premature or incomplete in development. In the first category would fall those nationalisms which are the product of the challenging and new-modeling forces operating *within* the society concerned, while the second would embrace those cases in which nationalism, at all events in its early phases, appears to be primarily a reaction to the *external* impact of forces which have not yet significantly affected the inner structure of the society itself.

An immediate objection to such an approach is that, from one standpoint, only the Western European initiators of the new era can legitimately be held to have produced a primary or original nationalism. For all others, and perhaps peculiarly for the non-European peoples, it could be contended that their nationalisms must be of a secondary or imitative variety since they are follow-ers in a second, third, or fourth generation and are all reacting to forces which came into being elsewhere. This is so evidently true as not to require more than statement, but one can argue that it obscures as much as it reveals. The forces brought into play by the revolution which spread out from Western Europe have operated in different ways in different countries and have had widely varying effects, even though the over-all results have been similar. The nature of the difference which is most characteristically involved can be illustrated by pointing to the contrast between, say, the Philippines and India on one side and Saudi Arabia and Ethiopia on the other. In the first pair of countries there has been a substantial penetration of the traditional order of society by the new. Westernized elements have emerged which are prepared and eager to push forward with further social transformations. This new-style elite has adopted democratic assumptions and practices, and the populace at large has a growing awareness of its own democratic claims and potentialities. In the second pair the traditional order has remained largely intact. The internal forces for change are still relatively undeveloped, the older dominant elites have in great part maintained their hold, and there has been both an avoidance of measures and appeals which would stir up the masses and a minimum of active popular participation, even by such middle class elements as have come into being. That the two pairs are already moving toward a greater resemblance to each other does not impair the fact that their experience of the age of European imperialism has been different in significant respects and that they have emerged from it with characteristic dissimilarities. The difference could be most concisely stated as involving the degree to which the *ancien régime* has been undermined and displaced.

Every kind and gradation of relationship to the imperial powers can be found at one or another point on the globe. Everywhere in greater or less degree the West has penetrated and disturbed the old order, although a few countries, such as Mongolia, Tibet, and Nepal, were sufficiently remote to limit Western contact to a minimum. The established ruling groups have almost everywhere been under some measure of attack, and only rarely have they been able to hold on to substantially unimpaired power and privilege. The term "quasi-colonial," applicable to, say, China, Thailand, Iran, and Liberia, points to the extent of imperial penetration under very different circumstances in four countries which never experienced colonialism. Again to suggest markedly divergent examples, Laos and Libya have both been influenced by their temporary subjection to European rule, and yet they could hardly be regarded as having had "long and intensive" colonial experience. The facts of the case establish a no-man's land in which the colonial shades off into the non-colonial with no clear line of demarcation to separate them. Political reality is diverse and recalcitrant, but colonialism has placed a distinctive stamp on those peoples whose destinies it has ruled.

CHAPTER XII

Colonialism as a School for Democracy

ALTHOUGH THE TIDE has of late begun to run in other directions, the uniformity with which colonial peoples turned to democratic institutions as they advanced toward self-government and independence remains one of the notable features of the last decades. In South and Southeast Asia, in Africa, and in the West Indies democratic constitutions were adopted, the franchise was widely extended, political parties sprang into being, and general elections determined the fate of governments. The affirmations of devotion to democratic principles by the nationalist leaders were repeated and continuous.

The sovereignty of the people, even though they were largely illiterate and little aware of the complexities of the great issues with which they were confronted, was enshrined in the preambles and opening articles of the new constitutions. In its second article the Philippine constitution stated: "The Philippines is a republican state. Sovereignty resides in the people and all government authority emanates from them." The 1945 constitution of the Republic of Indonesia, which Sukarno brought back into operation in 1959 as the instrument for his guided democracy, affirmed in its preamble, "We believe in democracy," and in its first article established that "Sovereignty shall be vested in the people." In similar vein, "We, the people of India," resolved in the constitution adopted in 1949, "to constitute India into a sovereign democratic republic." African leaders in a number of territories have asserted with a vigor equal to that of their Asian counterparts that they look to the building of democratic societies. The ever-present gap between constitutional principles and political realities has, however, been rudely emphasized by the recent abandonment of democratic pretensions in several of the new states.

The insistence of the rising nations on the democratic way derived from a number of sources. One fertile source, effective for both colonial and non-colonial peoples, was the general prevalence of such beliefs as that democracy is itself a good, that it is a superior form of government, that it is a symbol of maturity in the modern world, and that its adoption carries with it an assertion of equality. The ability to make a democratic system work appeared to be accepted by the nationalists as a significant element in disproof of the assumption of inferiority which they so bitterly resented. The Indian leader, G. K. Gokhale, explained the turn of Indian nationalists toward democratic and constitutional government in the following terms:

> We feel that you have contempt for us because we submit to personal and despotic government, and so we feel that it is not compatible with self-respect to acquiesce in it. You would disdain to be governed in that way yourselves, and so you despise those who submit to it.[1]

Other sources of persuasion toward democracy attached more peculiarly to the peoples who had been through the colonial mill. On the face of it the notion that subjection to the colonial yoke should be put forward as a school of democracy contains more than a scrap of ironic paradox. Yet much can be said for it even if the concession be made that a substantial part of the argument rests less on the positive contributions of colonial rule than on the democratic implications of the nationalist drive to oust the colonial rulers. In part, this paradox derives from the further paradox that, in the modern world over the long haul and with the exception of Tsarist and Communist Russia, the democracies are the ones which have scored by far the greatest imperial success. Britain, France, the Netherlands, Belgium, and the United States are the powers which have most effectively been able to expand and to hold their empires, whereas the colonies of Spain and Portugal, and of Germany, Italy and Japan have tended either to wither on the vine or to be wrested from them as the result of defeat in war. And the maintenance of empire by the first group of countries, despite dire predictions to the contrary, appears not significantly to have impaired their maintenance of democracy at home, although anyone so inclined may speculate what levels of democratic perfection might have been reached if the allegedly corrupting influence of empire had been absent. The historical record bears out neither the ancient dictum of Thucydides that a democracy cannot manage an empire nor the pessimistic assumptions that imperial autocracy would undermine domestic democracy.

Both theory and practice amply support the belief that democracy at the imperial center is a matter of real importance for colonial political development. The attraction to democratic forms which derives from the bare fact that the superior imperial authority itself operates democratically at home is enhanced by the double imperial assumption that democracy is the most advanced form of government and that immature colonial peoples are not to be trusted with it. Joseph Ralston Hayden extended this conception to the influence of nondemocratic imperial powers as well, contending that the Filipino revolutionary leaders at the end of the nineteenth century were fighting for the political heritage of the West. "The revolts of the Filipinos against Spain and even against America were evidence that although Spain had not granted liberty in the Philippines she unwittingly had taught it there." [2]

With the customary lag in overseas application, the doctrines and practices which evolve in the metropole will be applied in the colonies. The advance of constitutionalism and democracy at the imperial center leads both to an increasing presumption of the desirability of a rule of law which will provide equal protection and orderly administration for the colonial peoples and to a mounting uneasiness about the perpetuation of a system of alien autocracy. At the best a positive effort is made, as in the American control of the Philippines and the more recent turns of Western colonial policy, to enlist a growing measure of native participation and to equip the peoples for self-government through education and the provision of political institutions with something of a democratic base. Although the situation varies from colony to colony and has changed swiftly from year to year in the last decades, the Belgians stood out uniquely among the democratic powers in their earlier rejection in principle of any move in the democratic direction; but the Belgian resistance has now cracked. It should not go without mention that the colonial administrators have themselves grown up in a democratic environment, and not even the abrupt transition to power in an authoritarian colonial setting can wholly rid their minds of the social and political predispositions of the society from which they come. One need not wonder that the Spanish and Portuguese, unequipped with democracy at home, have made so little use of democratic institutions overseas.[3]

In addition to the example set by the imperial powers at home, the acquaintance with democratic societies gained by the colonials who visited the West, and such teaching of democratic principles as was contained in the colonial educational systems the most obvious source of familiarity with a Western style of political institutions was the political and administrative structures set up by the colonial authorities. Of these the easiest to spot, although by no means necessarily the most significant, were the councils and assemblies at all governmental levels from local to central-national in which the people were represented by appointment or election and were given an opportunity to participate in the management of their own affairs. In such councils it was possible to secure some experience of the public business and the ways in which it might be approached, of the give and take of politics, and of parliamentary procedure. The more extensive the range of powers and functions of these councils the more effective the experience was likely to be.

One standard and often somewhat stultifying sample of this type of body was the legislative council which has been so characteristic a feature of the British Crown Colony system.[4] Intended both to draw some leading local figures into association with the government and to tap sources of public opinion, the legislative council in its classic version was dominated by an official majority, composed of top civil servants who sat ex officio or through appointment by the Governor. The unofficial minority, often representing the Europeans more heavily than the indigenous population, was also far more frequently appointed than elected, although in some instances organizations such as Chambers of Commerce might nominate the persons to whom the Governor gave seats. Inevitably in such circumstances the charge was made, particularly as far as representatives of the native community were concerned, that the appointees were supporters of the colonial regime or, at best, tame critics of it who could be counted on to keep their opposition within staid and respectable limits. The official majority which constituted a steamroller always at the Governor's command, the shortcomings of the representation of the community at large, and the separation of legislative representation from the executive authority vested in the Governor and his executive council all worked to make the old-style legislative council an unsatisfactory instrument either of government or of education in democracy.[5] For all this it was a halfway house which gave some taste of democratic procedures and stimulated the demand for more. The interwar decades constituted a period of cautious experimentation of which the most significant phases were the share in power given to elected majorities in India and Burma, working within the framework of dyarchy, and the adoption of the legislative-executive committee system in Ceylon.

Under the pressures of the Second World War and its aftermath the old Crown Colony system began speedily to crumble as more radical approaches to democratic self-government were undertaken throughout the colonies. The process of transition to full-scale democracy on the parliamentary model was well under way in the postwar period when the official majorities, at first gradually and then with something of a rush, gave way to popularly elected majorities, and the executive councils were taken over by men drawn from and responsible to those majorities, as in Nigeria and the Gold Coast. A significant feature of the change was that it constituted a transition to the principle of "one man, one vote," and away from the prior tendency, still effective in African territories with white settlers, to build up a "corporative" representation of racial communities and major economic groupings, in which not numbers but current social-economic importance received the heaviest weight.

The British and American colonial systems offered the most fertile ground for the introduction of democratic procedures and institutions, but other colonial powers, including Australia and New Zealand, were making moves in the same direction. In the Netherlands Indies the Dutch, during the interwar decades, undertook a tentative approach to democratization at several levels. The central legislative body which they established, the *Volksraad*, was, however, limited in power, heavily overweighted in representation for the Europeans, and only partially elective on an indirect basis. Its effectiveness was further limited by the repressive measures adopted to curb the nationalists and Communists and by the tendency of the Indonesian nationalists to follow Gandhian tactics of noncooperation; yet the mere existence of the *Volksraad* and of electoral procedures provided a rallying point for the nationalists who demanded a full measure of democratic independence.

Despite the revolutionary tradition of liberty and equality, the French colonies offered little in the way of democratic institutions. The centralized character of the French system and the predominant assumptions as to assimilation limited the readiness of the French authorities to endow their colonial territories with political institutions which had in them the makings of autonomous self-government. At best the French created advisory councils of a dubiously representative kind with some financial and administrative powers but little general legislative competence. Even in the drastically changed climate after World War II and under the 1946 constitution which in its preamble pledged France to guide her colonial wards "toward freedom to govern themselves and toward the democratic administration of their own affairs," there persisted a marked hesitation to encourage the growth of colonial autonomy. Basic French inclinations and principles made it difficult to endow colonial representative bodies with the broad authority which flowed more naturally from British and American conceptions.

As in virtually all phases of the colonial problem, so in relation to the spread of democratic institutions the most difficult and intractable situations have arisen wherever a substantial alien settler element exists. This is most evidently the case where the settler group is made up of Europeans drawn largely from the ruling imperial power. For the Europeans settled in any part of Africa, the effective democratic faith tends to be limited to their own community, and their claim to democratic self-government blocks the similar claims of the far more numerous native masses.[6] If the solution is sought in the formula of partnership, as in British East and Central Africa, then the question arises as to whether one or another community is the dominant partner, and whether the partnership is one between communities regarded as equal in weight and status, though vastly disparate in number, or between individuals, each counting for one regardless of race or communal attachment. The corresponding effort of European settlers to secure recognition of a principle of cosovereignty in the French protectorates of Tunisia and Morocco met with vehement nationalist rejection. Certainly a democracy which rests upon a foundation of racial inequality and discrimination is not one which can long be acceptable to Africans, nor can the cynical manipulation of elections, as in postwar Algeria, serve as a useful school for democratic procedures. Both Spain and France bear witness to the danger that the highhanded and autocratic attitudes of North African settlers may have serious repercussions at home.

Education in the political process was obviously not limited to direct participation in the quasi-parliamentary institutions introduced by the imperial authorities. It flowed also from the development of political parties and movements which were associated with the expansion of elective councils but sometimes preceded and outran them. Themselves derived in large part from Western models, these parties reached out to the mass of the people, organizing them for the often contradictory purposes of taking part in the councils and of carrying on the struggle against the colonial regime. The variety of political experience which the parties offered was no less valuable than that which could be derived from the councils and assemblies. From his association with the Philippines, where the United States rapidly established democratic institutions, Hayden came to the conclusion that it is in their political parties "that subject peoples find the freest sphere of political action," and that in the Philippines, until the establishment of the Commonwealth in 1935, the parties "were primarily the instruments of liberty rather than of government." [7] This latter comment points to one of the problematical aspects of colonial political parties: insofar as their role is limited to powerless criticism (which was not the case in the Philippines), or their own view of their role is that of a disloyal opposition, battling for the overthrow of the existing order, the experience which they can gain may be dangerously negative and of little use in fitting them for the positive task of carrying on a government. On the other hand, the mere fact of

organizing and managing their own political instrumentalities in-
troduces an autonomously creative element, absent by definition
from an authoritarian colonial system. Once self-government is
accepted as a goal, the formerly "disloyal" may collaborate effectively with the colonial authorities, as in the case of the Convention
People's Party in the Gold Coast.

Political parties have come to be recognized as a necessary part
of any functioning democracy, but it is evident that the quantity
and quality of democratic practice within them vary greatly. In
the present age the names, symbols, and proclaimed objectives of
parties are likely to have a strongly democratic cast. Their structure and operations may, however, diverge radically from acceptable democratic principles. In many instances in the colonies, the
party barely exists in an organized fashion beyond, perhaps, a
leader and a select corps of followers. The Communists have furnished the model of the close-knit conspiratorial party whose
"democratic centralism" puts power in the hands of the few at the
top. In societies whose past has given them little acquaintance with
democracy, parties are prone to yield to the temptation to pay not
much more than lip service to democratic pretensions; and the new
elites, controlling the parties, are likely to look with some scorn
upon the illiterate mass whose interests they claim to represent. It
is one of the ironies of the situation that the colonial administrator,
persuaded of his natural right to rule over the lesser breeds of men,
may find his sense of superiority rivaled by the patronizing attitude
the Westernized nationalist leader adopts toward his own people.
But with this fundamental difference: while the alien official refers
elsewhere for the source of his power, the nationalist must in large
part draw his power from the support of the mass, and as the mass
advances it will seek to make its voice heard.

Political parties offer an obvious channel for the two way communication which is involved in the democratic process — from
the leaders to the mass and vice versa. The more the political system
comes to center about an elected parliament, the greater is the
opportunity for the ordinary man to make his needs and wishes felt
through the party organization. The effectiveness of the party as a
vehicle of democratic education and practice is, however, sharply
limited where its working control is held in the hands of a small

elite, as has been the case for the bulk of the Asian and African parties and movements. The point may be illustrated by two disparate examples. Even in the relatively free atmosphere of the Philippines a handful of leaders dominated the center of the stage when it was not wholly occupied by Manuel Quezon; shifting party alignments depended primarily on personal rivalries and attachments; and, for the country at large, the old-established tradition of rule from above left little room for the rank and file. The author of a book on Moroccan political parties claims to have scandalized a young Moroccan nationalist by asking him the numerical strength of the *Parti Démocratique de l'Indépendance*. The answer was: "But that has no importance at all. The support of the Moroccan mass and even its opinion have no importance at all for the P. D. I.!" [8]

In addition to the introduction of elective assemblies, with their direct bearing on the emergence of parties, a number of other aspects of the colonial governmental process feed into the democratic stream. One is the creation of a rationalized administrative system patterned after Western models. By itself the creation of an honest, impartial, and efficient administration is, of course, not necessarily a steppingstone to democracy since such an administration may quite as well serve an autocratic regime, but without it the emergent democracies cannot hope to survive. Its democratic bearing becomes more evident when other features of its development are taken into account. The recruitment of the civil service on the basis of merit rather than of traditional status, the separation of the public purse and business from the person of the ruler and his immediate entourage, and the assumption that all the people are entitled to equal treatment under the rule of law work in their different fashions to establish conditions essential for democracy. As the "nativization" of civil services progresses, more and more of the local populace are drawn into association with the government and secure training in the conduct of a modern state, no longer wholly vested in a remote and alien bureaucracy well above their heads. On this score, again, the British and American practices have been superior to those of the French who have notoriously staffed the middle and even some of the lower ranks of the colonial service with Frenchmen rather than with people of the country; while the

Dutch in the Indies fell somewhere midway between the two approaches.

Indirect rule interposed special barriers to the rationalization of the administrative system and complicated the transition to a modern democratic framework. Nonetheless, a few unreconstructed champions of the Lugardian principles of indirect rule still see it as the only means of saving Africa from ruin, and for them, indeed, the fact that it stands in the way of rationalization and Western-style democratization is one of the major points to its credit. The belief that Africans can advance successfully only on the basis of their traditional institutions was emphatically stated by Lord Altrincham, who, as Sir Edward Grigg, was Governor of Kenya from 1925 to 1931. To him the real issue in Africa lay in choosing "between a policy which would build up democracy in Africa with African goodwill on ancient African foundations, and a policy which would Europeanize Africa and destroy the democracy natural to it." [9] He contended that only a political system which accepted a tribal base could express the African genius, enlist popular participation, and call out the best leadership. The projected African nation-states could hope to survive only if held together by ruthless despotisms; and it was such despotisms — single-party rule of the Nazi or Communist variety — which would be the result of the foisting off of a centralized "national" parliamentarism on peoples for whom it was entirely unfitted. From these premises Lord Altrincham concluded that what was needed was a return to the principles of indirect rule under which each tribe and community (in areas of white settlement, such as Kenya, this would be equally applicable to the Europeans) would be given the widest possible sphere of self-government, only the absolutely essential central services remaining in the hands of the central authorities.

Is it perhaps a relevant commentary on these proposals that the former Governor portrays the vast majority of Africans as not wanting Europe's sophisticated life, clotted with regulations, machinery, and international troubles?

> They want, the cheerful mass of them, health of body and freedom to improve their lot as their elders and they think best upon the land they love, in sunshine unbroken by angry clouds from Europe, at the deliberate pace that suits their easy-going natures.[10]

This is by no means a lowly goal, nor is his further hope that the mass may remain "blessedly immune from the mental and moral upheaval that the uncertain outside world has caused in a few of them"; but both the outside and the inside worlds have moved too far and too fast to make the survival of that immunity possible. A part of the price for immunity and unbroken sunshine is the perpetuation of the white domination which the Kenyattas, Mboyas, and Kianos have determined to end.

The Africans who rise to leadership are not likely to remain satisfied with the traditional versions of African democracy and its tribal setting. Undoubtedly the native administrations which indirect rule preserved have been useful training grounds in administration and, as they came to be equipped with elective councils, in democracy as well. It can be argued further that by accentuating distinctive local elements and communities, indirect rule has provided potential cores of resistance to the rise of a dictatorial power at the centre. For the nationalists to accept a return to the traditional institutions, however, would be close to a surrender of their own claims to power since they would necessarily be entering into competition on their rivals' home grounds. In addition, they would be abandoning their chance of demonstrating that they can run a democratic system at least as effectively as the imperialists whom they are ousting.

CHAPTER XIII

The Colonial Nationalist as Democrat

NATIONALISMS WHICH DEVELOP under colonial conditions tend to have substantially more democratic roots than those which emerge in comparable non-colonial countries, even though the roots often do not go down very deep. In addition to the direct influence of colonial institutions, two major elements are involved which reflect the characteristic differences between colonial and independent countries. In the first place, colonialism creates a situation in which new persons and groups are pushed to the fore at the expense of the older traditional elites and must seek a new title to legitimacy, and secondly, if the rising nationalist leaders are to have the political as well as the moral and ideological strength to challenge the imperial authorities they must achieve at least a plausible facsimile of a popular mass base.

The subjection of any people to colonial rule inevitably entails the pushing aside or subordination of its preexisting powers-that-be. This may be accomplished in a variety of ways, but generally one of two courses is followed, both of which by circuitous routes come out at substantially the same place. The former dominant elements in the country are either so nearly wiped out as effectively to remove them from the scene or they are so thoroughly tarred with the colonial brush and so dependent upon alien support as to render them valueless for nationalist purposes. In either circumstance leadership in the anti-colonial revolution must fall to other hands.

Although deviations can be found on both sides of the fence, the rule seems clearly to be that a colonial regime undercuts the prestige and power of the old-established elite more drastically than does the more diffuse and unspecific intrusion of the modern West through other than colonial channels. The dominant groups in countries retaining their independence have obviously not been left undisturbed by the combination of Western revolution and Western imperialism, but the key fact that they have not had an alien government imposed on them has greatly enhanced their chances of holding on to power, possessions, and privilege. The total disappearance of the royal house of Burma under British rule and the discarding of the Indian princes after independence are typical phenomena of colonialism, as are the fate of Bao Dai in Vietnam and the fading into the background of Indonesia's traditional rulers with the exception of Sultan Hamengku Buwono of Jogjakarta. The emergence of Sultan Mohammed ben Youssef as a national hero in Morocco is close to being a unique event in modern colonial annals, requiring for its accomplishment the special circumstances of the Moroccan protectorate, singular maladroitness on the part of the French who exiled him in 1953, and much labor by the Istiqlal to win popular national status for him. On a lesser scale the British achieved similar results in Uganda when they withdrew recognition from the Kabaka of Buganda, also in 1953, and banished him from his own country.

The variations on this theme which occur in the multifariousness of actual practice are, of course, immense: protectorates and indirect rule maintain traditional authorities in the colonial sphere, while revolutions and modernizing innovations displace them in states without a colonial experience. Particularly in Africa the game is only partly played out, and it is not yet fully demonstrated that the waning powers of the chiefs will end in their complete displacement. To mention only the British West African territories, as late as 1949 the Coussey Committee wrote of the Gold Coast that "the whole institution of chieftancy is so closely bound up with the life of our communities that its disappearance would spell disaster"; [1] and the emirs of Northern Nigeria continue to have a strong hold. But Nkrumah in Ghana and Touré in Guinea, coming to independence, have wasted little sympathy on the chiefs in their domains.

A striking degree of uniformity can still be found in the general colonial picture, however. It is a rare event when the leadership of the anti-colonial, nationalist movement lingers in the hands of those who formerly held power. Unless destroyed or gravely crippled in the original imperial take-over, they are indeed the ones who lead the first round of resistance to alien encroachment, seeking to preserve the old society and their status in it. But when this round has come to its usually futile end, they are replaced by the newly risen, Westernized elements who take the lead in the drive for independence and modernization. The vanished member of the royal or aristocratic clan is no longer on the scene, and the prince, sultan, or chief whose continued majesty has rested upon subservience to the colonial authorities is regarded as one who has collaborated with the enemy. The king of Cambodia who abandoned his throne in 1955 to lead his party to victory in a national election signally stands out among his royal brethren. The explanation is to be sought not in the normal circumstances of colonialism, but in the facts that Cambodia was maintained as a protectorate, that it was relatively little developed by the French, and that King Norodom Sihanouk himself was a product of Western education and a man whose elevation to the throne was something of an accident of French policy.

Another country in which royalty has survived and the reigning families have adapted themselves to the nationalist era is Malaya. Here the Sultans retain their thrones and, under the 1957 constitution, elect one of their number as Supreme Head of the Federation. Malay political leadership has been drawn almost exclusively from the traditional governing class, as in the case of the two successive heads of the United Malay National Organization, Dato Onn bin Jafaar, British-educated member of the Johore aristocracy, and Tengku Abdul Rahman, brother of the Sultan of Kedah, British-trained lawyer, and first Prime Minister of independent Malaya. The answer is again to be sought in such special circumstances as that the British deliberately fostered the preservation of the Malay states and their established institutions, and, of even greater importance, that the Malay community has only belatedly and hesitantly entered into the modern world. The presumption must be that as the Malays develop their own middle class and intelligentsia and become more largely urbanized, a shift in internal power relationships will be inevitable. A similar shift will no doubt occur within the Chinese community as its lower strata are enfranchised, challenging the power of the well-to-do and generally conservative elements which have controlled the Malayan Chinese Association.

The Asian and African countries which retained their independence are inevitably a motley assortment of states, to be lumped together for the present purpose only because of the common negative trait of the absence of long-continued colonialism. If all have felt the breath of imperialism in varying degree, their common freedom from colonial rule has, nonetheless, enabled them to maintain their older political and social structure more nearly intact than the colonial countries. Even the rise to power of an upstart Reza Shah in Iran, seeking to force the modernization of his country in one great revolutionary spurt like Ataturk, was not enough to dislodge the established aristocrats, landowners, religious leaders, and tribal heads. His neighbor, Amanullah, made less headway still with reform in Afghanistan. Although Saudi Arabia, Yemen, and Ethiopia stand out in the absolutism which their rulers have anachronistically maintained, it is characteristic of the countries which have survived in independence that their privileged and propertied elites have often survived as well.

In the colonial setting the rising Westernized middle class elements have generally been able to take a clear political lead,[2] while similar groups in the non-colonial countries have had to make their peace with the still powerful elements of the old regime. It is evident that no black-and-white opposition between the two situations can be established. In colonial areas the men who have come into the Western orbit are sometimes the sons of the families which made up the older elite, while in non-colonial countries the traditional leading groups embrace a constantly increasing number of men who have had experience abroad and have received their education in Western schools and universities. They are usually wealthy enough to give their children a Western style of schooling and perhaps to send them overseas to make the grand tour and finish off their higher education. The prestige of the West has ensured that the opportunity is seized: the royal family and aristocrats of Thailand, the leading families of Iran and the Arab countries, and numbers of African chiefs, as well as countless others of lesser degree, have all recognized that contact with the West was an essential ingredient in the advancement of their children.

In all non-Western countries there is a clear and present danger that those who move over into the Western sphere will be infected by the prevalent germs of freedom, democracy, egalitarianism, and Marxism in one or another of its guises, but the attitude toward such infection is likely to be radically different in the non-colonial as contrasted with the colonial setting. In independent countries the established dominant elements continued to profit from a perpetuation of the old scheme of things; in the colonies, power and a large slice of the profits passed into alien hands. Furthermore, in the former case the title of the ruling groups to legitimacy remained unimpaired, at least as far as direct imperial attack on it was concerned, whereas the imposition of colonial rule profoundly disturbed the preëxisting system of legitimacy. In net effect, the colonial situation easily swings in a radical or revolutionary direction, while in the countries which maintained independence conservatism is at a premium. The colonial aspirant to power and privilege, as well as the idealist who repudiates imperialism, must see the "dangerous thoughts" of freedom and democracy as his allies. The leading groups in an independent country, on the other hand, however much they may be intellectually persuaded of the ultimate value of freedom and democracy, must see them as threats to the pattern of society which has put them where they are. It is alleged that Afghan students sent abroad for study are summoned by the government on their return and "warned, in effect, that they must forget any foreign ways they had learned and that they would be carefully watched in the future." [3]

In the dependencies an appeal to the masses for support against the alien few on top is the logical outcome of the situation; in independent countries a nationalist appeal to the people runs the risk of toppling the whole house down on the heads of the ruling few. It is asking too much of human nature to suggest that the response should be the same where the cards are so differently stacked.

Against this background one can easily see why colonial nationalist movements have so uniformly been cast in the democratic mold in contrast to the more aristocratic drift in countries not subjected to the peculiar pressures of colonialism. On the assumption that the imposition of colonial rule works to kill off the political efficacy of status in the traditional society, anyone who would challenge the imperial authority must build up both a new style of legitimacy and a new base of political power. Since a major ground for attack on the colonial authorities is that they do not derive from or represent the people they govern, the nationalists are necessarily concerned to establish their own popular base. It is in their asserted capacity as spokesmen for the national mass that the nationalist leaders find the justification for their demand to supersede the colonial rulers, and in their ability actually to command mass support they gather the political strength which makes their cause ultimately irresistible.

The necessity of seeking mass support is, however, by no means always recognized in the early stages of colonial nationalism. Indeed, the more frequent opening move is the creation of organizations which combine some of the characteristics of a study club, a debating society, and a genteel political party or pressure group. The leading figures in such organizations are likely to be men in the first generations of those to secure Western education, with a strong sprinkling of lawyers among them, who see their knowledge of the West as having peculiar values and virtues. Being a select few, they tend also to cherish their association with the alien governing elements to whom they are closer than the rest of their less privileged compatriots. They incline to hold themselves aloof from the mass and to assume that they are the proper custodians of the future, but in relation to their white superiors they remain burdened with the sense of inferiority which is so standard a product of colonialism. Far from driving to amass political power and to whip up public sentiment through demagogic appeals for a nationalist overturn of the colonial order, they seek to appeal rather in rational and constitutional terms, demonstrating that they are responsible persons rightly to be entrusted with a share in colonial management.

Thus in Burma in 1917 the chairman of the annual meeting of the Young Men's Buddhist Association, a forerunner of Burmese nationalism, pointed out the benefits of British rule and prayed that it would last forever.

We speak English and appreciate the Western way of life. We consider it a privilege and an honour to serve our rulers. We are gentlemen.[4]

The speeches of Caseley Hayford, a British-educated lawyer who was one of the outstanding early political leaders of the Gold Coast, admirably illustrate the position. Speaking at a meeting in London in 1920 as a delegate of the National Congress of British West Africa, he opened by reciting a resolution of the Congress which affirmed its policy of maintaining inviolate West Africa's connection with the British Empire. The men who promoted the Congress, he asserted, were "all men of responsibility," anxious to do things constitutionally. Mildly protesting that "it would not be accurate to say we were a primitive people emerging from barbarism," he appealed to "responsible authority to extend to us a certain amount of freedom in the government of our own country." [5]

The usual failure of such men to get an effective hearing for their case through rational argument and persuasion leads them or their immediate successors to the next phase, the effort to create mass parties or movements presenting a more radical challenge to empire. The democracy which they originally feared or scorned, save as a remote ideal, comes to be a political necessity for their further advance, and they are increasingly pressed from the rear as the society itself undergoes transformation. The process of social mobilization reaches beyond this tiny urban elite to lower middle class elements, the newly forming proletariat, and in due course the rural peasantry. Where the franchise is extended or universalized the appeal to the populace at large becomes inescapable, while the improvement of communications draws in a larger number of people and makes it possible to reach and organize them.

In India both the Congress and the Moslem League in their younger days represented this earlier type of quiet and urbane political activity, each protesting its loyalty to the established regime. It was not until the close of the First World War that either began to move significantly in the direction of the masses. In pre-1914 Indonesia, Boedi Oetomo, devoted to popular education and economic advance, and Sarekat Islam, aimed more against the Chinese than the Dutch, represented roughly comparable movements which only later turned to serious political operations. In the Gold Coast much the same phenomenon is found in the Aborigines Rights Protection Society, founded in 1897, the West African National

Congress after World War I, and even in the United Gold Coast Convention in 1947, so shortly to be overturned by Kwame Nkrumah. As contrasted with the role of Herbert Macaulay, "father of Nigerian nationalism" in the 1920's, the activities of Azikiwe who succeeded him in the later 1930's marked a similar development in Nigeria. One commentator has characterized the nationalism of the West Coast of Africa prior to World War II as "the esoteric pastime of the tiny educated minority of Lagos, Accra, Freetown, and Dakar," in contrast to the later efforts to popularize and energize the nationalist crusade.[6] The turning point in nationalist development, away from an elitist acceptance of the foundations of the colonial system and toward a radical affirmation of democratic challenge, comes as the Western educated handful grow in numbers and confidence, as they are joined by labor leaders and others, and as they come to increasing awareness that a restrained and responsible nationalism is unlikely to carry the day. It is characteristic of the new day that Tom Mboya of Kenya and Sékou Touré of Guinea should both have risen as labor leaders.

Although the evidence is too scanty to allow of any reliable forecast, the general trend in Asia and African countries appears to be in the direction of a continued narrowing of the gap between leaders and people. The political base is being widened in the sense that more people are rising to take some share in the political process and at the same time the door has been opened to the emergence of leaders with less Western education and orientation. In India, for example, the numerically superior but less educated lower castes as they come up in the world are cutting in on the political sway of the higher castes. What is happening, it has been suggested, is that the lower castes are taking over political control in much the same fashion as the immigrant nationalities — Irish, Italian, Polish, etc. — pushed aside the reigning Anglo-Saxon elite to establish their predominance in the politics of many American cities.[7] A similar elevation of formerly submerged elements is taking place in many other countries. Over the next decades both the face and the substance of political life are sure to be drastically changed, but one can have no confidence that the change will bring an effective extension of democracy, except, perhaps, in some plebiscitary sense. The role of the rising masses, still largely illiterate and politically inexperienced, may prove to embrace not much more than the right to say "yes" after having been duly indoctrinated. The political evolution of the more advanced Arab states, Edward Atiyah has remarked, "has been along the lines of a lame and stumbling democracy helped by military dictatorship." [8] The recent overturns in a number of the new states make it clear that it is not only in the Arab countries that democracy is unable to sustain itself as the mobilization of the masses gets under way.

It was part of my earlier argument that one of the factors which has promoted the democratic aspect of colonial nationalism has been the democratic background of the imperial powers themselves and the adumbrations of democratic institutions which they installed in their dependencies. This contention requires counterbalancing by another and basically contradictory aspect of colonialism which curiously works to the same end. In essence this is that, until very recent years, the colonial authorities have normally been concerned to hold on to power, and that nothing (save the whole process of development and modernization) so gravely threatens their position as the admission of democratic devices into the colonial political structure. Once it is conceded that the people are entitled to a significant share in the running of their own affairs, a wedge is introduced which will inevitably be hammered further in to separate the expatriate administrator from the community he governs.

In the version least flattering to the colonial official this is to say that he is the possessor of power to which he is prepared to cling by fair means or foul. In an equally realistic version, he feels that he has a job to do, the accomplishment of which is likely to be defeated by admitting to a share in power persons whose claim to participate comes from their being representatives of the people. Obviously such a line of argument is quite unacceptable if a substantial part of the job to be done is seen as the introduction of democratic self-government. In that circumstance the consultation of the people and the election of their representatives to positions of consequence is itself the fulfillment of the job; but this goal, as a working proposition, has been an infrequent one until the last decades. Even where it has been accepted, it has usually been with deep reluctance on the part of colonial administrations which have felt that their paternalistic management of a society still incompetent to manage itself would surely be impaired. In the Philippines, despite the American commitment to granting independence to a democratized country, the Commonwealth period found some American officials dismayed to surrender to Filipino control the system they had constructed to meet their interpretation of Philippine needs. It is the rare bureaucrat who welcomes the intrusion of the people at large to tell him what he should do and how he should do it. In this respect the colonial bureaucracy differs from any other bureaucracy only to the extent that it is less subject to local popular checks and that it regards itself as particularly superior in wisdom and experience to the people it governs.

Even though the colonial administrator may concede in some circumstances that he can gain from the presence of a representative body through which he can spread his program to wider circles and from which he can learn of popular grievances and desires, such a body is likely to come up with disturbing ideas of its own — particularly disturbing if it is equipped with power to do something about them. A chief or a rajah can be cajoled, persuaded, or pushed into compliance; an elected council is an almost impossible instrument for rule from above. Furthermore, a colonial government is subject to orders from home; with the recognition of democratic institutions in the dependency it finds itself caught between two fires, neither of which it can control. The colonial administrator, either lustful for power or out to do his job efficiently with a minimum of disturbance, is likely both to seek autonomy from home control and to ward off as long as possible the local politician and the popularly elected bodies from which the latter draws his most telling support. Since the prime ethical justification for the expatriate official's existence is that he knows better than the people themselves what they need, it can only upset applecarts if they start to speak with their own voice. This is all the more the case when their elected spokesmen are, as normally happens, persons whose representative character the official profoundly distrusts and disputes. The people whom a colonial administration would pick out as proper collaborators are rarely those whom the populace itself would freely elect, as the British have regularly found in moving from appointed to elected Legislative Councils. The corresponding

moral can easily be drawn by the nationalist opponents of the colonial government: if they can establish a popular mandate for their
claim to power, it becomes both difficult and dangerous to keep
them from the seats of the mighty. The colonial administrator is
inevitably in some measure the prisoner of the democratic ethos
which he represents but whose concrete application he has normally tried to postpone until some remote future.

Particularly in the last decades the imperial authorities have
introduced far too much in the way of democratic institutions to
justify any blanket charge that they have stood solely for a bureau-
cratic autocracy, but the more typical attitude has been that colonial officials should keep power in their own hands in order to carry
on the work of government. On this basis there was sound sense in
the earlier British assumption that the classic Crown Colony device
of an official majority must be kept intact if the ability to control
were to be kept commensurate with the responsibility to govern.
Once the elective principle has been accepted, the ways are greased
for a speedy and almost wholly irretrievable descent into the open
waters of self-government or independence. Safeguards and checks
may be introduced at a number of points in the new constitutional
machinery, but when the will of a majority has manifested itself
through recognized channels, they are unlikely to prove effective.
British experience has shown the reserved powers of governors and
other imperial authorities to be practically unavailable under ordinary conditions, and even in time of crisis they can be drawn upon
only at the cost of grave political and constitutional conflict. The
drastic reversal in 1953 of the constitutional advance which had
been made in British Guiana illustrates the possibility of reimposing
checks upon an achieved self-government, but it also emphasizes
the heavy price which must be paid. In the case of the Philippines,
the efforts of the Republicans, returned to power in Washington
in 1921, to reverse the concessions granted by President Wilson and
Governor-General Harrison caused a series of political deadlocks
and served only to delay for a few years the surge toward a complete Filipino take-over of the government. As contrasted with
British parliamentary conceptions, the American constitutional
system of a separation of powers renders somewhat more tolerable
a cleavage between appointed executive and elected legislature, but

nowhere can there be a long-continued conflict within the same government between two more or less equal sets of authorities deriving their power from totally different sources. In Okinawa the United States has run head on into trouble by trying to combine the autocratically determined needs of a great military base with a political system based in part on democratic elections.

To challenge the will of the elected representatives of the people is to run counter to the fundamental contemporary presumption of the sovereignty of the people. As it is the strategy of the nationalist to invoke this sovereignty on his behalf, so it must very frequently be the strategy of the colonial authorities to manipulate in such fashion as to evade its emergence in any active and formal guise.

In its standard form every colonial administration consists primarily of the hierarchy of officials who are shaping and executing policy. It is essentially an authoritarian system in which power flows from the top and from the outside. Even though its lower ranks and perhaps its middle range as well are staffed largely by local people, these as well as the expatriates at the top derive their legitimacy not from the people of the country they rule but from the external authority of the imperial government to which they are responsible. The record shows that officials of local origin have given their loyalty to the colonial government or to the service itself and have associated themselves in outlook with their alien superiors or have at least maintained political neutrality. This was strikingly exemplified in the Philippines in 1923 when the five Filipino members of the Cabinet resigned in the course of the conflict with Governor-General Wood over the reassertion of strong American control. For three and a half years Wood carried on the government through the permanent administrative officials who stayed at their posts and abstained from the political battle, enabling him to report that "the government moved on smoothly without interruption in any of its functions." [9]

Even though the local civil servants are by education and background usually the kind of people whom one would otherwise expect to find enlisted in the nationalist movement, their general tendency has been to stand aloof from it and to view it with some of the same suspicion as do their imported fellow officials. The men who have been most successful in their official careers are likely to grant the colonial system the largest measure of acceptance or tolerance. They become imbued with the morale of the service and look askance at those who seek to take over a government without firsthand administrative experience. In the accustomed fashion of the bureaucrat, they, like the expatriate officials, have grave doubts as to the ability of the people to know their needs and manage their affairs. The over-all consequence is, of course, that the local civil servants are often viewed with suspicion by the nationalists.

Where the colonial system rests upon indirect rule the situation is similar although with added complications. The same basic consideration is involved: there is a job to be done and the colonial official wants to be in a position to do it. Under indirect rule, however, it must be done with, through or around the traditional authority whose status has secured official recognition and who must somehow be brought within the working ambit of the system. It is a commonplace of the history of indirect rule in Africa that the Europeans regularly attributed to the chief a greater measure of royal omnipotence than was traditionally accorded him by native custom. In part, no doubt, this derived from the fact that the white man brought with him conceptions of royalty derived from European experience, but it also fitted well with the needs and convenience of the European officials who had to work with the chief. The diffused authority of a complex of elders, councils, and popular approval was an unhandy and perhaps a balky instrument through which to get things done, whereas the concentrated authority of a chief was relatively easy to manipulate — and if the particular chief proved recalcitrant, a more pliant successor could be installed.

The chief himself obviously had several angles to consider. At the outset the paramount fact was presumably that he had a colonial government imposed upon him and that white officials intervened in his affairs. But as time reconciled him to the fundamental change, he also found compensations. If his substantive power had largely passed into other hands, the formal range of his authority was often enhanced, he was protected in his style and dignity by the mighty imperial regime which had taken over, and, if he proved complaisant and reasonably effective, he was protected against the rivals who sought to dislodge him. The criterion of his ability to retain his rule could easily become the extent to which he pleased his colonial superiors rather than the satisfaction which he gave his people.[10]

With the rise of new elements in the society, including the Western-educated, new threats to both chiefs and colonial authorities began to appear. Basing themselves on the contention that the chiefs were an anachronistic force, the rising groups sought both to take over in the colonial hierarchy and to temper or, before long, to replace the power of the chief through the installation of elective councils.[11] They were confident that not only would democracy be served thereby but also that the democracy they wanted to call into being would recognize the justice of their own claims to power. In this triangular situation it is easy to see why the chiefs and the colonial officials should frequently have formed an alliance of mutual support against the newcomers. In entering such an alliance the chiefs, of course, opened themselves to continued charges that they had abandoned their proper position as leaders of their people to become mere agents of the colonial administration, as, in fact, they had to a considerable degree everywhere, and particularly in the way they were used by the French. It took no great shrewdness on the part of the chief to recognize that it was the colonial government which buttered his bread. Indeed, in the later stages, it might well be that he owed to the protecting authority even the survival of the chiefly institution, as the Indian princes survived only under the British wing.

For both chiefs and colonial officials there were corrupting aspects in this relationship. For the chief it meant subservience to the alien authority, perhaps at the expense of his people in such matters as the provision of a labor supply for white employers and more generally in the sense of an abdication of his individual and institutional judgment. In the case of the official it meant that he tended to align himself with reactionary elements in the society just at the time when the forces for change were beginning to come into prominence. In somewhat paradoxical fashion, the colonial official, who was willy-nilly the agent of the alien revolution which had been thrust upon the community, now joined with the chief and his entourage to bolster up the old order. For

some, prisoners of the dogmas of indirect rule, the maintenance
of an increasingly anachronistic traditional society tended to become an end in itself. This was, of course, not the case in the
many instances where the colonial authorities modified the structure of traditional authority through the introduction of elective
councils or other modernizing devices, or where their desire for
change and development clearly outran the ability of the old order
to satisfy it. As far as the British are concerned, in the last decade
or two the turn has been in the direction of "a realistic decision to
withdraw British support from the declining chiefly interest, and
transfer it to the rising African middle class and the new educated
elite." [12] The temptation was always present, however, to maintain the status quo against clamorous parvenus by forming a united
front with the chiefs. Wherever this happened the slogans of democracy, reform, and advance were likely to become the property
of the nationalists.

The issues involved here by no means relate solely to tropical
Africa, where the formalized conceptions of indirect rule originated, nor are they limited to the sphere of local administration to
which British practice has tended to confine the operation of native
authorities. The Malay Sultans who served to bolster both British
and Malays against the demands of the Chinese, the regents and
other native authorities of the Netherlands Indies, and the Indian
princes have all been utilized for the same purposes and found
themselves in similar situations. In Tunisia and Morocco the turn of
events was a peculiarly interesting one which lent itself, with a
little adroit manipulation, to the charge that democratic France
was the backer of autocratic monarchism whereas the absolute
Moslem rulers were the protagonists of democracy. The argument
in North Africa followed the same lines as elsewhere. Even apart
from the desire of Lyautey to preserve and work through the
established political and social structure of Morocco, French administrators inevitably found it more convenient to exercise their
control through, or, more accurately, in the name of, a single ruler
in each country than to complicate their lives by the creation of
popular assemblies which would become alternative centers of
power. The need to safeguard the rulers against the nationalist
threat to their royal prerogatives was paraded as a ground for the

denial of the democratic institutions which the rulers themselves had been persuaded to endorse. Given the close link in the two protectorates between the French administrations and the European communities established in them, the only type of democracy which the former would seriously contemplate was one in which the Europeans secured a factual predominance; but this involved a co-sovereignty which was politically unfeasible and violated the conception of a protectorate. In consequence, the slogans of democracy passed into the hands of the opponents of the French regime.[13] In this instance, however, the rulers as well broke with their alien protectors. The Sultan and the Bey, no doubt to their surprise and perhaps to their dismay, found that they had become the champions and symbols of a democratic movement which would substitute the sovereignty of the nations they headed for the supremacy of France. As a French writer put it:

> While a democratic state defended in Morocco monarchic and theocratic principles which were alien to it, the heirs of these principles, on the other, laid claim to the assimilation of democratic institutions in total opposition to their traditions.[14]

Of the depth, vitality, and staying-power of the democratic convictions of the Neo-Destour, the Istiqlal, and other North African parties there may well be legitimate doubt, but their success in capturing a monopoly on the claim to democratic virtue is unquestionable. That the French administration in Morocco should have been maneuvered into the position of embracing as reactionary a figure as El Glaoui as its principal ally only underlined the disastrous implications of the policy into which it had drifted.

CHAPTER XIV

Nationalism and Democracy in Non-Colonial Countries

T HE COLONIAL STAGE, as we have seen, has been so set as to tempt, or even to force, the rising leaders to create a mass base from which to operate, even though the resulting democratic institutions might prove short-lived. In the comparable non-colonial countries strong pressures have worked in the reverse directions: the surviving beneficiaries of the *ancien régime*, or some approximation of it, could call the masses into action only at the risk of their own necks. The democratic implications of nationalism were there for those who chose to read them, but the powerful and privileged in the countries which evaded colonialism have been tempted to ignore them as long as possible.

It is, of course, evident that the modern democratic tides have no more passed the latter countries wholly by than they have engulfed the countries with full-scale Western colonial experience. In their different fashions both sets of countries have been exposed to many of the same disturbing forces, and, in both, economic and other internal changes have brought about the emergence of nationalist elements with a leaning in democratic directions. Although the Western influence has normally been less direct in states which retained their independence, their leaders, like those in the colonies, have had the world prestige of democracy thrust upon them. Even where the people have been denied any significant share in power, old-style autocracy has not infrequently seen fit to parade itself in the outward dress of democratic institutions and may also, like the colonial nationalists, have found it politically expedient to seek a measure of popular support in the effort to throw off alien encroachment or win international favor.

Ever since the French Revolution first presented Europe with the challenge of a nation in arms, nondemocratic societies have been confronted by a peculiarly painful dilemma. The issue was then posed for Europe's monarchies and aristocracies, and most menacingly for the multinational Hapsburg Empire, as to whether it might be possible to enlist popular support in the war against France and yet maintain the established monopoly of power and privilege. In the succeeding century and a half the ruling groups in many countries have faced the same basic problem of seeking to tap the strength of the democratic and national revolutions without paying the revolutionary price.

JAPAN AND CHINA

There is no country whose effort to resolve this dilemma holds a larger measure of fascination than does that of Japan. Among the non-European peoples the Japanese stand out uniquely not only in the extent and success of their adaptation to industrialism but also in the mode of their transition to the modern national age. To an unprecedented and still unrivaled degree the Japanese leaders succeeded in achieving what might legitimately be regarded as the impossible: to impose from above a sweeping revolution which brought into being all the forces which characteristically promote democratic upheaval and yet to maintain the people in disciplined obedience.

Japan furnishes the ideal sample of a country besieged from without by Western pressures but not yet seriously penetrated by them, in which the established elite turns to nationalist symbols and slogans for defense against the mounting attack. It moved, however, far beyond the mere manipulation of such symbols and slogans: the Japanese nation was in actuality most effectively mobilized — ultimately in a literal sense which spelled its own ruin — to lend mass backing to the policies and purposes of those who wielded power.

In contrast to the standard colonial pattern Japan's swing toward Westernization cannot be attributed to the typical Western-educated intelligentsia or to a middle class brought into being by alien intrusion. In Japan these were the products and not the creators of the new era, although the old Japanese society was of its own motion producing somewhat similar elements. Some limited circles in the country had achieved a substantial degree of acquaintance with the West, but the closed feudal society of the Tokugawa era certainly had not been sufficiently disrupted by alien forces and ideas to compel the revolution which set the country on a new path. The changes which were taking place in Japan prior to the shock of Perry's appearance were essentially a response to the autonomous development of maladjustments and of altered social relations within the Japanese system itself. If they gave a new importance to groups such as the lower samurai and the merchants which could take the lead in the forced drive to erect defences against the imperialist threat, this was a turn of events not to be explained in terms of the prior intrusion of the West. It was not the already Westernized who spearheaded the national revolution, but offshoots of the old Japan who speedily came to the conclusion that the barbarians could only be expelled by turning their own weapons against them. That the late Tokugawa society should have produced a body of men able to take over as the crisis developed was Japan's good fortune. In the decade or two after 1868 the lower samurai, who led both the Meiji Restoration and the swing of Japan into the modern world, became advocates of Westernization, drawing heavily upon such key Western thinkers as Montesquieu, Rousseau, John Stuart Mill, and Herbert Spencer. In the distinctive setting of Japan these rising leaders were the equivalent of the Westernized intelligentsia of other parts of Asia who engineered their own nationalist revolutions. Where the Japanese outshone their counterparts in other non-colonial countries was in their grasp of the basic issues and in their determination to see the job through to a swift and coherent conclusion. That the Japanese social scene of the middle nineteenth century differed in significant respects from that of other countries confronted by the identical challenge has been elaborately established by later scholars, but in their own day these differences must have seemed far less evidently designed to serve as a bridge to the twentieth-century Japan which actually emerged.

Warned by China's helplessness in the face of Western power, the oligarchs of the Meiji period who had displaced their Tokugawa predecessors fashioned a country which preserved much of its past and yet was able to achieve a massive adaptation to the needs of a threatening and swiftly changing world. Although the Japanese people were deliberately roused to a passionate devotion to their national heritage and to a sense of their all-embracing duty to the nation, the explosive potential of a democratic nationalism, if not of a militant ultranationalism, was held firmly in check. In the new Japan the nation, with the Emperor restored as its supreme symbol, was raised to exalted place, but the transformation was enforced from above and the management of national affairs was reserved to the few at the top.[1]

Although the Imperial Oath of 1868, laying out the principles of the new government, seemed to point in a democratic direction with its pledge of the convocation of an assembly and its stress on public discussion, it does not appear that the dominant oligarchy was in fact at any time prepared to share its power with the people at large despite the very real interest which many of its members had taken in the principles of Western liberalism. The constitution of 1889, prepared in secret by the inner circle and unchanged until 1947, issued as an act of grace from the Emperor's sovereignty and preserved executive predominance over the popularly elected branch of the legislature. As Hugh Borton has put it, the constitution "created a political paradox — a parliamentary form of government, yet one in which the Emperor and his advisers retained autocratic control."[2] While the state, the economy, and the society at large were revolutionized by massive borrowings from the West, the consequent mobilization of the masses was denied anything approaching full democratic expression. Even the political parties which came into being gave only faint encouragement to mass participation and never fulfilled their democratic promise. In the early stages they were reduced to impotence by the principle of "transcendental cabinets," standing above the partisan fray, and later, in the period of party cabinets, were deeply compromised by the policies of corruption and infiltration adopted by the oligarchy and bureaucracy. For those excluded from the charmed circle a rise to power could be achieved only by a series of deals and compromises with those who were in it.

It was still necessary, however, for the ruling elite to make its peace in some fashion with the masses both in order to attain the vitally needed national solidarity and in order to guide the rising popular forces into acceptable channels. In his study of democracy in Japan, Robert A. Scalapino suggests that nationalism itself, brought into being by agrarian-military elements and dominated by symbols drawn from a primitive Japanese traditionalism, served the ruling group as a means of bringing the people into line. The place of democracy was taken by an elitist tutelage of the masses which utilized the modern instruments of mass communications and an educational system devised to teach the people their place in the mystical Japanese national polity and way of life.[3]

Within the dominant oligarchy itself, reënforced by the rise and coöption into it of elements deriving from the new Japan, serious conflicts often broke out, but the major contenders, such as the elder statesmen, the military, the bureaucracy, the industrialists, and even for the most part the party leaders, were rarely, if ever, prepared to undertake a large-scale appeal to the populace at large. Although the will of the nation, mystically embodied in the sovereign will of the Emperor, was to be the guiding star, the concrete formulation of the content of that will rested with the ruling circles. It remained the essence of the system that legitimacy flowed from the top down and was not bestowed by the favor of the people. In 1932 the hesitant approaches to liberal democracy of the preceding decade were swept away by the rise of ultra-nationalism and militarism — a counterpart but by no means a copy of the Fascist-Nazi surge in Europe. The defeat of 1945 and the American occupation reopened the door to democratic experimentation. How widely or permanently the door will be open is still unclear. Under the MacArthur-inspired constitution the Emperor lost his sovereignty and was reduced by its first Article to "deriving his position from the will of the people with whom resides sovereign power," but it was not long before Japanese voices were lifted to protest this violation of immemorial tradition.

In neighboring China the development of nationalism took a very different turn from that of Japan. Where Japan exemplifies, in its own unique fashion, the model of the non-colonial country, China somewhat curiously comes closer to fitting the colonial model. The heart of the matter is that in China's case, as typically

in the colonial countries, Western penetration had made deep in-
roads prior to the appearance of nationalism, while Japanese nationalism was rather a response to the external Western threat. In
consequence, China's nationalism found its stronghold in the new
Westernized middle class and the students whereas Japan drew
its nationalist leadership from elements more closely identified with
the old regime. It would, however, be easy to overstress this point of
contrast since the Chinese nationalists were in fact largely of
scholar-gentry background and hence associated with the former
ruling class. In Japan the lower samurai, on the other hand, had
little share in power prior to the Meiji Restoration and were genuinely in revolt against many features of the old order. Japanese
nationalism, despite the liberal currents which also flowed into it,
was predominantly authoritarian and elitist, while that of China
tended, colonial-style, to take on a revolutionary democratic cast.

To the absorbing question as to the causes of this immense
difference in development much attention has been devoted, and
if no complete answer is possible, a number of significant guide
posts have been established. Presumably the starting point for any
such inquiry must be the basic contrast between a vast and loose-
jointed Chinese empire, regarding its age-old civilization as the self-
sufficient world center, and a small and more compact Japan which
had already borrowed heavily from abroad and was aware that
it was only one people among many which existed in the world.
In terms of this contrast it is arguable that the transition to acceptance of the fundamental facts of life in an age in which nation confronted nation was a far easier spiritual and intellectual task for
the Japanese than for the Chinese. For the former it could be in
large measure an adaptation of well-established conceptions; for
the latter to reach a similar position a profound reorientation of
the entire *Weltanschauung*, ingrained through the millennia, was
required.

In a more manageable frame of reference, the particular circumstances of the two countries in the nineteenth century can be
drawn upon to explain why Chinese nationalism should have taken
a turn more closely akin to the typical colonial pattern. The first
and most obvious circumstance is that it makes sense to apply the
term "quasi-colonial" to China but not to Japan. From the middle

of the century China was teetering increasingly dangerously on the edge of the colonial abyss, and this produced close similarities between the Chinese situation and that which has been noted in colonial areas, particularly where colonialism was of the protectorate-indirect rule variety.

It is of importance that in Japan the throne was occupied by a native dynasty which could be used as the central symbol of national reconstruction in a fashion barred to China's alien Manchu dynasty. The Japanese Emperor served as the rallying point for the forces which sought to modernize Japan, whereas the Manchu regime effectively blocked China's passage into the modern world. Clinging to the ancient and intricate patterns of Chinese culture which it had adopted, the latter played a disastrous double game of trying at once to guard the country against foreign imperialist encroachment and to make deals with the imperialists when it was threatened domestically by recurrent waves of rebellion. Unable and unwilling to appeal to the still inchoate nation for mass support, it turned reluctantly to the foreigners who found it on the whole more expedient to work with the established order than to run the risks involved in collaborating with the rising popular forces. To the enemies of national regeneration must be added the principal instrument through which the Manchus ruled, the Chinese mandarinate — a scholar bureaucracy which "had become the jealous guardian of Confucian orthodoxy." [4] The deep commitment of this body of officialdom to the old order, including the traditional examination system to which it owed its peculiar essence, served to seal it off from the reformers and the nationalists.

In Japan lower levels of the old elite which had been excluded from power in the Tokugawa era moved swiftly and successfully to take over the government and to avert the disaster either of disintegration or of foreign conquest. In China the government made revolution inevitable by seeking to dam up the change which foreign intrusion brought with it. Unable to stall off the West and even suffering a singularly humiliating defeat by Japan in 1895, it likewise became less and less able to cope with the growing dislocation of Chinese society. If there were to be salvation, it must be sought in some other quarter. In China, as in the colonial areas, imperialism produced its own corrective in the new groups which it pushed to the fore. The old order discredited, the new must be brought into being by men who had achieved an acquaintance with some of the sources of power of the West; and, as in the colonies, both their legitimacy and their political strength must in large measure be derived from the people. The situation was further complicated for the Chinese by the fact that, in contrast to Japan, their national response was long delayed and did not effectively begin to operate before the last years of the nineteenth century and the opening of the twentieth. Indeed, it was not until the rising of May 4, 1919, directed against Western concessions to Japan in the peace settlement, that Chinese nationalism began to reach out into the masses of the people.

In the opening stages many of the reformers cherished the hope that the existing regime might be utilized to make the transition, but even this group assumed that the people must somehow be introduced into the process. Thus Wang K'ang-nien, looking to the political systems of the West, contended that democracy would make the nation the people's concern and would strengthen the Emperor's authority, bringing thousands of ears and myriads of eyes into play, enabling him to withstand the foreigner:

> In general, when the power of the empire comes from one person, it is weak. When it comes from millions of people, it is strong. . . . If people of all provinces are united to plan for a thing, then the spirit of the nation is integrated; otherwise, divided.[5]

Similarly, Liang Ch'i-ch'ao, a more influential publicist also associated with the Reform Movement of 1898, found the reason for European development and world progress to lie in "the stimulation and growth of extensive nationalist feeling everywhere," and pleaded for the necessity of throwing the virtue, wisdom, and power of China's four hundred million people into the scales against the foreigner.

The fate of the Hundred Days of Reform in 1898 indicated that this type of rational and moderate reformism, operating within the context of the existing institutions, was likely to meet with as little success in China as did the similar approach of early colonial nationalists in the colonial domain. The next stage, to a degree identified with Sun Yat-sen, involved a revolutionary turn against the old order, including the establishment of a Republic. At least in principle there was now a more radical dependence on the nation as a whole, in whose name the leaders claimed to act, but in practice the major contenders for power were more concerned with their mutual rivalries than with the establishment of a functioning democratic system.

In the eclectic and sometimes contradictory political philosophy of Sun Yat-sen democracy was joined with nationalism and the people's livelihood as one of the three fundamental principles of the people, but his version of democracy was not without its peculiar aspects. Although he found some democratic elements in the Chinese tradition, his argument rested much less upon them than upon the assumption that in adopting democracy China would not only be following — and improving upon — the political pattern of the West, but would also bring itself into line with what he portrayed as the world current flowing from theocracy through autocracy to democracy. To him, nationalism clearly represented the more important principle since a central feature of his plea for democracy was his belief that it could be used as an instrument to unite and strengthen the Chinese nation in its struggle against imperialism. Far from advocating democracy as a means of securing greater freedom for the individual, he laid his stress on China's need to secure a collective freedom for the people as an organized whole. The Chinese nation, now a loose sheet of sand which was becoming the slave and colony of all the world, should be pulled cohesively together on the basis of its family and clan groups. "If we want to restore China's liberty," he proclaimed, "we must unite ourselves in one unshakeable body; we must use revolutionary methods to weld our state into one firm unity." [6]

Besides abandoning an individualist base for democracy Sun also built much of his more applied consideration of democracy not upon the equality of men but upon their inequality in ability. In his picture of mankind, only a few have the ability to create or invent, a larger number can understand and follow the originators, but the mass can only carry out instructions. While this appears to be a permanent condition of man in his view, he found in China the added immediate handicap that the mass of the people, having been under tyrannical rule for centuries, had developed a servile mentality. As the means of bringing the Chinese people to the point where they could exercise the sovereignty with which his republicanism endowed them he prescribed a period of political tutelage by the revolutionary elite which would educate the people to such maturity as they could attain and help them to escape the confusions of Western democracy. This elitist outlook, combined with the prompt failure of his ill-organized first effort to reconstruct China on democratic lines, no doubt produced the frame of mind in which he was later ready to listen to the new gospel from Moscow and to remold the Kuomintang on the Bolshevik model.

In the succeeding decades the democratic path was regularly urged upon and promised to China from various quarters: the flowering of China as a modern democratic state was always just around the corner, but it was never here and now. C. P. Fitzgerald, who found all the fundamental requisites for democracy as it developed in the West lacking in China, attributed great importance to the crucial period of warlord rule from 1916 to 1925 when "democracy and with it all that the West hoped to see flourish in China had been discredited and cast aside." [7] Even after 1925, despite bravely democratic pronouncements, the enthusiasm in leading circles for any actual surrender of power to the people was at best lukewarm, and the absence of democratic experience joined with the pressures of the warlords, the Communists, and the foreign imperialists to lend plausibility to the maintenance of an authoritarian one-party government. Under Chiang Kai-shek the regime had an outward parliamentary form, but far from seeking a revolutionary translation of power to the masses, Chiang advocated a revival of the decorum and ordered stability of the Confucian social system in which the people would know their proper place. For many of those around him the maintenance of power, privilege, and wealth gave every appearance of becoming a more significant goal than drawing the Chinese people into an effective share in political life. [8] While Chiang and the Kuomintang increasingly rested their rule upon the conservative and propertied classes, the Communists went to the people, and it was their version of the New Democracy which ultimately swept the field.

As Japan serves to illustrate the inner dynamics of a country which escaped colonialism, so China illustrates other propositions which have been advanced. Since China experienced some of the aspects of colonialism it emerged with some of the results of colonialism, as, notably, the rise of a new-style business class and a Westernized intelligentsia which, with a growing proletariat as their storm troopers, became the spearhead of the attack upon the old order and the imperialist powers. Repudiating the *ancien régime* and aware of the new currents in the world, they spoke, as did their colonial counterparts, in the name of a democratic nationalism and sought some degree of popular support. But, since in China's case it was only a *quasi*-colonialism, undermining the old order without really laying the foundations of the new through the enforced experience of Western rule, there was as well only a *quasi*-democratic nationalism which tended to shed its democratic elements in the interest of preserving the well-being of those who had taken over power. These latter came to occupy much the same position and to hold much the same attitudes as those which are typical of the surviving old order in the non-colonial countries. Although the opening phases of the colonial cycle had been only very partially completed, the wheel had swung full circle, and the heirs of those who had achieved power and legitimacy as the spokesmen for the nation now shunned any full-scale appeal to the people of the nation because such an appeal would expose them to a revolution from which they were highly unlikely to emerge as the beneficiaries. This situation was reflected in reports of American Foreign Service Officers in China during the war. Thus, John Stewart Service in a report of June 20, 1944, stated that, in the face of a growing crisis, the Kuomintang was ceasing to be the unifying and progressive force in Chinese society:

> *On the internal front the desire of the Kuomintang leaders to perpetuate their own power overrides all other considerations.* The result is the enthronement of reaction. . . . Economically, the Kuomintang rests on the narrow base of the rural-gentry-landlords and militarists, the highest ranks of the government bureaucracy, and merchant bankers having intimate connections with the government bureaucrats. This base has actually contracted during the war." [9]

In contrast to this estimate of declining Kuomintang strength, both

Service and others found the Communists growing in strength because of their appeal to the people.

THE MIDDLE EAST

Despite the fact that Egypt and the former Arab Mandates had colonialism of a kind imposed on them, the Middle East as a whole belongs in the category of non-colonial areas which have developed an intense nationalism with only a partial realization of its democratic implications. Because of the variety and number of the countries embraced by it, no region offers a more fertile field as a laboratory for the study of political development.[10] All the forces characteristic of Western imperial predominance in the world have been at work in the Middle East, challenging the established order and compelling a basic reassessment of Islam. As elsewhere one of the major resultants of these forces was a nationalism which has become an all-embracing passion.

The old order was challenged, but where its leading members were for the time being themselves the principal figures in the anti-imperialist struggle, they were often able to maintain an anachronistic preëminence, demonstrating an extraordinary ability to cling to their threatened prerogatives.[11] Reforms looking to some equalization of wealth and privilege were blocked by the dominant groups who perpetuated their power. It has indeed been contended that in the Middle East the first effects of such steps as were made into the modern world, far from working toward a leveling out, were to make the rich richer and the poor poorer, or at least to make the contrasts between them more glaringly evident. More and more of late, however, the beneficiaries of the old order either have had to share power and privilege with the rising new elements or have been wholly elbowed aside. If the formal institutions of democracy are nonexistent or ignored with casual disrespect, the populace must be cajoled and taken into account by political leaders to a much greater extent than before. New and often dictatorial elites have risen to take over governments, but the time has come in some countries such as the United Arab Republic and Iraq, and is coming in others such as Iran and Saudi Arabia, when the ruling few must carry the people with them if they are to survive. A key point of strength for Egypt's Nasser was not only that he championed Arab unity against Western imperialism, but also that he promised domestic reforms which would lift the level of the lowly. The arts of the demagogue thus came to importance in an era which was far from being democratic and yet brought the masses into a new focus.

Among the Middle Eastern states democratic institutions have been able to secure a stable and durable foothold only in Israel. In this very special case — a democratic oasis in the surrounding Arab world — the dominant fact is surely that its political course was set by European Jews who brought with them the heritage of Western political thought and democratic assumptions even though their own experience of democracy may have been limited and unhappy. If Israel's leading elements had been drawn from the Jewish communities of the Middle East its political structure and history would presumably have taken a quite different course.

A possible rival for Israel in this sphere was Turkey but its ability to live up to its democratic pretensions has proved disappointing. Early in the nineteenth century the Turkish rulers became aware of the need to adapt Ottoman society, and at the outset particularly the armed forces, to the new currents flowing in Europe, but they were almost wholly unprepared either to reckon or to pay the price. The constitutional regime so fleetingly installed by Abdul Hamid in 1876 can be taken as a classic example of the effort to win a diplomatic success through the appearance of conversion to democratic methods, and the Young Turks who took over in 1909 did not do much better. The dictatorship of Ataturk, turning defeat to nationalist victory, later deliberately relinquished its authoritarian grip to encourage the existence of an opposition and a free electoral system. The democracy which was introduced has, however, had only occasional triumphs. The voluntary abandonment of a dictatorship is rare enough; the ability of a people suddenly endowed with political power to make democracy a working reality is perhaps even rarer.

Elsewhere in the Middle East the record of democratic experimentation is bleak, despite brief and scattered periods of success.[12] In a few countries — Saudi Arabia, Yemen, and some of the smaller Arab sheikdoms — there has not even been an approach to democracy; more generally the transition to nationalism has brought with it a swing in the direction of democratic institutions, but not an ability to get there. Writing of the Moslem world in 1932, H. A. R. Gibb asserted that "parliamentary government is accepted, in the present phase of political evolution, as the outward symbol of full nationhood." [13] The record of the succeeding years leaves no doubt that this acceptance was far from establishing the conditions under which parliamentary government could operate with even a minimum of stability, efficiency, and popular participation.

Two decades later Pierre Rondot could write that although a quarter of a century earlier the Middle East desired parliaments above all,

> today, almost everywhere, it is turning its back on parliaments. Once the national movements in the East considered the parliamentary regime as both the most efficacious means of self-expression and the most desirable political achievement they could offer their peoples. Not so today. . . . Far from considering it the instrument and the achievement of a policy of emancipation, many denounce it as an illusion if not a fraud.[14]

Among those who have capitalized on the failure of parliamentary institutions and have also on occasion dealt them the final blow are the military, who have been described as a political party equipped with weapons. Turkey and Iran had already demonstrated the possibilities for decisive military intervention when civilian forces proved unable to master a time of change, and these possibilities were further exploited as the Arab states, achieving independence, built modern-style armies. Edward Atiyah's description of the demise of parliamentarism in Iraq in the mid-thirties — the first of the Arab states to undergo a military take-over — may be taken as broadly representative of what has happened more recently elsewhere, as in Egypt and Syria, and again in Iraq. As he saw it, the key factors creating a political vacuum into which the army was drawn were the absence of an educated electorate and the lack of a long parliamentary tradition, accompanied by the intrigues of politicians competing for office and by growing social abuses which democracy proved unable to correct.[15]

That the army officers should have been the ones to undertake revolutions or *coups d'état* which proclaimed as their purpose the end of corruption and inefficiency and the introduction of social and economic reform is explained in part by the fact that the early recognition in the Middle East of the need for military strength made the army the first institution to be overhauled on modern lines. In consequence, the corps of army officers — Atiyah asserts their middle class origins in the Arab countries — became not a stronghold of conservatism, but a channel through which other aspects of Westernization could flow. It may well seem, one writer has suggested, that in the present circumstances of the Middle East, "the army remains the only instrument of popular aspiration that is capable of bringing about a social democracy." [16]

One central political concept which as a working matter has stayed constant in the Middle East is that rule properly rests with the few and not with the many, whether the few are the land-owners, the military, the politicians, or the reformers. Lord Cromer warned: "Do not let us for a moment imagine that the fatally simple idea of despotic rule will readily give way to the far more complex conception of ordered liberty." [17] Although new aspirants to power have rebelled against the landowners and others who are accused of using power in their own corrupt interest, they have much more rarely been prepared to act on the conviction that the people should be allowed to govern themselves. The fellahin and the other lowly may be romantically portrayed as the good and de-serving poor and the ultimate goal may be set as an ideal of democ-racy, but the tutelage of the mass by the enlightened is seen as the appropriate means to reach the goal. It is on grounds such as these that some observers have suggested that Communism with its frank avowal of a revolution imposed from above might have a strong appeal for many in the Middle East who have turned against the established order but find no adequate source of attraction in the liberal democracy of the West.

Of the Arab countries the one whose involvement with national-ism and its democratic implications reaches furthest back is Egypt. Because of the longer period of close contact with the West, the British protectorate, and other distinctive features in its develop-ment, the experience of Egypt differs in a number of ways from that of its Middle Eastern brethren, but it is also strongly marked by many of the elements which are characteristic of the non-colonial society. The temptation to enlist the Egyptian masses actively in national reconstruction and later in the struggle against British imperialism was counterbalanced by the fear that an aroused people might intrude too seriously upon the wealth and prerogatives of those who profited from the existing system.

Leaving aside Ismail's consultative assembly of 1866, the earliest significant move with democratic overtones was the rise from the junior officer corps of Arabi Pasha, himself the son of a fellah, who first gave expression to the idea of an Egyptian nation led by Egyptians. His own shortcomings and the mounting foreign pressure rendered his movement abortive, but the possibilities of a new course had been demonstrated. Under British control much was changed and yet much remained the same. With the rise of a middle class and of nationalist parties a multifaceted and intricate political game developed in which the king and his palace clique, the big landowners, the political leaders, the bureaucracy, religious factions, and the British were all complexly involved, but seldom to the benefit of the fellahin.

In 1919, as a result of war pressures and the profound disaffections which they left behind them in virtually all segments of society, the first popular rising took place, presenting the illusion that a new era of national unity and liberal progress had started on its way. In actuality the linking of the old order, only partially displaced by the British regime, with the glittering opportunities of the new served to corrupt and undermine the promised democratic advance and freedom which, as in China, were always just around the corner. The Wafd, starting its career as the nationalist champion of the Egyptian people, moved in due course into a cycle of attachment to wealth and power which in 1952 led to the sweeping away, in the company of the scandalous Farouk, of the entire discredited system of monarchy, parties, and parliament. Their place was taken by the Revolutionary Command Council, derived from the army and the disastrous Palestine war, which asserted an authoritarian guardianship over the nation.

In the new regime Colonel Gamal Abdel Nasser came shortly to tower over the rest and to lay claim to being the major spokesman for the Arab world. Denouncing the old party system as a minority ruling in the interests of the minority, Nasser proclaimed

as his goal a true democracy of the nation. To that end he prescribed a constitution by which "We, the Egyptian people," declared to be an integral part of the Arab nation, established themselves as a democratic republic and affirmed that "Sovereign power
is inherent in the Nation"; but the exercise of the nation's sovereign
power remained in the hands of the country's new rulers. The
plebiscitary character of the regime was demonstrated by the
election of June 23, 1956, in which Nasser was accorded the presidency of the Egyptian Republic by 99.9 per cent of those voting
and the new constitution was approved by a similar show of unanimity.

As Nasser saw it, the conquest of the Arab world by the West
had an immensely disturbing influence, shaking the people's sense
of their own national values without replacing them by Western
values. In the political sphere, Western patterns of democratic
government had become a veil for corrupt self-interest and dictatorship. These evils he and his associates were to sweep away,
establishing in their stead a government of national unity:

> Our ultimate aim is to provide Egypt with a truly democratic and
> representative government, not the type of parliamentary dictator-
> ship which the Palace and the corrupt "pasha" class imposed on the
> people. In the past, parliament was a body for blocking social im-
> provement. We want to make sure that in the future the senators
> and deputies will serve all the Egyptians rather than a few.[18]

The role which the new regime should play was explicitly
stated to be that of a guardian, guiding the people for a limited
time toward a new freedom to be won from the dual, and contradictory, political and social revolution in which they were engaged.
He compared the people to a caravan which seeks to follow a
certain route but runs into many diversions and dangers. When the
caravan's strayed and scattered parts have been gathered together
by the new regime and set on the one right path, it can be left to
proceed in peace and security on its own.[19] Such was part of the
creed which Nasser avowed as he moved from early concern with
domestic reform to anti-imperialist triumphs and asserted his bid
for Arab unity under Egyptian leadership. What remains to be
seen is whether the road to democracy, leading through plebiscitary
centralization of power, will arrive at its asserted destination.

THAILAND

Of the remainder of the non-colonial countries the only one which deserves specific comment is Thailand. Nepal and Tibet are just beginning to feel the impact of the modern world which is now crowding in upon them from India and Communist China. Ethiopia and Afghanistan have made at best only fragmentary approaches to the democratization of either their societies or their political systems, and in Liberia such democracy as has existed has been almost exclusively confined to the Negroes resettled from the United States. In Thailand the process of adaptation to the new forces is of old standing and has in many respects gone far, but it has been imposed from above with only passive participation by the Thai people. No breath of democracy was associated with the reforms introduced by the absolute monarchs since the middle of the last century. Even the revolution of 1932 was the work not of the people but of an aristocracy much of which was well versed in Western ways and outlooks. Although there have been occasional swings in more liberal directions the democratic potentialities of the revolution were smothered by the strongly authoritarian trend to which the military have increasingly contributed. Thai nationalism has been a growing force but its bearers have been the old upper crust: the people of Thailand have neither asserted themselves nor have they been invited by their ruling betters to join seriously in the management of the nation. As *The Economist* put it:

> The contented Siamese, traditionally uninterested in politics and with an ingrained talent for obedience, have never shown the slightest desire for democracy — a phenomenon disconcerting to well-intentioned western visitors. If they are now to enjoy the benefits of democracy, it is clear that these will have to be imposed from above.[20]

CHAPTER XV

The Erosion of Democracy in the New States

O F THE MANY democracies which have been born in the past century and a half, only a handful have survived. In the past years the casualties have been peculiarly heavy among the former dependencies of the West for the simple reason that these were the countries which were currently embarking on democratic experiments. The fragile mechanism of representative democracy which almost all of them adopted proved shortly to be unfitted to the needs and capabilities of most of them. In thus at least temporarily abandoning their democratic institutions the ex-colonies were demonstrating no singular weakness or instability but were following in what has been by far the more common experience of mankind.

Simon Bolivar, liberating Venezuela, was prophetic of the way the world has generally gone:

> It is a terrible truth that it costs more strength to maintain freedom than to endure the weight of tyranny. Many nations, past and present, have borne that yoke; few have made use of the happy moments of freedom and have preferred to relapse with all speed into their errors.[1]

And when he spoke of the people of the American hemisphere as having been purely passive for centuries with no political existence — "absent from the universe in all that related to the science of government" — he spoke for many other peoples around the globe as well.

The story which has repeated itself over and over is that

peoples have set out on the democratic path with revolutionary enthusiasm, but before long they have lost their way and settled back into authoritarian or dictatorial regimes. The real success of democracy has been confined to some of the peoples living in or stemming from Western Europe: the British, the Irish, the Belgians and Dutch, the Scandanavians, the Swiss, more dubiously the French, and overseas, the peoples of the United States and the older British Dominions. With these central exceptions each of the successive waves of democratic experimentation has ended in over-all failure. The revolt against European rule in Latin America in the nineteenth century brought into being an array of democracies whose record has been spotty and untrustworthy at best. The drive for self-determination which followed the defeat of the autocracies in World War I stimulated the emergence of democratic institutions in Central and Eastern Europe, but after a few years Czechoslovakia was the sole democratic survivor. Among the non-colonial Asian and African countries which tried out new political forms, only Japan, China, and Turkey could at any time have been seriously counted in the democratic ranks, and none of these three could be cited as a model of democratic behavior. The statistical odds against the survival of democracy outside the small circle of Western European peoples and their descendants overseas seem overwhelming.

For the non-European peoples it is, in the large, the former colonies of the West which have made the nearest approach to democracy, despite the serious defections which have recently taken place. The faith of their leaders in democracy was shown at the outset in the style of constitutions which they created; in a few countries, headed by India and the Philippines, these constitutions have so far maintained themselves as living realities; and even where democracy has gone into eclipse, as in Pakistan and Burma, the new rulers have pledged themselves to let it shine forth again promptly with a new splendor. Whether and when and by whom these pledges will be redeemed is a different matter. It must also be recorded that a ground swell of protest against the assumption that Western-style parliamentary institutions are appropriate for non-European peoples has been increasingly evident.

The push toward democracy which Western colonialism has

often given is not limited solely to Asia and Africa. In the Caribbean the democratic structure and stability of the dependencies of the United States, Britain, France, and the Netherlands stand out sharply against the dictatorial tendencies and political inconstancy of neighboring independent countries and indeed of Latin America as a whole. Puerto Rico, demographically akin to other Spanish-settled countries of the area, has, in its new Commonwealth guise, become a paragon of democratic advance as contrasted with the next-door Dominican Republic and Haiti. In the postwar surge of colonial reform the French Territories were converted into Departments of France, while the Dutch dependencies secured far-reaching self-government in association with the Netherlands. The British West Indies, having tried out representative institutions on an individual basis, have now moved on to a federal parliamentary structure. In estimating the current state of political development in these Caribbean territories it is, of course, a fact to be taken into the reckoning that none of them is currently independent, nor is independence contemplated for any other than those in the British orbit. How steadfastly they would maintain their present democratic posture as sovereign states can only be a matter of conjecture.

The contrast which still exists between colonial and non-colonial countries serves to confirm the presumption that a new look at Western colonialism and its contribution to the world is in order. From a number of standpoints colonialism is an intolerable evil, and its character as evil is attested by the passionate unanimity with which all colonial peoples seek to escape from it. Yet the effects which it has had in shaping the peoples on whom it has been imposed cannot be dismissed as solely bad.

The most striking and unexpected tribute to Western colonial practice came from Charles T. O. King, Liberian Ambassador to the United States. When Vice-President Nixon journeyed to the inaugural ceremonies for Ghana, reporters who accompanied him noted that Liberia was still largely primitive while the former Gold Coast was relatively well developed. Iconoclastically attacking all the truths concerning colonialism as oppression and exploitation which the liberals and the left have accepted as sacred and self-evident, the Ambassador explained that independent Liberia's backwardness stemmed from the fact that it had never had the advantages of colonialism:

> It is the difference between the home of a man who has had to accomplish everything by his own sweat and toil and that of a man who has enjoyed a large inheritance. . . . The United States did not care about a colony on the coast of Africa, and we were left alone and struggling to vegetate in the midst of developing European colonies.[2]

Not without a parallel to Adam Smith's dictum that the worst of all governments for a colony was government by a company, it might be argued that areas of the world, such as China and the Middle East, which have fallen victim to imperialism but have had no, or no effective, colonial regime imposed upon them have had the worst of the deal. The distortions arising from Western penetration are present, but not the positive contributions toward adjustment which colonialism has it within its power to make, even though it has by no means always made them. The stability of the states that emerged from the Indian Empire persuaded Bernard Lewis that the imperial peace was not without its merits:

> But there is little that can be said in defense of the half-hearted, pussy-footing imperialism encountered by most of the peoples of the Middle East — an imperialism of interference without responsibility which would neither create nor permit stable and orderly governments.[3]

Also drawing on India's example, Barbara Ward suggested that:

> China's ordeal was worse than India's, for India gained a hundred years of orderly administration and inherited in 1947 a functioning state and civil service, whereas China was left to drift like a sailless junk, its old equipment destroyed by the West but with no new machinery installed.[4]

A further illustration of the disadvantages of non-colonial imperialism might be found in the intervention of the United States in the affairs of the independent Central American and Caribbean republics in the opening decades of this century. Here likewise was interference without acceptance of responsibility, and the results which it produced were not unlike those in the Middle East. The relatively smooth functioning of the representative institutions of the Philippines, which was subjected to American colonial rule, contrasts favorably with the dictatorships and revolutions of Cuba which was spared it.

Depending on one's point of view, it may be counted among the virtues of colonialism that it has served in various ways to predispose the colonial peoples toward democratic political systems, or counted among its vices since it exposed peoples to the hazards of trying to live with institutions alien to their past. At all events we have good reason to question how deeply democratic conceptions and practices have penetrated and how long-lasting their effects can be expected to be. Already the contrast between the colonial and the non-colonial countries is fading. Once independence has been achieved the special forces and circumstances of colonialism cease to be operative, and the further the remove from colonialism the more attenuated the effects must be. In consequence, the ex-colonies find themselves in the same situation as the states which retained their independence; and one by one they have begun to drift away from the democratic standards they had originally set for themselves.

At the same time the non-colonial states are continuing, generally at an accelerated pace, their processes of adaptation to the modern world, of which one significant feature is "a high rate of recruitment of new elements into political activity" as a result of social and economic change.[5] Revolutionary innovations are taking place in the relations between the few at the top, the small but growing middle class, and the many at the bottom. Government will continue in most instances not to be *by* the people, but, recognizing the necessities of an era of "fundamental democratization," it must increasingly create the popular impression that it is *for* the people and responsive to their needs. In net effect, the two sets of countries whose recent history led them by divergent routes are now moving toward a common middle position.

As far as the former colonies are concerned, by far the most striking evidence of this shift is the open or only slightly concealed abandonment of the representative parliamentary institutions which came into being with the transition to independence. 1958 was the year of the great collapse. Within a few weeks of each other, Pakistan, Burma, and the Sudan surrendered their civilian governments into the hands of the military who in varying degree abrogated constitutions, postponed elections, and abolished or sidetracked political parties. In the Middle East, where Egypt and Syria had already made the transition, the revolution in Iraq installed a general in power, setting in motion the abortive American and British military interventions in Lebanon and Jordan, and Lebanon elected the chief of its army to the presidency. Ceylon was having its considerable troubles, and Indonesia, plagued by revolution and political feuding, retained only the remnants of parliamentary rule under the watchful eye of the military. In Ghana, Nkrumah and his associates ruled with a strong hand, cavalierly overriding the usual rights of the opposition. Guinea, thrust suddenly into independence, explicitly endorsed the one-party system and summed up its one party in the person of Sékou Touré.

The reasons for the erosion of democracy are not far to seek. Basically they are common to the new states even though the turn of events in each of them derives from a special set of circumstances which has produced distinctive results. The position of Ne Win in Burma cannot be equated with that of Mohammed Ayub Khan in Pakistan, nor can either of these two be identified with Abdul Karim Kassem in Iraq. Chief of Staff Nasution has not seized power in Indonesia, although he has a large say in the governing of the country, and in Ghana the army has played no political role — its loyalty to the new regime, it has been said, being guaranteed by the fact that its officer corps remains largely British. Yet, when all the differences are taken into account, many common elements stand out.

One among them is the lack of national unity which in virtually all the new countries threatens disruption and is met by enforced centralization. Nationalism is the dominant creed but the nations are still far from being consolidated. Of Pakistan it has been writtent that "no recollection of history and concord" binds the two wings, separated by a thousand miles of India [6]; in Burma inchoate civil wars have challenged the hold of the government since independence; and in Indonesia great stretches of territory remain under the control of Darul Islam, the Revolutionary Government which proclaimed its existence in 1958, and other dissident groups.

One country which has so far retained its democratic institutions despite great internal diversity is Malaya. Here, on the basis of what has happened elsewhere, the gloom-seeking prophet was and perhaps still is, entitled to assume that radical discord must soon bring open civil strife or strong man rule or both, but the governing coalition, the Alliance, has been able to hold the leading Malay, Chinese, and Indian parties together within the constitutional framework. The country has been independent, however, only since 1957, and the precedents suggest that the momentum derived from the colonial period and the *élan* coming from winning independence take a longer time than this to run down.

In addition to the lack of national unity, the most basic explanation for the failure of democracy in so many of the new states is the almost universal absence of what have been assumed to be the preconditions for its success. Although argument still rages as to precisely what these may be, the usually accepted list includes such items as mass literacy, relatively high living standards, a sizable and stable middle class, a sense of social equality, and a tradition both of tolerance and of individual self-reliance.[7] In virtually no instance are these conditions met in the colonial countries whose independence had led them into democracy. Instead these countries are characterized by peasant masses living at the subsistence level, overwhelmingly illiterate, unacquainted not only with the great world but even with their own country, accustomed to a high degree of social stratification, and with slight middle classes often strongly alien in composition. The representative government which emerges can be no stronger than the society which it represents.

Furthermore, the democratic institutions which were adopted were the work of the relatively small group which had come to significant acquaintance with the West. They were the product neither of the mass of the people, who inevitably had little understanding of them, nor of the evolutionary development of the society as a whole. Although social mobilization has been in full swing, the sudden universal enfranchisement of the peoples of Asian and African states differed sharply from the gradual adaptation to changing circumstances in the West where there was often a rough coincidence between the rise of new elements to economic and social consequence and their access to the ballot box. It is an immense added complication that while the democracies which came into being in the nineteenth and earlier twentieth centuries were concerned with the management of relatively simple political and economic systems in a still spacious world, the newly rising peoples seek full-scale social welfare states with most complicated mechanisms, plus the extra complexity of the drive for social and economic development, in a terrifying world of population explosion, superpowers, and nuclear weapons.

The increase in the numbers of those who were drawn into some measure of political participation did not necessarily enhance the prospects of democratic achievement. Poverty-ridden people in a climate of rising expectations are not likely to make their first concern the preservation of political forms and liberties whose meaning is obscure to them and whose promise may appear of less significance than other prospects held out to them. If democracy fails to produce results with adequate speed and if the politicians who manipulate the machinery come to be seen as self-interested and corrupt, the masses cannot be counted on to rise to the defense of unfamiliar political machineries.

The people at large lack not only the democratic tradition but also the more basic tradition of standing up to do battle for their rights against the remote and superior authorities which have through the ages pushed them around. Government, save at the local level where it was usually interwoven with old-established ties of family and status, has almost always been something imposed from above. What Gertrude Bell wrote of the Ottoman Empire half a century ago holds true for many other peoples:

> The government was still, to the bulk of the population, a higher power, disconnected from those upon whom it exercised its will. You might complain of its lack of understanding just as you cursed the hailstorm that destroyed your crops, but you were in no way answerable for it, nor would you attempt to control or advise it, any more than you would offer advice to the hail cloud.[8]

Sporadically the people have risen in revolt against abuses felt to be intolerable or at the urging of some popular leader, but little has come their way to imbue them with the sense that they are possessors of human rights and fundamental freedoms which they are entitled and able to defend. The democratic constitutions of the post-independence period have been almost as much imposed on them from above as any of the previous regimes, and in many instances it is probable that the people would feel more at home with a government which tells them what to do than one in which they must exercise freedom of choice.[9] Nasser, writing of the philosophy of the Egyptian revolution, has spoken of the pain and bitterness which tore his heart when he found that the leaders must continue to command because the "majestic masses" which should have joined in the hallowed march to the great end actually brought sloth and inertia and not the needed zeal and ardor.

If the newly enfranchised masses are uncertain defenders of the democratic institutions with which they have been endowed, what of the nationalist elites to whom the institutions owe their being? These elites are composed of men for the most part committed to the proposition that a radical democratization of their societies is in order, but their ability to live up to their proclaimed creed has already been demonstrated to be highly dubious. Even assuming that they or reasonably like-minded successors retain their hold, with what confidence can it be predicted that they will survive the temptation, baited by the insidious corruptions of power, to see themselves as a distinctive corps with closed ranks. A Burmese newspaper editor wrote of the leaders of the dominant political party in Burma that they have "a 'Messiah' complex by which they can justify deviations from democracy with the excuse that they must remain in power for the good of the country." [10]

The tendency of the nationalist parties and movements to be built around dominant personalities rather than on programs or ideologies has often been noted. The emergence of Fascism, the virtual deification of Stalin in the U.S.S.R., the return of de Gaulle to supreme power in France, the abundant Latin American experience, and even the wartime preëminence of Churchill and Roosevelt, among many other examples, make it absurd to regard this emphasis on personal leadership as in any way a peculiarly Oriental or African aberration. Its occurrence elsewhere, however, does not obscure the apparent need of the newly rising peoples to have a single personal focus of loyalty, symbolic of national unity: Gandhi and then Nehru in India, Jinnah in Pakistan, Quezon and

Magsaysay in the Philippines, Ngo Dinh Diem in Vietnam, Nasser in Egypt, Nkrumah in Ghana, and Sékou Touré in Guinea, to suggest only a few.

This personalization of loyalties and movements must be attributed in large part to the lack of political experience and sophistication of the mass of the people who require the personal figure of a leader to bring political abstractions down to the level of comprehensible reality. Another part may perhaps be linked to the general phenomenon of centralization of power in time of national crisis, as in the growth in stature of the American presidency in wartime. On such grounds it is not difficult to explain why the role of the leader should have expanded in Asian and African countries as they came to the critical struggles for independence, national consolidation, and economic development. It remains to be established, however, that leaders who have felt the intoxication of embodying the national will can be trusted to surrender its formulation to the people at large when the critical years are passed. The record of other parts of the world does not encourage the belief that the proclaimed adherence of such leaders to democratic principles is any guarantee that these principles will not be abandoned as the revolutionary tide ebbs and the attractions of power and privilege become greater.

The simple human inclination for those who have power to hold on to it is bolstered in Asia and Africa by the age-old assumption that the few at the top are rightfully masters of the people. "Most educated Asians," E. O. Reischauer has remarked, "simply take it for granted that they will be leaders." [11] The gap in awareness of the modern world between the Western-oriented elite and the largely unreformed mass furnishes additional justification for the exclusion of the mass from any effective share in political life. Until the gap is greatly lessened the claim of the educated few to manage the affairs of the society is as good — and as bad — as that of the colonial administrators who preceded them, with the one great difference that they operate within and not outside the national fold. The white man's burden thus finds its counterpart in the contention that those who know best should be the custodians of power.

This is an ancient dilemma, and one which Rousseau confronted in proposing the democratic concept of the general will as the source of law:

> How can a blind multitude, which often does not know what it wills, because it rarely knows what is good for it, carry out for itself so great and difficult an enterprise as a system of legislation? Of itself the people wills always the good, but of itself it by no means always sees it. The general will is always in the right, but the judgment which guides it is not always enlightened. . . . This makes a legislator necessary.[12]

In the Asian and African setting it can occasion no great surprise when the Legislator, willing the good of which his people are unaware, takes over from the struggling infant democracies, as he has so often taken over elsewhere. The Communists offer one version in their people's democracies: the dictatorship of the proletariat, exercised by the Party which is controlled by the one or the collective few at the top. Other versions range from some variant of Fascism through military rule to a more traditionalistic reassertion of older ways, and include always the possibility of mere degeneration into rule by a governing clique uninspired by any loftier ideology than clinging to its privileged position. As a species these are more akin to the Asian and African experience than are the parliamentary systems imported from the West.

The erosion of democracy in the new states has taken two characteristic forms: the seizure of power by the military and the turn to a one-party system. Whichever way the dice come up, a common feature is that politicians and political parties are denounced as corrupt, self-interested, and divisive betrayers of the public interest. Politics itself becomes an evil word, and Western-style democracy is publicly discredited by its fruits, or the lack of them. In contrast, the military or the single party are billed as representing the creative and unified national force which is needed to promote the common good and rescue the country from the disintegration with which the politicians and their parties threaten it. Thus Sukarno, himself a politician of note, sought to make the abolition of parties a feature of his guided democracy and portrayed Eastern democracy as "democracy accompanied by leadership"; and *Dawn* in Karachi hailed General Ayub Khan's coming to power as the end of a long winter:

The trees of our economic, social, and moral lives — withered and shrivelled by blasts of greed, corruption, self-seeking, and intrigue — are now beginning to blossom again into tender green leaves to herald the awakening of a glad and fruitful spring.[13]

The taking over of the government by the military in a number of the new states follows a pattern well established in other parts of the world. Although no dependency possesses significant armed forces of its own, as soon as it becomes its own master it moves to build them up as an essential symbol of sovereign manhood. Once the forces are available, the power they wield makes it exceedingly difficult for them to avoid playing a political role if any serious weakness develops in the civilian government. Where the civilian authorities stand firm as in India and the Philippines, or where a strong individual commands the scene as does Ngo Dinh Diem in Vietnam, the military can be kept within their proper sphere, but leading elements in the officers corps are almost certain to swing into action if the country seems threatened by corruption, administrative ineptitude, party or factional strife, or subversion. The wonder is not that the military have intervened as often as they have, but rather that they have so often stayed their hand. The presumption must be that we will see more and not fewer regimes dominated by the military in the years ahead as more governments are brought into being which are inadequate to the tasks confronting them.

Whether or not democracy is held to vanish when the military establish their control over the government or when a single party establishes a monopoly of power is a matter of definition. In Western terms democracy has gone by the board when a group of officers seizes the government, pushes the constitution aside, and abolishes or suspends parties and elections. The counterclaim has, however, been made, as, for example, on behalf of the government of Pakistan, that, since the basic concept of democracy is rule by consent, where a government has popular support it is by definition a democracy regardless of its structure.[14] This is a claim to be rejected. A government controlled by the military may be doing an admirable and necessary job, as in attacking corruption, undertaking land reform in West Pakistan, or cleaning up Rangoon, but it is debasing the currency of political terminology to call it a democracy, even though it has the honest intention of creating conditions under which democratic institutions can be restored.

A better case, or at least a different one, can be made for the regimes which have implicitly or explicitly adopted the one-party system — a single party which in most instances furnishes the vehicle for control by the one strong man at the center. The two most significant arguments, often blended together into one, are that Asia and Africa have their own democratic forms which differ from the parliamentary institutions of the West, and that, although representative bodies continue in existence, the need for national unity is too great to allow a dispersion of forces.

Increasingly it has been contended in recent years that the Western assumption of the majority's right to overrule a dissident minority after a period of debate does violence to conceptions basic to non-Western peoples. Although the Asian and African societies differ vastly among themselves in their patterns of customary action, their native inclination is generally toward extensive and unhurried deliberation aimed at an ultimate consensus. The gradual discovery of areas of agreement is the significant feature and not the ability to come to a speedy resolution of issues by counting heads. For the Chinese and other peoples among whom neither majority rule nor representative government had any traditional roots, the voice of the elders, the wise, and the specially qualified was entitled to extra or even decisive weight. As a symbol of the lack of relation between the concept of parliamentary opposition and the nature of West African decision-making, it has been asserted that "the word 'opposition' can only be translated into the majority of Ghanaian languages as 'enemy' (in the wars and bloodshed sense of the term)." [15]

The controversy has come to center in considerable part about the question of an opposition. A strong case can be made for the proposition that it is precisely the existence of an opposition which determines whether or not there is democracy. Only if an opposition party is available and is equipped with the rights essential to its free functioning can the ordinary citizen have any assurance that he is being presented with the facts and alternatives on which informed judgment can be based. Without the existence of an opposition he is inevitably forced to rely largely on the information which comes to him from the government and the governing party and to vote for the single slate of candidates officially laid before him. The freedom of choice which democracy implies is effectively denied him.

This conception of the role of the opposition has come under heavy attack. As one of the most articulate spokesman for a type of democracy with roots in local tradition Sukarno declared in 1957 that it was the adoption of the Western concept of an active opposition which gave rise to Indonesia's difficulties and brought people to think in a manner alien to the Indonesian way of life. Defeated in his proposal that parties be abolished, he asked for the representation of all parties in the cabinet and even more urgently advocated a program for the direct representation in the central councils of a wide array of social groupings, including the armed forces. These doctrines represented no recent conversion derived from his visit to Communist countries. As early as June 1,1945, in the speech in which he outlined the *Pantjasila*, the five principles of the Indonesian state, he expressed his distrust of the Western democracy which left the capitalists as bosses in Europe and America, and announced the need for a consultative body "which, together with the community, will be able to give effect to two principles, *political justice and social justice.*" [16] He has also never concealed his conviction that his role as president is actively to ensure the success of the Indonesian revolution.

In Africa south of the Sahara the one-party system has of late been endorsed in a number of quarters, following precedents well established in Egypt, Tunisia and Morocco. Although Kwame Nkrumah has not accepted the principle of a single party, he has asserted that

> Even a system based on social justice and a democratic constitution may need backing up, during the period following independence, by emergency measures of a totalitarian kind. Without discipline, true freedom cannot survive.[17]

In the drive for independence Nkrumah opened himself to charges of a high-handed and demagogic manipulation of power both personally and through the Convention People's Party, a party which has been described as a "Tammany-type machine with a nationalist ideology . . . composed of a militant elect who dominate and spearhead the nationalist movement." But David Apter, who so characterized the C.P.P., further contended that it was the charismatic leadership of Nkrumah which at least temporarily "endowed the structure of parliamentary government with legitimacy." [18]

After assuming power in independent Ghana, Nkrumah took a course which left the backers of democracy breathless but not without hope. Great attention was focused on himself, as in putting his image on coins and erecting a more than life-size statue of himself in Accra; the normal powers of government were stretched to secure the expulsion or suppression of elements of the opposition; and yet much of the democratic constitutional machinery remained at least temporarily intact. One American observer found that Nkrumah favored benevolent dictatorship and that neither he nor his associates had any liking for the parliamentary system except for the provisional use they could make of it and the unchecked power which it gave the dominant party,[19] but others saw no more resort to extraordinary measures than a critical situation called for.

In Nigeria, where each region has tended to develop a single party of its own, a more drastic attack was made on democracy by one Chike Obi, M.Sc. (London), Ph.D. (Cambridge), a mathematician at Ibadan's University College and founder of the politically inconsequential Dynamic Party. In his view the right question to ask was:

> What type of self-government has any chance within a short time to succeed in persuading the illiterate, ignorant, lazy, individualistic and undisciplined natives of Nigeria to make a great physical and mental sacrifice in military and labour camps for the defense of their country and the common good?

Since a people so described is obviously unready to make use of democratic freedoms, Obi saw salvation only in a planned and regimented Kemalism which would ensure that political power came to those "who will make the unavoidable dictatorship as benevolent and as short as possible." [20]

The vesting of a monopoly of power in a single party has found growing favor in both theory and practice in the present and former French territories of sub-Saharan Africa as they have moved to independence or more extensive self-government within the new French Community. In independent Guinea, Sékou Touré has accorded his Democratic Party, reaching out into the country through thousands of local committees, a monopolistic position and has declared that "Guinea cannot permit herself to disperse her forces, her energy, her will in political dualism." [21] In the Ivory Coast, Houphouet-Boigny, representing the right-wing of French African politics, has developed a one-party rule approximately as all-embracing as that of the more left-wing Touré in Guinea. The antiquity of this system in Africa is demonstrated in nearby Liberia where the True Whigs, continuously in power since 1878, are the only party and where President Tubman, in office since 1943, piled up 530,566 votes to his opponent's 55 in the presidential election of May 1959.

The single-party thesis was extolled by some of the spokesmen for French African territories at the Conference on Representative Government and National Progress held at Ibadan in March 1959. The flavor of their position can be garnered from a paper entitled "In the Phase of National Construction the Fusion of Parties Becomes a Categorical Imperative" which was presented to the conference by Alexandre Adande of Dahomey. Calling for prompt and bold action, he stressed the need for a unity not hampered by sterile sectarianism. Although he saw some people playing into the hands of a hard-pressed imperialism by raising the scarecrows of dictatorship, fascism, and totalitarianism, he contended that there should be no servile copying of European multiparty regimes.

> Beneath its "idealistic" appearance, every political party actually represents a definite class or definite economic interest which it must defend in parliament. The result of this is a squabbling among selfish oppositions that has nothing in common with the true and exclusive interest of the nation . . . they stop at nothing: lies, demagogy, compromise, corruption. . . . We have nothing to do with these poisons.[22]

This one-party philosophy was given the blessing of Guinea's Minister to Ghana who was reported as having spoken passionately in favor of "a united and democratic party without opposition," which would contain all the nationalists, maintain representative institutions, and encourage wide popular discussion. In good elitist fashion he asserted that the people must not be confused by a multiplicity of parties, at least in the first years of independence.[23] According to the usual single-party schemes, differences of opinion would be fully aired within the party, but once a party decision was reached, the Communist principle of democratic centralism would be applied.

In the former Asian colonies the trend has been somewhat the same as in Africa, although, as in the Middle East, the role of the military has been greater. In India the Congress has retained so dominant a position as to be accused of running a one-party system, but other parties have been given free play and the general elections which have been held were models of democratic procedure. The Philippines of Quezon's days had little in the way of party diversity, and Burma came close to being a one-party state under the sway of the AFPFL until that organization split in the spring of 1958, starting the series of events which brought Ne Win to power in the fall. In Vietnam and Korea opposition parties have had no encouragement to challenge the hold of the parties supporting the established regimes. Serious doubts about the desirability of Western parliamentary government for Ceylon have also been raised by Prime Minister Bandaranaike, although, oddly enough, his charge against the British parliamentary system was not that it encouraged the disruptive forces of the opposition but that it opened the door to cabinet dictatorship. In its place he proposed a series of executive committees, to one or another of which every member of parliament would belong — a plan drawn from one of Ceylon's colonial constitutions.[24]

The breakdown of Western representative institutions in so many countries has inevitably led to a renewed searching of souls both in Asia and Africa and in the West. The good sense of the West in proposing such institutions for underdeveloped non-Western peoples and of the nationalists in insisting on them in the first rounds of independence has been called in question.

What we are witnessing is the failure of a series of experiments in grafting an alien form of government on peoples whose background and circumstances are totally dissimilar from those among whom it originated, and who were, on virtually every count, demonstrably ill-prepared to make it work. The first phase of the post-colonial reaction to colonialism involved the copying of the institutions of the imperial West. The failure of those institutions and its aftermath constitute a second phase which may be expected to bring political systems more nearly akin to the experience, capabilities, and present needs of the Asian and African peoples. What the inarticulate masses wanted from the revolutions through which they were passing — insofar as they wanted anything other than to be left alone in peace — was presumably not constitutional democracy or parliamentary government, but economic and social advance under their own leaders within a framework of national unity and strength. Where the representative institutions could plausibly be accused of failing to move toward these goals, their overthrow would be accepted with indifference or even enthusiasm.

The rise of the strong man to power when governments are unstable and times are troubled is an age-old phenomenon. If he has to look for other sources of support than the armed forces, the single party is a convenient instrument for him in an era when the masses must be taken into political account. Even if the large assumption be made that democracy of a more or less Western variety is ultimately the best of all forms of government for all peoples, it is still not difficult to put together a case for the strong man in the present circumstances of most of the non-European world.

The peoples of the West advanced toward democracy by very slow and gradual stages which included long periods of rule by absolute monarchs and despots, benevolent or otherwise. The achievement of ordered societies, reasonably in agreement on those basic elements of social cohesion necessary for the functioning of democracy and well started on the path of economic development, was in good part the product of the firm authoritarian rule which bridged the transition from the Middle Ages to the contemporary world.

For a backward people precariously moving out from under colonialism into independence with all the problems of economic development still ahead of them, it is highly doubtful that the sovereign remedy is a full-scale installment of democracy as the latter has evolved in advanced and prosperous Western societies. Democracy implies far-reaching freedoms, and an opposition; but the prime requirement is not for more freedoms but for discipline and hard work, not for opposition but for a national consolidation of all forces and talents. This is all the more true in countries such as Nigeria or Malaya where the opposition is likely to be made up of parties formed on tribal, racial, or religious lines, deepening inner divisions at a time when the essential need is strong and unified management. The achievement of coherent national unity can properly be set as the first goal since it is an indispensable condition for internal order and security and for representative government as well. The premature exercise of an overabundant democracy, laying its stress on the rights of the opposition, can destroy the foundations on which a successful democracy may later be built. In a speech answering critics of his country's alleged departures from acceptable constitutional practices, Nkrumah asserted that Africa would stand by its own version of democracy, but added: "As a new and young government, our first responsibility has been to preserve the independence and security of our state." [25]

One issue habitually recurs. The swing away from democracy is justified in the name of democracy: powers vested in the people are removed from the people in order that they may later be restored for more effective use. Unquestionably a wise and effective authoritarian regime could do much in the way of establishing the preconditions which would make democracy viable in areas where it now is not, but that authoritarianism would either realize its potentialities for development or be prepared to relinquish its powers into popular hands is very far from being proved. An expert on Southeast Asia reported in 1959 that instability and disintegration had progressed so far in that region that Communism was bound to win, unless the military took over. In the officer corps he found men who are "the product of an unusual process of natural selection," devoted to their countries, committed to moral values, disciplined and yet accustomed to command, and progressively acquainted with the modern world.[26] That the military of the new states usually oppose Communism and also have much else to offer is undeniable, particularly when they are contrasted with corrupt and discordant civilian regimes, but can they be trusted to ward off corruption from their own ranks, to carry through development programs outside the range of their experience and training, and not to perpetuate themselves for selfish advantage? The historical record produces few affirmative answers to questions such as these.

A functioning democracy must rest upon a judicious mixture of two potentially antagonistic principles of individual and collective rights. Wherever nationalism is the main driving force, the collective principle is likely to ride roughshod over individuals and minorities whose counterclaims seem to threaten the solidarity of the nation. This, however, gives no clue as to how the collectivity is to be represented: specific content must be given to the national will, and those who formulate it must be singled out. Rousseau's *volonté générale*, only accidentally identified with the concrete wills of actual human beings, must somehow be brought down to earth. Whose voice speaks for the national will? The soul of the nation may reside in the simple peasants and workers who constitute the democratic majority, but their ignorance, and lack of experience render them, it is likely to be contended, unable to give it true expression. In their stead, an elite or a charismatic leader takes over as the emanation of the national will which, in the vocabulary of Rousseau, is the *real* will of the individuals although not one they can be trusted to discover for themselves. The nation is sovereign but the exercise of the sovereignty, so the argument runs, should for the good of the nation itself be entrusted to those who can use it rightly. By this time national democracy has been transmuted into nationalist autocracy; and it was down this road that the German people were stampeded into the disaster of Nazism. It is not my intention to predict that a comparable fate will befall any or all of the presently democratic Asian or African peoples, although some of their neighbors, if they have not already succumbed, are at the least dangerously close to it. The democratic tides still run strongly in the world, but it would be folly to ignore the fact that they have often been turned aside, as in the Communist version which combines the name of democracy with the reality of totalitarian control. How much credence may be given the pessimistic tone of Guy Wint in his survey of British territories in Asia?

> Easy come, easy go. The liberal civilization came more or less by chance from the association of the ancient world with Great Britain,

and as easily it may go. It is perhaps simpler to turn Oriental man into an imitation Bolshevik, competent and ruthless, than into an imitation Western liberal.[27]

Save for a chosen few, democratic institutions have not been able to establish the conditions under which democracy could survive the buffetings of the world. It remains to be seen whether authoritarian rule can do better. Dynamic forces are in motion to bring the preconditions of democracy into being, and the drive toward social and economic development has its inescapable democratic implications. Even authoritarian regimes will have to take the people at large more into account than in the past and make use of plebiscitary symbols — the familiar frauds of an age which so frequently can neither take democracy nor leave it alone — but with no certainty that they will progress beyond symbolism. The best of all safeguards for the survival of democracy or for a return to it would be the mobilization of a populace vigilant to defend its rights and manage its own affairs. "Since the beginning of time," Adlai Stevenson has said, "governments have been mainly engaged in kicking people around. The astonishing achievement in modern times in the Western world is the idea that the citizens should do the kicking." [28] The future hangs on the question as to how many of the Asians and Africans will want to do the kicking when the chance comes their way.

SELF-DETERMINATION

CHAPTER XVI

The Principle of Self-Determination

In its wilsonian heyday self-determination seemed to many a simple and straightforward proposition consolidating under one rubric a number of nineteenth-century liberalism's most cherished propositions as to freedom and democracy and the rights of individuals and peoples. Its subsequent history has been a checkered one, both in its practical application and in the theorizing concerning it. It has tempted the sophisticate to display his wit and learning by demonstrating its inadequacies and contradictions and forced many statesmen to shake their heads in dismay at its uncouth proportions. Neither the skeptical sophisticate nor the perturbed statesman, it should immediately be added, has had any significant bearing on the revolutionary drive of peoples to achieve their independent destiny in their own fashion.

A summary glance at the experience of the world with self-determination since World War I will indicate its curious career. Brought to explicit formulation by Woodrow Wilson and the Bolsheviks in the course of the war, it became one of the fundamental principles of international society, and yet it found no place in the League Covenant. It served as a guideline for much of the reshaping of states in the peacemaking that followed close on the heels of the war, but after that process was completed the only new states to emerge on the international stage in the interwar decades were Eire in Europe and Iraq and Saudi Arabia in Asia. (The short-lived Japanese puppet state of Manchukuo may properly be ignored in this context, as may Hitler's creations in Central Europe.)

The experience of the Second World War and its aftermath

is in many respects the reverse of the first. Although the Atlantic Charter paid appropriate homage to self-determination in a somewhat indirect fashion, the Allies, leaving aside the restoration of peoples overrun by the Axis, were not only divided as to the application of self-determination but had also largely lost their enthusiasm for it as anything approaching a panacea. For the Soviet Union the aim in relation to its Western neighbors had become one of absorption or domination, and for the colonial powers self-determination meant self-destruction of empire. Hence, although the principle of self-determination of peoples now figured among the purposes of the United Nations Charter, it played only a scanty role in such peacemaking as took place. As a sorry substitute for a peace settlement, the cold war indeed worked to produce national partitions at some of the key points on the new-style international frontier. In Germany, Korea, and Vietnam the pleas of nations for unity were subordinated to the high strategy of international politics with the result that each had a jealously guarded barricade erected across it to demarcate the spheres of the two great opposing blocs; and China underwent a division between the mainland and Formosa. In each instance there were two bitterly opposed regimes, one Communist and the other non-Communist, each claiming to represent the national will under its own symbols.

Self-determination was still very much alive but its locus had shifted from Europe to Asia, the Middle East, and Africa, with the anti-colonial powers tending to insist that it was for practical purposes an issue which had relevance only in the colonial realm. In 1919, even though the Versailles peacemakers could frequently do little more than ratify states of fact already accomplished by the peoples directly concerned, the reordering of Central and Eastern Europe was carried on under the auspices of the victorious Allies essentially at the cost of their enemies and Russia. In 1945 and thereafter self-determination was a weapon aimed primarily at the victorious imperial powers themselves, and was under their control only in the sense that they could either fight it outright, as in Indochina and Indonesia, or yield to it with greater or less grace, as in the Philippines, India, Burma, and Ceylon. In contrast to Iraq's lonely eminence in the interwar decades, a host of new Asian and

African states were added to the international family in the years following the Second World War; and more are in process of being created out of the dwindling colonial empires.

The principle of self-determination derives from a familiar set of doctrines, whose apparent simplicity conceals a multitude of complications. The prime starting point is presumably the eighteenth-century proposition that governments must rest upon the consent of the governed, to which the nineteenth and twentieth centuries added the assumption that, since man is a national animal, the government to which he will give his consent is one representing his own nation. For full-blown self-determination to emerge it was only necessary to secure recognition of a new principle of natural law which entitles nations to possess their own states and, as the other side of the coin, renders illegitimate states with a non-national base. As Woodrow Wilson put it, the Central Empires had been forced into political bankruptcy because they dominated "alien peoples over whom they had no natural right to rule." [1] With the aid of a little sleight of hand the original claim that individuals must consent to or contractually establish the governments ruling them is thus transmuted into the natural right of nations to determine their own statehood.

The difficulties of self-determination become most serious when the doctrine is brought down from abstraction to working reality and when an effort is made, as in the United Nations' covenants on human rights, to translate it from ethical and political precepts to binding legal norms. In the current temper of world opinion no one can in principle oppose what has come to be the almost self-evident right of peoples to dispose of their own destinies, but it is unfortunately equally impossible to formulate this right in such terms as to make it meaningfully applicable to reality. Who can say the nations nay, and yet who can say what nations are and when and how they may assert themselves?

A RIGHT OF REVOLUTION

If the issue is put in its most drastic terms, to accept the right of self-determination in blanket fashion is to endow social entities which cannot be identified in advance with a right of revolution against the constituted authority of the state, and even to obligate the state to yield to the demands of the revolutionaries.

As for the first part of this proposition, little need be added to what has already been said about the vagrant character of our knowledge concerning what are and what are not nations. The matter becomes even more tangled when the Charter of the United Nations endorses the self-determination of *peoples*. Any number of questions come immediately to mind, and virtually none of them have answers which can be relied upon. How are the people to whom the principle applies to be defined? [2] Is it applicable only to people constituting a majority in a certain territory, or has a minority people an equal right? And if a majority decides one way today, may the whole or a segment of it decide differently tomorrow? Who speaks for the people in order to set the process in motion, and under what circumstances and by what methods may they press their case? What degree of maturity and political experience is needed to qualify a people to make an informed and responsible choice and to maintain the independence for which it may opt? That these are not idle academic questions can be illustrated by a host of examples. In addition to the whole troubled experience of the effort to sort out the European peoples on national lines there may now be added such Asian and African examples as Palestine, the partition of India, claims to Kashmir and Pushtunistan, the Karens in Burma, separatist movements in Indonesia and the West Irian issue, the divided peoples of Nigeria and the Sudan, the claims and counterclaims of China, Formosa, and the Formosans, the racial complexities of Malaya, tribal peoples in many areas not yet brought within any national fold, and the uncertain allegiance of the Arabs.

This is one key facet of the question — that peoples and even nations are uncertain quantities which from time to time assert themselves with irresistible force but which cannot be known in advance with any assurance. Even if nations are taken for granted as given — a not unreasonable assumption since nations will at all events make themselves heard in their own good time — when they come to self-determination they are inevitably exercising a revolutionary right. In its most extreme version the right of self-determination could mean the right of any group of disaffected people to break away at their pleasure from the state to which they presently belong and establish a new state closer to their heart's desire. As far back as 1793 in the setting of the French Revolution Carnot reported to the National Assembly that:

> If . . . any community whatever had the right to proclaim its will and separate from the main body under the influence of rebels, etc., every country, every town, every village, every farmstead might declare itself independent.[3]

Even though it is obvious that this *reductio ad absurdum* could not find acceptance, the problem still remains as to whether and how the right can be incorporated in any reasonably orderly and predictable scheme of things, within an acceptable framework of law.

Self-determination constitutes formal recognition of the principle that nation and state should coincide, but the plain fact is that the state structure derived from the past only occasionally and accidentally coincided with the national make-up of the world. That is, indeed, what all the furor was about. To bring the states into line with man's new-found national aspirations required a major act of political reconstruction. No question of sympathy with the desire of states to continue in existence in their present form need be involved in the contention that the exercise of self-determination is ordinarily an exercise of the right of revolution. The overturn and reconstitution of states to bring them into harmony with the demands of "the changing content of natural law" may be a highly praiseworthy achievement, but this necessitates appeal to a higher law which supersedes and seeks to nullify the established legality of states and governments. The states are the creators and maintainers of law in the ordinary sense, and a challenge to their own existence must have some other basic point of reference. At this stage there emerges a clash of rights derived from different sources: the state has an indisputable prerogative and duty to defend its own existence, and the nation comes likewise to be endowed with a right to overthrow the state.

It is, of course, conceivable that the right of self-determination should be explicitly embodied in the constitutional structure of individual states or of the international community as a whole. There is a ring of fundamental improbability to the notion that states will in advance concede their own potential dissolution. It may be that the Jeffersonian defense of occasional revolution is an admirable thing, but it defies constitutional formulation. The only examples of a preordained acceptance of self-determination which I have been able to find are contained in the constitutions of Burma and the Soviet Union, and for the French dependencies in the constitution of the Fifth Republic. The grant of a right of secession to the constituent republics of the U.S.S.R. can be dismissed as a piece of window dressing which lacks all political reality save its propaganda value. From Lenin on, it has been made clear that the needs of socialism override the claims of nations. Already embraced within the Communist fatherland, the peoples have achieved their *summum bonum*, and, by the easy logic of Communist dialectics, any recalculation of their destiny is to be undertaken by the hierarchy of the single and monolithic Party. As W. K. Hancock adroitly put it in a dictum which has wider applicability than merely to the Soviet Union: "The apostles of secession have unfettered freedom as nationalists, but they will be shot as revolutionaries." [4]

The case of Burma is a slightly more realistic one. Under the constitution of 1947 the states representing the minority peoples within the Union of Burma, with the exception of the Kachins and by later constitutional amendment the Karens, were given the right to secede after an interval of ten years from the time the constitution came into force, and, in contrast to the Soviet model, the processes by which this might be accomplished were spelled out in some detail.[5] Although it is unlikely to be put to the test, this is a unique model of a constitutional provision establishing self-determination as an operative constitutional right.

On the international stage the most significant earlier effort to institutionalize self-determination was that of Colonel House and Woodrow Wilson in preliminary drafts of the League Covenant. What was essentially involved in their proposal was an effort to square a continuing right of self-determination with the Covenant's guarantee of the territorial integrity and political independence of the League's members. In brief, it provided that, subject to League approval, territorial readjustments might be undertaken to meet "changes in present racial conditions and aspirations, pursuant to the principle of self-determination." [6] After going through several drafting stages the proposal was dropped under a variety of understandable pressures, and the guarantees of the famous Article X were allowed to stand without impairment by what the President had earlier called "the sacred right of self-determination." As might easily have been expected, this meant simply that the territorial integrity of states took priority over the potential aspirations of nations.

THE UNITED NATIONS

Considering its intrinsic importance, it is surprising how little attention the framers of the United Nations appear to have devoted to the loose language in which self-determination was incorporated in the Charter. The earlier Dumbarton Oaks version of the Charter made no mention of it, but at San Francisco the four sponsoring governments introduced it as amendments to existing articles, at the suggestion, it has been stated, of the Soviet Union.[7] This clause moved tranquilly on its way and ultimately made its appearance in both Articles 1 and 55 as "respect for the principle of equal rights and self-determination of peoples." That at least one of the basic problems involved was not wholly ignored is evident from a Committee report which affirmed that the principle of self-determination was desired by peoples everywhere and should be clearly enunciated in the Charter, but held that "the principle conformed to the purposes of the Charter only insofar as it implied the right of self-government of peoples and not the right of secession." [8]

To those who had their doubts it must have been consoling to have secession thus ruled out (even though it was not specified whether the break-away of a colony constituted secession) as it was also consoling to have self-determination recognized only as a principle to be respected and not as a right. The harsh reality remained that self-determination very often involved secession and that what was labeled as a principle was sure to be asserted as a right. Nor could much reliance be placed on the denial in Article 2:7 of the right of the United Nations to intervene in matters of domestic jurisdiction. Put to the working test of UN practice, this supposed bulwark of state's rights was soon found to have as many holes in it as the majority in the organ concerned was prepared to open up.

Since San Francisco the concern of the United Nations with problems of self-determination has been continuous and many-faceted. In very considerable part it has focused on one or another aspect of colonialism, including involvement in specific cases such as that of Indonesia, Algeria, or Cyprus, but the debates swirling around the effort to draft Covenants on Human Rights have also provoked much searching discussion of more general considerations. Even when the latter has been the actual or nominal intent, however, the problems of colonialism are so evidently the central issue that they habitually intrude themselves.[9]

This was apparent when the General Assembly in 1952 decided to include in the Covenant on Human Rights an article which should read, "All peoples shall have the right of self-determination," and stipulated that, in particular, states having responsibility for non-self-governing territories should promote the realization of the right in relation to such territories. A little later in the year the Commission on Human Rights obeyed by elaborating the proposed article in the following fashion: "All peoples and all nations shall have the right of self-determination, namely, the right freely to determine their political, economic, social and cultural status." To this the Commission added both a special injunction in relation to non-self-governing and trust territories, and a Chilean proposal which broadened self-determination to include permanent sovereignty over natural wealth and resources. Not satisfied with these actions, the Commission recommended a further resolution, to the profound pain of the colonial powers, which not only specified that the demand for colonial self-government should be ascertained through a plebiscite held under UN auspices, but also roundly declared that "slavery exists where an alien people hold power over the destiny of a people."[10]

There is no occasion to pursue in detail here all the ramifications of the ensuing battles over self-determination, colonialism, and the proposed Covenants. Generally the Western powers and their friends, normally including the United States, took an increasingly dim view of the entire matter, while the Asian-African and Soviet blocs, aided by some of the Latin Americans, pressed their case as vigorously as possible. The charge of slavery was eliminated and other terms were softened, as, for example, in the decision of the Assembly in December 1952, that the administering powers should facilitate the exercise of the right of self-determination by colonial peoples, "the wishes of the people being ascertained through plebiscites or other recognized democratic means, preferably under the auspices of the United Nations." The majority, however, continued to back the main lines which had been worked out. As the debate wore on, it became increasingly clear that Covenants including the disputed self-determination provisions were exceedingly unlikely to secure the adherence of the Western powers. To add to the already ample array of problems, from the Human Rights Commission and other sources came proposals to establish some type of organ which would be empowered to look into, and perhaps act upon, allegations of a denial of the right of self-determination.

One of the difficulties in the situation is that, although the United Nations might help to make it so, self-determination is not a right which finds any place in international law. The leading case on the subject, a singularly clear-cut one, has not lost its validity. Immediately after World War I Sweden laid claim to the Aaland Islands which, together with Finland, it had lost to Russia early in the nineteenth century. When Finland achieved independence in the course of the Russian Revolution the islands continued to form a part of Finnish territory. It was not seriously disputed that over 95 per cent of their inhabitants were "altogether Swedish in origin, in habits, in language, and in culture," and informal plebiscites as well as other evidence confirmed their desire for incorporation in Sweden. The Swedish claim was considered by the League of Nations in its earliest days, just after the adoption of self-determination by the peacemakers as a major principle in the reshaping of Europe. Despite the unassailable case that had been presented as far as self-determination for the islanders was concerned, the claims of peoples to disrupt states were flatly rejected.

Two key passages may be cited from the League's documents dealing with the matter. In 1920 a Committee of Jurists, appointed by the Council, reported that national self-determination was not recognized by positive international law: "In the absence of express provisions in international treaties, the right of disposing of national territory is essentially an attribute of the sovereignty of every State."

A Commission of Rapporteurs gave a similar verdict to the Council in 1921, even though it conceded that the islanders feared Finnish even more than Russian domination. Asking whether it were possible to have a general rule that a minority can separate to join another state or become independent, it stated:

> The answer can only be in the negative. To concede to minorities either of language or religion, or to any fractions of a population, the right of withdrawing from the community to which they belong, because it is their wish or their good pleasure, would be to destroy order and stability within States and to inaugurate anarchy in international life; it would be to uphold a theory incompatible with the very idea of the State as a territorial and political entity.[11]

These are not novel considerations — nor are they in the least persuasive to those who deliberately seek to overturn the stability of the present order in the name of what they assert as a higher principle. It is the normal and expected procedure that the state authorities should proclaim their right to maintain things as they are whenever a segment of the people seeks to secede or to overturn the existing state. As the Pope protested French incorporation of Avignon in the Revolution, so Metternich held that for the powers to recognize the inclinations and repugnances of provinces within states would be to introduce a new and limitless confusion, bringing the social body to the point of an overpowering anarchy. In similar language Abraham Lincoln, confronted with the threatened secession of the South, laid it down in his first Inaugural: "Plainly, the central idea of secession is the essence of anarchy." Stressing the rightness of the principle of majority rule, he warned that government must cease if the minority refuses to acquiesce, and that the new confederacy would itself be threatened by arbitrary secessions.[12] To make it clear that the hesitations as to self-determination are not confined solely to the Western world, let me add a single example from India. The Indian nation had successfully asserted its right of self-determination as against British rule, but at the cost of a further secession in Pakistan which pointed to dangers like those of which Lincoln had warned. The demand in

India for a redrawing of the map of the country on the basis of linguistic states has, since independence, had to yield priority to the prime need of maintaining unbroken national unity. The 1955 report of the States Re-organization Commission stated firmly that, so far as the component parts of the Indian Union were concerned, there could be no question of a right of self-determination regardless of other factors and circumstances. The Commission held that if self-determination were the governing principle, the possible demand for separate States would be unlimited. "Every linguistic or other minority group might demand a State for itself, and the wishes of the people could be swayed by purely temporary considerations." [13] An outspoken champion of self-determination on the international stage, India's devotion to it breaks down, and very sensibly so, when it comes to its application within India itself. Nehru's handling of the question of Kashmir has been equivocal, and to the untutored eye India's suppression of the risings of the Naga tribesmen was not easy to distinguish from the colonial method of dealing with such problems. That other Asian and African states would in the normal course of events act in the same fashion seems not open to question, even though the Bandung Conference of 1955 gave its full support to the principle of self-determination as basic to all fundamental human rights.

In his memoirs former President Truman, referring to the nationalist movements in Asia and Africa, affirmed that the American people have always accepted without "ifs" the right of a people to determine its own destiny.[14] This was an admirably forthright position, but it has the fatal defect of not coinciding with the facts for either President Truman or his predecessors who have hedged in the right with considerable care. The United States has moved beyond the days when President Coolidge could defend his veto of a bill calling for a Philippine plebiscite with the contention that it would be trifling with the sacred feelings innate in humankind to ask the Filipinos with which state they wished to be associated, but the American position is still a cautious one. The standard form has come to be something approximating the Pacific Charter appended to the SEATO agreement: self-determination is to be promoted for countries "whose people desire it and are able to undertake its responsibilities"; or the joint Eisenhower-Eden declaration of February 1, 1956, that they had dedicated themselves "to the goal of self-government and independence of all countries whose people desire and are capable of sustaining an independent existence." Not, in other words, self-determination for all who may seek it, but for those who are regarded as qualified for it. Even in the latter category it would not be difficult to demonstrate that the United States, like all other states, has inserted "ifs" where other political considerations appeared to make them desirable. The wishes of the people of Okinawa will be given less than full credence where they run counter to the American estimate of military needs.

All too often self-determination is a right to be defended in lofty terms when it is politically advantageous and to be rejected when it is not. Despite occasional surface appearances to the contrary, the issue is not one which divides East and West in any of the meanings of that geographical expression. Pakistan is as enthusiastic for free self-determination for Kashmir as is Afghanistan for Pushtunistan; and neither Nationalist nor Communist Chinese give evidence of profound concern over the self-determination of the Formosans, nor is the United States prepared to acquiesce in the choice of the form of government made by the mainland Chinese. The Soviet Union finds it an excellent right for use against the West and its colonies as the West holds it eminently applicable to the peoples of the U.S.S.R. and its satellites.

The Communists are, however, more frankly selective in their use of self-determination than is the rest of the world. Lenin and Stalin made it clear that self-determination was good where it involved a breach in the imperialist structure and intolerable where it involved separation from the Communist fatherland. In the days before he was read out of the brotherhood Trotsky defended the Soviet take-over of Georgia with the active participation of the Red Army and went on to state the general principle under which he and his colleagues acted:

> We do not only recognize but we give full support to the principle of self-determination, wherever it is directed against feudal, capitalist and imperialist states. But wherever the fiction of self-determination, in the hands of the bourgeoisie, becomes a weapon directed against the proletarian revolution, we have no occasion to treat this

fiction differently from the other "principles" of democracy per-
verted by capitalism.[15]

In brief, the Soviet Union gives all-out backing to the right of
self-determination except where it threatens to impair Communist
interests. No right of self-determination was invoked on behalf
of the people of the Kuriles and southern Sakhalin, taken over
from Japan after World War II, although it is to be applied to
everyone else's "salt-water" dependencies.

It is no accident that self-determination, as a new tenet of
natural law attacking the existing state structure, should be associated in its practical manifestations with wars and the aftermath
of wars. In rare instances it has been accepted in wholly peaceful
fashion, as in the separation of Norway and Sweden, the attainment
of independence by the Philippines, or Britain's readiness to speed
some of her colonies to independence after 1945, but the great run
of cases are linked to violence or to such fundamental changes in
power relationships as occur most notably as a result of wars. The
wars of the French Revolution and Napoleon started it on its way
in Europe; the unification of Germany and Italy required war;
Central and Eastern Europe were reconstructed as a consequence
of the first World War; and the Second World War opened the
door to self-determination for Asia and Africa. It has often been
argued, though with dubious validity, that the full-scale application of self-determination will bring peace, but it would be impossible to argue that self-determination itself has normally been
achieved by peaceful means or in generally peaceful situations. An
added threat to peace and friendly relations among nations appears
wherever third parties intervene to back the claim of a people to
break away from the state to which they are presently attached.

The right of self-determination has as yet found no stable
place in the international legal structure nor has it been accepted
by states as a policy to be applied consistently and across the
board.[16] Indeed, I would suggest that it is essentially miscast in
the role of a legal right which can be made an operative part of
either domestic or international systems. It is a force of incalculable
importance which has already brought immense changes and will
presumably continue its triumphant sweep as long as nations born

and unborn feel their destiny incomplete. To recognize it as one of the basic forces shaping the modern world is, however, by no means to say that it can be tamed and brought within the limits of a constitution, treaty, or covenant. It is distantly conceivable that under the United Nations or otherwise the states of the world might give it working legal and political status, but it is much more probable that its revolutionary implications will keep it outside the constitutional framework.

It must be regarded as a clear gain for mankind whenever legal and orderly procedures of peaceful change are substituted for the violence of war and revolution, but it is folly to think that any such gain has been achieved by the mere issuance of loose pronouncements of the "all peoples" variety. If the right of self-determination is to be made meaningful, it must be sharply delimited. The more strictly the peoples to whom it is to be applied are defined, the more possible it becomes to make something of it as a right which can be stated with reasonable precision and given institutional expression.

NON-SELF-GOVERNING TERRITORIES

For present purposes, in the light of the actual concerns of the United Nations, the most significant illustration of this possibility involves the non-self-governing territories which have so largely monopolized UN attention. Although there may be arguments at the fringes, as in relation to the incorporated overseas territories of France or Portugal, the colonies constitute relatively fixed and identifiable bodies of people. Here certainly it would be possible, although still politically difficult enough, not only to legislate into existence a formal declaration of the right of colonial peoples to self-determination under specified conditions but also to establish procedures through which the international community would decide by whom and when and how the right would be exercised, and the rights and obligations of third parties.

There has in fact already been a substantial movement in this direction in the United Nations, building on the two basic principles that non-self-governing territories are an international responsibility for which the administering authorities are to be held accountable and that their proper goal is self-government or independence, even though the Charter mentions independence only for the Trust territories. The Mandates System constituted recognition that the extension of colonialism on the old terms was no longer acceptable, and the United Nations, in addition to tightening up some of the provisions of that system, took the bolder step of bringing all non-self-governing territories within the sphere of international concern. Under the pressure of the anti-colonialists in the General Assembly the Trusteeship System has come to be seen increasingly as a vehicle for the realization of self-determination by the peoples embraced in it, who should in the interval be given ever greater responsibility in democratically constituted governments. Reaching well beyond the limited language of Chapter XI of the Charter, the Assembly has attempted to apply essentially the same principles to all the dependencies as have been applied to the Trusteeships. Even though the Assembly's formal powers to act in this broader sphere are scanty and uncertain, it has among other things affirmed the right of non-self-governing territories to self-determination, recommended the setting of target dates as in the model of the ten year trusteeship established for Italian Somaliland, asserted a claim to decide whether self-government has been achieved, and explored in detail the factors to be taken into account in reaching such a decision.

Secretary-General Trygve Lie said of the Trusteeship System that its success would afford "a reassuring demonstration that there is a peaceful and orderly means of achieving the difficult transition from backward and subject status to self-government or independence." [17] Such peaceful and orderly means, however, have not yet been devised for the colonial peoples in general. Their drive to achieve self-determination has reached a stage beyond that of merely having the sympathetic approval of the world at large, but it has not reached the status of international acceptance of a right fortified by established procedures, nor do the conditions attached to the amendment of the Charter make it likely that that desirable goal will be achieved in any foreseeable future.

The steps which the United Nations has taken have met with the vehement objection of several of the colonial powers. Among the counterclaims is that of the Belgians who have attempted to meet the attack of the anti-colonialists by undertaking an offensive of their own. The so-called Belgian thesis, repudiating the notion that all colonial regimes automatically deserve condemnation as evil, claims to find non-self-governing peoples scattered widely over the earth's surface, and by no means only in what are customarily accepted as colonies. It attacks the "salt-water fallacy" according to which rule over an alien people separated from the mother country by open sea is intolerable and subject to international control whereas similar rule over an alien people on an unbroken stretch of dry land is neither suspect nor a matter for international concern. It is further contended that colonialism, far from being inherently bad, is in fact frequently freer, more enlightened, and more progressive than some of the regimes imposed on peoples embraced within the territory of sovereign states. In illustration of this theme a number of familiar cases are cited, such as the position of the Indians in several Latin American countries, of the Africans in the Liberian hinterland, and, on a grand scale, of the non-Russian peoples within the Soviet Union. For all of these and others like them, it is argued, international attention is at least as pressing a need as it is for any colonial people. On this basis the Belgians have protested their full loyalty to the principle of self-determination, but have been insistent that they cannot go along with resolutions which single out colonialism as the only enemy worthy of attack.

To all of this ingeniously worked-out line of argument there is perhaps no wholly satisfactory answer, but it carries scant conviction to those who have set out to do battle on the colonial front. Without a shadow of a doubt the conditions in many non-colonial countries are worse than in many colonies and as deserving of international attention, including the application of self-determination, but it is idle to think that the well-established category of colonies, or, in UN terms, of non-self-governing territories, can be merged with the other comparable evils of mankind. The argument almost wholly fails to meet political realities. The anti-colonialists rightly fear that the net effect of an acceptance of the Belgian thesis would be to divert public interest from the colonial question, and to introduce so many additional confusions and obstacles as to make it virtually certain that nothing would be done about any of them. The United Nations has good reason to attempt to deal with the problems of oppressed and under-privileged peoples in independent states through programs of minority protection and other devices. The issues of colonialism, however, deserve consideration separately and in their own right.

A FEW ILLUSTRATIVE CASES

Some of the major ways in which the path to self-determination is blocked or obscured may be illustrated by a glance at a few recent examples of the application or nonapplication of the principle in relation to Asia and Africa.

In the Arab world self-determination got off to a singularly bad start after World War I. Here the Allies demonstrated how great was the contradiction between their professed adherence to the principle and their actual readiness to ignore it when it interfered with their imperial interest. From the Arab standpoint the three principal issues involved were the partition of the Arab peoples, the subordination of some of them to British and French control, and the acceptance of Zionist ambitions in Palestine. To these actions, regarded by the Arabs as a shocking failure of the West to act in accord with its promises and its own proclaimed principles, must be attributed much of the anti-Westernism which has recently characterized the Arab world. However one may choose to interpret the tangled record of the negotiations, documents, and conversations of the war years, every word and implication of which have been examined with microscopic care and passionate partisanship, there is an immense gap between what the Arab leaders wanted and thought they were being promised and what the Allied statesmen thought they were promising and were in fact prepared to do when it came time to pay the bill. As far as the Arabs are concerned, all the subtleties of interpretation which have been invoked lose their significance in face of the bare fact that Arab leaders believed, not without reason, that they had been promised an independent Arab state in Asia, with only minor geographic limitations. Instead of such a state they were presented with the carving up of vital parts of the Arab territories in accord with secret wartime agreements and the imposition of French or British colonial rule upon some of the resulting entities. It was cold comfort to the Arabs that the colonialism which was substituted for the independence they had expected was dressed in the guise of the new-style Mandates System.

At no point in the proceedings were even the minimum decencies of self-determination observed. Whether the Arabs could have overcome the divisions in their own ranks to the extent of setting up and maintaining a single Arab state is highly debatable, but certainly they were given no chance at it nor, alternatively, to shape their own multiple state system. What actually happened was as clear a process of imperial dividing and ruling as has been seen. The mandatories who, with the League's blessing, appointed themselves to guide the Arabs to a surer footing in the modern world were by no means those the peoples would have chosen for themselves, and, in the case of the French in Syria and Lebanon, were rejected with vehemence. Furthermore, the Arabs promptly claimed that they were quite as well fitted to govern themselves independently as were the Balkan peoples when the latter achieved their independence from Ottoman rule: if full independence in one case, why not in the other? To this contention there was added the reverse peculiarity that a status of tutelage was imposed upon precisely those Arabs who had the most intimate and long-continued contact with the West and hence might be regarded as best able to stand by themselves, while the less "advanced" Arabs of the peninsula, still largely nomadic and unacquainted with the modern world, were acknowledged to possess sovereign independence. At a later date, after World War II, exactly the same kind of question was being asked in connection with other Arab territories; if the former Mandates could have independence, and, particularly, if Libya could be made an independent state by formal international action, what excuse could there be for holding Morocco, Tunisia, and Algeria?

These were unanswerable questions which the Arabs in due course answered in their own fashion by rising against alien domination. Here as elsewhere Western imperialism worked to produce its own antibodies.

ZIONISM

The acceptance of Zionist aspirations in Palestine was, however, a very different matter. Instead of working to correct itself,
it grew always worse and more threatening from the standpoint
of the Arabs who had from the outset lacked faith in the solemn
assurance that their rights and position would not suffer. The
conception of creating a Jewish national home in Palestine could
not possibly be squared with the principle of self-determination,
or, for that matter, of democracy, on the basis of any of the generally accepted criteria. Aside from the fact that many Jews wanted
to establish themselves there, the only claim which had any conceivable status was that Palestine had been the ancient Jewish
homeland many centuries ago; but to accept the legitimacy of
claims to self-determination whose basis is possession broken off
two thousand years earlier would be to stir up such a host of
conflicting and unrealizable demands as totally to discredit the
principle. It is, of course, true that some small number of Jews
had continued to live in Palestine or had at some point returned
there, but at the time of the Balfour Declaration and the introduction of the Mandate the Jewish community in Palestine was
vastly outnumbered by the Arabs whose occupancy dated back
to the remote past. If self-determination were to be applied in the
customary fashion of seeking out what the people of the country
wanted, there could be no doubt where the overwhelming majority
lay nor of the rejection by that majority of both Balfour Declaration and Mandate. The Zionist program could be carried through
as a decision of policy only if someone were prepared to enforce
it in the face of bitter opposition.

The Arabs were neither slow nor bashful in bringing these
and similar points to the world's attention, and as early as August
1919, they received neutral support from the King-Crane Commission sent by President Wilson to ascertain the state of affairs
in Syria and Palestine. Asserting that the Zionists looked to practically complete dispossession of the non-Jewish inhabitants of
Palestine, this Commission found nearly nine-tenths of the population to be non-Jewish and emphatically opposed to the entire

Zionist program. With specific reference to the Wilsonian principle of self-determination, the Commission held:

> To subject a people so minded to unlimited Jewish immigration, and to steady financial and social pressure to surrender the land, would be a gross violation of the principle just quoted, and of the people's rights, though it be kept within the forms of law.[18]

As the Jews saw it, what now happened was not only the opening to them of a haven of refuge, but also their rightful return to an ancient homeland to which they had never surrendered title. To the Arabs it was a prolonged and tragically successful invasion of an Arab country by an alien people under Western imperialist auspices, ending in the expulsion of most of the people whose country it was. No suggestion of a plebiscite accompanied the General Assembly's proposal that Palestine be partitioned. Since the establishment of Israel and the reduction of the Arab population to some 10 per cent of the whole, the Arab states have insisted that Israel is a totally illegitimate creation, overriding the natural right of the Palestinian Arabs to their own country, and that it has no existence which they are prepared to tolerate and recognize.[19]

CYPRUS

In the same part of the world another imperial denial of self-determination which has attracted global attention in recent years concerns the island of Cyprus. Here the basic circumstances were not unlike those of the Aaland Islands, at least in the sense that the great bulk of the population was of one ethnic stock and sought union with its national country. Four-fifths of the half million inhabitants of the island were Greek and were claimed as devoted adherents of union with Greece, which country with increasing insistence demanded the island's cession; but the remaining fifth was Turkish and hostile to such a merger. On the basis of a count of heads the verdict of self-determination was clear, but geography, history, and high strategy all combined to confuse the issue. Geographically, the island lay only some forty miles off the Turkish coast, and ten or more times that distance from Greece. On the score of history it was Britain's pleasure to insist that Cyprus had been Egyptian, Persian, Roman, Genoese, and Turkish, but never Greek except for a short period in the fourth century B.C. It fell into British hands as the result of an Anglo-Turkish treaty of 1878 whose avowed purpose was the defense of Turkish possessions against Russian aggression, and this cession was reconfirmed by the 1923 treaty of Lausanne to which Greece was also a party. Strategically, the loss of Palestine and the Suez base left Cyprus as the only base from which the British could defend their still considerable Middle Eastern interests and commitments. To counter the argument as to the precariousness of a base located in the midst of a hostile population, and the consequent moral that the demand for self-determination should be granted, the British pointed unhappily to what self-determination had done to their holdings in Egypt and elsewhere. The Turks, who also had an obvious strategic and political concern, protested that history and geography made it clear that, if the island were to change hands again, its prior owner had claims which could not be ignored.

The issue was one of relatively old standing. In 1931 the Cypriot demand for union with Greece took a sufficiently violent form to lead the British authorities to suspend the legislature and govern from that time forward through the Governor aided by an Executive Council. Later British efforts to secure acceptance of more liberal constitutions were rebuffed by leaders who would take no substitute for union.[20] When Greece raised the issue in the United Nations in 1954 Britain promptly pleaded domestic jurisdiction in an effort to keep it off the Assembly's agenda, with the lack of success which has customarily attended such efforts. Although it presumably carried little conviction save to those already converted, there was more substance to Britain's protest that the endorsement of the Greek attempt to interest the United Nations in its claims would undermine international stability by encouraging states to seek the incorporation of related peoples beyond their frontiers even though those frontiers had been accepted by treaty.[21] This was an authentic echo of the classic objection to self-determination, but it was harder to take seriously the British contention, backed by the Turks, that self-determination was not really involved because what the Cypriots wanted was a merger with Greece and not independence. On the basis of this contention, however, several states shifted their support from *enosis* to independence for Cyprus. The final solution of the controversy which the British, Greek, and Turkish governments agreed upon in 1959, ruled out both partition and union with Greece, called for the establishment of a Republic of Cyprus organized about the Greek and Turkish Cypriot communities, and safeguarded British control of military bases and installations.

The Cypriot claims, backed by terrorism as well as by political action, raised a complex series of questions not lightly to be brushed aside. Do history, geography, and economics play a role, or is the popular majority the sole determinant? What are the rights and duties of minorities and of the third states which are the national states of those minorities? One further issue may be mentioned which never came quite clearly to the fore in the Cyprus case although the British tried to put it there in claiming the base as necessary for the fulfillment of Britain's free world commitments against Communism: At what point, if any, does a genuine international interest supersede the right of a nation to determine itself and its territory in any fashion that it may choose? This was an issue which was also laid squarely on the table in Colonel Nasser's nationalization of the Suez Canal Company in 1956.

BRITISH GUIANA

In British Guiana in 1953 there appeared another aspect of the impairment of self-determination in a colonial setting, and one whose shadows reached far afield. The essential question at stake was: how large is the freedom of an advanced colonial people to choose for itself the kind of institutions which it wants? What if such a people selects a political and economic system which the administering power regards as a betrayal of the real interests of the people for whom it still has responsibility?

When the crisis erupted, British Guiana, despite poverty, illiteracy, economic imbalance and racial diversity, appeared to be moving successfully ahead through the stages on the road to self-government which were becoming standard for British colonial policy. On the basis of the Waddington Commission report of 1951 and to meet growing political agitation, a new constitution had been granted which created a bicameral legislature composed of an appointive second chamber and a House of Assembly of twenty-four members elected by universal adult suffrage plus three official members — the Chief Secretary, the Attorney-General, and the Financial Secretary. In the Executive Council, presided over by the Governor, sat the three official members of the Assembly, six ministers elected by the Assembly and placed in charge of departments of government, and one minister without portfolio elected by the second chamber. The political effect of this reform was to place a very large measure of control in the hands of the elected majority. In April 1953, the first elections were held under this new instrument, resulting in a substantial sweep by the People's Progressive Party, headed by Cheddi Jagan, which won eighteen of the twenty-four elective seats in the Assembly. With this victory, which incidentally gave the party a larger hold in the Assembly than its share in the popular vote, the P.P.P. could count on dominating both legislature and executive.

In a few months the British authorities came to the conviction that the colony was being taken over by the Communists as represented by the P.P.P. leadership in general and Jagan in particular, and was threatened by violence and revolutionary overturn. The Governor was equipped with the reserve powers which had been so very charily exercised where elected majorities had come into power elsewhere under similar constitutions; but to draw upon them meant not only to reverse the stream of political advance but also to challenge the recently expressed will of the people. Confronted by this dilemma, the Governor took the drastic step of suspending the constitution and reintroducing authoritarian colonial rule, thus precipitating a clear-cut issue.

As Jagan presented it, that issue was not one of Communism: "It is really whether any people — colonial people — have a right to rule themselves." [22] To bolster his case he threw into the scales the Atlantic Charter's pledge to respect the right of all people to choose the form of government under which they will live and the assertion in the UN Declaration of Human Rights that "the will of the people shall be the basis of the authority of government."

It was beyond dispute that the expressed will of the people had been flouted, but the Commission appointed by the British government to investigate the constitutional controversy in effect came to the conclusion that the people of Guiana were not yet in a position to make political choices in a responsible fashion. Lacking the prerequisites for democracy and having neither an effective two party system nor an understanding of economic realities, the people were exposed to the likelihood of one-party rule. Because of its broader bearing as well as its specific reference to Guiana, the Commission's estimate of the political prospects might usefully be cited.

> In these circumstances the alternatives seem either that rival parties of comparable strength will compete for the homogeneous popular vote by simply vying with each other in the design of programmes which will promise the voter what he wants rather than attempt a serious treatment of the country's problems; or, as events have shown, that a single party will command such support among the immature and undiscriminating electorate that having no immediate and effective rivals for office it may safely ignore the rights of minorities and, by abuse of its powers, so consolidate its position that the risk of eventual defeat by the democratic process is eliminated.[23]

Should democracy be allowed to destroy democracy? What right has any people to determine the life of another, and if such a right exists, at what point does it cease? Where the exercise of self-determination remains for the moment in the control of the colonial power, or of organs of the international community, should it be conceded if there is good evidence that human rights and fundamental freedoms will be impaired rather than protected and advanced? These are speculative questions of great moment for self-determination, and it must be evident that they have no easy answers. The democrat may find himself torn between his acceptance of self-determination and his devotion to democracy itself.[24]

One concrete issue with which the British were embarrassingly faced in Guiana concerned the next steps to be taken. The tight colonial control which had been reimposed could not be maintained indefinitely, while the restoration to power of a popularly elected majority would run head on into the danger that the prior official attack on the victorious party had worked to enhance its prestige as the champion of the people against the imperialists.

With due deliberation, giving time for a cooling-off period, the British introduced a new constitution which abolished the post of Chief Minister and gave the Governor power to appoint enough members of the Legislative Council to balance the elected members if this should prove necessary. Again Jagan and the P.P.P. came out on top, winning nine of the fourteen elective seats, three more of which went to a rival offshoot of the P.P.P. The Governor was presented with the choice of overriding the popular mandate or of recalling to power the man who had been the center of the earlier storm. Jagan was asked to form a government and, as leader of the majority party, assumed the position of virtual Chief Minister although his official post was that of Minister of Trade and Industry. His wife, Detroit-born Janet Rosenburg, whom he met while studying dentistry at Northwestern University, became Minister of Labor, Health, and Housing. With the Governor's substantial reserve powers in the background, Jagan promised moderation and respect for the existing constitution although he reserved the right to agitate against it through the normal democratic processes. To all outward appearance peace has reigned in this second and modified venture in constitutional progress for Guiana.

The lessons of British Guiana were widely studied elsewhere. As might be expected, they were generally taken by the anti-colonialists as justification of their fear that imperial promises of self-government were not to be taken at face value: self-government would be tolerated only where it worked within patterns acceptable to the imperialists. In a different setting this fear was further substantiated in the year following the Guiana crisis when the government of Guatemala, accused of being part of the international Communist conspiracy, was overthrown by invading forces which gave every evidence of outside support while the United Nations and the Organization of American States stood amicably by in a state of some confusion. On the other side of the fence, the imperial authorities saw the events in Guiana as justifying *their* fear that the end of colonialism might mean a taking over by Communism. The Guiana experience was cited by the British as furnishing grounds for moving slowly in Cyprus, and it no doubt forced second thoughts about self-government for

Singapore where it was an obvious risk that the main beneficiaries would be the Communists.

THE TWO TOGOLANDS

The complexities of self-determination in a colonial setting even where the desire to maintain empire plays only an incidental role is well illustrated by the recent history of the two Togolands, later paralleled in the case of the Cameroons. The problems of the Togolands were brought to a head not by imperial intransigence but by the British decision to grant independence to the neighboring Gold Coast. Spared only the extra hazards presented by European or Asian settlers, these two Trust Territories encompassed approximately every other type of division and inner differentiation which Africa and colonialism could provide. A survey of some of the highlights of Togoland history will lend concreteness to the contention that the principle of self-determination offers no self-evident answers to the problem it is supposed to deal with.

Togoland was wholly a German colonial creation, brought into being in the last years of the nineteenth century and existing as a single political entity only until 1914. Even such scanty unity as German rule brought to the disparate peoples lumped together in a colony arbitrarily carved out from the African landscape was lost in the equally arbitrary partition between Britain and France after World War I. From that time forward the people on the two sides of the line were subject to very different influences, including education in two different European languages. Since the two Togolands shared the typical ethnic make-up of their West African neighbors in the sense of a sharp distinction between the peoples of the northern hinterland and those of the coastal regions, both Britain and France undertook an administrative separation between the northern and the southern portions of their territories. The political consequences of this division are reflected in the comment of James S. Coleman that "until the last five years the overwhelming majority of the peoples of northern Togoland were unaware of the existence of Togoland." [25]

A further point of differentiation arose from the fact that while French Togoland was administered as a politically distinct unit, not merged with next-door Dahomey, British Togoland was treated as an integral part of the adjoining Gold Coast, north Togoland being joined to the Gold Coast's Northern Territories and the south to the Colony. In consequence, British Togoland had virtually no independent existence of its own. French Togoland, despite its political separateness, was for all practical purposes run on the standard French colonial lines, involving the usual processes of assimilation.

In addition to these political and administrative separations and linkages, tribal groups overflowed all the European-imposed boundaries and maintained some sense of communal identity even though they had been cut off from each other by imperial surgery. The most significant and vocal group were the Ewe people of the south, numbering some 700,000, who covered an area reaching from the Gold Coast across British Togoland into the French territory. As early as 1919 a number of the Ewe chiefs protested to Lord Milner, Secretary of State for the Colonies, against handing over part of Togoland to the French on the ground that it meant separating members of the tribe from their brethren in the Gold Coast. "The feeling of your Lordship's petitioners," they concluded, "will be more clearly understood when they are considered side by side with those of the inhabitants of Alsace and Lorraine at the time of their annexation to Germany in 1871." [26] But this early effort to oppose self-determination to imperial bargains proved of no avail.

In its long and tangled United Nations career the Togoland problem was subject to drastic swings of sentiment and interpretation, due in part, no doubt, to lack of knowledge as to the realities of the situation but in part also to the fact that the Togolanders were divided among themselves and changed their minds from time to time. The widening out of the circle of those who had an awareness of social, economic, and political issues led to a heightened consciousness of the distinctions which separated the Togolese from each other.

Three major types of proposals successively dominated the deliberations of the United Nations. The first was based on the assumption that the most urgent matter was Ewe unification, but the Trusteeship Council and the Assembly in the exercise of its jurisdiction over the Trusteeship System had no proper concern with the Gold Coast where a substantial portion of the Ewe lived and of which British Togoland was an integral part. Nonetheless, in 1950 the Assembly in Resolution 441 (V) recognized "the great importance of the Ewe problem" and urged that an adequate solution be speedily found for it in full accord with the real wishes and interests of the people concerned. In the next round the Assembly moved on to a clearer linking together of the inescapably related questions of Ewe unification and of the unification of the two Togolands. By 1952, the latter issue had come to predominance, with the result that the Assembly in Resolution 652 (VII) concluded that "the unification of the two Togolands is the manifest aspiration of the majority of the population of both Trust Territories," and urged Britain and France to work toward as large a unification as possible.

Very shortly, however, it became apparent that with the approach of independence for the Gold Coast a new star was rising whose magnetic attraction could not be ignored in any future deliberations about Togoland. The matter came to a head with the British announcement in 1954 that when the Gold Coast achieved independence it would be impossible for Togoland to be administered as in the past. Almost everyone could join in rejoicing that an African state was coming to independence, but this new state of affairs raised an array of problems concerning both Trusteeship and self-determination. A strong case could obviously be made for the proposition that small and unviable Togoland, already factually integrated with the Gold Coast, should now be formally merged with the latter when it became independent. The Trusteeship purists, however, protested that such a move was in violation of the basic precepts of the System since they viewed the Trust Territories as permanently separate units whose only proper goal was full independence. Furthermore, the evidence indicated that while the northern section of British Togoland wanted to become part of the Gold Coast, the people of the south had serious reservations. In particular, the adherents of Ewe unification feared that integration would mean permanent separation from the Ewe people of French Togoland. Those who had become convinced of the desirability of the unification of the two Togolands were necessarily disaffected; and it was evident that any far-reaching move in British Togoland must have serious consequences for its French neighbor.[27]

Despite these varied doubts and objections the Assembly in 1955 adopted Resolution 944 (X) which provided for a plebiscite to be held in British Togoland under United Nations supervision, in which the people would be consulted as to their wishes in regard to

(a) the union of their Territory with an independent Gold Coast; or
(b) Separation of Togoland under British administration from the Gold Coast and its continuance under Trusteeship pending the ultimate determination of its future.

In May 1956, this plebiscite was held, setting a precedent for the future evolution of other Trust Territories. From a technical standpoint it appears to have been an outstanding success, but as to its substantive bearing and interpretation there is room for some measure of skepticism. The verdict was for integration with the Gold Coast, 93,095 votes being cast for the first alternative on the ballot as against 67,492 for the much more vaguely defined proposition that British Togoland should continue under Trusteeship until some other unspecified decision should be reached by somebody. The vote in the two major sections of the Territory diverged markedly: while 79 per cent of the northerners endorsed integration with the Gold Coast, only 45 per cent of the voters of the more populous south were for it. In a number of instances the votes in nearby wards differed so greatly as to leave little doubt that the determining influences were rather purely local considerations or the pressure of local chiefs or other leaders than a weighing of the larger issues. A further complicating factor was that some among the Ewe voted against integration in the hope that at a later stage they might be able to join with their fellow "nationals" in French Togoland and perhaps bring the entire Ewe people into Ghana. A number of others, it was asserted, would have been ready to join the Gold Coast on a federal basis but rejected submergence in the unitary state on which Nkrumah insisted, fearing Ashanti separatism.

In the earlier United Nations deliberations on the plebiscite the inescapable question had been raised as to whether the Territory should be treated as one consolidated block or should be divided in accordance with the popular vote in its different parts. Despite the disparities in opinion which the voting disclosed, both the Trusteeship Council and the Assembly came to the conclusion that the whole of British Togoland should be merged with the Gold Coast. The principal arguments for this sensible decision were that any further partition would produce even less viable entities and that everything possible should be done to bolster the fortunes of the first sub-Saharan African colony to win independence. These arguments were unpersuasive for the southerners in general and the Ewe in particular since they claimed that the unity of British Togoland was a fiction, that they were quite distinct from and more advanced than the northerners, and that their ethnic allegiance tied them to the French territory as well as to the Gold Coast. Their plea to the Assembly later in 1956 to divide British Togoland in two along the lines which had been administratively accepted from the start made no headway, however.

As for French Togoland, the effect of these developments was to spur France on to similar actions. In the resolution which sanctioned the British plebiscite the Assembly noted the French intention to introduce political reforms and to consult the Togolese as to their wishes for the future. The Assembly hoped that this consultation might also be conducted under UN supervision. In July 1956 the French representative in the Trusteeship Council presented the outline of a new statute intended to establish an autonomous Togoland Republic within the framework of the French Union and requested the appointment of UN observers for the forthcoming referendum on the territory's status. The Council, however, refused to associate itself with the referendum on the two major counts of uncertainty as to the statute's final form and doubts as to the adequacy of the self-government it provided. Furthermore, the voters were to be given no chance to opt for independence since they could only accept the new statute, which would involve termination of trusteeship, or continue the existing trusteeship arrangements.[28] The proposal that the package to be offered the Togolese should embrace their later right to choose full independence was rejected by the French, presumably with a wary eye to the effect on Algeria and other French colonies.

Despite this rebuff by the Trusteeship Council and strong protests from some political groups in Togoland, France put its plan into effect. In September the Autonomous Republic of Togoland was officially brought into existence, equipped not only with a Premier and a Cabinet drawn from the legislature but also with an anthem and a national flag.[29] A month later the promised referendum was held, but without UN supervision and in face of a boycott by some opposition elements. Although more than 70 per cent of those who voted approved the new status, the circumstances leading up to and surrounding the referendum could leave neither the Togolese nor the United Nations wholly content with the result. Behind the infant republic lurked the same kind of difficulties as those which had come more openly to the surface in British Togoland: the unresolved problems of the Ewe and other tribal groups, the question of Togoland unification and independence, and the attractive force of a Gold Coast about to secure independence.

Fortified by the report of a Commission which visited the Territory early in the year, the General Assembly in November 1957, decided to elect a Commissioner to supervise Legislative Assembly elections in French Togoland which would, for the first time, be based on universal adult suffrage. The French announced their intention of enhancing Togoland's autonomy by transferring to local control all powers save defense, foreign affairs, and currency. To the surprised dismay of France the voting in April 1958, went heavily in favor of the opposition parties and particularly in favor of the *Comité de l'Unité Togolaise*, headed by Sylvanus Olympio who had been a frequent spokesman before UN for the All-Ewe Conference. This swing toward independence and away from the pro-French party which had controlled the Togoland government from the time of the adoption of the new statute was to be attributed primarily to such factors as universal suffrage and the unprecedented readiness of French administrators, supervised by a corps of UN observers, to refrain from manipulating the electoral machinery. The outcome may also have been influenced by the action of the Accra conference of independent African states, held just before the election, in criticizing

French policy in Togoland and claiming the right of self-determination for the territory.

The intricate affairs of the two Togolands throw light on a number of facets of the problems which self-determination brings with it, but still others deserve mention. Among them is the minor but potentially troublesome question of the disposition of tiny dependencies, such as the American Virgin Islands, miscellaneous Pacific islands, and the smaller African colonial holdings, which have a real measure of separate identity but for which sovereign independence seems no sensible answer. Here a doctrinaire application of self-determination is far less in order than the use of inventive ingenuity to devise solutions fitted to the wide variety of particular circumstances. A number of models now exist to which it is possible to turn for inspiration, not only for the smaller territories but for larger ones as well. Several former French dependencies have come to self-government as at least formally indistinguishable and integral parts of France; a new type of integration with Britain has been proposed for Malta; Puerto Rico's commonwealth status establishes a unique association with the United States; and the Dutch Antilles are similarly linked with the Netherlands. In all such cases the obvious danger must be faced that the fate of the smaller unit will in fact be determined at the pleasure of the larger, but this is a danger against which it should be possible to erect safeguards, as the General Assembly has sought to do in its deliberations on the factors involved in self-government.

Of broader importance is the fact that the application of self-determination in the colonial sphere inevitably comes to be tangled with the continuing backwardness of some of the non-self-governing peoples whose political inexperience makes it highly doubtful that the issues involved in self-determination can be presented to them in meaningful terms. It is one thing for President Sukarno to assert on behalf of the Indonesian nation that it is "the law of nature . . . that West Irian will return to us, return to the fold of our Motherland," [30] but it is quite another thing for the inhabitants of West Irian, still living in primitive isolation, to decide between the Indonesians, the Dutch, and independence, not to mention some form of trusteeship. Can it be seriously contended that the people of Southwest Africa are in a position to make an informed and responsible choice between annexation by the Union of South Africa, the maintenance of the Mandate or the creation of a Trusteeship, or some other solution to be devised, perhaps, in the chambers of the United Nations? Despite assurances by South African leaders that the chiefs in Southwest Africa applauded the idea of merger with the Union, the UN General Assembly in its first brush with what has become a perennial problem held in Resolution 65 (I) adopted in 1946 that:

> the African inhabitants of South West Africa have not yet secured political autonomy or reached a stage of political development enabling them to express a considered opinion which the Assembly could recognize on such an important question as incorporation of their territory.

Even if this were not the case and the chiefs knew what they were approving — which might be taken in substance as almost a denial of self-determination, placing them and their people within the jaws of *apartheid* — a further question would immediately arise. How much credence should be given to the claim of a small dominant minority, be it the old-style chiefs or the new-style Western-trained middle class, to speak in the name of the people as a whole? The burden of proof should certainly rest upon those who deny the capacity of a people to decide its destiny for itself — a capacity which in some cases is clearly still lacking or woefully inadequate. It stretches a good point too far to accept the contention of a Venezuelan delegate to the United Nations that "The mere fact that a people had expressed a desire for self-government should be rcognized as sufficient evidence that they were ready for it." [31]

Where the capacity to make an effective choice is lacking it is plausible to assume also a lack of ability to maintain independence effectively without extensive outside support. The political validity of this argument is, however, seriously impaired by the fact that the anti-colonialists and nationalists backing independence for almost any people can point to others whose independence has been accepted, but whose maturity and experience are not demonstrably ahead of those whose right to self-determination is being questioned. No survey of the states and peoples of the world could sustain the contention that independent statehood has necessarily been reserved for those who are most advanced and capable of sustaining it while colonialism has been the lot only of the most backward. It must also be asked whether the good of the world is promoted by the multiplication of weak and perhaps irresponsible states. Whatever answer the statesman or the philosopher may give to this question, the working answer is presumably the same: if other peoples, no better qualified for it than we, have been allowed to clutter up the international stage, why should a new set of rules now suddenly be invoked to deny us our equal right?

CHAPTER XVII

Self-Determination in Plural Societies

For those embraced within the national community nationalism is an immensely powerful uniting force, but the counterpart of its success in binding men together on this side of the fence is its intensification of their sense of separation from those on the other side. This has notoriously been the case on the international stage at large. The coming of nationalism to a society which is politically united but made up of communities divided from each other by race, language, religion, or historical development often works to produce very much the same effect, emphasizing inner cleavages and setting one community against the other. Where distinct peoples, each wakened to a consciousness of its separate identity, live on the same territory and lay claim to the whole or a part of it, as in the case of Jews and Arabs in Palestine, or where a nation claims to contain within it peoples who assert their own distinct nationhood, as the Indian nation claimed to include all India's Moslems within itself, the issue can become one to be settled only through a trial by battle. As J. S. Furnivall has put it, "Nationalism within a plural society is itself a disruptive force, tending to shatter and not to consolidate the social order." [1] What is basically at stake is the control of the state which will itself thenceforward direct and control the lives of those within it. In a state composed of diverse and perhaps hostile peoples this question must be translated in simple language to read: who rules whom?

Where there are such conflicting claims, an appeal to the principle of self-determination is useless since that principle establishes no criteria by which to judge between them. "All peoples shall have the right of self-determination," but if the peoples dispute among themselves, the doctrine of devil take the hindmost is as good as another. The nearest approach to a criterion to be found within the framework of self-determination is the customary majoritarian formula of counting heads instead of breaking them, but in this setting it has only dubious applicability even though the idea of self-determination is itself derived from democratic roots. Phrased abstractly, the prime defect of decision by majority where a mixed or plural society is involved is that it relies upon one of the central instruments of the democratic process despite the absence of the foundations on which democracy rests. In any working democratic society there must be a strong sense of community which brings with it tacit agreement that the issues which divide men are of less importance than those which unite them. On this basis it is possible for the minority to accept with good grace the verdict arrived at by the majority, particularly in view of the presumption that the majority is a shifting one which may give way to the minority at the next election. Where the issue is one of fundamental national allegiance, and, at least in principle, of permanent subordination of the minority people to the majority nation which wins the state, no such agreement can be read into the situation; and the majority decision carries with it no necessary implication of ethical validity and binding force. If it is legitimate to assume that the sense of common nationality represents the core of the tacit agreement on which modern democracies rest, then the weakness of the majority principle when nations contend against each other is all the greater.

The crux of the matter in a plural society is that it is not one people which is determining itself but two or more, and it should not be ignored that the United Nations Charter speaks in the same breath of self-determination *and* of the equal rights of peoples. If they are actually to be equal, then the subordination of one to another is evidently ruled out. As the international system has been built around the doctrine of the sovereign equality of states, so likewise nations assert themselves as separate and ultimate entities which cannot legitimately be subjected, particularly in the great issue of independence or state allegiance, to the action of majorities which they regard as alien. For the general international scene, Inis L. Claude, Jr., has put it in the following terms, which are equally applicable to the more limited horizons of a society divided within itself:

> Majority rule works only when the minority has such confidence in the ultimate reasonableness of the majority and such conviction of the ultimate community of majority and minority interests that it can afford to respect the right of the majority to rule without undue obstruction. . . . Indeed, majority rule has no valid claim of legitimacy apart from the existence of a basic moral consensus.[2]

Whatever the proper theoretical base, it is very clear on the record that the Sudeten Germans did not accept the validity of the Czech majority, that the Jews were unpersuaded of the rightness of the Arab cause by the latter's majority in Palestine, and that the outnumbering of the Moslems by the Hindus in India did not mean that the dream of Pakistan must be abandoned. Even though plebiscites may in some cases serve as a useful device to indicate the appropriate allocation of a disputed territory, it is against both logic and history to believe that peoples can be generally counted on to abide by the result of a vote when they deny that the majority has any moral claim on them. The great issues of nationalism and self-determination have been settled not by the genteel processes of votes and majorities but by the revolutionary rising of peoples and the successful waging of wars, which have carried history with them.

Luckily for the peace of mankind, the occasions on which the minority is prepared to do battle for its views are relatively rare. Minorities are of many kinds,[3] of which only a few are so constituted or situated as to make full-scale self-determination a plausible possibility or even something to be desired. Not infrequently the minority acquiesces indifferently or reluctantly in its fate. Where a minority is so small, scattered, or backward as to have no real chance in the world on its own, the best it can hope for is either nondiscriminatory acceptance into the larger society or nondiscrimination combined with some measure of protection for its separate identity. The most troublesome cases are often those in which a minority, too weak to be able to act effectively for itself, looks for salvation to a neighboring national state to whose people it is ethnically related and which may be prepared to intervene on its behalf. If the Sudeten and other Germans outside the Third Reich's frontiers offer a dramatic illustration of this situation in the recent past, it is certainly within the bounds of possibility that the overseas Chinese and Indians may become the illustrations of the future.

A surprising number of cases also arise in which the relationship between the peoples involved are imprecise or in flux because the composition of the nation itself remains undetermined. The basic element needed to create such a situation is the existence of an actual or potential nation made up in whole or in part of peoples closely related to each other and yet marked off by some significant points of difference, as in language, religion, or historical experience. In many such instances the peoples concerned are of a size and importance to warrant a claim of independent statehood, but the question remains open in which direction they will move or be pushed. A variety of possibilities are at least speculatively available, and the actual outcome depends on the attitudes and actions both of the potential minority and of the majority. At one extreme such a minority may, if the opportunity is opened to them, be prepared to merge into a larger national community as an integral but distinguishable part of it, preserving intact for the foreseeable future those cultural elements in which they differ from their compatriots, but turning their backs on any claim to a separate sovereign existence of their own. At the other extreme they may, as the result of internal and external pressures, move increasingly firmly toward an insistence on their separate nationhood, coming to demand self-determination in their own right. In between there are all kinds and gradations of minority status.

Situations of this sort test most severely the skill and patience of the statesmen on both sides. Assuming — as it can by no means always be assumed — that both sides have some desire to consolidate a broader national unity, the choice of the means to be utilized is likely to present great difficulties. To insist on a uniform national pattern across the board may be to drive into rebellion communities which could be held within the nation by generous recognition of their desire for differentiated treatment, but to yield too much and at the wrong time may be to encourage separatist forces which likewise shatter the nation. What the minority regards as its obvious due in the way of offices and prerogatives may be taken by ardent adherents of the majority community as a betrayal of their own rightful claim to national predominance. Gandhi was, it should be remembered, assassinated by a Hindu communalist and not by a Moslem.

Examples of this type of indeterminate relationship of peoples to nations with which they are in some fashion associated can be found at many points on the globe. One version of it is presented by the Ukrainians who appear prepared on the whole, despite the pronouncements of Ukrainian nationalists abroad, to accept membership in the broader Russian nation if their language and cultural differences from the Great Russians are given free play. Both pre-partition and post-partition India are rich in examples which cover virtually every phase of the possibilities. Large numbers of India's Moslems came in the 1930's and 1940's to intransigent rejection of the proposition that there was a single and indivisible Indian nation while others continued to accept it; within the resulting Pakistan substantial cleavages have developed, particularly between its western and eastern provinces; and post-partition India has found itself plagued by the demands of the linguistic communities as well as by some reassertion of caste attachments. The several peoples which compose a Burmese nation still in the making have had serious difficulties in settling down in peace with each other, and in independent Ceylon the Sinhalese and Tamils have been at each other's throats. Indonesia's national existence has perhaps not been threatened, but leading groups in Sumatra, Celebes, and other islands have resented Javanese control to the point where they rose in abortive rebellion against the existing Jakarta government. Afghanistan, Iran, Libya, and considerable stretches of the Arab world continue to be faced by tribal and other divisions which place roadblocks of greater or less consequence in the way of national consolidation. Although the processes of nation-building in Africa south of the Sahara have not yet evolved far enough to make clear outlines of the shape of the future visible, every country and colony is evidently divided within itself on tribal and clan lines, if not on lines of race. The spread of political activity in Africa has sometimes stimulated the development of a more local tribal consciousness which impairs potential national unity. In the British West Indies communities shaped on the basis of both islands and races make difficult the emergence of a West Indian nation which would serve as the firm foundation for the West Indian federation.

Almost everywhere one finds plural societies in which distinct communities are in some fashion asserting their separate identity. Operating sometimes within and sometimes outside the dominant nation, these communities react in very different ways to their different settings. Occasionally the communities are sufficiently divided on a geographic basis to make a partition of the disputed territory possible; more frequently and more painfully the peoples are intermingled to the point where no separation is possible except at a shocking cost, as in India or Palestine.

A significant attempt to work out a method of approach to the problem of predicting in which direction plural societies may turn is that of Karl W. Deutsch whose *Nationalism and Social Communication* proposed a series of quantitative and statistical tests intended to furnish evidence as to the trends in the formation and reshaping of communities: are these particular peoples moving more closely together or is each community tending to consolidate within itself? Given the necessary factual and statistical materials, this scheme of investigation points the way toward objective and scientifically based predictions concerning, say, the national future of Burma or French West Africa in terms of growing or declining intercourse and communication between its regions and peoples. There can be no doubt of the desirability of substituting this type of more rigorous and quantitative analysis as far as possible for the looser and more subjective evaluations which have hitherto been employed, although ample room is still left for the subtle task of appraising human emotions.

Short of the techniques suggested by Deutsch it cannot be said that significant advance has been made toward the goal of enabling us to predict with any acceptable degree of accuracy. For the most part, what has been offered has involved little more than a restatement of the original problem in more complex or elegant language. Useful distinctions in terminology have been introduced as, for example, that a community is a body of men whose members see it as an end in itself in contrast to a society composed of communities which see the larger body as a means to their separate ends; but this formulation offers no ready means of determining whether, say, the Achinese in Indonesia or the Kikuyu in Kenya are moving toward or away from the larger political societies of which they are a part. Nor does a survey of the vast historical record appear to offer much more in the way of usable criteria. Peoples have united and divided under the most diverse of conditions, and elements, such as language, culture, or religion, which have been of major consequence in one time or place recede into the background in another.

THE CLASH OF RACES

If one were to pick out a single element which more than any other is likely to be brought to the surface by the coming of nationalism and to bar the way to national unity, it would presumably be diversity of race. The concept of race is, for eminently sound reasons, in disrepute, but this disrepute unfortunately does not touch the fact that, for much of mankind, the major divisions of the human species, as determined by skin color and other external physical characteristics, continue to be of central significance. Where there is a clear racial separation, as between Negro and white, or Chinese and Malay, there must be a strong presumption that the knitting together of a single nation with actual equality for all will be a long and hazardous project at the best. But even here the historical record will certainly sustain nothing approaching a blanket assertion that a nation of mixed races is impossible. Without seeking to explore the question as to the extent to which more ancient racial mixtures underlie the apparent homogeneity of present-day nations, it is evident that nations of more recent origin have with a greater or less degree of success been able to break the racial barrier, although never without continuing strains and tensions. Particularly in the Americas many races have been thrown into the melting pot from which the American nations have emerged and are still emerging: native Indian stocks, European whites, Africans, and smaller numbers of Asians from many countries. The verdict as to the success of racial amalgamation into national homogeneity remains a debatable one and varies from area to area. The attitudes, policies, and results, as well as the component elements of the original problem itself, differ greatly in, say, the United States, Mexico, Brazil, and Peru, but enough has been accomplished to make it clear that race constitutes no wholly insuperable obstacle. There has also been enough of failure and shoddiness in the efforts of the United States and other American countries to secure racial integration to establish that racial cleavage is a singularly difficult one to bridge.

In the colonial setting this has become abundantly evident as the advance of nationalism in plural societies has forced consideration of the fundamental question: self-determination for whom? White settlers, if they are present in substantial numbers, initially pose the gravest difficulty for a colonial people in moving toward self-determination. At a later stage the frequently much larger number of alien Asian settlers may raise even more serious problems, but in the first round or two the Europeans most decisively block the path because of their political, social, and economic predominance and their easier access to those who wield power both in the colony and at home. In sheer self-protection and seeing themselves as the natural superiors of the "natives," they are likely to seek a form of self-determination which will put them in command. For the settler minority to accept either self-determination or self-government on a democratic majority basis is to cut out from under its feet the ground on which its privileged position rests. As a former Governor of Kenya, Lord Altrincham, put it, "every white man or woman with the brains of a rabbit knows that security for white settlement must in the end prove incompatible with sincere efforts to enable Africans to qualify in increasing numbers as voters on a Common Roll." [4]

Given the vastness of the gulfs which usually divide the races, the settlers' demand for predominance, and perhaps even for a self-determination of their own, may be inescapable, but for the imperial authorities the matter always involves other considerations than merely the desires of the settlers. One of the major considerations was admirably stated as far back as 1832 by the British government when it was petitioned by the planters and merchants of Trinidad to grant them representative government. In reply Lord Goderich posed the question as to whether the granting of their request would provide for the necessary identity of interest between a legislature elected by slave proprietors and a society in which the great mass of the governed were slaves. The general tenor of his answer remains as valid today as it was then:

> Society in Trinidad is divided into castes as strongly marked as those of Hindustan, nor can any man who has but an ordinary knowledge of the history and general character of mankind, doubt what must be the effect of such distinctions when in addition to their other privileges, the superior race are entrusted with a legislative authority over the inferior.[5]

In the West Indies the British have recently moved step by step to carry out one of the possible implications of this statement by granting increasingly representative and responsible government to the people as a whole in each of the islands, and full self-determination for the West Indian federation is not far distant. Despite its doubts and pains the formerly dominant white community has accepted with reasonable grace the fact that the far more numerous descendants of other races and racial mixtures now hold political power.

In British East and Central Africa the full impact of the nationalist era is still to be felt, although the tensions between European settlers and Africans have been growing for decades. Both African leadership and the African masses are still only in process of developing the political maturity which will enable them to express their grievances and their sense of separate identity effectively. The Mau Mau movement, African protest against the Central African Federation, labor disturbances with racial roots, and many other such signs indicate the dangerous potentialities which lie immediately ahead. The combination of a speeding up of African development with the introduction of freer political institutions is likely to enhance rather than to diminish the political distance between the major racial communities, particularly where white racialism helps to evoke an African counter-racialism.

In its dealings with these African colonies the British government has been torn between the demands of the settlers and its obligations to its African wards. In Kenya the imperial authorities in 1923 proclaimed that "the interests of the African natives must be paramount" and asserted that they could not delegate the trust which they exercised on behalf of the African population. Although this stout affirmation has since been watered down, the imperial center has refused to yield ultimate power to the Kenya settlers. Lord Hailey was, however, undoubtedly justified in his comment that at one time the European farming interests "were able to exercise an influence over the formation of policy hardly less than that which they might have possessed had they been the dominant party under a fully developed form of Responsible Government." [6] The net effect has been to postpone self-determination for anybody since London would accept neither a white dominion ruled by a tiny minority of Europeans nor a democracy in which a few thousand white settlers would be overwhelmed by millions of African voters. On April 23, 1959, the Colonial Secretary formally stated that the British government, responsible "to all the inhabitants of Kenya of all races and communities, both backward and advanced," could still not foresee the date at which a single Kenya nation might be granted full self-government on the parliamentary model. [7] The attitude toward London in Kenya is, however, in process of undergoing a dramatic shift. As the Africans have grown in political maturity and strength they have looked with increasing distrust on the Colonial Office, which they formerly saw as their protector against settler rule, and are now demanding democratic self-government on a one-man one-vote basis.

The Central African Federation marked a larger breach with the principle that settler self-determination was ruled out, as had Southern Rhodesia earlier, although some safeguards were retained against complete domination of the African majority by the local white minority. It is the evident fear of the Africans that the Federation, already infected by the racialism of Southern Rhodesia, will repeat the tragic experience of the Union of South Africa. That some 7,000,000 Africans in the Federation will long rest content with a political framework which gives a quarter of a million Europeans a great preponderance of political power is grossly unlikely, particularly when the dominant Europeans use their power to found much of the society on flagrant segregation and discrimination. The aim of the Capricorn Africa Society to create a common African patriotism without racial discrimination and based on Western standards of civilized society is admirable, but its achievement will require far greater tolerance and understanding than can be reasonably expected on the basis of the past. African distrust of the professed good intentions of the Europeans found expression in the protest against the creation of the Federation. Subsequent political developments, including armed suppression of the disturbances in Nyasaland in 1959, have not allayed their fears. As in Kenya, African leaders are more and more looking to their own political action rather than to protection by the authorities in London.

In Tanganyika, slated to become a predominantly African state, African voices were also raised to question the acceptability of parity of representation in the legislature on racial-communal terms for 8,000,000 Africans, 70,000 Asians and 22,000 Europeans. The overriding of African opinion concerning Federation, the acute tensions of neighboring Kenya, and fears of being drawn into a white-dominated East African union were among the causes of Uganda's troubles in 1953, in which the separatist claims of Buganda were the central feature.

The grim potentialities of racial issues came closest to complete realization in the Union of South Africa, the continent's one full-scale experiment in white self-determination. The results do not encourage repetition of the experiment, despite the fact that the Union has made the largest economic strides of any country in Africa. Here the Afrikaners have manipulated the machinery of parliamentary government to establish a virtual monopoly of power, using their Nationalist Party majority to remove political and constitutional restraints which stood in the way of their program. Under the label of apartheid they have sought to build white supremacy permanently into the structure of the Union, segregating the Africans and keeping them in their place. In its ideal version apartheid would completely separate white and black peoples, honorably divide the country between the two, and let each develop in its own fashion. It is evident that no such separation can take place without forcing upon the white community so extensive an economic ruin as to compel the Afrikaners to pull back; nor has it presumably ever been seriously contemplated by the more hardheaded among them. In its practical implementation apartheid has meant the removal of the non-whites from any pos-

sible access to power in the white man's world, the abusive treatment of Africans who earn their living as workers or hangers-on
in that world, and the establishment of more or less self-governing
Bantu "national" units in the rural areas, so-called Bantustans. These
tribal units are to send representatives to the urban areas who will
have the function of restoring the ties of the urban proletariat to
its tribal origins. As one interpreter portrayed these schemes, their
effect would be to vest such political power as is left to the Africans
in the hands of the most conservative and least Westernized elements, and to continue the economic integration of the urban
Africans with the European community but to prevent them from
becoming socially, psychologically, and politically integrated with
it.[8] In this best of all possible Afrikaner worlds African national
unity and resistance is fragmented, and African labor remains a
cheap commodity for the white employer.

What lies ahead for South Africa is not pretty to contemplate.
For some years to come the Afrikaners, commanding the instruments of force and repression, should be able to hold the positions
they have won and even extend them. It is improbable that the
opposition United Party, representing largely the British-descended
elements in the population, would seriously oppose them in time
of crisis although it takes a somewhat more moderate position on
the racial question. Given the mood of Africa, as reflected in the
conferences at Accra, and the anti-colonialism of the great bulk of
the world, it appears inevitable that the present white rule of South
Africa should be swept away in a vast revolutionary surge if the
Afrikaners persist on their course. Perhaps the most hopeful prospect is that the Afrikaner community may gradually recognize the
need for policies more in keeping with the modern world as more
of its members are drawn into urban industrial and commercial
life.

As far as the French colonies with significant bodies of settlers
are concerned, the West Indian holdings have been constitutionally merged into metropolitan France and all their people endowed
with an equal French citizenship, although equality in living
standards is still remote. In Tunisia and Morocco, after many years
during which the settlers largely had their way, the French yielded
to the demands for independence. There can be little doubt that

Algeria, where the settler problem is the largest and most acute, must eventually be conceded a similar self-determination. The nine-to-one majority of Moslem Algerians has rejected the fiction that it constitutes an integral part of the French nation, and increasing numbers of French spokesmen have acknowledged the need to recognize a distinct Algerian personality in one or another guise. It is hard to see a future for the artless notion which had found some official acceptance that France must retain its authority in Algeria in order to provide an impartial arbiter between the two communities.

The question which lies ahead concerns the future fate of the European minorities who have held so privileged a position in Africa under colonialism. Up to now the balance or imbalance which has been established represented not only the fact that a European power had taken over political control of an African territory but also, in very rough terms, the actual social-economic balance between the communities. The white man's position rested only in part on his possession of superior physical force, although that was not a trifling consideration; it rested also on his superiority as a scientist, technician, producer, and organizer. As the great African majorities take over some of the white man's attributes and assert themselves politically, white privilege must surely go; but how much else will go with it? If the model is to be the nationalism of Egypt or Indonesia, the prospects for peaceful coexistence are not bright. Partnership is an appealing word, but as the American South attests, some bitter truth lingers in the comment of H. V. Hodson that "Man is a political animal only by education; he is a racial animal by birth." [9]

The white settlers raise peculiarly acutely the problem of the lack of that national homogeneity which any simple version of self-determination presupposes, but they are only one phase of the problem and not necessarily the most important in the long run. Everywhere there are mixtures and interpenetrations of peoples, derived from folk wanderings and earlier non-European imperialisms. Where the melting pot of history has done its work inadequately, it has often proved an impossibility to evade the blunt question as to who rules whom and the next question as to what happens to the left-overs who are effectively denied self-determination. As the European experience laid bare the impossibility of any tidy working out in Central and Eastern Europe of the principle that each nation should have its own state to itself, so the spread of self-determination to the non-European parts of the world has demonstrated that they are at least equally plagued by basic ethnic diversity. Particularly in Africa a variety of alternative community linkages may threaten the stability of the new states as the principle of self-determination becomes the touchstone for the political organization of peoples who have not yet coalesced into nations, and perhaps never will.

The ending of colonialism by itself eliminates no more than the problems arising directly from alien control, dumping even the question of the white settlers, so closely linked to colonialism, into the lap of the new regime. Independence, in prospect or achieved, cannot be counted on to weld disparate peoples into national homogeneity, and may in fact aggravate rather than allay discord. In one set of circumstances the divergent strands of the population may be assimilated to a general national norm through such instrumentalities as a unified educational system and communications network; in other circumstances similar forces will serve only to crystallize and solidify the minority. Freedom for one community may imply for another oppression which it regards as more intolerable than continued colonial rule.

When nationalism comes to prominence in any society, and particularly when it comes in a democratic guise, it works to provoke a consciousness of ethnic diversity. Under an autocratic regime, be it colonial or indigenous, the component parts of a plural society may be able to live in a reasonable facsimile of peace with each other, but the transition to self-government raises immediately the question as to the "self" which will be doing the governing. "An autocratic state," Sir Ernest Barker has said, "might in the past be multi-national, uniting by the one will of the autocrat a number of nations that were merely social groups. A democratic state which is multi-national will fall asunder into as many democracies as there are nationalities, dissolved by the very fact of will which should be the basis of its life." [10]

The approach of independence, relaxing external pressures and calling in question the foundation of the existing political system, forces a choice of allegiances. As growing numbers of people are brought into active participation in the affairs of the larger society and as their social and political consciousness is widened and intensified, an increasing awareness of the things which unite them with and divide them from their fellow men is certain to follow. If the differences are emphasized by the creation of communal electorates or other devices which officially mark off one community from another, the divisive effect of democratic institutions is aggravated because of the implicit denial that the society involved is one single body with common interests and purposes.

MOSLEM AND HINDU IN INDIA

All other illustrations of the theme that the approach of self-government in a democratic guise promotes division in a plural society pale to insignificance in the face of the immense and tragic experience of India. Whether the lion's share of the blame be attributed to the inherent facts of the situation or, less plausibly, to the divide-and-rule policies of the British, the introduction of freer political institutions in India corresponded strikingly with the growth of communal-separatist demands among the Moslems. Hindu-Moslem antagonism inevitably grew with the growth of Indian nationalism as the Moslems recognized that they would be submerged in a free Indian democracy.

The theory, so indignantly repudiated by spokesmen of the Indian National Congress, that India contained two nations, Hindu and Moslem, dates back at least to the latter part of the nineteenth century, and it regularly emerged to the political surface when questions of representation and election forced attention to the fact of the Hindu majority. Perhaps the first version of it in its modern dress appeared in 1883 when the distinguished Moslem leader, Sir Syed Ahmed Khan, a pioneer in leading his Indian co-religionists into the modern world, successfully insisted that Moslems should receive separate nomination to the partially elected local government bodies which were being reconstructed by Lord Ripon. Conceding that elections were no doubt the best means of securing the representation of the majority in a homogeneous country, he protested that in a country with India's divisions of race, creed, and caste, "the system of election, pure and simple, cannot be safely adopted. The larger community would totally override the interests of the smaller community, and the ignorant public would hold Government responsible for introducing measures which might make the differences of race and creed more violent than ever." [11] Given this position and his aristocratic outlook, it was wholly logical that he should oppose the demands of the newly formed Congress for larger installments of representative government, holding them "exceedingly inexpedient for a country which is inhabited by two different nations"; and that he should predict open conflict between the two nations for domination if the British were to leave India to its own devices.

The next serious move came in 1906 after the partition of Bengal and at a time when the Congress was beginning to make itself felt with greater political vigor. The immediate occasion for Moslem concern was the proposal of the imperial authorities, later to emerge as the Morley-Minto reforms of 1909, to undertake a substantial extension of the elective principle for Indian councils. In October 1906, a large and distinguished Moslem deputation, headed by the Aga Khan, waited upon the Viceroy, Lord Minto, to present essentially the same arguments as those which Sir Syed Ahmed Khan had earlier urged on Lord Ripon, and to plead for special safeguards for the Moslem community. The latter should not only have separate access to the legislative councils through communal electorates but should also be awarded representation beyond its numerical strength in order to protect it from being a wholly ineffective minority and to give recognition to its political importance, its contribution to Imperial defense, and its past rule over India. In reply Lord Minto stated that he was entirely in accord with the contentions that had been brought forward, and saw as "doomed to mischievous failure" any electoral representation in India "which aimed at granting a personal enfranchisement, regardless of the beliefs and traditions of the communities composing the population of this continent." [12] The principle of communal representation was thus accepted into the Indian scheme of things; and in December of the same year the Moslem League held its first meeting.

From that time forward the communal issue was of central

importance for the Indian political scene and the progress of the nationalist movement. In 1916 the Congress and the League were able to come to agreement at Lucknow on a program for India's future, which included acceptance of communal representation, and at the close of the war the Khilafat Movement joined with Gandhi's new political drive to produce a short-lived united front, but the general trend was toward a worsening of relations between the two communities. With the advance of nationalism and of democratically inclined constitutional reform the Moslems increasingly asserted their separate identity and distinctive claims. It was a considerably more bitter pill than the Congress leaders were prepared to swallow, but evidence mounted that the nationalist movement must reckon with two nations and not one.

Indeed, in his presidential address to the Moslem League in 1930 Sir Muhammad Iqbal, although he also cast doubt on the compatibility of nationalism and Islam, pointed to the Moslems as the only Indian people who could be described as a nation since the Hindus had not been able as yet to achieve a similar homogeneity among themselves. Of greater consequence, it was in this address that Iqbal, denying that the model of British democracy could be of use in a country of many nations, proposed that Indian unity should be preserved by explicit recognition of national diversity in a federal system which would give sharply limited powers to the central government and as large freedom as possible to the constituent units. Concretely he presented the idea of joining the Punjab, the Northwest Frontier Province, Sind, and Baluchistan into a single state, which would meet the needs of the Moslem majority of that corner of India and constitute one of the members of the loose Indian federation. Here appeared the germs of the idea of Pakistan whose name was still to be created. Both in this speech and in his presidential address of 1932 Iqbal emphasized that democracy could work only if modified to suit India's conditions.[13]

It was also in 1930 that the Simon Commission attributed the growing communal conflict to "the anxieties and ambitions aroused in both communities by the prospect of India's political future," to the struggle for political power and the opportunities which power confers. So long as British authority was firmly established, the Commission suggested, a large measure of communal peace

could be maintained by a neutral bureaucracy, and it pointed out
that much the same situation could be found in the Indian states.

> But the coming of the Reforms and the anticipation of what may
> follow them have given new point to Hindu-Muslim competition.
> . . . The one community naturally lays claim to the rights of a
> majority and relies upon its qualifications of better education and
> greater wealth; the other is all the more determined on those ac-
> counts to secure effective protection for its members; and does not
> forget that it represents the previous conquerors of the country.[14]

The succeeding years of political agitation, round table conferences, commissions, and reports inevitably worked to heighten
political consciousness on all sides. For the development of Moslem
separatism the most significant single event was undoubtedly the
bringing into force in 1937 of the principle of provincial autonomy
provided by the Act of 1935. In the eyes of the Moslem leaders
the Congress governments which took over in a number of the
Provinces were essentially instruments utilized by the Hindu community for its own advancement and to harass the Moslems. If it
was improper to write off the Congress, as the Moslem League
inclined to do, as a Hindu communal body, it was evident that the
Hindus constituted the great bulk of its membership, that Hindu
far more than Moslem outlooks and attitudes lay behind its policies,
and that its actions, as reflected in the work of the Provincial
Congress governments, were bound in some instances to be offensive to many of the Moslems. The Moslem League, then greatly
broadening its scope under Jinnah's leadership, claimed to represent
the entire Moslem community; the Congress governments, on the
other hand, took the position that while they would welcome
Moslem colleagues in their ranks, the latter would be acceptable
only if they foreswore the League and came into the ministries as
members of the Congress. In full accord with Jinnah's increasing
stress on the two-nation theory, one Moslem writer summed the
matter up in the following illuminating terms:

> Whether the Congress was good, bad, or indifferent is irrelevant;
> for good government is no substitute for self-government. If good
> government were the right criterion, then no Indian political party
> would be justified in clamoring for self-government or Swaraj. Na-
> tional freedom or sovereignty is a good in itself. It has an absolute

value, for which good government by an alien people is no substitute, and Hindu Raj, by the Congress or by the Mahasabha, is alien
rule to the Muslims.[15]

When the Congress governments in the Provinces resigned
because of Britain's decision that India was a belligerent in the war,
Jinnah declared that December 22, 1939, should be observed by
all Indian Moslems as the day of deliverance and thanksgiving
which would demonstrate their relief that the Congress regime
had come to an end, freeing them from tyranny, oppression, and
injustice. In March 1940, under the leadership of Jinnah, the Moslem League in its annual meeting at Lahore came to its clearest
affirmation of the idea of Pakistan — although the major resolution
which was adopted on this score was still filled with ambiguities.
In addition to a demand for effective protection of all minorities,
the League resolved that no constitutional plan would be acceptable
unless it were based on the principle that:

> geographically contiguous units are demarcated into regions which
> should be so constituted, with such territorial readjustments as may
> be necessary, that the areas in which the Muslims are numerically
> in a majority, as in the North-West and Eastern zones of India,
> should be grouped to constitute 'independent States' in which the
> constituent units shall be autonomous and sovereign.[16]

It is possible, looking back, to see that this resolution and the
preceding years of Congress supremacy marked a point of no return, although a federal system might still have been worked out
which would have enabled Hindu and Moslem to live within a
single political framework.

The essential stumbling block was that the leaders of the
Congress and of the Moslem League set off from fundamentally
irreconcilable positions, of which a central feature was their opposing views of the nation. In his reflections on the Pakistan problem,
B. R. Ambedkar, leader of the Untouchables, gave a good clue to
what was at stake in his comment that "a community has a right to
safeguards, a nation has a right to demand separation." [17] He found
the roots of the distinction in a sense of ultimate destiny. The
community, in his use of the term, feels its ultimate destiny to be
one with that of other communities in the state of which it is a

part, whereas when one nation rises against another, the conflict involves the assertion of a separate ultimate destiny and hence can be settled only by the disruption of the state, not by any reforms in its government. The Congress saw the Moslems as constituting a community which could be manipulated within the framework of India, while an increasing number of Moslems, under the relentless leadership of Jinnah, came to the conclusion that life within an undivided India was intolerable and that only through securing a Pakistan of their own could their ultimate destiny be safeguarded.

Gandhi and his associates expressed a readiness to go to almost any length to meet Moslem demands for a protected position within a single India, but they reached a limit beyond which they could not or would not pass when the demand was put in terms of a wholly separate Moslem nation standing in equality beside the Indian nation. In the eyes of the Congress leaders the sacred cause to which all else must give way was the struggle for independence from Britain; once that had been achieved it would be possible to move on to secondary matters such as the status of Moslems and other minorities. For Jinnah and the League, on the other hand, the independence from Britain of a single Indian nation was even a dangerous and undesirable thing since it would mean the subordination of the Moslem minority to the good pleasure of the Hindu majority. The only political timetable which the Moslem leaders would accept reversed that of the Congress in giving first priority to Hindu recognition of the separate equality of the Moslem nation; when that had been secured the Moslems would be prepared to join in the struggle of the *two* nations against Britain. At the 1940 League meeting in Lahore, after laying out his version of the unbridgeable gulf between Hindu and Moslem, Jinnah concluded:

> To yoke together two such nations under a single state, one as a numerical minority and the other as a majority, must lead to growing discontent and final destruction of any fabric that may be so built up for the government of such a state.[18]

To round out the story with a slightly ironical touch, it might be added that in 1956 Prime Minister Suhrawardy declared that the creation of Pakistan (despite the presence of a larger number of Hindus in the country) put an end to the two-nation theory since "All of us, Muslims or non-Muslims, are Pakistanis, first and last." [19] Here, once again, is an illustration of the familiar theme that self-determination is rarely, if ever, accepted as a continuing right.

India presents the greatest as well as the most costly example of the plural society separating off into its component elements as one of the consequences of its entry into the modern world, but it is far from being the only one. With some measure of exaggeration Tibor Mende has contended that in the area from Pakistan through the Philippines, there is, almost without exception, "a tendency to fragmentation latent in the administrative units left behind by Western man." [20] It was his argument that the imperially created administrative units are larger than the people of the several countries are competent to manage on their own, and that separatism represents an attempt to escape "to the manageable proportions of an area united by religious or linguistic kinship." That a tendency toward separatism exists in various countries is undeniable but the facts of the case make possible flatly contradictory judgments as to its reach and significance. With the exception of Pakistan the only point at which there has been a breaking-up of the preëxisting units is in Indochina where the federal superstructure erected by the French gave way to a reassertion of the separate identity of Vietnam, Cambodia, and Laos, and where Vietnam itself underwent a division in the modern style into a Communist north and a non-Communist south. In none of these cases does the lack of administrative capacity to run a larger area appear to play any role whatsoever, although the pull of religious or linguistic kinship is certainly of central importance. For the rest of the area the threats and risings of dissident communities or regions have produced considerable smoke, most notably in Burma and Indonesia, but nowhere have they flared up in the fire of actual partition.

THE BRITISH WEST INDIES

On the other side of the world, progress toward self-government produced similar results in the British West Indies, and particularly in those territories — British Guiana and Trinidad —

which had a large proportion of East Indian as well as of African-descended inhabitants. In relation to the proposed federation the Indian position has been at best reluctant for understandable reasons: to enter into the federation was to run the risk of becoming submerged in the general West Indian population, whereas, by staying out, control of each of the two territories might come into Indian hands. Internally in both Guiana and Trinidad there is a widespread feeling among the other elements of the population that the Indians have not only held aloof from joining in a broader West Indian society but have also had direct support from India in so doing. Although it did not touch upon this latter accusation, the Constitutional Commission sent to investigate the crisis caused by the rise to power of Indian-descended Cheddi Jagan and his People's Progressive Party in 1953 reported that:

> Guianese of African extraction were not afraid to tell us that many Indians in British Guiana looked forward to the day when British Guiana would be a part not of the British Commonwealth but of an East Indian Empire.[21]

This Commission cited the comment of its predecessor, the Waddington Commission of 1951, to the effect that the Indians were coming up in the world and demanding positions not previously sought; that this Indian challenge had stimulated the other races to close their ranks; and that race, easily identifiable with nationalism, was a powerful slogan ready at hand to be used by unscrupulous men as a steppingstone to political power. The 1954 Commission went even further in pointing to the tendency for racial tension to increase as the Indians rose in education and in the economic sphere and as the independence of India stimulated their self-assertiveness. In cautious language it expressed its doubt that "a comprehensive loyalty to British Guiana can be stimulated among peoples of such diverse origins." Here again the effect of social and political advance has on the whole been to divide rather than to unite. The People's Progressive Party itself split into two factions, of which the predominantly Indian one headed by Jagan proved stronger than its largely Negro rival.

AFRICA

In the case of Africa the returns are still far from being in. North of the Sahara the divisive forces within the several countries appear generally to have been overcome by the drive for national unity, although the integration achieved within Libya is tenuous at best and in Algeria the Moslem-settler conflict promises to have a long life. In particular the French expectation that it would be possible to separate Arab from Berber and thus establish a firmer foundation for continued French rule was defeated by a joining of the forces of the two ethnic groups. In this instance identity of religion, long living together, and common hostility to the alien overlord surmounted such influences of language and culture as continued to divide Arab and Berber. The maladroit French efforts boomeranged to strengthen the nationalist movement and national solidarity although the 1958–59 risings in the Rif indicated that Moroccan national unity still left something to be desired. Since Morocco and Tunisia achieved independence they have speculated increasingly on the possibility of some type of North African federation, and in 1957–58 Morocco showed its expansive tendencies in laying claim to French Mauretania — a mixed borderland between North Africa and *l'Afrique noire* — on its southern frontiers.

It is in Africa south of the Sahara, with its still fluid lines of community, that the advent of nationalism and self-government is most likely to cause a searching of hearts which might bring drastic changes in any presently foreseeable political ordering of the continent. To counterbalance pan-African dreams at one end of the scale, at the other end are found the surviving realities of tribal and other communities which attach more closely to the African past. Surveying the emergence of African political parties, James S. Coleman saw in Africa, as in Southern Asia, a tendency for broad and loosely knit nationalist coalitions to disintegrate into religious, tribal, or socio-economic parties as independence approached.[22] The trend toward a democratization of political institutions brought increasing numbers of people into the political arena and made it necessary for anyone aspiring to leadership to reach out into the masses, both urban and rural. In consequence, the forward sweep of the broader nationalist movements was accompanied by the restoration to the older communities of an importance which the early nationalists generally denied them, giving an apparently dying tribalism a vitality which must still be reckoned with.

The forces working toward this end are manifold and complex. In part, no doubt, they are contained in the assertion by a Nigerian writer that while the African nationalist leaders have a bourgeois liberal orientation, the mass of the people seeks to combine with political, economic, and educational advance the preservation of African institutions and "is extremely unwilling to sacrifice its basic African heritage." [23] But this insistence of the mass on its African heritage is only one facet of the story. For the Westernized vanguard itself nationalism has brought the conviction that Africans must take pride in their own past and their own culture, no longer accepting the earlier European evaluation of the African record as adding up to little more than an accumulation of ignorance, superstition, and barbarism. The effort to reconstruct an African past of worth and consequence inevitably leads back to the tribal foundations in which most Africans have lived their lives. From this position an ambivalence of attitudes is likely to follow: the African past, including its tribal anchorage, is to be praised and cherished, but at the same time it must not be allowed to get in the way of modernization which will remove from Africa the stigma of inferiority and primitive backwardness.

Nor was this the only factor. As the numbers of the urbanized, and in some measure detribalized, increased, there was a search for forms of community which would fill the void created by their transplantation. For many the solution was found in the formation in the urban centers and elsewhere of tribal associations which brought together people with a common background and offered a means of keeping in touch with and influencing developments at home. Although they have played a particularly significant role in Nigeria, Georges Balandier pointed out that similar groupings, which he termed *association d'originaires*, have also been of importance for the French African colonies. He suggested that since the town represents a recent reality, still in process of continual transformation, the city dweller continues to orient himself in relation to the rural society from which he came and frequently conceives his role as leader of his "racial brothers." [24]

Inevitable political repercussions were felt from the fact that the Africans who moved from their home base to the towns or elsewhere so often found that their tribal ties retained an importance for them which they neither wanted to nor could shake off. If the tribes had an emotional and social hold upon them, it was equally true that these urban offshoots were constantly at work to bring about a modernization and democratization of their traditional tribal institutions. In the earlier stages this brought them into conflict with the chiefs and colonial officials, but the nature of the conflict appreciably changed as some of the chiefs themselves began to be reached by Western education and as British colonial policy shifted away from the more rigid dogmas of indirect rule.[25]

This renewed emphasis on the tribal communities was supplemented from a quite different direction as democratic processes of election to legislative councils and other bodies were introduced and as nationalist movements and political parties spread from the urbanized few to the popular mass. Basically what happened was that the more abstract vision of the nation held by the early nationalists was forced to compromise with the realities of the existing social scene as soon as politics came down to the street, the market place, and the village. If mass political support was to be secured, the people must be reached in their own setting, and, particularly where indirect rule had maintained the tribal structure, through the channel of their traditional institutions.[26] The latter was all the more in order where the electoral system was linked by one or another device to the officially recognized native authorities and their councils, as, for example, through indirect election. In such circumstances it became essential for the political leaders and the parties to spread their tentacles out into the countryside, to seek to come to terms with the chiefs, and to take into account the surviving tribal loyalties of the people. The new style of political life also gave the chiefs an inducement to enter the political arena in self-protection, although in so doing they risked departing dangerously from their traditional role. For both the chiefs and the political leaders who were in process of taking over, the balance to be achieved between the two disparate elements was of crucial importance. Like Indian castes, African tribes have provided built-in political organizations and constituencies which the politically minded cannot ignore.

NIGERIA

Because of its size, the ethnic heterogeneity of its people, and the conditions under which its several pieces were brought together to constitute a single colony, Nigeria furnishes the most striking African example of the tendency for nationalism appearing under democratic auspices to stir pluralistic forces into existence.[27] Margery Perham has portrayed what happened by suggesting that, while European rule was imposed like a steel grid over the cellular tissue of tribal Africa, opening up the possibility of peaceful intercourse between the peoples embraced within Nigeria, a half century of peace "does not make two hundred or more tribes into a nation." Furthermore, the prospect of the removal of the steel grid holding them together "at once sets each group reckoning up what natural strength it will have to protect itself or dominate its neighbors when all are left to find their own levels of power." [28]

Although the parallel should obviously not be pushed too far, some observers have suggested that significant resemblances can be found between Nigeria and India-Pakistan. In both instances the original assumption of the existence of a single nation tended to give way to the assertion of inner separatisms as political activity began to reach the people and in both the Moslems represented the less advanced community which held back from the drive for national independence, with the great difference that in Nigeria the Moslems decided to stay within the state. Like India, though on a far smaller scale, Nigeria, which did not achieve administrative unity until the North and South were linked together in 1914, embraces a wide range of ethnic and linguistic diversity. Each of the three Regions into which the country has been divided includes a number of tribal or other groupings, but the political spotlight has focussed on the Moslem peoples of the north and in the south on the Yorubas and the Ibos.

Although political activity can be traced substantially further back, the present constellation of forces in Nigeria began to take shape toward the end of World War II under the typical circumstances of a political ferment caused in part by proposals for the introduction of a more liberal constitution. It was reasonable to expect that the predominantly Moslem North, whose emirates had furnished the classical setting for Lugardian indirect rule, should view with a suspicious eye political advance for a single Nigeria in which the Southerners were so likely to take the lead. While the Yorubas and the Ibos had made relatively rapid strides into the modern world, the North had generally clung close to its traditional institutions. To the conservative Moslem leaders the northward movement of considerable numbers of southerners, bringing with them the disruptive and "progressive" influence of Western ideas and techniques, seemed ominously to foreshadow where power would rest in a self-governing Nigeria and what directions it would take. When democratization threatened both their own position and the traditional order, the ruling elements organized a political party, the Northern People's Congress, which had less the look of representing the people at large than of a hedging operation which enabled the dominant elite to take part in the new political game without abandoning its status or undermining the social structure from which it derived.

In the South the rivalry between the Yorubas, who made the first strides into modernity, and the Ibos has come to be almost as characteristic a feature of Nigerian politics as the split between both of them and the North. The most dynamic figure in this development was Nnamdi Azikiwe, better known as Zik, who broke the Yoruba monopoly of professional and political leadership. Returning to Nigeria in 1937 after more than a decade of education in the United States and journalism in the Gold Coast, Azikiwe revolutionized Nigerian political life. He became not only the outstanding Ibo leader and in due course Premier of the Eastern Region, but also a major contender for predominance in the general Nigerian national movement. "Zikism" became the philosophy of the rising national forces, and was spread far and wide through his political activities and through the exuberant journalism of his newspapers. The National Council of Nigeria and the Cameroons, which held its first meeting in 1944, became his principal political instrument.

Despite its broader national title, the NCNC has in fact been very largely an Ibo affair, although in the 1954 federal election it scored an unexpected success in also winning the largest number of seats in the Western Region, the Yoruba stronghold. The role of the Ibos and their place in Nigeria, as Azikiwe saw it, emerged with reasonable, if flamboyant, clarity, from the presidential address which he delivered in 1949 to the Ibo State Union at its first meeting at Aba. In this address, entitled "Self-Determination for the Nation," it was his contention that he could safely recommend only one road:

It is the road to self-determination for the Ibo nation within the framework of a federal commonwealth of Nigeria and the Cameroons, leading to a united states of Africa. . . .

It would appear that the God of Africa has specially created the Ibo nation to lead the children of Africa from the bondage of the ages.

Otherwise is it not fortuitous that the Ibo nation is one of the few remnants of indigenous African nations who are still not spoilated by the artificial niceties of Western materialism . . . one of the select few to have escaped the humiliation of a conqueror's sword or to be a victim of a Carthaginian treaty? . . .

Instead, there is record to show that the martial prowess of the Ibo nation, at all stages of human history, had enabled them not only to conquer the others but also to adapt themselves to the role of preserver of all that is best and noble in African culture and tradition.

Placed in this high estate by the God of Africa, the Ibo nation cannot shirk its responsibility from its manifest destiny.

Within the Ibo nation he found some twenty dialectical regions, also referred to as "Ibo nationalities," which could become the provinces of an Ibo state; and the latter would in its turn "exist as a separate nation in a federal commonwealth of politically free and equal nations." One last quotation from this address will round out at least the bulk of the intricacies of the Nigeria which Azikiwe at that time envisioned:

With the Hausa, Fulani, Kanuri, Yoruba, Ibibio (Iboku), Angus (Bi-Rom), Tiv, Ijaw, Edo, Urhobo, Itsekiri, Nupe, Igalia, Ogoja, Gwari, Duala, Bali, and other nationalities asserting their right to self-determination, each as separate as the fingers, but united with others as a part of the same body, we can reclaim Nigeria and the

Cameroons from this degradation which it has pleased the forces of European imperialism to impose upon us.[29]

It can come as no surprise that the Yorubas, in response to Azikiwe's attitude and seeing the advantages of their head start slipping away from them, should have sought to build similar bulwarks for themselves. Their leading figure was British-educated Obafemi Awolowo, who has played much the same role for the Yorubas as Zik for the Ibos, though in less strident fashion. His principal political instruments have been the Egbe Omo Oduduwa and the Action Group, which are roughly the Yoruba counterparts of the Ibo State Union and the NCNC. The Egbe Omo Oduduwa, whose name means the "Society of the Descendants of Oduduwa," the mythical founder of the Yoruba race, was the tribal union of the Yorubas, while the Action Group functioned as a political party whose base was primarily in the Western Region, of which Awolowo became Premier.[30] Where Azikiwe saw the Ibos as being peculiarly discriminated against by the British, Awolowo made precisely the same protest on behalf of the Yorubas; and where the former proclaimed the Ibos as the God-given leaders of Africa, Awolowo laid it down that "The fact can be taken as admitted, or cannot be honestly disputed, that in Nigeria the Yoruba are pioneers in every field of human endeavor." [31]

As the Gold Coast neared independence similar tribal divisions threatened the country's unity. The obvious heart of the matter was that, as in Nigeria, the original ethnic units were based not on the imperially established frontiers, which ran from the coast northwards, but on a horizontal layering of peoples running from east to west. This has confronted each potential West African nation with the problem of integrating the Negroid peoples of the coastal South with the Sudanic and largely Moslem peoples of the North as well as with the demographic layers in between. As in other West African territories, the pre-colonial ethnic distinctions were aggravated by the fact that the peoples on the coast underwent relatively long and intensive contact with the West while those in the hinterland came under European rule only at a much later period. In the Gold Coast, more compact than Nigeria, the division in its broadest outlines was between the more "advanced" coastal strip, the Ashanti, and the Northern Territories. The speedy sweep into self-government under the leadership of Nkrumah and the Convention People's Party, with independence just around the corner, produced its reaction in fears that the proud heritage of the Ashanti would be lost in the shuffle and in charges that the Ashanti cocoa producers were being exploited for the benefit of the dominant political group in Accra which controlled the Cocoa Marketing Board and other important political-economic instrumentalities. The demand for a federal structure which would enable the peoples of the interior to manage their own affairs with a larger role for their chiefs and traditional institutions was buttressed by the accusation that British colonial rule was being replaced by a new black imperialism and that the British expatriate officials were giving way to what were termed local expatriates, or, in American terminology, carpetbaggers. What Nkrumah described as a feudal revolt against a democratic way of life, the leaders of the opposition National Liberation Movement portrayed as a legitimate search for self-determination, in a federal guise, as a safeguard against alien oppression.

Similar problems of tribal diversity are to be found everywhere in Africa, the original differences between the tribes often having been aggravated by a different type and length of exposure to Western influences. Thus in Kenya it was the Kikuyu, the instigators of the Mau Mau movement, who had the first and largest exposure to Western civilization, and other tribes such as the Luo have only slowly caught up with them. In both the French and the Belgian Congos tribal differences were in varying degree involved in the troubles which broke out early in 1959. As it has been denied that Togolanders were aware of the existence of Togoland, so it has been asserted that Tanganyika has political significance among the Africans for only a small though growing number of civil servants and political activists. The political awareness of the overwhelming majority of Africans in Tanganyika was held to extend at best to tribal horizons and sometimes to be limited to lesser units within the larger tribes.[32]

To cite one last case, the Sudan embodies full-scale the problems of seeking to build a nation from widely divergent materials. As arbitrarily carved out of the African terrain as the other ex-colonies, the ethnic ties of its people reach out across its frontiers in every direction. In particular, it is divided between its immensely disparate northern and southern regions, the former attaching more closely to Egypt, the latter to sub-Saharan Africa. The difficulties of all kinds which independence inevitably emphasized found strong expression in the report of a Commission appointed by the Sudanese Minister of the Interior to investigate a 1955 rising in the south against northerners present there, which cost a number of lives. According to this report, although the northern administration in the south is not colonial, the great majority of southerners regard it as such. In seeking out the causes of the disturbance, the Commission concluded that the less developed Southern Sudanese, primarily tribal in loyalty, look upon the Northern Sudanese as their traditional enemies. It found that:

> there is very little in common between Northern and Southern Sudanese. Racially the North is Arab, the South is Negroid; Religiously the North is Muslim, the South is pagan; Linguistically the North speaks Arabic, the South some eighty different languages. This is apart from the geographical, historical, and cultural differences.[33]

PART FIVE

BY WAY OF CONCLUSION

CHAPTER XVIII

Traditionalism and Communism

In 1912 Lord Crewe, Secretary of State for India, proclaimed that he could see no future for India in moving toward self-government on the model of the Dominions. It was his opinion that the experiment of extending self-government practically free from parliamentary control "to a race which is not our own" was one which could not even be tried:

> There is nothing whatever in the teachings of history . . . or in the present condition of the world which makes such a dream even remotely probable. . . . Is it conceivable that at any time an Indian Empire could exist, on the lines, say, of Australia and New Zealand, with no British officials, and no tie of creed and blood, which takes the place of these material bonds? . . . To me that is a world as imaginary as any Atlantis.[1]

Four decades later, when the inconceivable had passed into reality and India, partitioned to provide also for an independent Pakistan, was well established in its full sovereignty, another British colonial authority — Lord Milverton, Governor of Nigeria and of other colonies — could say, not of the ancient cultures of Asia, but of darkest Africa:

> Whether Africans are ready or not for self-government, whether independence is reasonable or not, has become irrelevant. Africa is in a hurry and in no mood to wait. . . . The nascent nations of Africa do not accept Western timetables of the proper or prudent timing of independence, and when we talk of the premature grant of self-government, the adjective presupposes a point of view which is not admitted by the Africans.[2]

The vast gulf between these two statements symbolizes the

distance the world has moved in what is, as history is reckoned, a very short span of time. Nations whose very existence was denied before the First World War and which were held in subordinate attachment to Europe's imperial dominance have, in the aftermath of the Second World War, established their claim to be their own masters. The nationalists who then barely merited the attention of serious statesmen have now become the heirs of empire. As if to give formal notice to all the world of the new order of legitimacy, no longer derived from white sponsorship or protection, twenty-nine Asian and African countries gathered at Bandung in Indonesia ten years after World War II to declare that "colonialism in all its manifestations is an evil which should speedily be brought to an end."

Of the forces which have created the nationalisms of Asia and Africa it is possible to give a reasonably accurate account. When the inquiry turns to the shape and direction which these nationalisms are likely to take in the years ahead, it moves into a speculative realm where flatly contradictory hypotheses can be buttressed with arguments which have a look of equal validity. The inevitable starting point is the record of the past, but immense new elements have been brought into play through the coming of independence, the progress of social and economic development, and the impact of outside events. Particularly in the case of the peoples emerging from alien rule, the experience of colonialism is still too near and too potent a force for them to have been able as yet to find their own feet in their own fashion.

Merely to list some of the major factors which have entered into the shaping of Asian and African nationalism is to suggest potent sources of future discord and basic realignment. Most of the vital Asian and African movements of the present day must trace a large part of their brief ancestry to Western sources, particularly if it be taken into account that the negative and destructive aspects of what the West brought have played as large a role as its positive contributions. I have in mind not only such matters as the brutality, exploitation, and race discrimination which have accompanied imperialism, driving non-Europeans to assert themselves in sheer self-defense, but even more the disruption of traditional communities. The atomization of the older close-knit society, which found a counterpart in the isolation of the Westernized intelligentsia, and showed its worst face in the sprawling slums of the urban centers made it inescapable that new forms of community should come into being to meet the deep human need for social roots and to secure reintegration. As in the West in similar circumstances, the nation is the community which has established its preëminence, offering an escape from frustration and a reconstituted social bond to link the atoms together.

Despite Western protests that nationalism has outlived its day, an increase rather than a decline in its hold can be expected in most of the non-Western world. Development along modern lines draws larger and larger numbers of people into a sense of national consciousness. The multiplication of the educated and partially educated creates a mass audience which is potentially manipulable through the channels of mass communications and to which the symbols and battle cries of nationalism offer the easiest means of access. It has already been pointed out that the more restrained and part-time nationalism of the earlier leaders, relying largely on rational persuasion with little attempt to secure broad popular participation, has regularly given way to more militant mass-based movements led by men who make politics their full-time career. Of these we will hear much more.

The turn of events in the last few years in Ceylon, and in particular the general election of 1956, may be used as a sample of probable future developments in other areas. As compared with the more turbulent experience of many countries, Ceylon's progress to independence had been relatively smooth and painless, yet there was growing popular disaffection with the first Prime Minister, Sir John Kotelawala, and his United National Party, under whose aegis independence had been secured in 1948. In part, no doubt, this represented only the usual swing of the political pendulum away from a governing group which had had a long lease on power, but other matters were also involved. It was charged that the government was overly elitist, had lost contact with the people, and betrayed the Buddhist religion. More particularly, the feeling existed that the "country is still run by a thin layer of English-educated people" who effectively excluded rising elements of the Sinhalese-educated lower middle class from the jobs to which they were entitled.[3] Villagers who wanted urban opportunities for their children felt that they were blocked off by language and other barriers. Both the spread of education in the vernacular and the Buddhist cultural and religious revival had the effect of reëmphasizing a communalism which many people had wishfully believed to be outgrown. For the 1956 elections a victorious coalition of left-wing parties and Buddhist monks was formed under the leadership of S. W. R. D. Bandaranaike (himself an Oxford graduate), which drew its strength from the villages and discontented student and religious groups. In foreign policy it advocated a turn toward India's neutralist position and cancellation of the agreements which allowed the British to establish military bases. The key issue, however, appeared to be the demand that Sinhalese be made the official language, a demand which worked against both the urban elite whose command of English was one of its titles to authority and the large Indian or Indian-descended minority whose native language was Tamil. In the result the nationalist effect was threefold: a broadening of the popular political base through the drawing in of less Westernized elements; a swing leftward toward a more independent foreign policy, moving the country away from the Western orbit; and a further division in Ceylon's plural society, emphasizing the gap between the Sinhalese majority and the several minorities and leading to bitter and bloody battles with the Tamils.

The experience of Ceylon calls attention to one phase of the problem which is certain to be of increasing importance. Everywhere the gap between the mass of the peasantry and the dominant Westernized few continues to be immense, and must surely be narrowed as time goes by.[4] With rare exceptions, however, it still remains true that the backwardness of the villages and their isolation from each other and from the urban centers has prevented the rural elements from mobilizing sufficient strength to challenge the dominant leadership.

What will be the mood and the outlook of the rising masses of Asia and Africa as they come to awareness that at long last they can have a determining say in their own destiny and that of their rulers? In part the answer must depend upon the balance between the attachments of the people to their traditional ways of life and their effective desire for speedy movement into the modern world.

Even if it be taken for granted that the inherent strength of the Western revolution, tapping almost illitimable sources of power of many kinds, will make the ultimate spread of that revolution to the rest of the world irresistible and inevitable,[5] it is also to be expected that in the short run many people will reject it or refuse to pay the price for it.

While the fruits of a higher standard of living and of enhanced national power, to mention only two aspects, are generally desired, serious resistance is likely to be met when it comes to a reckoning of the costs in terms of a threat to established cultures, religions, and communities. Inertia and conservatism often have strong champions among the older elites, the religious leaders, and other beneficiaries of the existing order. Aspirants to political leadership, becoming aware of the new situation, may well succeed in rousing popular passions by appeals to the traditionally minded among the rural and urban masses to thwart those who would destroy the national heritage by alien innovation. One version of the national goals and values, derived from the past, would thus come to be sharply opposed to another version, aimed at a different style of future.

Such traditionalist appeals have had little practical effect at early stages of political development when a thin layer of the Westernized spoke almost unchallenged for the nation, and the mass of the people were still illiterate and little aware of their potential political power. Traditionalist appeals might again be of little effect at some future stage when education has spread widely and the electorate has come to greater sophistication. Another outcome, however, might appear in the intermediate situation which lies just ahead for a good many countries, in which the illiterate or only partially educated mass, prodded into keener acquaintance with its political potentialities, would be aroused to block the reforming zeal of its present leaders and seek to set the clock back or at least hold it where it is. Resenting the current sacrifices being imposed upon it for the sake of uncertain future gains and fearing the disintegration of its familiar world, this mass might bring about a serious reversal in the drive for development.

A sample of part of this process can be found in Egypt in the decades following the First World War.[6] In the 1920's the nationalists in the first flush of the new day's liberal enthusiasm introduced a system of parliamentary constitutionalism, taken over intact from Western Europe with virtually nothing in the way of adaptation to Islam or to the peculiarities of the Egyptian scene. The optimism of the liberal nationalists was, however, shortly challenged by two different but interacting sets of forces. On one hand, the new constitutional order failed to function as it should because the society on which it was imposed possessed so few of the prerequisites essential to its success. Instead of producing a rational, efficient, and progressive government, it produced intrigue, corruption, and a dismal struggle for power and profit. The result was to cast discredit on Western ideas and institutions which were blamed for Egypt's unhappy state. On the other hand, as the Egyptian masses were drawn more actively into the political arena, their religious conviction, in part expressed through the Moslem Brotherhood, came to be of central importance for the political life of the country. The secular assumptions of the Western-oriented leadership of the 1920's had to come to terms with the popular devotion to Islam. The Moslem world had fallen disastrously from the high estate divinely accorded it. To restore it to its proper place required the revitalization of Islam morally, socially, and politically, and such a revitalization, involving a return to traditional sources, was a key feature of Egyptian popular demands. In the end result the revolution of 1952 and the authoritarian rule of Nasser reached something of a middle ground: liberal constitutionalism was abandoned, but the Moslem Brotherhood was also suppressed.

A widespread reactionary swing would work to substantiate the contention of F. S. C. Northrop that the Asian peoples are not pursuing nationalist aspirations as the West understands them, but

are working toward the resurgence of their respective submerged civilizations. What Western reporters have described as the coming of Western nationalism to the Middle East and Asia is really the return of Islamic and Far Eastern ways and values. . . It is culturalism rather than nationalism that is the rising fact of the world today.[7]

Although Professor Northrop added the qualification that there is also an ingrafting from the West of the factors needed to raise living standards, the record to date does not sustain his view that the revival of cultural traditions has been the principal concern of those who have so far called the tune. Gandhi was not wholly alone in his traditionalist-religious position, but the overwhelming majority of the contemporary Asian and African nationalists have been oriented toward large-scale adaptation of their societies to the West; and in Gandhi's own country it was the essentially modern-minded Nehru who succeeded the Mahatma. The emergence of the masses, however, brings a new force to bear which might promote a turn in the other direction.

It must be assumed that such a search for the past would be rendered short-lived by the inevitable forward surge of the more dynamic modernist forces. Whether or not it will come to pass at all, other than as a sporadic protest movement, depends in each country both on the response of the people to the pressures being brought on them and on the ability of the present generation of leaders and their immediate heirs to move ahead on the road of reform and industrialization. Where it proves possible to carry through the bold new development programs with relative despatch and a minimum of pain, the Western-oriented nationalists may be able to hold their power and to keep the future within the type of patterns they are seeking to impose upon it.

The difficulties which stand in the way of speedy realization of development have been too elaborately examined to require further exploration here. It is my own inclination to fear that the task of bringing Asian and African societies into a modern Western-style world will, in general, be long and hazardous, accompanied by almost as much backsliding as advance. Recognizing that the temper of the times has undergone dramatic changes and that a new magnitude of energy is being turned to development, it remains the fact that the earlier experience of non-Western peoples in their efforts to rationalize and industrialize their societies is not encouraging, and the brief postwar record is spotty at best. There is, furthermore, no reason to assume that the nationalist leadership which has come to the fore is particularly well equipped for the work which must now be undertaken. Its demonstrated ability to perform the political function of rallying the people against imperial domination can give no guarantee of ability to perform another and quite different job, although a strong case can be made for the proposition that the basic social changes which economic development calls for can only be got across to the people by the politician and not by the expert or bureaucrat.[8] Certainly also, the overthrow of an ineffective democratic regime by a more authoritarian one gives no assurance that the latter will handle the problems involved with any greater measure of competence.

Nationalism by itself gives the answer to virtually none of the particular problems which the development programs pose, and, indeed, to very few of the broad array of questions which confront peoples coming to independence.[9] Its most vital contribution is in the realms of the intangibles of the spirit: the restoration of self-respect, the building up of morale, and the stimulation of social solidarity. Insofar as it helps to produce national unity and to furnish the drive and the readiness for sacrifice which are essential for advance and perhaps even for survival, it is of central significance. It does not, however, determine the choice between alternative values, each legitimately put forward as embraced within the national destiny, or establish the institutions necessary for further progress. Nationalism may actually serve as an impediment to advance, as, for example, in curtailing access to alien goods, skills, and capital. Where a government is under attack for a failure to produce results, it is not unlikely to exploit nationalism in order to divert attention from domestic inadequacies by pointing to the need for national solidarity in the face of external danger; and the opposition can use the same device to blacken the record of a ruling group accused of betraying the national interest.

The effort to achieve economic development within a liberal-democratic framework may impose strains which prove unbearable. To single out only one familiar item, the struggle to accumulate capital from a base of poverty is a difficult task under any conditions, and to try to do it by democratic means may be asking more than human nature can stand. The record of many countries furnishes ample proof that there is no necessary link between liberalism and economic development, and Japan demonstrates that even a technically backward country can reach a high level of development without resorting to Communist methods.

A clash between democratic machineries and the pressures of

economic development, however, opens wide a door through which Communism can enter. It goes without saying that the Communists rank close to the top among the threats to the existing order in the underdeveloped countries, at least in the sense that they have a good chance of becoming the ultimate beneficiaries of future disturbances and overturns. Combining patterns which have already been suggested, a conceivable development is that a present Western-style leadership might be replaced by a resurgent traditionalism, and that the latter would in its turn be forced to yield to a new and tougher modernizing drive under Communist auspices. This pattern was at least partially foreshadowed in China in Chiang's turn back toward Confucianism and the subsequent triumph of Mao.

In terms of economic development the appeal of Communism is evident since it not only offers a set of blueprints showing how the advanced countries can be overtaken but also points to the concrete achievements of the Soviet Union and China which have lifted themselves up by their bootstraps and shown that industrialization can be accomplished without surrender to the alien capitalist. When Khrushchev and Bulganin took to the road in South Asia in 1955 the wares which they had to display were in many ways highly impressive. They made adroit use of their opportunities in their insistence that the Soviet Union had no desire to impose Communism on other peoples or to secure a common political front and wanted only to be of service to its South Asian brethren who, faced by the same problems and the same enemies as those which the Bolsheviks had overcome, happened to be less far advanced along the road than the Communist states.[10] Even the brutal suppression of the Hungarian rising of 1956 did less to mar the altruistic pretensions of the Soviet travelers than might have been expected, because much of Asia and Africa tended to see Hungary as a far-off European country whose affairs could not be encompassed within the stock categories of colonialism or imperialism and were therefore of little direct relevance. Striking far closer home, the Israeli and Anglo-French attack on Egypt served to blanket Hungary from the public view. For peoples who have had so scant an experience of freedom the Communist promise of prompt relief from the present evils of poverty, backwardness, and inequality is not necessarily impaired by the heavy authoritarian hand which accompanies it. The escape from freedom may under appropriate circumstances come to have charms of its own.

There has of late been a significant drift of opinion to the effect that Marxism in modern dress is no longer primarily a matter for the proletariat of the highly developed capitalist countries but rather for the peasants, workers, and some of the bourgeoisie of the underdeveloped areas. Although Moscow has often appeared to alternate its attention between the industrialized and the underdeveloped countries, between Europe and Asia, it is in the latter that it has made its greatest gains and presumably sees its largest future. While the workers in the highly developed capitalist countries have made unprecedented advances in living standards, social status, and political power, the masses of Asia and Africa have for the most part had little more than an increasing awareness that good things were available of which virtually no share was coming to them. In consequence, it is the latter and not the former who are now attuned to a revolutionary appeal.

To this turn in current political realities the contention has been added that the real doctrinal role of Marxism was to combine the essentially anarchist nature of peasant protest against the oncoming industrial society "with an intense cult of technology and a conviction of the historical necessity and blessings of industrialism. . . . It expresses all the grievances of the Industrial Revolution, and it shows that industrialism is necessary and must be submitted to." [11] In this reinterpretation Marxism seems well fitted to deal with the problem posed by J. S. Furnival in his comment that the tropical peoples coming to self-government "can get what they want only if they want what in the conditions of the modern world they *must* want." [12]

It is one of the more peculiar twists of the present day that Marxism, which boasts its materialist base, owes a large part of its appeal to noneconomic elements, while the West and particularly the United States, claiming greater concern for the dignity and spiritual well-being of man, has tended to concentrate its attention abroad on economic development and armaments. The Communists, of course, continue insistent that they command the secrets of industrialization and material advance. Having achieved a significant propagandist victory in spreading the Leninist identification of imperialism and capitalism, they represent themselves as the bearers of an alternative and more effective mode of access to the modern industrialized world which will maximize the good and minimize the evil.[13] But, in addition they stress such seductive themes as social solidarity, racial equality, and true national independence. A significant consequence has been that Communism has generally appealed at least as much to the rising intelligentsia as it has to the workers. There is suggestive truth in the conclusion reached by H. J. Laski thirty years ago that "Communism has made its way by its idealism and not by its realism, by its spiritual promise, not its materialistic prospects." [14]

In the simplest political terms, drawing on the old maxim that the enemy of my enemy is my friend, the bare fact of long and bitter animosity between the Communist countries and the imperial West is by itself persuasive evidence to many that Communism must have virtues worth investigating. Subject to the swings of the party line, the Communists have since the earliest days of the Russian Revolution professed their devotion to the victims of imperialism and their eagerness to bring freedom to the oppressed and exploited of the world. The theoretical counterpart of this position is that in the age of imperialism class warfare has been in part translated into international warfare between the bourgeois capitalist nations and the oppressed proletarian nations to whose defense the workers' fatherland has rallied. As Marxism in its earlier variants served to give the industrial proletariat a sense that the scientifically determined laws of history foretold the speedy triumph of the workers, so do the later variants give similar assurance to the non-Western peoples.

Here the links to nationalism become self-evident. Whatever the doubts of Marx and his successors as to the correctness of pushing nationalism into the foreground, a prime condition of such success as Communism has won in Asia and Africa has been its advocacy of national aspirations. From his special vantage point the Indian ex-Communist, M. N. Roy, has described the present phase in the following terms:

Communism in Asia, essentially, is nationalism painted red. . . . The Leninist program was to regard nationalism as an ally; now communism plays the role of nationalism, and appears in its most extreme form, having a corresponding share of all its vices — racism, cultural revivalism, intolerance, jingoism and resistance to Western bourgeois influence. This nationalist degeneration is a general feature of postwar communism, and assumes its most pronounced form in Asia.[15]

In its particulars this may be an extreme and biased statement, but in its broad lines it is not too remote from the facts. The Communists have inscribed anti-colonialism on their banners in large letters, and anti-colonialism carries with it endorsement of the rights of nations to independence. That this endorsement has very serious limitations is evidenced not only by the denial of any second thoughts on independence to countries brought within the Communist orbit but also by the assumption, more evident in Stalin's day than after his death, that independence gained under other than Communist auspices was necessarily suspect and presumably fraudulent. Thus a number of years were required before it could be acknowledged that independent India was not merely a dupe of the imperialists. Nkrumah in the Gold Coast was similarly viewed with pain as an ally of colonialism. When the Soviets finally endorsed non-Communist independence, as in post-Stalinist acceptance of India, it came as a considerable blow to the local Communist party which was committed to all-out attack upon a government now given authoritative blessing. Whatever their difficulties in particular cases, the Communists have had considerable success in spreading the belief that they are the only trustworthy guardians of the national interests of peoples overrun by imperialism. The role of Communism as the champion of nationalism may be perverse in theory and unreliable in its results; but there is far from universal agreement with the warning of the Filipino statesman, Carlos P. Romulo, that the colonial peoples could more easily "wrest their freedom from a dying imperialism than from a vigorous new one — that is, Communist imperialism." [16] For much of the non-Western world, imperialism is by definition Western and capitalist.

As Americans are inclined to fear that Asians are inadequately aware of the dangers of Communism, so Asians are inclined to doubt that Americans pay enough attention to the evils of colonialism. Not without reason the charge is that the United States headlines any act of Communist violence, as in Hungary or Tibet, but passes indifferently by colonial warfare in Algeria or the suppression of nationalists in Nyasaland. It has been remarked that Indians "regard a Chinese Communist as a great deal more free than, say, a black South African; and they have not noticed any great Western excitement over the freedom of the blacks in Africa." [17]

To point out the attraction which Communism has for the rising Asian and African countries is merely to underline the obvious and is a far cry from predicting a swing into the Communist camp for any particular country. Such a swing must depend both on the internal developments in different areas and on the turn of events in the world at large. The outbreak of war could destroy the foundations of the most scientifically worked out estimate. The prestige attaching to one or another camp will surely be of large moment, and the Communists can boast that, since they established themselves in Russia, they have nowhere suffered significant and lasting defeats, except for Tito's defection, while they have successfully weathered a great war and moved ahead to spectacular triumphs in both Eastern Europe and Asia. The policy of the West has been to contain, but nowhere has there been any rolling back.

Edwin O. Reischauer has said of the take-over in China: "Communism did not conquer Chinese minds; rather the Chinese seized upon Communism as the most obvious and available panacea to replace political dreams that faded with time." [18] If dreams fade elsewhere, through the failure of non-Communist programs in such countries as India, Indonesia, Egypt, and Ghana, the Communist panacea will surely be looked to as furnishing a proved alternative answer. It is an ominous sign that in many instances the students, who may be regarded as a weather vane of future trends, have adopted Communism as the fashionable creed. What an Australian has said of Burma is presumably of much wider applicability: "As for the younger generation in this economic frontier region, the cry most apt to be heard by the political hopeful is 'Go Left, young man.' " [19]

Of the reality of the Communist threat we can have no question, but it is an equally real fact that the immense victory in China has so far been accompanied or followed by the establishment of Communist regimes only in North Korea and North Vietnam, both, it might be noted, areas which were not "liberated" by one of the Western powers in 1945. Given the dimensions of the Asian and African revolutions, the often chaotic conditions under which they have taken place, and the intensity of the sentiment against Western colonialism, it is on the whole more surprising that Communism has made so few conquests than that it has made so many. To the masses it promises a revolutionary attack upon their stark poverty, to the intelligentsia it offers a chance to consolidate their elitist tutelage of the people through strong and centralized instruments of power, and to the disaffected and disinherited it gives solidarity, action, and a fervent creed. Yet, up to the present time such forces as nationalism, democracy, religion, and traditionalism have held the line against Communist advance. In varying degree the Communist movement has penetrated everywhere, and in many quarters China and the Soviet Union are viewed with a sympathetic eye, but domestic Communist parties have been more frequently fought than accepted. Although Nehru's neutralist noncommitment may from time to time have seemed to lean benevolently toward the Communist bloc, he has not been prepared to take any nonsense from the Communists at home and he reacted sharply to the Chinese attack upon Tibet in 1959. In the Philippines and Burma there have been pitched battles with the Communists, and in Indonesia the Communist rising at Madiun in 1948 was suppressed by force although the party has more recently made substantial gains, particularly in Java. Despite increasing Communist pressure in the Middle East, including an expansion of trade and the furnishing of both military and economic aid, none of the Middle Eastern countries has as yet taken its way into the Communist orbit, although rumors that one or another country was about to succumb have abounded in the last years. Local Communist parties have generally found little encouragement. As far as Africa is concerned, evidence of a growing Soviet interest is available, yet the record is barren of any notable achievement. It is significant that Kwame Nkrumah, himself accused of earlier Communist attachments, as Sékou Touré has been in Guinea, should in 1954 have announced in the Gold Coast Legislative Assembly that Communists would not be employed in certain branches of the government because their loyalty went to an alien and threatening government. The Prime Minister declared that all would agree that:

> the first loyalty of all of us must be to our own country, and that the government has a duty to protect our people from the insidious attacks of those who, at the very time when we are freeing ourselves from one form of imperialism, seek to undermine and destroy us or bind us to another one which would swiftly undo all the work that has been done in recent years to foster the growth of the Gold Coast as a free and independent nation.[20]

CHAPTER XIX

The Virtues of Nationalism

In MAGISTRAL language and with his customary profusion of capital letters, Arnold Toynbee, seeing Nationalism as "the outcome of a perversion of Industrialism and Democracy through the impact of these new forces upon the old institution of Parochial Sovereignty," denounces it as "this disastrous corruption poisoning the political life of our modern Western society." [1] He is, if anything, more unhappy about the spread of nationalism to other parts of the world than about its rise in the West, finding it even less congruent to their needs and circumstances; some part of the accusation of anti-Semitism which has been leveled at him arises from his sense of betrayal by the Jews who turned from their proper sphere of religion to the political-nationalist creed of Zionism. Mr. Toynbee charges that the nation is an ill-fitting mold for many of the peoples who have tried to thrust themselves into it and that nationalism is a limited and self-centered force, falling far short of the universalism which is conceivably man's ultimate destiny.

Few would be concerned to deny such charges as these and even fewer to deny that the nation and the nation-state are anachronisms in the atomic age. But it must still be asked whether in lesser philosophic reaches than those inhabited by Mr. Toynbee something should not be said in praise of nationalism. Its sins and shortcomings are sufficiently notorious to make it unnecessary to linger over the question as to whether nationalism is an absolute and ultimate good. The real question is whether, within a more limited framework of time and space, it can furnish some of the answers to the ills of some of the world's peoples. Many hundreds of millions are still flocking to its banners: are they wholly deluded in their folly?

Conclusions that make sense for peoples who have had relatively elaborate experience of nationalism may be completely out of order for newcomers to the national era, standing on the other side of what might be called the Bandung Conference divide. The West, having sown its own national wild oats in the past, is now sometimes inclined to look with a combination of dismay and superior wisdom on the upstart countries which assert an allegedly anachronistic desire to follow the same course. With Indochina gone and much of Africa slipping away, the French have been especially insistent that this is supposed to be a century of interdependence and not of national separatisms. "Nationalism," Foreign Minister Christian Pineau told the General Assembly in the 1957 debate on Algeria, "whatever some of you may think of it, is no longer a sign of progress." [2]

However great the disenchantment of Europe with nationalism, the colonial nationalist is little likely to be persuaded by an argument so easily identifiable with the interest of the West in maintaining some facsimile of its older relationships in a world swiftly sliding out of its grasp. He is, furthermore, exposed to the vulgar temptation of suggesting that if the relinquishment of national sovereignty is really as good as it is made out to be, why have not the Western powers made more venturesome use of it for themselves before urging it upon their overseas clients. Even if it be conceded that nationalism fails to furnish the foundations for an acceptable world order and has outlived its usefulness for the advanced, thoroughly "nationalized," countries of the West — a point which many in the West would vigorously dispute — it has by no means exhausted its contribution to the development of the non-Western peoples. Nationalism, I have contended in earlier pages, has a chronology of its own derived not from the calendar but from the stages of the gradually spreading impact of the revolution which originated in Western Europe. It appears to have an essential role to play for peoples undergoing the kind of social and psychological transformation which that revolution imposes on them. One can plausibly argue that in the different but related stages of the cycle in which Asia and Africa are now engaged nationalism intrudes itself not only with an aura of inevitability but also as the bearer of positive goods.

Such a view carries with it no implication that everything ticketed with a nationalist label should be taken as desirable. The profoundly evil potentialities of nationalism have been amply demonstrated in the West by Fascism, Nazism, and many less globally disastrous movements. There is no reason to assume that its Asian and African variants are less likely to plunge into intolerable excesses. Japan's imperialism, the slaughter accompanying the partition of India, and the pretensions of Mossadegh, Nasser, and other Middle Eastern leaders are clues enough to the directions in which Asian nationalism can turn. Renan's idealized version of the nation as a soul and a spiritual principle is not wholly devoid of meaning, but it needs to be balanced by the harsh reality of national politics and prejudice and by taking into account the many millions whose poverty and ignorance exclude them from any effective share in the nation.

If we have no occasion to assume that nationalism is always right, we have equally little to take it as representing the ultimate good to which peoples should aspire. The double question which must be asked is as to the significance of nationalism for peoples at certain stages in their development and the extent to which it lays the indispensable foundations for building toward a more acceptable order than it can itself provide. The prospect of lingering for all eternity with nationalism would be appalling, but if it can be regarded as a steppingstone and if we could know with greater assurance where the steppingstones led, we might view its present evils with less apprehension — or, conceivably, with more.

To peoples emerging from imperial overlordship the major immediate contributions of nationalism are a sense of independent worth and self-respect and a new social solidarity to replace the traditional bonds. It is the sword and shield of those who are achieving independence. From being "natives" they rise to the honorable title of nationals. Through national self-assertion they achieve the spiritual satisfaction of demonstrating that they can make their own the forms on which the superior imperial powers pride themselves. They achieve also the more tangible satisfaction of overcoming that lack of social-political cohesion which earlier played so large a role in rendering them unable to resist the imperial pressure of consolidated nations.[3]

For a dependent society to come to a sense of its own national existence is to make a substantial start along the road of equality with its alien rulers. The spokesmen for the imperial powers have habitually been concerned to insist that the peoples whom they govern have never constituted and do not now constitute nations.[4] If the latter can be written off as no more than geographical expressions, owing such meager unity as they possess to alien rule, a large part of the justification for that rule is already established. The French, for example, have been much concerned to spread it on the record that the people of Algeria had no claim to being a nation at the time of the French take-over, even though that fact, assuming it to be proved up to the hilt, is irrelevant to their national status today. As the reverse side of the coin, to secure acceptance as a nation is to establish a people as having arrived in the modern world with a *prima facie* claim to all the benefits which may flow from self-determination. For Indian Moslems to win acknowledgement that they constituted a nation was regarded as an important step toward the achievement of Pakistan.

Colonialism has in many respects changed its spots of late, but the basic fact remains that, as a system, it involves the assertion of alien supremacy and the denial of the right and ability of peoples to manage their own affairs. Colonialism created not only the conditions which made nationalism possible, but also, as a complex of relationships subordinating "natives" to expatriate officials and employers, the conditions which made it an appropriate response for those who would regain their self-esteem. At least until the most recent times the white man who went out to any of the imperial domains assumed automatically the privileged position which the imperial order assigned him and which the people of the country were obligated to respect. Writing of Indochina, Paul Mus referred to the "colonial axiom" that the first of the Annamites should come after the last of the French.[5] The assumption that colonial status is degrading was illuminated by the comment of the President of Burma, looking back to his days at Cambridge, that while Japanese, Chinese, and Siamese students were accepted as equals, "Indian and Burmese students were merely tolerated, if not treated with open contempt." [6]

Where this principle is explicitly linked to race — as in South

Africa's apartheid, the legislation and practices of Southern Rhodesia, or the white taunt in Kenya that the Kikuyu came down from the trees only fifty years ago — the humiliation which is inflicted runs so deep as to be almost beyond repair. What is involved is no longer an accidental or historically conditioned backwardness which may be overcome, but a charge of inherent inferiority against a race as a whole. To make matters worse this charge is often brought most vigorously by white settlers who have taken over the land and prerogatives of the people whom they condemn and who in this fashion seek to justify their position to themselves and to the world at large. The colonial peoples were not slow to point out that the racialism of empire ran very close to that of the Nazis which the imperial democracies were denouncing, and Nehru contended that the whole ideology of British rule in India was that of "the herrenvolk and the master race." [7]

Even for the French, who have boasted their freedom from Anglo-Saxon race prejudice, racialism has been by no means wholly absent. While it is open to question that Algeria could under any conditions have been successfully assimilated to France, the overt assumption, particularly of the *colons*, that the Moslems were an inferior breed which must be kept in its place made the spread of nationalism an inevitability. The transition of Ferhat Abbas from his reliance on France and his denial of the existence of an Algerian nation in 1936 to nationalist leadership in 1943 coincided with growing disbelief in the possibility of achieving other than subordination to France. Despite brave French pronouncements and much new legislation the postwar years only worked to confirm the disbelief.

Imperial arrogance and racial discrimination have been the prime sources of the vehemence of Asian and African nationalism. Tragically they have also given currency to the conviction that the West, despite its pretensions of having reformed, continues to live by a double standard which justifies acting toward non-white peoples in a fashion that would not be tolerated for the white man. Thus, the United States is accused of seeing it as fitting to drop atom bombs on Asians but not on Europeans, and the West in general of being deeply concerned with sufferings inflicted on white men but casually indifferent to far more widespread sufferings of men of darker shades. As one sample among many, the whole complex of suspicions and resentments boiled to the surface in the speech of the Lebanese delegate on the Hungarian question in the General Assembly on November 21, 1956. With somewhat curious but characteristic disregard of other contemporary UN actions, he asked whether French and British bombs were less deadly than those of the Soviet, and why the fate of Arab refugees in the Gaza strip was ignored while attention was showered on the Hungarian refugees:

> Are Egyptian lives, Algerian lives, Cypriote lives and the lives of other subjected peoples worth less in the scales of the United Nations than the lives being lost in Hungary? . . . For when the rights of a European or a Westerner are affected, even though it be at the hands of another European, the whole world becomes indignant. But when the rights of an African or an Asian are at stake, the United Nations' conception of man becomes so different that one is led to believe that contrary to the principles of the Charter, man is not the same everywhere.[8]

Whether or not it is justified by the objective imperial record, the plain fact remains that this attitude is generally shared by those who have been on the receiving end of imperialism. Propaganda has, of course, made the most of all the points it could score in this domain, but the significant element is not that propaganda has whipped sentiment up, but that peoples have been conditioned by their experience to be immediately responsive to appeals couched in such terms. "We have gone forward to build a strong Egypt. We go forward towards political and economic independence." said President Nasser in his speech of July 26, 1956, announcing the nationalization of the Suez Canal Company. "But, whenever we look behind, we do so to destroy the traces of the past, the traces of slavery, exploitation, and domination."[9]

The contributions which nationalism can make are presumably most significant for peoples still in process of establishing their freedom, but even for the older-established nations it retains not only charms but also virtues. The retreat from nationalism in France in the period of the outbreak of World War II was far from presenting a pretty spectacle. Apart from such general contentions as that the nations remain vital centers of free and creative diversity in a world threatened by drab uniformity, more specific claims can be put forward. It is, after all, largely to nationalism that the West looks for a shattering of the Soviet empire, welcoming every nationalist gesture of the Yugoslavs or Poles, Hungarians or Ukrainians, and hoping for the appearance of a Tito among the Chinese. A resurgent nationalism inspired the resistance movements of the European countries overrun by Hitler. Churchill led a Britain whose young men had forgotten that they would not fight for King and Country. There is a ring of authenticity to the comment of the *New Yorker*'s London correspondent on the British reaction to Eden's decision to attack Egypt in October 1956:

> There has been, too, an undoubted profound psychological pleasure throughout England in seeing, as you hear people say, "the old lion wag its tail again"; and the fact that the old lion was wagging this much-docked appendage with no directives from a ringmaster in Washington was certainly balm to national feelings.[10]

Nationalism can give a lift to the spirits of even the oldest of nations, although, as in the British case, it may also leave some bad effects for the morning after.

A stark contrast exists between the ever-present egocentrism of the nation as a whole and the self-sacrifice which it demands from the individuals within it. The readiness and ability of the nation to override other peoples in terms of its own survival or advantage is matched by, and in fact rests upon, the readiness of its members to forego their own interest in its behalf, even to the extent of giving up their lives. "Greater love hath no man" tends to be translated in modern times to mean that devotion to the nation should know no limits. Reinhold Niebuhr has pointed out that while patriotism is a high form of altruism as compared with more parochial loyalties, from an absolute standpoint it is simply another form of selfishness, and he added that "civilization has become a device of delegating the vices of individuals to larger and larger communities." [11]

Here is a fundamental dilemma which offers no hope of escape within its own terms since the counterpart of the unity of the nation's "we" is the deep gulf of separation from the "they" of other peoples. It has been wisely said that the price of nationality is war:

and yet what is bought at that price is also of great value. The brotherhood of man finds much of its working expression within the nation.

In the large the nation continues to be the most extensive community to which men give their effective allegiance. To seek to undermine it by insistence on its shortcomings could create a worse rather than a better situation unless preferable forms of community which people were prepared to accept were ready at hand. I would myself take it to be a foregone conclusion that the nation, like other forms of community which have preceded it, will lose its priority — whether because of technological change, rational persuasion, or the dialectical unfolding of its inherent contradictions. Such a change may indeed lie just around the proverbial corner, but is at least hidden far enough around to make it impossible to see the form and nature of the nation's successors; nor is there any necessary reasons to assume that if the nation were to lose its hold the next stage would mark any appreciable advance toward a more desirable world order.

Despite the pressure of great objective forces which work to render the nation obsolete in the contemporary scene, countervailing forces tend to enhance its hold. Nineteenth-century liberalism and laissez faire have given way as the dominant creed to planning, social welfare, and collective controls, all of which expand the range of the nation-state and make it more indispensable to its members.[12] The rising peoples of Asia and Africa rely upon it as the only instrument effectively available to them for the achievement of the planned development to which they are committed. Assuming even a moderate degree of success, the net result must be to link the people more closely to the national framework which determines so many phases of their existence.

In relation to the newly rising countries a further point must be added. While in the West the nation has come to represent the actual outer limits of communal allegiance for most men or sets limits which are already found too confining, in Asia and Africa the nation constitutes a great potential widening of the working social and political horizons of most of the people. Far from holding men in, it opens new doors to them. Where men's lives have traditionally been bounded by tribe, clan, or caste, by village, locality, or petty state, the emergence of nationalism creates pressures which force them into larger communities. That the lesser communities can put up strong resistance to full absorption into the nation, or what claims to be the nation, is demonstrated by many evidences of growing pains such as the revolts in different parts of Indonesia and Nigeria's troubles with its regions and peoples. In some instances, as in Pakistan's split from India, the claim that a single nation embraces the peoples concerned may even be successfully denied. Undoubtedly for many individuals and groups considerable time will elapse before their social consciousness expands to the new national limits, but Western precedents establish a strong presumption that, as the older and narrower communities are undermined, the nation will in general take over in their stead and provide some measure of adjustment to the changing circumstances. The nation is itself still far removed from meeting the needs of an age of mass production, jet planes, and intercontinental ballistic missiles, yet it is at least an advance in social magnitude over what preceded it. Certainly where national solidarity is lacking the new states have a hard road ahead of them and may even lack the essential conditions for survival.

In a shrinking world wracked by two great wars, impoverished by the armaments race, and constantly threatened with new and more disastrous wars, the burden of proof must fall back on the defender of the nation. He can sustain his case only if he can demonstrate that the nation itself offers substantial hope of escaping from the dilemmas which it poses. Can the nation be regarded as a point of transition to a more acceptable order? Two different but closely related types of affirmative answer to this question have been given. One has had its claim to validity shattered by the actual historical development; the other, more modest in its pretensions, can still make a respectable bid for credence. The former sees the realization of national self-determination as leading directly into the succeeding international phase while the latter sees it as a necessary pre-condition of further advance but as not itself ensuring that such advance will take place.

Although the more skeptical have described nationalism as one of the major causes of war, its advocates have frequently portrayed it as the open road to world peace. In the liberal creed of the nineteenth century the national idea was so intimately linked with freedom, democracy, and progress as to make it almost inconceivable that a free people, united within its proper national domain, could threaten its neighbors. Once men had been democratically sorted out into their national communities, the parliament of man became a practicable vision. The heart of the argument was that peace must be endangered so long as national injustice continued, but that the basic harmony of interests would find free expression when the nations came into their own. Within this impressive, if less than wholly viable, body of doctrine, the nation became a building block of the world's peace and not a hindrance to it.

For Mazzini as for many others the virtue of nationalism lay at least as much in the belief that it would be a bridge to the brotherhood of man as in the calculation of the benefits it would bring to the particular nation concerned. The ordering which Woodrow Wilson imposed upon his Fourteen Points had at least symbolic significance: when the presumption of liberal international intercourse had been stated and the requirements of self-determination met, it then became appropriate to move on in the concluding Point to the formation of a general association of nations, "affording mutual guarantees of political independence and territorial integrity to great and small states alike." Claiming that he found it very difficult to follow those who drew a distinction between nationalism and internationalism, Wilson represented the last plateau of confident belief in the preceding century's liberal doctrine, of which acceptance of the national idea was an integral part. It is doubtful that even for Wilson himself the belief survived the pains of peacemaking wholly intact.

Early nationalists in many countries have been inclined to argue their case in part on the contribution to a peaceful world which the realization of their demands would embody. The contention of J. A. Hobson that "Nationalism is a plain highway to internationalism" is one which spokesmen for the rising nations have regularly found congenial. Thus, Masaryk held with Mazzini that

> Between nationality and internationality there can be no antagonism, on the contrary, agreement: nations are the natural organs of humanity . . . it will be the liberation of the nations which will make

possible the organic association, the federation of nations, of Europe and of all mankind.

Sun Yat-sen saw cosmopolitanism growing out of nationalism: ". . . if we want to extend Cosmopolitanism we must first establish strongly our own Nationalism." And Ghana's first Prime Minister has declared his belief that "true internationalism is rooted in the national independence of all countries." [13]

It is easy to dismiss such contentions as only a tactical device to win support for the national cause; in fact they have more significant roots. One of these roots is the naive conviction of the ardent nationalist, young in a new-found faith, that his nation's aspirations are so evidently right that they must not only command the world's favor but also contribute to the achievement of such other good things as peace and harmony. The conflict of which he is passionately aware derives from the ills inflicted on his nation: put an end to those ills and conflict will vanish as well. Only with the Fascists and Nazis does nationalism swing the full cycle from the idealism of Mazzini and Wilson to the crude programmatic assertion of the nation as the sole measure of good and evil, thus realizing the dire prophesy of Lord Acton that the course of the theory of nationality would "be marked with material as well as moral ruin, in order that a new invention may prevail over the works of God and the interests of mankind." [14]

Time has dealt harshly with the optimistic dream that the principle of nationality is the avenue to peace. There remains a less exalted version which rests upon the conviction that only free men and free societies will cross their frontiers to collaborate in achieving peace and well-being. In the first draft of the *Social Contract* Rousseau, attacking the fashionable cosmopolitanism of his day, asserted that "The building of little commonwealths sets us dreaming of the great, and we do not really become Men until we have learnt to be Citizens." [15] Whether or not people will cooperate when the decision is freely theirs is a matter dependent on many other circumstances, but a chance exists that they may be voluntarily enlisted, whereas compulsion will breed evasion, resistance, and revolt. It was the verdict of the twenty-nine Asian and African countries gathered at the Bandung Conference of 1955 that "Freedom and peace are interdependent."

This is so familiar a theme as to need little in the way of illustration or emphasis. Peoples under colonial domination have asserted countless times: if you want our good will and friendship, if you want us to join in larger enterprises, then give us the freedom to make our own choices. Looking back to the 1930's Nehru saw as one of the key problems how India might bring its nationalism and its internationalism into line in a world so largely bounded by Nazism, Communism, and British imperialism. It was, he believed, the lesson of history that nationalism was sure to win in any contest with internationalism, particularly in a foreign-dominated country with its bitter memories of struggle and suffering. But he evidently did not see the door to internationalism as closed since he added that "Internationalism can indeed only develop in a free country, for all the thought and energy of a subject country are directed toward the achievement of its own freedom." [16] With the outbreak of war in 1939 one facet of the issue took on burning urgency: the Indian nationalists demanded independence as the pre-condition of India's joining in the great anti-Fascist coalition which was being shaped.

As far as its theoretical formulation is concerned, nowhere has the idea that national freedom sets the stage for internationalism found more explicit endorsement than in Communist doctrine which contains the best contemporary approximation of the nineteenth century's belief in the harmony of national interests. Under the aegis of "the noble principle of proletarian internationalism," the Communists assert the impossibility of significant contradictions or conflicts in the relations between Socialist states — Tito and Hungary to the contrary notwithstanding. Bourgeois nationalism is, of course, reactionary and aggressive, but, as the Chinese Communist theoretician, Liu Shao-chi, put it, the revolutionary nationalist liberation movement is not only consistent with proletarian internationalism but is "a great step forward along the path of the proletarian internationalist cause," and "the genuine patriotism of the masses of the people in all countries" is intimately connected with true internationalism. [17]

The working out of the Communist position on the national problem caused bitter controversy, but under Lenin's leadership the conclusion was ultimately reached that national self-determination, including the right of secession, was a proper and necessary prelude to the consolidation of proletarian internationalism. The Communists maintained that peoples suffering under a sense of national oppression and inferiority could not be expected to collaborate in building the new world society. Nonetheless, as in all Marxist thinking on nationalism, no doubt existed at any point that the attainment of national goals was subordinate to the needs of Socialism and of the proletariat. Both aspects found expression in the apparent paradox of the Leninist injunction that the Socialists of the imperial states must demand full freedom of separation for the oppressed nations while in the latter the Socialists must seek unity and fusion with the workers of the countries oppressing them. To the argument that only in a free country could the workers be counted on to pursue their true class interest was added the further contention that no nation which oppresses another people could itself be seen as free.

The hope that freedom might achieve what could not be achieved by compulsion was one of the important elements in the policy adopted by the Bolsheviks toward the nationalities of the disintegrating Russian Empire in the early phases of the revolution. As Lenin put it in May 1917:

> The greater the freedom in Russia, the more decidedly our republic recognizes the right of non-Great-Russian nations to separate, the more powerfully will other nations be drawn into a union with us, the less friction will there be, the more rarely will actual separation occur, the shorter the period of separation of some nations from us, the closer, the more permanent — in the long run — the brotherly union of the workers' and peasants' republic of Russia with the republic of any other nation.[18]

This was a theme which Stalin picked up and carried further. For the Soviet Union itself he asserted that the revolution could not have succeeded without the aid of the peoples freed from Tsarist imperialism and that the flowering of the several national languages and cultures was an essential condition for ultimate merger into a common Socialist culture with one common tongue. For the rest of the world he held that the revolution had dealt a mortal blow to the legend that peoples could only be freed through bourgeois nationalism with its attendant national antagonisms: "The *prole-*

tarian, international method of liberating the oppressed nations" had been shown to be the only correct method, demonstrating "in practice the possibility and expediency of a *fraternal alliance* between the workers and peasants of the most diverse nations on the principles of *voluntarism* and *internationalism*." [19]

The historical record belies this claim. On one side of the fence much evidence exists of unsatisfied national aspirations in the Soviet Union as well as of antagonisms between the Soviet Union and its satellites; on the other, in many instances the realization of freedom in a non-Marxist setting has resulted in friendly collaboration. The most striking of the latter is the success of Great Britain in maintaining a Commonwealth of freely associated states composed of former British colonies. As the colonial pressure for separation rose, the British wisely decided not to seek to hold the imperial line by force but to shape a new society of autonomous communities "equal in status, in no way subordinate one to another," conceding a right of secession far more real than that constitutionally proclaimed in the U.S.S.R. In its first phase this was an association of peoples of common descent inhabiting the older Dominions, but the more recent additions embrace the very different peoples of India, Pakistan, Ceylon, Ghana, and Malaya, with others still to come. If Ireland and Burma departed, the rest remained; and it is a plausible guess that freedom achieved what would have evaded compulsion. On a lesser scale the United States has come to comparable results in the diverse cases of Puerto Rico and the Philippines.

Such examples as these indicate that it is not merely a romantic dream to think that freedom may, under proper circumstances, create a climate of confidence and good will in which nationalism will temper the rigor of its demands. Enough examples, however, point other morals to curb any undue optimism. The reshaping of Eastern and Southeastern Europe through self-determination brought little enough of peace and good will to that part of the world. At all events, the issue is now flatly posed. In the last years hundreds of millions of peoples have emerged from dependence to form their own sovereign independent states. The question is now before them, as it has earlier been for other independent peoples, whether they will make use of their freedom to move on beyond nationalism or merely consolidate their gains in clinging to as much sovereignty as states can cling to in the present world. The claim that granting nationalism's demands encourages a turn toward internationalism is exposed to its greatest and final test.

Certainly the achievement of independence by Asian and African peoples has meant no retreat into isolationalism. On the contrary, it has everywhere been accompanied by one or another variant of internationalism. Membership in the United Nations and the specialized agencies has been eagerly sought by all the newly independent states, well aware that they need peace to make their independence meaningful. Undoubtedly their eagerness is to be explained partly in terms of prestige: admission into the United Nations is a symbol of coming of age and of equal acceptance into the family of nations. It also represents recognition of the special advantages which collective security and mutual aid offer to relatively weak newcomers still wary of imperial encroachment. Regrettably, for them as for all other members there is the painful question of what happens when the shoe begins to pinch. Assaults upon the peace, deserving of international censure, are always made by other states; one's own actions are the response of a peace-loving people to intolerable provocation.

To the former victims of imperialism the principle of collective restraint is laudable and self-evident when applied to the "Powers" in general and the imperialists in particular; they are likely to find that the principle loses some of its luminously self-evident quality when applied to one of their own number. Thus in the Suez crisis of 1956 Egypt found it wholly appropriate that British and French aggression should be checked, but welcomed with no similar enthusiasm the suggestion that her own freedom to act as she chose might be called into question or the canal subjected to international control. At a time when his country was itself contributing troops to the United Nations Emergency Force in Egypt, Nehru repudiated the proposal that a UN force might supervise the UN-sponsored Kashmir plebiscite (which he also rejected): "India will not tolerate the stationing of foreign troops in any part of her territory under any circumstances." [20]

The rush on the part of the new states to join the United Nations is both a tribute to that body and clear evidence of internationalist inclinations, although some have doubted that the result is entirely good from the standpoint of international society. It is desirable that international organizations should embrace as universal a membership as possible, yet at an explosive moment in history there are obvious dangers in having so large a proportion of the UN's membership made up of weak states, unversed and perhaps uninterested in democracy and inexperienced in world affairs. The issue is in many respects the same as that confronting a state which extends political power to a hitherto inexperienced segment of its population. The answer in both instances is presumably a twofold one: first, that the newcomers can only learn by doing although they may cause some havoc in the process, and, second, that their elders and betters themselves have, after all, made a considerable mess of things.

The difficulties are enhanced by the fact that, as a working matter, both international law and international organizations function best in maintaining the established status quo — even though the end result may be to pile up discontents which will ultimately topple the entire structure. Attractive as is the conception of peaceful change, it has not been possible to clothe it in acceptable institutional forms. The drive of the new states, however, is inevitably toward a revision of the old order, looking to the elimination of the remnants of colonialism and to a recasting of the international society in such fashion as to curb the power and pretensions of the imperial West. Understandable as it is that peoples coming out from under should have difficulty in determining the nature of their relations with their former overlords, this does not contribute to their ability to join responsibly in constructing a stable international system. The world has had good reason in recent years to holds its breath while it teetered on the several brinks to which the cold war led it. The multiplication of new states has added a further reason.

In addition to membership in the United Nations, the Asian and African countries have demonstrated their internationalist inclinations in a number of meetings among themselves. Of these the largest and most spectacular was the 1955 conference of twenty-nine states at Bandung, which repeatedly stressed the need for international cooperation in all spheres. This conference was the culmination of a series of smaller prior sessions, and stemmed directly from a meeting of the five so-called Colombo powers: India, Pakistan, Ceylon, Burma, and Indonesia. More recently several conferences have been held in Cairo and Accra, either of Asians and Africans jointly or of Africans by themselves. Although both the Accra conferences of 1958 set up loose machinery for further consultation, the results in the way of continuing organizations have been slight. Only the Arab League, whose solidarity has been subjected to drastic strains, has a fixed charter, secretariat, and other established organs. Within the United Nations the Bandung countries have to some degree operated as a bloc, particularly in relation to colonial issues.

Colonialism's barriers to neighborly intercourse are being broken down, but the usual disaffections to be expected among neighbors crop up among Asian and African peoples. Despite agreement on the final communiqué, the Bandung Conference — to the open delight of considerable segments of American opinion which had feared a neutralist or even pro-Communist sweep — left no doubt that there were ample grounds for rivalry and dissension among the disinherited who were now claiming their own. Those who either cherished or feared the illusion that the victims of imperialism must all be of one mind soon found that the normal hazards of international intercourse prevailed among them as among other states.

While the new-found freedom of Asian and African peoples has led them into international activity of many kinds, one type of international collaboration which colonialism and the cold war have combined to make peculiarly difficult is the establishment of limited pacts or alliances centering about the Western imperial powers. Colonialism has left behind it a bitter residue of hostility and suspicion. If Cromwell's memory still lives on in Ireland, is it likely that his imperial successors in India and Indonesia, Algeria and Madagascar will be so soon forgotten? The colonial and ex-colonial peoples are far less persuaded that colonialism is dead than are the Western powers.

As the United States and its Western allies see it, an irrefutable case can be presented in favor of creating a united front on the widest possible basis against Communist imperialism. Many of the non-Western states not only make a very different estimate of the nature of the Communist threat, but also shy away from any arrangement which would tie them too closely to the former imperial masters. The neutralists contend that military pacts promote rather than lessen the likelihood of war and tend to thrust them into wars in which they have no real concern. They fear that the allegedly benevolent intentions of such agreements in fact conceal the machinations of the same old imperialists, trying new tricks to win back the substance of the power they have recently lost. What Krishna Menon had to say about SEATO was representative of a widespread sentiment concerning this and other similar groupings:

> It is a curious combination of former imperial countries and former colonial countries. It is, more or less, a return in a pact form to colonial rule. It is our view that these helpless countries, militarily weak countries, by joining these military alliances, simply bring back all the attributes of colonial rule in a different form.[21]

It was very largely fears of this variety which doomed the earlier proposals for a Middle East Defense Organization; Nasser regarded the suggestions for international control of the Suez Canal as tantamount to renewed surrender to imperialism; and Mossadegh and many other Iranians felt the same about the proposals for an international oil consortium to operate in Iran. An internationalism whose principal sponsors are the Western imperial powers looks to numbers of the non-Western peoples like the spider's invitation to the fly. The national sovereignty and equality so newly acquired are jealously guarded against the danger that the white man's burden might once more be assumed under a different set of symbols.

This is, of course, not the view of all of free Asia and Africa. The Philippines, Thailand, and Pakistan joined in the SEATO enterprise; Pakistan, Iran, Iraq, and Turkey were included in the Baghdad Pact although the 1958 revolution put an end to Iraq's effective membership; and the United States has entered into special bilateral arrangements with several other countries as well. It is open to legitimate doubt that these pacts and agreements constitute a net gain for either the general peace or the free world cause. Inevitably outright alignment with one of the poles of the bipolar world divides neighbor from neighbor, while the arming of a chosen few (by no means necessarily the most democratic and "peace-loving") upsets the existing balance and leads to a search for arms elsewhere on the part of those who are out of favor, as in the case of the United Arab Republic. Even if these bulwarks against Communism were stronger and less penetrable than they are, they would still be only dubious compensation for the disaffections which have been stirred up locally. The charges of Moscow and Peking that the West is playing its old imperialist game of divide and rule, although good propaganda, seriously misrepresent both fact and intent. The consequence of the pacts has, however, undeniably been to rouse suspicions and to make regional collaboration more difficult. As the cold war was thrust deep into it the Arab world threatened to come apart at the seams. The arming and flattering of Pakistan further impaired her relations with India and heightened India's suspicions of the armed coalition which Washington headed.

At this uncertain point in history no definitive answer can be given to the question whether the nationalism of Asia and Africa will turn out to be a blind alley, leading nowhere except to ultimate disaster, or the path leading toward internationalism which nineteenth-century liberalism proclaimed nationalism to be. Gunnar Myrdal opened an attractive prospect with his comment that

> Only when all these underprivileged nations, with their great multitude of peoples with different racial features, color of skin, religions, folklores, and cultural heritages, have risen to equality of opportunity will the world become integrated.[22]

But it remains a wide-open gamble whether freedom and equality will, in fact, be turned toward the end of world integration.

CHAPTER XX

The New Nations and the International Community

WHETHER THE NEWLY rising nations turn into apostles of internationalism or, like their Western colleagues, remain nationalist sinners, they must come into contact at many vital points with the international society in which they live. Of these, two may be singled out: the role of the new nations as producers of trouble and their role as consumers of international aid and guidance.

When colonial peoples move to open nationalist agitation, the disorder they create is often held to demonstrate their immaturity and irresponsibility: the underprivileged are discredited by depicting them as disturbers of the peace.[1] The colonial authorities have time and again met nationalist resistance or resort to force not only by repressive measures but also with denunciations of the ringleaders as betrayers of the loyal unsophisticated mass. In addition it is usually maintained with righteous indignation that it is impossible to deal with rebels while fighting or civil disobedience is still under way. The clear implication is that, once peace is restored and legitimate authority recognized, then reforms will meet such grievances as may actually exist; of course the views of the authorities and the nationalists as to what those grievances are and how they may properly be dealt with are likely to differ monumentally. Furthermore, the restoration of peace can itself be taken as establishing that there really was no general popular disaffection. A stand is made on the high line: "We cannot yield to force"; yet when force is absent or abandoned, why yield at all?

Traditionally it has been by making trouble — at the extreme by turning to revolution in the fashion inaugurated by the Americans — that dependent peoples have called attention to their demands. If they made enough of a nuisance of themselves, holding on to them ceased to be worth while. Only since World War II has the ending of colonialism found anything approaching general acceptance as the present goal of colonial policy. In Britain's dependencies in Asia, West Africa, and the West Indies, in the Dutch West Indies, and, most recently, in the French African territories other than Algeria, this has brought the innovation that overt resort to violence is no longer necessary, but well-organized nationalist movements and the threat of violence in the background are still useful instruments with which to prod hesitant governments. Is there any reason to think that Tunisia and Morocco would have moved as far and as fast as they did if the nationalists had not brandished the weapons of agitation and force which they possessed?

Self-determination when self-exercised involves revolution. With revolution confronting them, the colonial or imperial powers resorting to repression have habitually pleaded that they were doing no more than enforcing the law or treaties legally made whereas the nationalists were carrying on illegal activities which deserved the full authorized penalties. Within the limits of the existing order this is a position whose formal correctness cannot be challenged any more than can the proposition that, in normal circumstances, a government must and will defend itself against attack. This invocation of legality is, however, irrelevant and unimpressive to the nationalists against whom it is invoked since they deny the validity of both the source and the content of the law or treaty to which the governing power turns for justification. They may be branded as rebels by the imperial authorities, although they see themselves as patriots. Formally they are lawbreakers or treaty violators; in a larger and more realistic view what is actually involved is the clash of two fundamentally opposed systems of law: the positive law of empire and the "higher law" of the nationalists. For the members of the Indian National Congress it was a point of pride to have been imprisoned by the British, and Nkrumah and his followers in the Gold Coast took to themselves the title of Prison Graduates.

In illustration of this age-old conflict between established order and revolutionary aspiration one might turn to a debate in 1956 on the Algerian question. The French representative in the Security Council, denying the competence of the United Nations, stated:

> France is doing no more in Algeria than exercising one of the most normal attributes of domestic sovereignty. It is endeavoring to maintain public order which has been disturbed by rebellious citizens; it is trying to prevent, or, if that has proved impossible, to punish the killings, the brutalities, fires and robberies which certain French Algerians are committing against other French Algerians, whether Christians or Mohammedans.[2]

Speaking for the thirteen states which had brought the matter up, the Iranian representative contended on the contrary that, since the Algerian question was purely colonial, it was squarely within the UN domain. As he saw it, the right of the Algerians to self-determination was inalienable, and he suggested that the legitimacy of many of the states present, including the United States, rested upon a revolutionary base. To the Algerian nationalists who were carrying on the struggle in the field the position was clear: they were prepared to negotiate with France the terms on which Algerian independence would be secured, but not to recognize French sovereignty or the law flowing from it.

A more rational principle should no doubt have been established than that a state or people attracts attention to its grievances by making trouble; regrettably there is little evidence that it has. In general it remains true, as I. L. Claude put it, that "states are likely to get what they want if they raise a sufficient fuss and unlikely to get it if they fail to do so." He added that to insist on rebelliousness as a prerequisite for the satisfaction of demands is a poor way to bring up children or put peaceful change into action: "The United Nations would do well to make itself useful, as a matter of principle, to disgruntled states which do *not* press their demands in such fashion as to engender a threat to the peace." [3] At least until the unlikely event of the creation of an international organ empowered to decide when and how each colony should attain self-government, the dependent peoples who receive an international hearing will usually be those who have resorted to self-help. Whatever the strength of Indonesia's claim to independence, the factor which clinched her right to international consideration was the

outbreak of open warfare — in that instance launched not by the
nationalists but by the Dutch under the suspect label of police
action.

The demand for independence or equality is only one of the
kinds of trouble which the newcomers can bring to the international
scene and one which, by definition if not wholly in actual fact,
vanishes when the demand is satisfied. The aftermaths of imperialism are many and the sources of potential trouble vast. One of the
major causes of trouble is that the former imperial states continue
to have important interests in all the corners of the earth to which
they have penetrated, whereas the erstwhile underdogs have no
countervailing interests in Europe and America. When the United
States surrendered its sovereignty over the Philippines it left behind
it large-scale investments, business connections, missionary enterprises, and military installations. Furthermore, it became senior
partner in an alliance and the rich uncle furnishing aid and setting
the terms on which aid would be given. It is evident that American
influence will be felt in the Philippines as far ahead as one can see
and that, despite all feelings of good will, the Filipinos must have
a nagging sense of resentment against the former ruling power
which continues to play so important a role in so many aspects of
their lives.

The frictions inevitably caused by these material survivals of
Western world predominance are aggravated by the psychological
debris of imperialism. The peoples who have been through the
imperial mill will for long bear the scars of the inferiority and
subjection which were thrust upon them and dread a return of
alien encroachment. Precisely the opposite attitudes linger among
those who have so recently lost their dominant position. In their
hearts they are often unpersuaded that they are not in fact superior
to peoples of darker skins, and they are understandably reluctant
to surrender the privileges and prerogatives of empire.

The Suez-Egyptian crisis of 1956 brought out in the open, on
a scale almost bigger than life, the tensions that characterize a world
emerging from imperialism. Although they had step by step dis-
engaged themselves from Egypt, the British still had many interests
in the country and even more in the maintenance of unimpeded
passage through Suez. While France's interests in Egypt, Suez,

and beyond were far smaller, it was inclined to attribute to Nasser a large share of the blame for its troubles in Algeria. Egypt, jealous of her sovereignty and humiliated by decades of British control, welcomed any chance to assert herself and strike back at the imperialists. By getting rid of the unpopular Suez Canal Company, an obvious survival of the days of Egypt's subordination, the Nasser regime could demonstrate its strength to its people and to the Arab world in general — and perhaps also distract attention from its domestic shortcomings. The ouster of the Company was denounced as improper and illegal by the Western powers, who also made it plain that they regarded the Egyptians as incompetent to run the canal efficiently and equitably. In the background stood the Soviet Union ready to applaud and aid every anti-Western move.

Leaving the Israeli share in the matter aside, the French and British attack on Egypt could be regarded as either a recrudescence of imperialism or as one of the early reactions to the post-imperial period. The former interpretation was obviously the one with the greatest appeal to the Bandung anti-colonialists: the attack confirmed all their fears of a still threatening colonialism. Although the methods used by the British and French were all too reminiscent — save for the fumbling hesitation with which they were applied — of those characteristic of the days of Western imperial domination, the second or post-imperial interpretation is more plausible and more revealing. It seems clear that neither Britain nor France wanted any extension of power or domain and hoped at best not to lose too much of what they had formerly had. What was essentially at stake was that each felt that the time had come to call a halt to the attack upon what it considered its legitimate interests. Seeing Nasser as a dictator who would push his advantage as far as he could and fearing that his nose-thumbing example would inspire others to go and do likewise, the British and French governments determined to demonstrate that there were limits to the amount of pushing around they would take. In the existing climate of anti-colonialism they could see nothing but ever-mounting frustration in further reliance on diplomatic negotiations. Their immediate aim was the replacement of Nasser by an Egyptian regime more amenable to what they regarded as reason. Their long-range aim was to stop the anti-colonialist drive from turning into an uncontrollable stampede which would trample down not only what was left of imperial domination but also the other rights and interests of the Western powers.

The anachronistic unwisdom of their course and the immense change which had come over the world were unmistakably demonstrated in the UN reaction to the attack and in the necessity which they themselves felt to withdraw their forces before they had won any of their objectives. The use of force, once so easily indulged in, had now become more damaging than helpful and had lost its stamp of legitimacy. The evidence indicated that the anti-colonialists could take to arms to better effect and with greater impunity than could the once mighty Europeans. At the same time, however, the Soviet Union crushed the Hungarian national rising with no apparent concern for UN condemnation.

The reversal of values which has tied the hands of the Western powers and given such free rein to their former underlings can be dated back to the later 1920's. In the United States the new outlook found expression in the Good Neighbor policy, the abrogation of the Platt Amendment in 1934, and the abandonment of the policy of keeping small Caribbean countries in line by sending in the Marines. A striking manifestation of this change was the peaceful handling of the crisis in the 1920's caused by the Mexican moves under the revolutionary constitution of 1917 to take over control of American petroleum holdings in Mexico. Here the pattern was set for quiet remonstrance and adjustment or acquiescence.

A British counterpart can be found at the same period in the new readiness to recognize that Chinese nationalism and anti-imperialism, for the first time winning wide popular support, were forces to be taken seriously. In December 1926, when the nationalist contingents had started their northward move, the changing British position found expression in a memorandum distributed to the interested governments which proposed that "the Powers should make it clear that . . . they desire to go as far as possible towards meeting the legitimate aspirations of the Chinese nation. They should abandon the idea that the economic and political development of China can only be secured under foreign tutelage." [4] Faced by increasingly bitter Chinese attacks, including a boycott against which military measures were essentially useless, the British turned from resistance to conciliation in such key matters as tariffs, extraterritoriality, and concessions. Early in 1927 the British concessions in Hankow and Kiukiang, already in Chinese hands, were formally handed over to China in accordance with agreements reached with the Nationalists. From that time until the Japanese attack threw everything into disarray in 1931, the British and the other Western powers were in a mood to curtail their special privileges in China rather than to protect and extend them by the forcible means which had prevailed before.

In the exuberantly expansive decades preceding the First World War Western foreign offices and international lawyers frequently asserted the existence of an international standard governing the treatment of foreign investments, property, and persons. This was a standard, never spelled out in a detailed code, which was concocted by the advanced states and enforced by them unilaterally against their weaker and more backward brethren. Its effect was to impose upon the latter an obligation to provide the conditions under which trade and investment could be securely carried on. An American version of it was bluntly put forward by Theodore Roosevelt in a message to Congress in 1904. Asserting that the United States might be forced to exercise "an international police power," he warned Latin America that

> chronic wrong-doing, or an impotence which results in a general loosening of the ties of civilized society, may in America, as elsewhere, ultimately require intervention by some civilized nation.[5]

As forced labor for colonial natives was justified by the contention that they were being taught the dignity of labor, so the rights of private property and capitalist enterprise were explained to Asians, Africans, and Latin Americans, if need be, by blockade, bombardment, and occupation. Where lesser measures were inadequate, peoples were wholly taken over by a colonial regime which itself saw to the provision of the necessary conditions. Such techniques conveyed the lesson that the resources of backward countries were not to be locked up by them but were to be made available to the world through one of the imperial powers which would take its fee for the service rendered. Any society or state which wanted to retain its independence had to be able to provide the necessary guarantees for modern economic enterprise, including adequate legal, police, and administrative systems; if it could not, it faced the likelihood of forcible intervention.

In laying down criteria for the survival of states coming to independence now, one might be tempted to revert to this recent past and suggest that they must be able to furnish similar guarantees or live up to some general standard of good conduct, but the anti-colonial sweep has outmoded such ideas. The old methods of forcible intervention by the powers directly involved no longer work, and the UN Charter bars the threat or use of force, thus removing the old sanction behind the international standard. As a consequence, attacks upon foreign persons, property, and interests which a few decades ago would have brought swift retaliation can now be indulged in with impunity save for diplomatic protests and, perhaps, the cutting off of benefits, such as grants or loans, which might otherwise have been received.

China turns Communist and sweeps aside the whole body of Western interests, imprisoning Western missionaries and others. Indonesia takes over Dutch property within its territory. Iran nationalizes its oil industry in which Britain has so large and politically established a stake. Jordan dismisses the British general who has organized and commanded its armed forces. Haiti enters into a turmoil of *coups d'état* and instability. Such actions do, of course, carry their own partial sanction in discouraging tourists, trade, and particularly foreign investment which might have promoted development; but where private investment is regarded as the opening wedge of capitalist imperialism this is scarcely a serious deprivation. Diplomatic and economic pressure is also by no means wholly useless. Sometimes much can be salvaged for the Western powers, as in the case of Iran where they secured a satisfactory oil agreement in 1954 and aided in the installation of a government sometimes accused of being more responsive to Western desires than to the Iranian people. When all the protective steps which have been taken are laid end to end, however, they still constitute only a series of rearguard actions, covering a constant and irreversible retreat by the West from its advanced positions.

On one side, the imperial prerogatives are either gone or being whittled away; on the other side, the peoples who have experienced Western imperial penetration are in process of building up their rights of territorial sovereignty to as much of an absolute as they can achieve. Captain Mahan, in good nineteenth-century vein, justified expansionism by his belief that "an obligation to repress evil external to its borders rests upon a nation, as surely as responsibility for the slums rests upon the rich quarters of a city." [6] By the middle of the twentieth century the "obligation to repress evil" had ceased to attach to the imperial powers and, save insofar as it had been transferred to the United Nations, had become a domestic function of each of the states, new as well as old. For the new a primary evil which they sought to repress was any Western intrusion. A state which acted in a harsh or discriminatory fashion toward foreign interests within its borders could reject protests on the ground that its sovereignty gave it the right to act as it desired. A link between territorial sovereignty and the key doctrine of self-determination was achieved by the Bolivian addition to the Covenants on Human Rights, which, to wide acclaim, laid it down that

> The right of peoples to self-determination shall also include permanent sovereignty over their natural wealth and resources. In no case may a people be deprived of its own means of subsistence on the grounds of any rights that may be claimed by other states.[7]

In all this there was nothing very new as a matter of principle. Sovereignty, domestic jurisdiction, and exclusive control of the national territory and resources were, after all, old standbys of the Western powers, even though they denied them to non-Western societies. What was startling in the situation was that the latter societies now insisted on using their sovereignty for their own purposes. In an article on the Post-Imperial Age, inspired by the Egyptian crisis, D. W. Brogan answered his own question as to the nature of the basic problem:

> It is the sudden appearance on the stage of scores of new nations, most of them inadequately and some completely unequipped for the exercise of total sovereignty, and this at a moment when such sovereignty is both more complete and more dangerous than at any time in modern history.[8]

The dangers arise not only from the fact that governments are inexperienced and unequipped but also from other considerations which have already been mentioned: the temptation and provocation provided by extensive Western interests within the territory of the new states, of which petroleum holdings are presumably the most striking example; the survival in the West of notions of superiority and of habits of acting as if the world were still its oyster; the post-imperial touchiness of the peoples who dread a return to colonialism in any guise; and Communist readiness to make the best use of any trouble which may break loose. It might be added that sovereignty takes on a new meaning in practice when most states look, not to free, private enterprise systems, but to planned, centrally managed, socialist economies. The unscrambling of the imperial eggs is as delicate and hazardous a task as any one might ask for.

Yet another source of trouble is the continued existence of gross differences in degree of development between the advanced and the underdeveloped peoples. It was, after all, these differences which gave rise to colonialism. On a mass scale the bulk of "black Africa" lingers far behind the advanced West; other even less developed areas such as New Guinea still live in a quite different era. Asia and Africa are technically more backward now in relation to Europe and North America than they were a century ago, though China, India, and other countries have been driving forward. While the West has been making scientific progress at jet plane speed, most of the rest of the world has advanced at no better than the speed of a motor car. The brief span of European rule in Africa has introduced extraordinary changes, but, as Kenneth Robinson has suggested, it has not obliterated the poverty, political fragmentation, and technological backwardness which made Africa the colonial continent par excellence.[9]

In Asia as in Africa and elsewhere in the non-Western world only a small fragment of each of the peoples has been drawn into the main stream of modernity. If one reads into imperialism the function of spreading to the rest of mankind the distinctive outlooks and achievements deriving from Western Europe, it is evident that its task is most inadequately done. New-style solutions must be found for the tangled debris of problems left behind.

Nationalism can furnish only part of the answer. The new states which have come into existence, such as Ghana or Indonesia, or the old ones which have reasserted themselves, such as Thailand or Afghanistan, can certainly not be ordered around on the old imperial terms, but neither can they cope singly with the overwhelming tasks which confront them. The most intransigent of nationalisms must live in a world of which interdependence has become a central feature; no state acting alone can guarantee its own security or assure its own well-being.

The task which lies ahead for the Asian and African nations in adapting to the modern world, and for the rest of the world in adjusting to their new status, is vast enough to occupy the best efforts of mankind well into the future. In tackling it vital aid might come from the organized international society, taking over from a dying imperialism. Up to now, however, that society has been able to offer only a fraction of what is needed, partly because of its own basic shortcomings and weaknesses, partly because of the deep cold-war cleavage within it.

On the latter score the one obviously sensible answer would have been for the Communist and non-Communist states, whatever their remaining conflicts, to join forces for the advancement of the underdeveloped peoples — a goal to which both professed devotion. Such good sense is beyond the capacity of the enemies who glower at each other across the barricades of the cold war. Each feels that the only acceptable development is one which takes place under its own auspices and symbols. The West is suspicious of any Communist moves in the direction of the former imperial domains, as shown in the fears aroused by the direct Soviet approach to India, Burma, Egypt, and Iraq. Even the Soviet decision in 1953 to take part in the UN technical assistance program was greeted with dismay in some quarters despite the earlier jeers that Moscow had not contributed one red ruble. Indeed the more amiable countenance which post-Stalin Russia turned to the world sometimes seemed more menacing than the forbidding one which had preceded it. The Communists can, however, legitimately be accused of the major responsibility for blocking united international action, demonstrating less interest in aiding peoples to develop themselves than in scoring propaganda triumphs over the imperialists. As the

U.S.S.R. had previously confined its participation in UNRRA mainly to the promotion of its own cause or that of its client states, so in the dealings of the United Nations with the Asian and African countries it has shown a minimum of interest in collaboration for the assumed common purpose. The dream that a joint effort on behalf of the underdeveloped peoples might serve as a bond between the two great blocs proved as futile as the hope that Communists in national legislatures might join forces with other parties for the common good. The role of the international organizations in relation to the new states, significant as it has been, has fallen far short of a general mobilization of the resources of the international community.

From the split between the Communist and non-Communist states the newcomers have, of course, been able to draw some profit by playing one off against the other and perhaps enjoying subsidies from both. They have also been losers in being forced to start their new lives in a disorganized world of massive armaments and constant threats of war. Such a world is conducive neither to sensible handling of the aftermath of imperialism nor, for that matter, even to bringing imperialism to an end, as the peoples emerging from the imperialist shadows are apprehensively aware.

While the United Nations provides an indispensable meeting place for the pursuit of peace, it is all too evident that the pursuit cannot be counted on to be successful. Much the same can be said of the UN's function of presiding over the liquidation of colonialism, with the added complication that the colonial powers and their supporters deny that any such function can properly be read into the Charter. The claims of the anti-colonial majority — the Bandung states, the Communist bloc, and assorted others — as to the extent of UN's powers and responsibilities in this sphere have constantly grown, but the organization's ability to have a decisive say has shown no corresponding increase.

Although UN was significantly involved in the determination of the future of the Italian colonies, Indonesia, Israel, Togoland, and the Cameroons, in the case of most of the countries which have come to independence since 1945 it has done no more than welcome them to membership. Only in relation to the Trust Territories does UN have a reasonably clear role; for the remaining non-self-governing territories the process of achieving independence continues a haphazard one. The effort to impose a system of international accountability on the colonial powers has been met by them — unless like Portugal they deny that they are colonial powers — by a counterattack which first denies UN's jurisdiction and then asserts that the backwardness and bias of many of the members render the organization an untrustworthy instrument to ensure either the maintenance of acceptable colonial standards or the orderly liquidation of what is left of colonialism. The United Nations has neither clarified the jurisdictional limits within which it operates nor convincingly established the case for making itself the arbiter of colonial issues.

The third major sphere of international action in the post-imperial era, in addition to the maintenance of peace and the liquidation of colonialism, is that of development. The methods of imperialism are repudiated, but the transformation of mankind's way of life which was going on under its hegemony is being pressed more vigorously than ever in the new dispensation. After World War II the underdeveloped countries were insistent on rising levels of living and access to the instruments and techniques of power which the West had evolved. The West itself was prepared to concede, as President Truman put it in his inaugural address of January 20, 1949, that the time had come "to embark on a bold new program for making the benefits of our scientific advances and industrial progress available for the improvement and growth of underdeveloped areas."

Neither grants, loans, and investments nor technical assistance were by any means novelties in the world, but they grew in significance after the war and clothed themselves in new and more elegant forms, replacing the colonialism which had previously been a major source of such activities.[10] The Peoples of the United Nations, in the preamble to their Charter, expressed their determination "to employ international machinery for the promotion of the economic and social advancement of all peoples," and the international community assumed an array of new functions.

The International Bank both as lender and as analyst of national economies and needs; the technical assistance program of the United Nations and the specialized agencies; UN's regional commissions and other development activities; American grants and loans and the Point Four program; and the Colombo Plan — however short they may have fallen of the immense size of the task — are all manifestations of the new trend. The underdeveloped peoples might legitimately complain of the scantiness of the available international resources, of the early concentration of the Bank and the United States on the reconstruction of the already advanced countries, and of the American desire to attach political strings and press constantly in military directions. Nonetheless, an impressive start is unquestionably being made toward filling one of the gaps left by the decline of imperialism and toward meeting new needs. As a counterpart to these international activities, Britain and France adopted large-scale schemes for the financing and promotion of development within their own colonies.

Evidence of the extraordinary flowering of interest in development was available on all side. In UN, development problems and prospects became central themes of debate. Overtly recognizing that the demise of the colonial system created special vacuums which international action might usefully fill, Secretary-General Hammarskjold proposed in 1956 that UN furnish a new variant of technical assistance in the form of a career service of trained administrators available for employment in the public service of less developed countries.[11] Great Britain has sought to meet the needs of newly independent colonies through an Oversea Civil Service which can be drawn upon by the new governments to tide them over the period of most acute staffing problems. In many other countries foreign advisors and advisory groups were drawn into the developmental process.

As far as the supply of capital is concerned, the nationalism and the waywardness of the underdeveloped countries have made necessary a large degree of reliance on governmental sources, both national and international. Imperial and colonial policies had been aimed at establishing conditions which would encourage private as well as governmental investment to flow into backward areas. With the elimination of imperial controls the need for capital increased because the new national governments embarked on far more ambitious plans for development and social welfare than had been conceived before. Frequently, however, all but the boldest of private investors were scared off by the lack of political and administrative stability, the threat of nationalization, foreign exchange difficulties, and the widespread hostility to capitalism in general, and to alien capital in particular. Nationalist movements have played too heavily on the dangers of alien domination and on the links between capitalism and imperialism to allow an easy acceptance of foreign investment. These difficulties were augmented by the generally ample investment opportunities at home in the Western countries and by the need in the underdeveloped areas for basic facilities and services which would themselves bring in little or nothing in the way of cash returns. Consequently, an unexpectedly large share of responsibility for development has been placed in the hands of either international agencies whose resources are sharply limited or of foreign governments tempted to tie strings to their financial operations.

All the circumstances make it inevitable that a great part of the burden of overcoming backwardness should fall upon the West, whether each of the powers acts separately or whether they jointly channel their efforts through the United Nations or other international organizations. It is one of the cheerful illusions of our day that economic and social development will surely redound to the benefit of the West. Confusingly enough, the U.S.S.R. cherishes the same illusion for itself in relation to its own developmental activities. The fact of the matter is that if the West is to devote itself seriously to development it must undertake several acts of faith of varying dimensions. Some of these are equally shared with the non-Western peoples, but since the latter are receivers and not givers their position is in many respects different.

Two preliminary and fundamental acts of faith which are required of both parties are belief in the feasibility and in the desirability of development of a Western variety. As for feasibility, presumably the essential issue is whether a Western-style, rationalized, industrialized society can be brought into being in environments so radically different from those in which this type of society originated; and, if so, within what time periods and at what cost, spiritual as well as physical, to the people concerned. A pessimistic view as to feasibility is not currently in fashion; yet the fact remains that, with the usual exception of the Japanese and perhaps one or two other marginal cases, none of the non-Western peoples has as yet made its way far into the modern world.

The issue of the desirability of development on the Western model stirs up a host of questions, many of which can be answered only on subjective grounds. How much of the traditional way of life of non-Western societies, including the entire religious setting, can be combined with how much and what aspects of Western civilization? Until recently it was widely assumed, as by those who accepted the doctrines of indirect rule, that peoples should not be radically divorced from their established patterns of life and that colonial policy should work through the instrumentalities of the old order. This doctrine has been generally repudiated by the leaders of the non-Western peoples themselves. Although there are a variety of other possible bases, faith in the desirability of development now rests most conveniently on the almost unanimous insistence of the nationalists that they want to modernize their societies and want international aid in the process. Whether their peoples as a working matter share their enthusiasm for development and its implications cannot be told with any certainty until the process is further advanced.

For the rest the necessary acts of faith largely concern the benefits assumed to flow to the West from developmental activities. Such benefits need not be sought if the position suggested by Captain Mahan is accepted: that is, if it be agreed that the wealthy states of the world have the same type of responsibility for the poor states as the rich quarters of a city have for the slums. That the well-to-do must not only be charitable toward their poorer fellow-citizens but may also be taxed for their benefit has come to be standard practice in the advanced states, although, somewhat oddly, less so among the underdeveloped. It is not a principle which has as yet reached beyond the nation to embrace the incipient international community. Even within the alleged Arab nation, the oil-rich Arab states have not been prepared to share their wealth with their poorer Arab neighbors.

The easiest version of Western benefit to defend, but certainly not the most important as a present motivating force, is the assumption that the economic development of underdeveloped countries will aid the trade and investment of the advanced parts of the world.

Although industrialization would obviously cut in on certain markets which the West has held up to now, the over-all effect would be to multiply the opportunities for mutually profitable economic exchange. Despite all the restrictive devices which human ingenuity has been able to create, economic intercourse has flourished best between the richer and more developed countries. To put the matter crudely, Asians and Africans in their hundreds of millions can become good customers only if they are producing the wealth to pay for the goods the West wants to sell them, and to produce effectively they must modernize their economic systems.

Such economic calculations undoubtedly play a real role, but the West, and particularly the United States, pays larger attention to the political consequences which are presumed to accompany development. The three major ones are the laying of stable foundations for presently unstable societies, curbing the appeal of Communism and making friends for the West, and eliminating dangerous threats to the peace. Regrettably, an irrefutable case can be made out for none of these.

As for stability, there is little reason to believe that the drastic processes of economic transformation sought by the promoters of development can be counted on to produce it. The rise of new classes and ultimately of the masses has normally been accompanied by profound disturbances, as in the revolutionary waves which swept Europe from 1789 on. Conceivably, stability will be the remote end product of a period of radical social-economic change in Asia and Africa, but the historical evidence suggests that such change is not likely to stabilize existing social relations. The best that can be hoped — and it is a somewhat utopian best — is that political attitudes and institutions may be developed which will allow peaceful constitutional change and revolutions through orderly processes on the model of a handful of Western countries. The presumption of instability, however, is all the greater where the normal processes of social adjustment have for decades or even centuries been dammed up or turned into unnatural channels by colonial rule. If economic development really takes hold, it cannot help but operate as a profoundly revolutionary force, the results of which may not be in the least to the West's liking. It is a familiar

story that the industrialization of Germany, Japan, and Russia produced no triumphs of liberal democracy. Is there really plausible
ground for assuming that China, Indonesia, Iran, and Nigeria will
emerge with results more satisfactory to the West?

The type of instability against which the West is peculiarly
concerned to guard is Communist overturn. For societies in the
kind of ferment of change in which most of the non-Western
world is now caught up, the Communist creed holds many attractions. The social upheaval which development brings with it produces not only the proletariat but also the uprooted intelligentsia
to whom Moscow and Peking have an immediate appeal, particularly when Marxism comes dressed in the garb of nationalism.
Aside from the general propaganda effort to publicize Communist
sins and free-world virtues, the West hopes to be able to counter
this appeal through two different aspects of the development
process. One of these is the hope of winning the good will of the
non-Western peoples by the provision of aid which will demonstrate who their true friends are. The United States in particular
continues to have a wistful yearning to be loved and finds it difficult to believe that its motives can be suspected and its benevolence
unappreciated. The outlook for gratitude among nations is not
encouraging. States are likely to accept aid where they can find it,
without too scrupulous examination of the source, as witness India,
Egypt, and Guinea among others. So good a friend of the West as
President Bourguiba could declare in 1957 that Tunisia must have
arms "no matter what the price," making it clear that the price
of turning to the Communists was not too high.[12]

The other aspect of Western aid programs is the hope that they
will begin to eliminate the poverty and frustration which might
otherwise lead peoples into the Communist camp. Here again the
hope cannot be much more than a gamble even apart from the
menace of unchecked population growth. Can development move
fast enough to meet rising expectations? What are the prospects
that it generates dislocations and discontents without providing
enough new openings to absorb rising elements? One characteristic
focal point for discontent is the situation which Gunnar Myrdal
regarded as almost endowed with the dignity of an economic law,
"that the poorer the country, the greater the difference between

the rich and the poor." [13] The richer countries, he suggested, are ruled by governments effectively controlled by the people while the poor ones are often ruled by wealthy oligarchies. In such circumstances the proceeds of development, and a share of foreign aid as well, are likely to move into the pockets of the rich without substantially changing the condition of the poor except, perhaps, to impose more labor upon them. When the fat grow fatter, as has often been the case in, for example, Latin America and the oil countries of Arabia, the potential anti-Communist effect of development may swing into reverse.

The third of the acts of faith which justifies Western aid to development is that it promotes peace. Just as it is held that peace and a denial of human rights cannot coexist, so it has become a commonplace that marked disparities in conditions and standards of living are a fruitful source of war. In fact, it would be difficult to establish that the backwardness and poverty of most of the world have had any direct relation to the large-scale wars of modern times. The major conflicts have been between the advanced states, as in the two World Wars of the present century. Although the powers snarled and bared their teeth at each other about their imperial pretensions, as in the British and French clashes over Siam and at Fashoda and the Anglo-Russian tangles in the Middle East, they were not prepared to risk a major showdown about them; and when it came to the two great wars of recent times these three powers were allies. Leaving aside the small-scale Boer and Spanish-American wars, the one clear-cut exception to the principle that the powers did not go to war over imperial spoils was the drive of Japan into China and Southeast Asia, which brought her into full conflict with the United States and Britain and, at the last possible moment, with the Soviet Union as well.

The great wars which have seriously threatened mankind in recent history have taken place within the fraternity of the rich and developed states. Can there be any clear assurance of a gain for peace in the multiplication of well-to-do, industrialized states, modeled precisely after those which have been the principal warmakers of modern times? As for the smaller, colonial-style wars, something may still be said for the suggestion of Adam Smith that if the backward peoples grow stronger or the Europeans weaker, the inhabitants of all the different quarters of the world may arrive at the equality of courage and force which, by inspiring mutual fear, can alone overawe the injustices of independent nations into some sort of respect for the rights of one another.[14]

Such little peripheral wars have not themselves, however, been the ones which have endangered the general peace; and the mutual fear has now come to be inspired by nuclear fission.

In the past the existence of poor and defenseless peoples has been no more than a minor added temptation to war. It may be that the current global clash of the great blocs based on Washington and Moscow has introduced a basic change. The struggle for dominance in a world increasingly lacking elbowroom, makes any gain of territory or allegiance by one side appear to the other side as constituting both a loss in prestige and an actual danger. In principle, this does not refer more particularly to the underdeveloped areas than to the rest of the globe. Their relative weakness and instability, however, give them at least the appearance of being easier to take over, and their present allegiance, as demonstrated by the neutralism of many of them, is uncertain. As the controversies over China, Korea, Vietnam, and the Middle East show, neither Washington nor Moscow can allow the other to carry off one of these prizes without loud outcry, perhaps including the threat of massive retaliation. Any falling out among the client states of the great may also bring the superpower principals into belligerent action.

This state of affairs, which is aggravated by the increased need for the raw materials of Asia and Africa, gives new force to the proposition that the coexistence of rich and poverty-stricken peoples is incompatible with peace. Even so, it is still by no means certain that the growth of the underdeveloped countries to strength and modernity would significantly diminish the threat of war. The industrialization and modernization of India and Indonesia, Egypt and the Congo would enhance their ability to maintain their independence and hence lessen their availability as easy prizes, but would have no necessary effect in bringing Moscow and Washington to lie down in peace together or to look less eagerly toward winning new adherents. Indeed, the stronger and wealthier any of the presently underdeveloped countries become, the greater their value as prizes and the more their shift into either camp would affect the balance of power.

These are some of the considerations which justify a skeptical attitude toward the benefits presumed to accrue to the West from development. It would be tragic, however, if skepticism were to prevent or corrode the West's creative participation in a process which marks one of the great turning points in history. The chances that development will move in acceptable directions are far better if the West is actively engaged in the process than if it either grudgingly holds back or lays its emphasis too heavily on military goals. Although some unhappy circumstances may still conspire to make it so, the heart of the issue is not Communism or anti-Communism. It is that the lives of peoples all over the face of the earth are being transformed by the working of forces which had their origin in Europe. This is a process which cannot be halted, unless we use our new-found atomic wisdom to wipe mankind off the map; it can be hastened or retarded, eased or made more difficult, and guided in one direction or another. If the advanced countries do not join in promoting development, they are likely to prove the principal losers. Self-interest demands that the West have the courage to undertake the acts of faith required to link it with the aspirations of the rising nations. Western aid may spell the difference between a relatively free and voluntary transition to modernity and one driven forward by dictatorship. Furthermore, if the West were to join in full-scale attack on the problems of helping others to help themselves, its own somewhat hesitant unity might be inspired by a new sense of common purpose.

However great the aid provided them, the Asian and African states inevitably remain uncertain quantities, precariously perched between several worlds. The nature of their evolution and in what direction and in whose company they will travel, remain questions to which we can have no confident answers. At the moment it is only possible to hazard a mildly instructed guess whether they will grow in independent strength, sink back into lethargy, or follow China's lead to some destination behind the iron curtain. Each will surely take a different road from the others. China, India, and Afghanistan, Syria, Liberia, and Madagascar stem from such different universes and have had so diverse an experience of the age of

Western dominance that it would be absurd to expect them now to produce an identical pattern of response. All must somehow make their peace with the world which is insistently crowding in upon them. The terms of that peace will vary greatly.

One key factor common to all of them is that they have presented themselves to the world as nations — even though the observer may have occasional doubts as to how widely and deeply the sense of nationhood has penetrated. The nation has been taken as the measure of the state, in Asia and Africa as in the West. Once that premise has been established the goal of policy inevitably becomes the promotion of the national interest, however that uncertain concept may come to be defined. One of the greatest of the unanswered and still unanswerable questions, frequently posed in the pages of this book, is whether nations can supersede themselves, merging in some fashion in the pursuit of a larger common interest. The logic of the atomic age, unless it leads toward total destruction, leads irrefutably in the direction of an international society; but nationalism and logic have often parted company before this. A brilliant case can be made for the proposition, advocated by Lord Acton nearly a century ago, that the idea of nationality should be divorced from the state, making room for not one but many nations within the state, as there is now room for many religions. Who is prepared to make the first move to attack the menacing pretensions of nationalism, no longer compatible with survival, through abandonment of national sovereignty? And is there in fact an international society into which peoples seeking to break out of the narrow bounds of the nation can move?

Even given the most honorable intent on the part of Asian and African nationalist leaders to use independence to promote not only the national interest, but also the concerns of humanity as a whole, the climate of the period in which they have achieved freedom is scarcely one to inspire confidence in the international spirit. If the postwar world had seen a general sweep toward the consolidation of the community of mankind, the new nations might have welcomed an opportunity to take their equal place in a working global system. An organized international society which could guarantee peace, supervise the orderly liquidation of colonialism, and provide for the pooling of resources to promote economic and social progress would have an immense appeal for weak, unstable, and impoverished peoples. A divided world of hostile sovereign states holds out scant inducement, particularly when the surrender of national prerogatives carries with it the danger of renewed subordination to the imperial West or of satellite status in the Communist orbit.

Nations have arisen from the ashes of empire. Must they follow the ruinous course of their cantankerous predecessors upon the national stage?

NOTES
INDEX

Notes

CHAPTER I. INTRODUCTION

1. "Future historians will say, I think, that the greatest event of the twentieth century was the impact of the Western Civilization upon all the other living societies of that day. They will say of this impact that it was so powerful and so pervasive that it turned the lives of all its victims upside down and inside out — affecting the behavior, outlook, feelings, and beliefs of individual men, women, and children in an intimate way, touching chords in human souls that are not touched by mere external material forces — however ponderous and terrifying." A. J. Toynbee, "Encounters Between Civilizations," *Harper's Magazine*, vol. 194, no. 1163 (April 1947), p. 290.

2. Sir Percival Griffiths, *The British Impact on India* (London: MacDonald, 1952), p. 15.

3. *Physics and Politics*, ed. Mrs. R. Barrington (London: Longmans, Green, 1915), pp. 29, 139. This work was first published in 1872.

4. L. M. Kaganovich in a Moscow broadcast, *New York Times*, November 7, 1955, p. 8.

5. The Supreme Court of the United States, in handing down its decision on the segregation cases on May 17, 1954, remarked as to the status of public education at the time of the adoption of the 14th Amendment in 1868: "In the South, the movement toward free common schools, supported by general taxation, had not yet taken hold. Education of white children was largely in the hands of private groups. Education of Negroes was almost nonexistent, and practically all of the race was illiterate. In fact, any education of Negroes was forbidden in some states." *Brown v. Board of Education*, 347 U. S. 483, 489, 490 (1954).

6. "Political Development in the Congo," *The Belgian Congo To-Day*, vol. V, no. 4 (October 1956), pp. 140, 141.

7. Demetrius C. Boulger, *Lord William Bentinck* (Oxford: Clarendon Press, 1892), p. 154.

8. *Development for Free Asia* (Fair Lawn, N.J.: Essential Books, Inc., 1956), p. 1.

9. *Nationalism in Colonial Africa* (London: Frederick Muller, Ltd., 1956), p. 17.

10. "Reflections on Colonialism," *Confluence*, vol. IV, no. 3 (October 1955), p. 263.

CHAPTER II. THE ERA OF THE TWO WORLD WARS

1. Robert Delavignette, *Freedom and Authority in French West Africa* (London, New York, Toronto: Oxford University Press, 1950), p. 149.

2. A relatively large-scale but abortive revolt was planned in Indochina in 1916. See Ellen Hammer, *The Struggle for Indochina* (Stanford: Stanford University Press, 1954), ch. iii.

3. *The Background of India's Foreign Policy*, ed. Dr. N. V. Rajkumar (New Delhi: Indian National Congress, 1952), pp. 37–38, 39–40.

4. *Survey of International Affairs*, vol. I: *The Islamic World* (London: Humphrey Milford, Oxford University Press, 1927), p. 1.

5. *Burma's Fight for Freedom* (Dept. of Information and Broadcasting, Government of the Union of Burma, n.d.), p. 32.

6. Winston S. Churchill, *The Second World War*, vol. IV: *The Hinge of Fate* (Boston: Houghton Mifflin Co., 1950), p. 209.

7. H. Michel and B. Mirkine-Guetzévitch, eds., *Les Idées politiques et sociales de la Résistance* (Paris: Presses universitaires de France, 1954), p. 339. "The very term 'self-government' figures in English in the text like some foreign body, utterly indigestible and alien to French language and thinking." Herbert Lüthy, "The Crisis of French Colonialism," *The Atlantic Monthly*, vol. CXCVII, no. 5 (May 1956), p. 63.

8. *The United Nations Conference on International Organization: Selected Documents* (Washington: U.S. Government Printing Office, 1946), p. 695.

9. C. P. Fitzgerald, *Revolution in China* (London: The Cresset Press, 1952), p. 208.

CHAPTER III. THE REJECTION OF COLONIALISM

1. *Egypt Since Cromer* (London: Macmillan & Co., Ltd., 1933), II, 358. In his comment on placid contentment, Lord Lloyd was presumably challenging the precisely contrary stand which had been taken in 1918 by the Montagu-Chelmsford Report on Indian constitutional reforms (Cd 9109). The authors of this report stated their profound belief that the sheltered existence given to India could not be prolonged without damage to her national life, that she should move forward to nationhood within the Empire, and "that the placid pathetic contentment of the masses is not the soil on which such Indian nationhood will grow, and that in deliberately disturbing it, we are working for her highest good." p. 126.

2. Lord Lloyd, II, 4–5.

3. For a detailed exposition of this problem in one area, see Bruno Lasker, *Human Bondage in Southeast Asia* (Chapel Hill: University of North Carolina Press, 1950).

4. *Report of the Commission of Enquiry into the Disturbances in the Gold Coast* (London: His Majesty's Stationery Office, 1948), Colonial No. 231.

5. Cited by D. R. Williams, *The United States and the Philippines* (New York: Doubleday, Page & Co., 1925), p. 137.

6. Cited by Anup Singh, "Storm over India," *Far Eastern Survey*, vol. XII (March 22, 1943), pp. 57–62.

7. H. V. Hodson describes what he sees as the fourth and last stage through which an imperial bureaucracy passes in the following terms: "It

falls behind the march of social and political progress and requires, if it is to justify itself, the divorce of administration from policy, which must pass to different and more experimental hands." *Twentieth-Century Empire* (London: Faber & Faber, 1948), p. 53.

8. The Governor of Nigeria, Sir Arthur Richards, commented on this remark in an address to the Nigerian Legislative Council on March 20, 1947: "A generation ago a Filipino politician is reputed to have said that he would prefer to go to hell with a government of his own than to heaven under alien guidance. Possibly so. But there are the silent millions of the people to be considered, and the reply to him was that if premature independence were to be hell it would be little consolation to tell the victims that the fire had been lit by their own countrymen." Cited by Joan Wheare, *The Nigerian Legislative Council*, vol. IV of Studies in Colonial Legislatures, ed. Margery Perham (London: Faber & Faber, Ltd., 1950), p. 251.

9. W. R. Thayer, *The Life and Times of Cavour* (Boston and New York: Houghton Mifflin Co., 1914), I, 424.

10. J. R. Seeley, *The Expansion of England* (Boston: Roberts Brothers, 1883), p. 234.

11. William E. Gladstone, *Political Speeches in Scotland — March and April 1880*, rev. ed. (Edinburgh: Andrew Elliot, 1880), p. 289.

12. In her Christmas Day broadcast from New Zealand in 1953, Queen Elizabeth referred to what she termed an entirely new conception of the Commonwealth, bearing no relation to the empires of the past: "To that new conception of an equal partnership of nations and races, I shall give myself, heart and soul, every day of my life."

13. *Behind God's Back* (New York: Harcourt, Brace & Co., 1941), p. 466.

14. *Asia and Western Dominance* (London: G. Allen & Unwin, Ltd., 1953), p. 157.

15. *Nationalism* (New York: The Macmillan Co., 1917), pp. 24–25. Speaking of Cecil Rhodes in Africa and Cromer in Egypt, Hannah Arendt concluded that "Aloofness became the new attitude of all members of the British services; it was a more dangerous form of governing than despotism and arbitrariness because it did not even tolerate that last link between the despot and his subjects, which is formed by bribery and gifts. The very integrity of the British administration made despotic government more inhuman and inaccessible to its subjects than Asiatic rulers or reckless conquerors had ever been. Integrity and aloofness were symbols for an absolute division of interests to the point where they are not even permitted to conflict." *Origins of Totalitarianism* (New York: Harcourt, Brace & Co., 1951), p. 212.

16. A vigorous statement of the shocking conditions of the life of the Africans who remain in the traditional society is contained in the address of the Vice-Governor General of the Belgian Congo to the *Conseil de Gouvernement* in 1947. "We are in an impasse: by the side of prosperous European enterprises, the native economy vegetates." He stated that the natives of the bush were naked, badly housed, badly nourished, sick; that, despite the prosperity of the Europeans, nothing real had been done for the prosperity of the natives; and that development had been for the aliens.

"But for the mass of those in the interior what have we done? Go to a real village in the bush; you will find there primitive people, who, except in relation to forced labor, the corvée, and taxes, live substantially as they always have, eat what they have always eaten. . . Always the same fatalistic conclusion: they are too poor to feed themselves; too badly fed to work; too inefficient to earn more." *Discours du Vice-Gouverneur Général L. Pé-tillon; Statistiques,* Congo Belge, Conseil de Gouvernement 1947, p. 78.

17. Lord Lloyd, II, 4.

18. Merle Fainsod sees the position of the Soviet-trained native intelligentsia as one of the most serious points of tension in Soviet policy, and draws an explicit comparison to Western colonial territories. *How Russia is Ruled* (Cambridge: Harvard University Press, 1953), pp. 495–496.

19. A similar position is strongly taken by W. R. Crocker, *Self-Government for the Colonies* (London: George Allen & Unwin, Ltd., 1949). "People do not like being exploited but they can put up with it. What they cannot put up with is being considered inferior" (p. 8). "Let us not deceive ourselves; the essence of the colonial grievance is not economic. For the biggest fact of all in the colonial world today is not poverty, but passion — passion about the colonial relationship" (p. vi). Setting off from the Arab world, Albert Hourani defines imperialism as the imposition of alien control upon an unwilling people and holds it to be "strictly irrelevant" whether or not Asian and African countries have benefited materially from Western rule. "The essence of imperialism is to be found in a moral relationship — that of power and powerlessness — and any material consequences which spring from it are not enough to change it." "The Decline of the West in the Middle East," *International Affairs,* vol. VII, no. 2 (January 1953), p. 31.

20. Jawaharlal Nehru, *Toward Freedom* (New York: John Day, 1941), pp. 352–353.

21. "The Characteristics of Urban Centres in the East," ch. vi of *Eastern and Western World,* ed. S. Hofstra (The Hague, Bandung: W. van Hoeve Ltd., 1953), p. 95. Georges Balandier finds that urban contact gives a special orientation to the relations between the races in Africa: the political awakening of the African city-dweller is speeded by the gap between the races, the dominant role of the Europeans, and the striking disproportion between the style and level of life of the two communities. "In the city social relations are less personal relations (which are often established in a rural milieu in view of the small number of Europeans who live there) than relations between groups; this wiping out of relations of a personal kind contributes to the affirmation of antagonistic reactions." *Sociologie des Brazzavilles Noires* (Paris: Librairie Armand Colin, 1955), p. 266.

CHAPTER IV. COLONIAL POLICY AND NATIONAL MOVEMENTS

1. Marvin Harris, "Portugal's African 'Wards' — A First-Hand Report on Labor and Education in Moçambique," *Africa Today,* vol. V, no. 6 (Nov.–Dec. 1958), p. 35. See also Lord Hailey, *An African Survey: Revised*

1956 (London, New York, Toronto: Oxford University Press, 1957), pp. 1371–1375; Basil Davidson, "Africa's Modern Slavery," *Harper's Magazine*, vol. 209, no. 1250 (July 1954), pp. 56–63, and his *The African Awakening* (London: Jonathan Cape, 1955), chs. XIX and XX; and James Duffy, *Portuguese Africa* (Cambridge, Mass.: Harvard University Press, 1959), chs. XI–XIII.

2. *Inside Africa* (New York: Harper & Brothers, 1955), p. 590. L.-P. Aujoulat accused Portugal's assimilation policy of "an excessive and suspect cautiousness" and of establishing almost insuperable barriers to the rise of Africans in the social scale. *Aujourd'hui, L'Afrique* (Tournai, Paris: Casterman, 1958), p. 167. See also Lord Hailey, pp. 228–233.

3. Marvin Harris, pp. 16, 6.

4. See J. H. Huizinga, "L'Evolution du Congo Belge," *Le Monde*, August 24, 1958. Huizinga contrasts the heavy contribution made by the French taxpayer to French colonial welfare and development with the lack of similar contributions by the Belgians.

5. See Pierre Ryckmans, "Belgian 'Colonialism,' " *Foreign Affairs*, vol. 34, no. 1 (October 1955), p. 94. In 1957 another Belgian Governor General warned that the great difference in social and economic standards between Europeans and Africans in the colonies was justified only so long as the Europeans represented a superior culture. It became illegitimate as soon as the civilizing mission had done its work and differential standards rested only on differences in race. *Discours du Gouverneur Général L. Pétillon; Statistiques*, Congo Belge, Conseil de Gouvernement 1957, pp. 13–14.

6. *Discours*, Congo Belge, Conseil de Gouvernement 1954, p. 35.

7. "Enlightened Colonialism," *The Reporter*, January 27, 1955, pp. 34–39. Finding that prophetic religious movements have been most extensive in the Belgian Congo since World War I, Georges Balandier contended that such Negro churches have come to the fore in areas where Christianization was most intensive, racial discrimination was most pronounced, and a modern economy was introduced through the early development of mining. "Here then is a zone where the causes of social change are more numerous and more pervasive, a zone where the position of being *dominated* is endured with greater difficulty." *Sociologie actuelle de l'Afrique noire* (Paris: Presses universitaires de France, 1955), p. 419.

8. *The Belgian Congo To-Day*, vol. V, no. 4 (October 1956), pp. 139–146. The original appeared in an African-owned newspaper, *Conscience Africaine*, July 1, 1956. The closing lines of the manifesto were: "With whole-hearted sincerity and enthusiasm we say: Long live the Congo! Long live Belgium! Long live the King!" For comments on this manifesto and other political declarations concerning the Congo which appeared at about the same time, see *African News*, vol. III, no. 8 (October 1956).

9. See James S. Coleman, "The Emergence of African Political Parties," *Africa Today*, ed. C. Grove Haines (Baltimore: Johns Hopkins Press, 1955), pp. 225–256.

10. *Discours*, Congo Belge, Conseil de Gouvernement 1956, p. 19.

11. The text of the King's Message and the Government's Declaration on January 13, 1959, are given in "The Belgian Congo's Political Future,"

Belgian Congo 59, special edition (Brussels: The Belgian Congo and Ruanda-Urundi Information and Public Relations Office, [1959]).

12. *Address to Foreign Policy Association, February 28, 1957*, Speeches and Press Conferences No. 90 (New York: Ambassade de France, Service de Presse et d'Information, February 28, 1957), p. 5. A French denial of nations is not a wholly new thing. On June 20, 1866, Marx wrote to Engels concerning an International Council at which some of the French representatives saw all nationality and nations as antiquated prejudices. In particular Marx said that he pointed out to Lafargue that the latter, entirely unconsciously, seemed to understand the negation of nationalities as "their absorption into the model French nation." *Marx-Engels Gesamtausgabe: Dritte Abteilung*, vol. III: *Briefwechsel* (Berlin: Marx-Engels-Verlag G. M. B. H., 1930), p. 342.

13. Cited by Raymond Leslie Buell, *The Native Problem in Africa* (New York: The Macmillan Co., 1928), II, 81.

14. *Address on Togoland and Black Africa*, Speeches and Press Conferences No. 85 (New York: Ambassade de France, Service de Presse et d'Information, January 1957), p. 7. "Is it not an edifying spectacle," he also asked, "to see before you a Minister of the French Republic, member of a Government under Socialist leadership, an African who follows the customs of matriarchy, a plain middle class African, leader of the largest democratic popular movement in French Black Africa?" p. 3. Some Africans failed to be edified by this type of absorption of the elite into the French society, and expressed their opinion of it in the more standard nationalist phrases. One African, denouncing it as treason to a people living under the colonial yoke, proclaimed the proper function of the elite to be "that we are first of all at the service of Black Africa and that we will merit the respect of the world only in proportion to our total loyalty to our country." Kader Fall, "Problème de l'élite en Afrique Noire," *Les Etudiants Noirs Parlent* (Paris: Présence Africaine, 1953), p. 38.

15. Félix Houphouet-Boigny, "Black Africa and the French Union," *Foreign Affairs*, vol. 35, no. 4 (July 1957), p. 597. See also François Mitterand, *Présence Française et Abandon* (Paris: Plon, 1957), part IV, chs. iv and v; Paul-Henri Siriex, *Une nouvelle Afrique* (Paris: Plon, 1957), part V.

16. Senghor has taken the position that "we are willing to assimilate what you offer us, but not to be assimilated by you." Cited by Robert Delavignette, *Freedom and Authority in French West Africa*, p. 50.

17. *Le Monde*, September 28, 1957. In 1949 J. H. Huizinga wrote of France's conceptions for Africa: "There is to be equality of status in the marriage; the one-sided obligation to honour and obey is to be gradually erased from the contract as the dusky child-wife is growing up. But there is to be no divorce. Those whom God — who is well known to be French — has joined together no man shall put asunder." *Manchester Guardian Weekly*, March 24, 1949.

18. For facts and figures on the voting, see *Birth of a New Community of Free Peoples*, French Affairs No. 71 (New York: Ambassade de France, Service de Presse et d'Information, October 1958).

19. *Le Monde*, October 1, 1958.

20. *Lord Durham's Report on the Affairs of British North America*,

ed. C. P. Lucas (Oxford: Clarendon Press, 1912), II, 38. The Report continued with language applicable to any number of colonial relationships: "The French complained of the arrogance and injustice of the English; the English accused the French of the vices of a weak and conquered people, and charged them with meanness and perfidy. The entire mistrust which the two races have thus far learned to conceive of each other's intentions, induces them to put the worst construction on the most innocent conduct; to judge every word, every act, and every intention unfairly; to attribute the most odious designs; and reject every overture of kindness or fairness, as covering secret designs of treachery and malignity." This would serve as an admirable description of Anglo-Indian relations in the interwar decades.

21. *The Dual Mandate in British Tropical Africa* (Edinburgh and London: W. Blackwood and Sons, 1922), p. 618.

22. Madame Pandit wrote, "The spirit of Britain that endures in India is that of her democratic institutions and traditions, her sense of fair play and her celebrated justice." Vijaya Lakshmi Pandit, "India's Foreign Policy," *Foreign Affairs*, vol. 34, no. 3 (April 1956), p. 437.

23. A. D. C. Peterson has pointed to the "curious spectacle" of the British struggling to create a nationalist movement in Malaya. "It is only in Malaya that you see the extraordinary sight of British officials more interested in the spread of the national flag, the national anthem, a national army, a national police force, and national schools, than are the people of the country themselves." "The Birth of the Malayan Nation," *International Affairs*, vol, XXXI, no. 3 (July 1955), p. 311. For discussion of a similar problem in an African setting, see David E. Apter, "Political Development in Uganda," *Current History*, vol. XXX, no. 177 (May 1956), pp. 269–278.

24. This point has been well made by David E. Apter, *The Gold Coast in Transition* (Princeton, N.J.: Princeton University Press, 1955), pp. 306–307 and elsewhere.

25. For the complete statements of these two leaders, see *Ghana Today*, vol. I, no. 8 (June 12, 1957) and *West Africa*, no. 2128 (January 25, 1958), p. 93.

26. Cited by Buell, I, 381–382.

27. Lord Altrincham, *Kenya's Opportunity* (London: Faber, 1955), p. 33.

28. W. Arthur Lewis *et al.*, *Attitude to Africa* (Harmondsworth, Middlesex: Penguin Books, 1951), p. 49.

29. J. Z. Savanhu, "Challenge to Sir Roy Welensky," *New Commonwealth*, vol. 28, no. 1 (July 8, 1954), p. 9. In the 1958 election for the Federal Parliament, 1,764 Africans were registered as voters of a total African population of nearly 7,000,000. *The New York Times*, October 12, 1958.

30. *A Petition to Her Majesty Queen Elizabeth II against Federation made by Chiefs and Citizens of Nyasaland* (London: The Africa Bureau, 1953), p. 6.

31. *Africa's Challenge to America* (Berkeley: University of California Press, 1956), p. 81. The opposite case was presented by the President of the Federation of Colonists in the Congo in a speech of June 1953, when

he argued that what should be done was "to people the Congo with inhabitants of the white race so as to realize its potentialities and raise the level of its populations and, to preserve the peace inside the country, to place those who govern under the eyes of the blacks and in direct personal contact with them." Cited in *Africa in the Modern World*, ed. Calvin W. Stillman (Chicago: Chicago University Press, 1955), p. 285.

32. *Report of the United Nations Visiting Mission to Trust Territories in East Africa, 1954, on Tanganyika*, U.N. Doc. T/1142, Dec. 23, 1954, p. 185. The earlier citation from the Report is from p. 188. Mr. Nyerere appeared before the Trusteeship Council on March 7, 1955. The Meru Citizens Union is cited as taking the position that "when the time for self-government comes, it will not be a multi-racial government but a government for the Africans and by the Africans." *Report*, p. 120.

33. "Development Through Democracy," *The Annals of the American Academy of Political and Social Science*, vol. 285 (January 1953), p. 2. The Netherlands gave a status similar to that of Puerto Rico to their territories in the Western hemisphere at about the same time.

34. *Ghana* (Edinburgh, New York, Toronto: Thomas Nelson & Sons, 1957), pp. 162–163.

35. "The Passing of the European Order," *Encounter*, vol. IX, no 5 (November 1957), p. 7. The italics are Lüthy's. This is a far more acceptable judgment than the exalted pronouncement of a former Governor of Kenya, Sir Philip Mitchell, that "The processes now called 'colonialism' have been, beyond question, the most beneficent, disinterested, and effective force which has ever been brought to bear on Africa in all its history. That it might have been better, that it has its blemishes and faults, does not alter that plain statement of fact." "Africa and the West in Historical Perspective," *Africa Today*, ed. Haines, p. 22.

36. H. J. van Mook, *The Stakes of Democracy in Southeast Asia* (New York: W. W. Norton & Co., 1950), p. 75.

CHAPTER V. THE NATURE OF THE NATION

1. An effort to reduce the element of subjective guesswork and to introduce objective scientific criteria, making quantitative measurement possible, has been undertaken by Karl W. Deutsch, *Nationalism and Social Communication* (Cambridge, Mass.: Massachusetts Institute of Technology Press, and New York: John Wiley & Sons, Inc., 1953). For a critical review of the concepts and criteria suggested in this book, see Herbert Goldhamer, "Fashion and Social Science," *World Politics*, vol. VI, no. 3 (April 1954), pp. 394–404.

2. For further citations from Mazzini and others who hold the nation to be created by God, nature, or other mystical forces, see Boyd C. Shafer, *Nationalism: Myth and Reality* (New York: Harcourt, Brace and Company, 1955), chap. ii, "Some Metaphysical Myths." In a contemporary version of this doctrine, Chancellor Adenauer, meeting in Moscow with Soviet leaders, protested that "The division of Germany is abnormal. It is

against human and divine law and against nature." *The New York Times*, Sept. 10, 1955.

3. See Crane Brinton, *From Many One* (Cambridge, Mass.: Harvard University Press, 1948). "Neither the German nor the French nation is an entity predestined by nature, any more than the American nation is. They all, as well as the national consciousness which animates them, were formed by historical forces." Hans Kohn, *The Idea of Nationalism* (New York: The Macmillan Company, 1944), p. 22. Ortega y Gasset attacks those historians who "suppose that France and Spain pre-existed as unities in the depths of the French and Spanish soul. As if there were any French or Spaniards before France and Spain came into being! As if the Frenchman and the Spaniard were not simply things that had to be hammered out in two thousand years of toil!" *The Revolt of the Masses* (New York: W. W. Norton and Co., 1932), p. 179.

4. Cited in Luigi Sturzo, *Italy and Fascismo* (London: Faber and Gwyer, 1927), p. 13.

5. *The New York Times*, October 4, 1955.

6. Jean-Marie Domenach, "Les Nationalismes," *Esprit*, vol. XXIII, no. 224 (March 1955), p. 344.

7. "Nationality," *The History of Freedom and Other Essays* (London: Macmillan and Co., Limited, 1909), p. 292.

8. See Werner Levi, *Free India in Asia* (Minneapolis: University of Minnesota Press, 1952), chap. iii.

CHAPTER VI. PEOPLE, TERRITORY, AND STATE

1. See Bernard Joseph, *Nationality, Its Nature and Problems* (London: G. Allen & Unwin, ltd., 1929), p. 84, and Arnold van Gennep, *Traité Comparatif des Nationalités* (Paris: Payet, 1922), p. 143.

2. *Speeches and Statements of Iqbal*, compiled by "Shamloo" (Lahore: Al-Manar Academy, n.d.), pp. 204 ff.

3. Arnold Toynbee suggests that for this part of the world the morally devastating effect of the impact of nationalism was aggravated by a vein of archaism which based itself not on the national attachments of the living generation but on the territorial claims of an ephemeral past reaching back many centuries. *A Study of History* (London: Oxford University Press, 1954), VIII, 191, note 2.

4. *Asia and the West* (New York: Institute of Pacific Relations, 1953), p. 288.

5. See the statement made by Prime Minister Macmillan in the House of Commons on June 19, 1958. For the final settlement, see *The New York Times*, Feb. 24, 1959.

6. *Nationalism and Culture* (New York: Covici-Friede, 1937), p. 200.

7. *The Revolt of the Masses*, p. 180. In even more cautious vein: "Once the most primitive communities have been left behind, the origin of any common political feeling, as well as the factors of common language, traditions, beliefs, and laws, is in a large number of cases to be found in subordination at some period in the past to the influence of some common

political organization." Royal Institute of International Affairs, *Nationalism* (London, New York, Toronto: Oxford University Press, 1939), p. 4.

8. *Weltbürgertum und Nationalstaat*, 6th ed. (Munich and Berlin: R. Oldenburg, 1922), p. 3.

9. Hans Kohn in his *The Idea of Nationalism*, p. 329, attempts a differentiation of dubious validity. He suggests that in the Western world, including the United States and the British dominions, nationalism was a predominantly political occurrence, preceded by the formation of the future national state or, for the United States, coincident with it. In the rest of the world, including central and eastern Europe, he contends that nationalism came generally at a more backward stage of political development: "The frontiers of an existing state and of a rising nationality rarely coincided." Nationalism grew as a protest against the existing state pattern and sought to reshape political boundaries to meet ethnographic demands.

To limit comment on this proposition to Asia, such examples as those of Japan, China, Korea, Thailand, Burma, Iran, and, in a somewhat different setting, India, Indonesia, and the Philippines indicates that the coincidence of state and nation has in fact been very marked and extensive. There are, certainly, significant differences to be pointed out between Western Europe and much of the rest of the world, but this does not appear to be one of them.

10. This was strongly put by the Argentine Foreign Minister, José Maria Cantilo, at the Pan-American Conference in Lima on December 10, 1938: "Our nationalities are administrative creations of the crowns of Spain, France and Portugal. The frontiers of most Spanish American republics are frontiers of old vice royalities, provinces or administrative departments." *The New York Times*, December 11, 1938.

11. Karl Marx, *Capital, The Communist Manifesto and Other Writings* (New York: Modern Library, 1932), p. 333.

12. A recent analyst of the British influence on India seeks out the common elements in three opposed nationalist leaders, Gandhi, Jinnah, and Sri Subhas Chandra Bose. "What had these three men in common? Certainly not religion, nor native language, nor family customs, nor way of life. They shared, indeed, in a common Indian culture, which has never been overlaid by religious or provincial differences, but most of all they were united by a demand for liberty, the belief in the parliamentary system and the conviction that all men had equal rights before God and the law. Every one of these ideas was the direct result of British administration; none of them had ever existed in ancient or medieval India." Sir Percival Griffiths, *The British Impact on India*, p. 229.

13. See Joseph Ralston Hayden, *The Philippines: A Study in National Development* (New York: Macmillan, 1942), pp. 9–10.

14. See *The Indonesian Review*, vol. I, no. 1 (January 1951), pp. 13, 46.

15. "The English found in Burma a country already unified under one Crown and, although the outlying provinces were at first glad to be freed, in metropolitan Burma the people remembered past glory and forgot past misrule. In India, nationalism was a product of British rule; in Burma it was ready-made." Philip Woodruff, *The Guardians* (New York: St. Martin's Press, 1954), p. 136.

16. T. L. H., "Anatomy of African Nationalism," *West Africa*, no. 1977 (January 15, 1955), p. 36. Much the same point is made for French North Africa by Ch.-André Julien who sees Algeria, Tunisia, and Morocco endowed with a sense of both separate nationalism and regional unity. *L'Afrique du Nord en Marche* (Paris: René Julliard, 1952), p. 25.

17. "The Bases of Arab Unity," *International Affairs*, vol. XXX, no. 1 (January 1954), pp. 44–45.

18. See G. Balandier, "Contribution à l'étude des nationalismes en Afrique noire," *Zaire*, vol. VIII, no. 4 (April 1954), p. 381.

19. *An African Survey: Revised 1956*, pp. 251–252. Diedrich Westermann has denied that nationalism can have the same meaning in Africa as in Europe where it is the desire of a nation for unity. "In Africa it simply means independence from European domination. In Africa there are no nations, but only tribal groups." "Cultural History of Negro Africa," *Cahiers d'Histoire Mondiale*, vol. VII, no. 4 (1957), p. 1003.

20. Address to the Nigerian Council, cited by James S. Coleman, *Nigeria: Background to Nationalism* (Berkeley and Los Angeles: University of California Press, 1958), pp. 193–194.

21. Obafemi Awolowo, *Path to Nigerian Freedom* (London: Faber and Faber, 1947), pp. 47–48.

22. Cmd. 505 (London: H.M.S.O., 1958).

23. "The Cameroons Question," *West Africa*, no. 1969 (November 20, 1954), p. 1093. For a similar point regarding Togoland, see the *Special Report of the First Visiting Mission to the Territories of Togoland under British Administration and Togoland under French Administration on the Ewe Problem*, U. N. Doc. T/463, 1950, pp. 35–36.

24. "Resolutions of the All African People's Conference held at Accra, Ghana, December 5–13, 1958" (Washington: Embassy of Ghana, Information Section, January 19, 1959), pp. 7–9.

CHAPTER VII. LANGUAGE

1. Edward A. Freeman, "Race and Language," *Historical Essays*, 3rd series (London: Macmillan and Company, 1879), p. 203.

2. *A Study of History*, VIII, 536.

3. André Martinet in his preface to Uriel Weinrich, *Languages in Contact* (New York: Publications of the Linguistic Circle of New York, 1953), no. 1, p. vii, stresses the importance of "linguistic allegiance" as one of the determinants of languages, suggesting, for example, that different allegiances rather than actual material differences make two separate languages of Czech and Slovak. See also H. Munro Chadwick, *The Nationalities of Europe and the Growth of National Ideologies* (New York: The Macmillan Company, 1946), p. 14.

4. *Essays on Nationalism* (New York: The Macmillan Company, 1926), p. 47.

5. In Indonesia independence brought with it a prompt shift from Dutch to English as a second language, and similar shifts are under way elsewhere, arising in part from a desire to facilitate closer contact with

neighboring Asian countries through the possession of a single *lingua franca*.

6. Cited in *The New York Times*, September 24, 1955. On the other hand, the dangers involved in drifting too far away from the use of English have been pointed out by Nehru himself, and in 1959 a special committee on higher education opposed a too hasty change-over from English as the medium of instruction in Indian universities. *The New York Times*, October 16, 1955, and February 16, 1959.

7. See Tao-tai Hsia, "The Language Revolution in Communist China," *Far Eastern Survey*, vol. XXV, no. 10 (October 1956), pp. 145–154. Tradition won out, however, in a 1957 ruling of the Ministry of Education that students must write the Chinese characters and with the standard brushes, not fountain pen. *The New York Times*, July 8, 1957.

8. L. Szabe, "Regression or New Development? Twenty Years of Linguistic Reform in Turkey," *Civilisations*, vol. II, no. 1 (1952), p. 50.

9. *Marxism and the National and Colonial Question* (Moscow: Foreign Languages Publishing House, 1940), pp. 5–6.

10. I. Potekhin, "De quelques problèmes méthodologiques pour l'étude de la formation des nations en Afrique au sud du Sahara," *Présence Africaine*, no. 17 (December 1957–January 1958), p. 62.

11. *The New York Times Magazine*, April 20, 1958, p. 9.

12. "The Question of Language," *The Unity of India* (London: Lindsay Drummond, 1941), p. 241.

13. These figures are drawn from the opening pages of the *Census of India, 1951* (New Delhi, 1954), Paper No. 1. That the compiling of a linguistic census is impeded by other than merely technical problems is indicated by the reason given (pp. 1–2) for the failure to give a separate figure for those whose mother tongue is the official language, Hindi. It was necessary to lump the speakers of this language together with Urdu, Hindustani, and Punjabi because in five states "the replies to the language question were extensively falsified as a result of public agitation," with the result that the returns were so vitiated by controversy as to force a lumping together of the languages. In one district a man was murdered in the ensuing disturbance.

14. Stalin, *Marxism and the National and Colonial Question*, p. 184. For a more scholarly and scientific version of the same conception, see Deutsch, *Nationalism and Social Communication*, pp. 110–111 and Appendix III.

15. *The Unity of India*, pp. 243–244.

16. Cited by Selig S. Harrison, "The Challenge to Indian Nationalism," *Foreign Affairs*, vol. XXXIV, no. 4 (July 1956), p. 621. On the general problem, see also Marshall Windmiller, "Linguistic Regionalism in India," *Pacific Affairs*, vol. XXVII, no. 4 (December 1954), pp. 291–318.

17. *Report of the States Re-organization Commission* (New Delhi, 1955), p. 43.

18. See Marshall Windmiller, "The Politics of States Reorganization in India: The Case of Bombay," *Far Eastern Survey*, vol. XXV, no 9 (September 1956).

19. Selig S. Harrison, *The Most Dangerous Decades: An Introduction to the Comparative Study of Language Policy in Multi-Lingual States*

(New York: Columbia University, Language and Communication Center, 1957), p. 9. This pioneer study contains bibliographies on linguistic-political problems in several parts of the world.

20. See *An African Survey*, ch. iii. Lord Hailey indicated the shortcomings of knowledge about African languages by citing the varying estimates of scholars that of a possible total of 2,000 languages in the world, Africa is responsible for some figure between 700 and 1,000. P. 79. A Unesco publication itemized 369 languages and dialects in British African territories alone. *The Use of Vernacular Languages in Education*, Monographs on Fundamental Education, no 8 (Paris: Unesco, 1953).

21. "Matchet's Diary," *West Africa*, no. 2081 (March 2, 1957), p. 196.

22. Resolution 329 (IV), adopted on December 2, 1949.

23. The assimilationist doctrines of France and Portugal dictated that education at all levels in their dependencies should be carried on in the language of the metropolitan power. In Ethiopia, where 35 languages and dialects are said to be spoken, there is a similar insistence on Amharic as the sole national language. W. H. Lewis, "The Ethiopian Empire," *Middle East Journal*, vol. XI, no. 3 (Summer 1956), p. 257.

CHAPTER VIII. CULTURE AND RELIGION

1. Ernest Renan, "Qu'est ce qu'une nation?," *Discours et Conférences* (Paris: Ancienne Maison Michel Lévy Frères, 1887), p. 286.

2. *Nationalism: Myth and Reality*, p. 54.

3. *The Discovery of India*, 2nd ed. (London: Meridian Books Limited, 1947), p. 288. Characteristically, Nehru followed this passage with the comment that India's past, "in all its variety and greatness, was a common heritage of the Indian people, Hindu, Moslem, Christian, and others, and their ancestors had helped to build it."

4. "It is not merely that you and I, the general public, are expected to recognize certain peoples as definitely backward. It is that these peoples are being summoned to *think of themselves* as backward." William Ernest Hocking, *The Spirit of World Politics* (New York: Macmillan, 1932), p. 4.

5. Confronting the difficulties involved in this situation, Thomas Hodgkin, writing of African nationalism, decided "to use the term 'nationalist' in a broad sense, to describe any organization or group that explicitly asserts the rights, claims and aspirations of a given African society (from the level of the language-group to that of 'Pan-Africa') in opposition to European authority, whatever its institutional forms and objectives." *Nationalism in Colonial Africa*, p. 23.

6. "History of African Nationalism," *Proceedings of the First Annual Conference of the West African Institute of Social and Economic Research* (Ibadan, Nigeria: University College, 1952, reprinted, March 1957), p. 31. See also P. Mercier, "Evolution of Senegalese Elites," *International Social Science Bulletin*, vol. VIII, no. 3 (1956).

7. "African Nationalism: A Critical Portrait," *Dissent*, vol. III, no. 3 (Summer 1956), p. 277.

8. *Nations Nègres et Culture* (Paris: Editions Africaines, 1955), p. 19.

9. *Afrique Ambiguë* (Paris: Libraire Plon, 1957), p. 280. Dika Akwa's book, to which Balandier refers is *Itinéraire de la pensée nègre*.

10. "Resolutions of the All African People's Conference held at Accra," pp. 6–7, resolutions on Tribalism, Religious Separatism, and Traditional Institutions.

11. *Pan-Africanism or Communism? The Coming Struggle for Africa* (London: Dobson Books Ltd., 1956), p. 373.

12. See Kenneth Little, "African Culture and the Western Intrusion," *Journal of World History*, vol. III, no. 4 (1957), pp. 941–964.

13. "The Conflict of Culture in Africa," *Phylon*, vol. XVI, no. 4 (4th Quarter, 1955), p. 392.

14. Hans Kohn formulated a "universal sociological law" which he saw as signifying the transition from medieval to modern forms of organization: "religious groupings lose power when confronted with the consciousness of a common nationality and speech." *Nationalism and Imperialism in the Hither East* (London: Routledge, 1932), p. 229.

15. See *A History of Nationalism in the East* (New York: Harcourt, Brace and Company, 1929), chap. ii.

16. *Nationalism in Colonial Africa*, p. 114. See also Georges Balandier, "Messianismes et Nationalismes en Afrique Noire," *Cahiers Internationaux de Sociologie*, vol. XIV (1953). Balandier (p. 64) suggests that one of the factors involved in the origin of separatist and Messianic Christian sects is the contrast between Christian teachings and the actual situation which Christian colonialism creates.

17. *Pakistan, or the Partition of India*, 3rd ed. (Bombay: Thacker, 1946), pp. 18–19.

18. *Current Digest of the Soviet Press*, January 25, 1956, p. 9.

19. Cited by Jean A. Curran, Jr., "The RSS: Militant Hinduism," *Far Eastern Survey*, vol. XIX, no. 10 (May 17, 1950), pp. 95–96.

20. *The Meaning of Pakistan* (Lahore: M. Ashraf, 1944), p. xii. Durrani preceded this comment by the injunction that the purposelessness and selfish greed of India's Moslems must now be replaced "by a fierce fanatical passion for the service of our people."

21. This proposition has been well stated by W. Norman Brown, who remarked that, although Gandhi abhorred Hindu-Moslem communalism and partition, he still contributed to them. The argument which is developed is that no one could be leader of a mass party in India without being religious, that Gandhi could not be religious without being a Hindu, and that his Hinduism inevitably made him suspect to the Moslems. *The United States and India and Pakistan* (Cambridge, Mass.: Harvard University Press, 1953), p. 90. R. Coupland summed the matter up by saying that, however all-embracing Gandhi's charity toward other races and creeds, he belonged to the Hindu tradition: "he would be out of place among the heroes of Islam." *The Indian Problem*, vol. II: *Indian Politics 1936–42* (New York, London, Toronto, Bombay: Oxford University Press, 1944), p. 193.

22. *The Autobiography of an Unknown Indian* (New York: Macmillan, 1951), p. 432.

23. *Social Background of Indian Nationalism* (Bombay: Geoffrey Cumberlege, Oxford University Press, 1948), p. 271.

24. *The New York Times*, May 18, 1958. Nehru's modernism is reflected in a report of a speech he made at the opening of a dam in Bihar. Here he proclaimed that temples, mosques, and churches were not the only places of worship, but that dams, built by the labor of the Indian people, "were also to be regarded as Centers of worship. . ." *Indiagram* (Washington: Information Service of India), no. 807 (October 19, 1955). On another occasion in the same year Nehru said that the time had come "when we have to consider the service of India as our first religion, whatever religion each one of us might profess." *Indiagram*, no. 673 (April 11, 1955).

25. Cited by Keith Callard, *Pakistan: A Political Study* (New York: The Macmillan Company, 1957), pp. 157–158.

26. Sayyed Abulala Maudoodi, *Nationalism and India*, 2nd ed. (Pathankot, Pb.: Maktaba-E-Jama' at-E-Islami, 1947), pp. 12, 40. For an examination of different aspects of the relations between Islam and Pakistan, see Callard, *Pakistan: A Political Study*, chaps. ii and iii; and Leonard Binder, "Pakistan and Modern Islamic-Nationalist Theory," *The Middle East Journal*, vol. XI, no. 4 and vol. XII, no. 1 (Autumn 1957 and Winter 1958).

27. *An Arab Tells His Story: A Study in Loyalties* (London: John Murray, 1946), p. 1.

28. Wilfred Cantwell Smith, *Islam in Modern History* (Princeton: Princeton University Press, 1957), p. 75.

CHAPTER IX. ECONOMICS

1. Demetrio Boersner, *The Bolsheviks and the National and Colonial Question* (Geneva: Librairie E. Droz; Paris: Librairie Minard. 1957), p. 36.

2. Joseph Stalin, *Marxism and the National and Colonial Question*, pp. 6–7. The continued hold of Stalin's 1913 definition is shown by the use of it by the Soviet Africanist, I. Potekhin, who comments also that "if there is not a national market, there is not a nation." "De quelques problèmes méthodologiques pour l'étude de la formation des nations en Afrique au sud du Sahara," *Présence Africaine*, no. 17 (December 1957–January 1958), p. 72.

3. *The Right of Nations to Self-Determination* (Moscow: Foreign Languages Publishing House, 1951), p. 10.

4. Karl Marx, *Capital, the Communist Manifesto and Other Writings* (New York: The Modern Library, 1932), p. 340.

5. "Ausland," *Weltwirtschaftliches Archiv* (Jena: Verlag von Gustav Fischer, 1930), p. 68. The entire question is more elaborately examined in his *Nationales Gemeinschaftsgefühl und Wirtschaftliches Interesse* (Leipzig: C. L. Hirschfield, 1929).

6. "The wave of nationalism in the underdeveloped countries has created the desire of having a national economy which presupposes national independence." V. B. Singh, "Keynesian Economics in Relation to Underdeveloped Countries," *Science and Society*, vol. XVIII, no. 3 (Summer 1954), p. 228.

7. Concluding a survey of Arab-Jewish relations in Palestine, W. K.

Hancock asserted: "The one thing which is crystal clear is the dominance of national feeling over economic calculation." *Survey of British Commonwealth Affairs* (London, New York, Toronto: Oxford University Press, 1937), I, 465.

8. *Imperialism and World Economy* (New York: International Publishers, 1929), p. 119. In his Introduction Lenin renewed his attack on Kautsky and on the idea that capitalism might rise beyond national imperialism.

9. *Die Nationalitätenfrage und die Sozialdemokratie* (Wien: Verlag der Wiener Volksbuchhandlung, 1924), p. 105.

10. *The Right of Nations to Self-Determination*, p. 9. The study group of the Royal Institute of International Affairs came to much the same conclusion in summarizing its survey of developments in Europe: "As far as it is humanly possible to judge, the national movements would not have arisen, or would not have merited the title of 'national,' if it had not been for the growth of the capitalist system and the Industrial Revolution." *Nationalism*, p. 112.

11. *Economic Planning and International Order* (London: Macmillan and Co., Ltd., 1937), p. 55.

12. *Freedom vs. Organization* (New York: W. W. Norton & Co., Inc., 1934), p. 213. Recognizing the dualistic nature of the problem, Russell also commented: "It is true, of course, that conflicts between nations are very largely economic, but the grouping of the world by nations is itself determined by causes which are in the main not economic." P. 199.

13. *Colonial Policy and Practice* (Cambridge: Cambridge University Press, 1948), p. 157.

14. *Africa's Challenge to America*, p. 304.

15. *Die Nationalitätenfrage und die Sozialdemokratie*, p. 263. Chapter 18 is devoted to "Capitalism and National Hate."

16. *News from Viet-nam* (Washington: Embassy of the Republic of Viet-nam), vol. III, no. 21 (May 31, 1957), p. 3.

17. "Ideological Background of the Asian-African Conference," *United Asia*, vol. VII, no. 2 (March 1955), p. 44. In Burma Premier U Nu told the Chamber of Commerce: "Burma has been for over a century under Imperialist domination, and Capitalists have during the entire period been regarded as the handmaids of Imperialism. During the entire course of our struggle for freedom, therefore, Capital and Imperialist domination have been closely associated in the minds of all of us who have taken part in the struggle, and it has been impossible to view the two in isolation." *From Peace to Stability* (Rangoon: Ministry of Information, 1951), p. 75.

CHAPTER X. THE WEST AND NON-WESTERN NATIONALISM

1. "The 'Modern State' in Africa and Asia," *The Cambridge Journal*, vol. VI, no 1 (July 1952), p. 592.

2. "The most important arena (apart from Holland) is England, be-

cause it is in England, with its new geographical position as the entrepôt between Europe and America, its achievement of internal economic unity two centuries before France and two and a half centuries before Germany, its constitutional revolution, and its powerful *bourgeoisie* of bankers, shipowners, and merchants, that the transformation of society is earliest, swiftest, and most complete." R. H. Tawney, *Religion and the Rise of Capitalism* (New York: Harcourt, Brace and Company, 1926), p. 8.

3. *Mémoires . . . Laissés par le Prince de Metternich*, 2nd ed. (Paris: E. Plon et Cie., 1881), III, 262. The "Profession de Foi Politique," from which the earlier citations are taken, is in the same volume, pp. 425–445. See also Heinrich Srbik, *Metternich: Der Staatsmaan und der Mensch* (Munich: F. Bruckmann, 1925), I, 380–381.

4. *A Study of History*, VIII, 338. For Lenin it is "the bourgeoisie which naturally comes out as the hegemon (leader) in the beginning of every national movement." *The Right of Nations to Self-Determination*, p. 32. See also International Institute of Differing Civilizations, *Development of a Middle Class in Tropical and Sub-Tropical Countries* (Brussels: 1956).

5. See James S. Coleman, "Nationalism in Tropical Africa," *American Political Science Review*, vol. XLVIII, no. 2 (June 1954), p. 414. For a somewhat variant view, in relation to Southeast Asia, see Erich H. Jacoby, *Agrarian Unrest in South East Asia* (New York: Columbia University Press, 1949), especially chap. viii, "Agrarian Unrest and National Movements."

6. David Mitrany has pointed to the same moral with special reference to Eastern and Southeastern Europe. *Marx Against the Peasant* (Chapel Hill, N.C.: University of North Carolina Press, 1951), p. 139.

7. *The Hill of Devi* (New York: Harcourt, Brace and Co., 1953), p. 137.

8. "Presidential Address to the Indian National Congress, 1936," *India and the World* (London: George Allen and Unwin, Ltd., 1936), p. 77.

9. Ivor Jennings asserts that "experience in Asia suggests that nationalism becomes prominent in the third generation of the English-educated." The first generation is a small one, mainly composed of Eurasians and feudal landlords; the second is made up largely of clerks and interpreters, though some secure greater eminence; while the third, infiltrating into the higher civil service, also produces the nationalist movement. The fourth generation achieves self-government. *The Approach to Self-Government* (Cambridge: Cambridge University Press, 1956), pp. 138–139.

10. *San Min Chu I* (Shanghai: China Committee, Institute of Pacific Relations, 1927), p. 16.

11. *L'Afrique du Nord en Marche*, p. 24. See also pp. 144–145.

12. *The Discovery of India*, pp. 324–325. The same conclusion is reached by A. R. Desai, *The Social Background of Indian Nationalism* (London: Oxford University Press, 1948), p. 284, and Sir Percival Griffiths, *The British Impact on India*, pp. 101–103. See also Hugh Tinker, "1857 and 1957: The Mutiny and Modern India," *International Affairs*, vol. 34, no. 1 (January 1958), pp. 57–65.

13. Saw Tun, "A Burman Speaks," *Asia and the Americas*, vol. XLVI, no. 8 (September 1946), pp. 412–413. Another example is the rising of the

Rif tribesmen against both Spain and France in the 1920's. Of their leader, Abd-el-Krim, Robert Montagne writes: "He represents authentically the old Morocco of the tribes and everything which distinguishes it from the countries of Asia and Egypt led by their semi-modernized elites. . . . Abd-el-Krim is the man of the past, of an epoch which was no doubt heroic but is ended today. The forces which made his grandeur are not those of our time." *Révolution au Maroc* (Paris: Editions France-Empire, 1953), pp. 152, 175.

14. James S. Coleman has undertaken an analysis of African nationalist movements and other similar phenomena in a series of articles: "The Problem of Political Integration in Emergent Africa," *Western Political Quarterly*, vol. VIII, no. 1 (March 1955), pp. 44–57; "Current Political Movements in Africa," *Annals of the American Academy of Political and Social Science*, no. 298 (March 1955), pp. 95–108; "The Emergence of African Political Parties," *Africa Today*, ed. C. Grove Haines, pp. 225–256; "Nationalism in Tropical Africa," *American Political Science Review*, vol. XLVIII, no. 2 (June 1954), pp. 404–426.

15. "African Growing Pains," *African Affairs*, vol. LII, no. 208 (July 1953), p. 195.

16. Dankwart A. Rustow gives some Middle Eastern examples of anti-Western nationalist movements which turned to Westernization. "New Horizons for Comparative Politics," *World Politics*, vol. IX, no. 4 (July 1957), p. 538.

17. Sjahrazad (pseud.), *Indonesische Overpeinzingen* (Amsterdam: De Bezige Bij, 1949), p. 22.

18. *Toward Freedom*, p. 264.

CHAPTER XI. NATIONALISM AND DEMOCRACY: BACKGROUND AND FOREGROUND

1. *The Idea of Nationalism*, p. 3.

2. *Man and Society in an Age of Reconstruction* (London: Kegan, Paul, Trench, Trubner & Co., Ltd., 1940), p. 44.

3. Maurice Duverger suggests that paternalist policies in the colonies have produced results comparable to those which shook Europe in the nineteenth century: "Les transformations économiques entraînent des transformations sociales, lesquelles conduisent à un bouleversement politique. Que la classe moyenne soit créée par le progrès technique ou par la colonisation, les résultats sont les mêmes au point de vue des structures politiques." "Une Course contre la Montre," *La Nef: Où va l'Union Française?*, vol. XII, cahier no. 9, nouvelle série (June 1955), p. 216.

4. *World Politics and Personal Insecurity* (New York, London: McGraw-Hill Book Co., Inc., 1935), p. 97.

5. Alfred Cobban, *National Self-Determination* (London, New York, Toronto: Oxford University Press, 1945), p. 6. This view reached far beyond the liberal camp. Speaking of the period around the turn of the century, Richard Pipes states: "The principle of 'national self-determination'

was generally recognized by socialists in Europe and Russia as a basic democratic right, like, for instance, the principles of equality of the sexes or freedom of speech." *The Formation of the Soviet Union* (Cambridge, Mass.: Harvard University Press, 1954), p. 33.

6. The Asian-African Conference at Bandung adopted this position in its final Communiqué of April 24, 1955: "The Conference declared its full support of the principles of self-determination of peoples and nations as set forth in the Charter of the United Nations and took note of the United Nations resolutions on the rights of peoples and nations to self-determination, which is a pre-requisite of the full enjoyment of all fundamental Human Rights." *The New York Times*, April 25, 1955. The latter part of this statement repeats the words of the first "Whereas" of the General Assembly Resolution 637 A(VII) of 1952.

7. The material in this and the succeeding paragraph is drawn from the opening pages of chapter xvi, "Of Nationality, as Connected with Representative Government."

8. *Liberalism* (London, New York, Toronto: Oxford University Press, 1945), pp. 135–136. See also his *Democracy and Reaction* (New York: G. P. Putnam's Sons, 1905), pp. 157 ff. Cobban comes to precisely the contrary conclusion: "We are bound to conclude that the association between nationalism and democracy and therefore the theory of self-determination itself, may have been the result, not of their innate interdependence, but of historical accident." *National Self-Determination*, p. 7.

9. "The rise of nationalism accompanied the growth of democratic sentiments and of democratic instrumentalities." R. M. MacIver, *The Web of Government* (New York: The Macmillan Co., 1947), p. 169.

10. Alexander Dunlop Lindsay, *The Essentials of Democracy*, 2nd ed. (London, New York, Toronto: Oxford University Press, 1935), p. 45. He added that "it is a commonplace that successful political democracy on a large scale implies something that we call nationality."

11. *Government and the Governed* (London: Christophers, 1939), p. 169. "Englishmen thought nationalism a subordinate manifestation of liberalism." Raymond J. Sontag, *Germany and England* (New York: Appleton-Century Co., Inc., 1938), p. ix.

CHAPTER XII. COLONIALISM AS A SCHOOL FOR DEMOCRACY

1. Cited by L. S. S. O'Malley, ed., *Modern India and the West* (London, New York, Toronto: Oxford University Press, 1941), p. 758. Writing of Southeast Asia Kenneth Landon stated: "The political forms of the West can no more be rejected during this period of Westernization than could the Hindu theory of the divine king have been rejected during the period of Hinduization. Each is an integral part of an organized way of life." *Southeast Asia, Crossroad of Religions* (Chicago: University of Chicago Press, 1949), p. 177.

2. *The Philippines*, p. 30. Manuel Quezon said that Englishmen and Dutchmen in the Philippines at the beginning of American rule told the Americans "how foolish it was — and how *dangerous* — to attempt the experiment of 'shooting' democracy into the fabric of 'Oriental' minds.

These critics overlooked the fact that more than three hundred years before the Spaniards *did* shoot — and successfully — the Christian religion into the souls of the Filipinos, and that Christianity had prepared us for democracy since Christ's teachings were indeed the essence of democratic ideals and principles." *The Good Fight* (New York, London: D. Appleton-Century Co., 1946), p. 113. The Revolutionary Malolos Filipino Constitution of 1899 provided that "Sovereignty resides exclusively in the people," and that the government of the Republic should be popular, representative, and responsible. *Report of the United States Philippine Commission* (Washington: Government Printing Office, 1900), I, 189–190.

3. Regarding the state of democratic institutions in Portuguese Africa, see the despatch from Lourenço Marques in the *New York Times*, March 2, 1956, which reports the establishment in Mozambique of a Legislative Council. "However, the Council's powers are slight" and its members are either appointed by the Governor General or elected under a strictly limited franchise from a list which is "government-approved and unopposed at the polls. . . . Portuguese officials say it is not inconceivable that a qualified native may one day take a seat in the Council."

4. See the series of Studies in Colonial Legislatures, edited by Margery Perham, which opened with a general survey by Martin Wight, *The Development of the Legislative Council, 1606–1945* (London: Faber & Faber, Ltd., 1946).

5. E. W. Evans, *The British Yoke* (London, Edinburgh, Glasgow: William Hodge & Co, 1949), p. 123, denies that Crown Colony government can serve as a training ground for responsible self-government. "Like the art of flute-playing, which, as Aristotle observed, can only be learned by playing the flute, the art of government can only be learned by the process of governing." He suggests that the limit of achievement for the local member of the Legislative Council is that of the good debater and committee man.

6. Similar views obviously linger on vigorously in some quarters of the American South. In the Declaration of Constitutional Principles issued by ninety-six Southern Congressmen in relation to the school segregation problem, it was laid out, for example, that: "Without regard to the consent of the governed, outside agitators are threatening immediate and revolutionary changes in our public school systems." *The New York Times*, March 12, 1956. No great ingenuity is required to determine which racial section of the governed feels that its consent should be secured. In relation to the colonies Henri Brunschwig has suggested that the situation has grown more difficult since World War II because the imperial centers, inspired in part by uneasy consciences, have moved toward more generous attitudes while "the colonists overseas retained their easy conscience and their superiority complex toward the natives." "Colonial Imperialism," *Confluence*, vol. IV, no. 2 (July 1955), p. 224.

7. *The Philippines*, p. 316.

8. Robert Rézette, *Les Partis politiques marocains* (Paris: Librarie Armand Colin, 1955), p. 358.

9. *Kenya's Opportunity* (London: Faber & Faber, Ltd., 1955), p. 64.

10. *Kenya's Opportunity*, p. 60.

CHAPTER XIII. THE COLONIAL NATIONALIST AS DEMOCRAT

1. *Report to His Excellency the Governor by the Committee on Constitutional Reform* (London: H.M.S.O., 1949), Colonial No. 248, p. 9.

2. A curious feature of the regime established by Nkrumah in the Gold Coast is the charge that he has been unready to welcome into the dominant elite the students returning from England and the United States. Bankole Timothy attributed this to Nkrumah's effort to bring in the day of the common man, combined with a deliberate belittling of the intelligentsia. *Kwame Nkrumah* (London: Allen & Unwin, 1955), p. 118. See also Apter, *The Gold Coast in Transition*, p. 296.

3. Arthur Bonner, "The Russian Moves in Afghanistan," *The Reporter*, vol. XIV, no. 7 (April 5, 1956), p. 34.

4. Cited in Maung Maung, *Burma in the Family of Nations* (Amsterdam: Djambatan, Ltd., 1956), p. 81. The author added that Burmese nationalism in the first decades of the twentieth century "remained very much a gentleman's affair, courteous and calm and cautious, and most of the leaders were lawyers who had been trained in England and had great love for English institutions, and businessmen and journalists who had plenty of spare time on their hands." P. 82.

5. See the collection of Hayford's speeches edited by Magnus J. Sampson, *West African Leadership* (Ilfracombe, Devon: Arthur H. Stockwell, n.d.), pp. 39–41.

6. James S. Coleman, "Nationalism in Tropical Africa," *American Political Science Review*, vol. XLVIII, no. 2 (June 1954), p. 408. For the later period some of the difference is indicated in the suggestion of Thomas Hodgkin: "The spiritual ancestors of the Convention People's Party are Rousseau and Tom Paine; the ancestors of the United Gold Coast Convention are Locke and Burke." Cited by Bankole Timothy, *Kwame Nkrumah*, p. 68. For further comment on the development of African parties, see Coleman, "The Emergence of African Political Parties," *Africa Today*, ed. C. Grove Haines, pp. 225–256, and Hodgkin, *Nationalism in Colonial Africa*, pp. 139–168. Coleman's *Nigeria: Background to Nationalism* presents the Nigerian story in detail.

7. I am indebted to an unpublished manuscript on India by Lloyd I. and Susanne H. Rudolph for this comparison.

8. *The Arabs* (Harmondsworth, Middlesex: Penguin Books Ltd., 1955), p. 239.

9. See J. R. Hayden, *The Philippines*, p. 136.

10. In the Gold Coast the Watson Commission reported: "The fact that destooling — once the absolute privilege of a dissatisfied people, if need be exercised capriciously and violently — has been made the subject of a well-defined code under the supervision of the Government is itself the object of grave suspicion. The view is advanced that as long as a chief accepts and supports the Government policy he will receive Government support however much he has become the object of dislike to his people." *Report of the Commission of Enquiry* (London: H. M. S. O., 1948), Colonial No. 231, p. 3. The debate in the Gold Coast Legislative Council on the Native Administration Ordinance of 1927 throws much light on this

issue. The Ordinance, introduced by a chief and defended by other chiefs as well as by the government, was attacked as "taking away the traditional safeguards of the people against the development of the natural system of democratic monarchical rule into a system of autocratic rule." For this and other related materials I am indebted to the unpublished doctoral dissertation of Amon Nikoi, "Indirect Rule and Government in Gold Coast Colony, 1855–1954" (Harvard University, 1956).

11. Hubert Deschamps contends that in French Africa the installation of elective councils at higher levels and particularly the broadening of the franchise worked to strengthen the power of the chiefs. The basis of his argument is that the restricted franchise favored the *évolués* of the towns whereas the wide franchise brought in the peasantry among whom the chiefs had great influence. *L'Eveil Politique Africain* (Paris: Presses Universitaires de France, 1952), p. 99.

12. Hodgkin, *Nationalism in Colonial Africa*, p. 42.

13. For Morocco this position was stated by Ahmed Balafrej, who was Secretary General of the Istiqlal Party, and was shortly to become first Foreign Minister of the newly independent Moroccan state: "The Moroccan people cherish the hope of exercising the attributes of effective sovereignty and of seeing a régime of liberty, equality and democracy established in their country. They expect to enjoy freedom of expression, thought, assembly and movement such as exists in independent sovereign nations. They aspire, in other words, to a respectable way of life." "Morocco Plans for Independence," *Foreign Affairs*, vol. XXXIV, no. 3 (April 1956), p. 483. Note that democracy had now come to be identified with "a respectable way of life."

14. Rézette, *Les Partis politiques marocains*, p. 28. In a speech from the throne, on the twenty-fifth anniversary of his accession, the Sultan of Morocco proclaimed in November 1952: "No one can ignore the fact that we are living in an age of equality and democracy. Representative government is today regarded as the characteristic sign of the maturity of nations and their crowning achievement. We wish to organize the country on the basis of a constitutional monarchy. Our devotion to this principle is the greater in that it is sanctioned, or rather ordained, by Islam." For the corresponding developments in Tunisia, see Julien, *L'Afrique du Nord en Marche*, pp. 210, 260 ff.

CHAPTER XIV. NATIONALISM AND DEMOCRACY IN NON-COLONIAL COUNTRIES

1. E. Herbert Norman, *Japan's Emergence as a Modern State* (New York: Institute of Pacific Relations, 1940), p. 102.

2. *Japan's Modern Century* (New York: Ronald Press Co., 1955), p. 201. Norman said of this constitution that "it was conceived in a spirit of benevolent autocracy and has remained as the inflexible instrument of absolutism." P. 188. The political paradox to which Borton refered was also to be found in the constitution of Bismarckian Germany to which the Japanese turned for guidance in shaping their own constitution.

3. *Democracy and the Party Movement in Prewar Japan* (Berkeley and Los Angeles: University of California Press, 1953), p. 390.

4. Norman, *Japan's Emergence as a Modern State*, p. 30. William W. Lockwood remarked that whereas elements in the Japanese upper class, strategically located to bring Japan into the modern world, were influenced by new value orientations, the Chinese mandarinate, presenting a solid front, "faced backward, not forward, through the nineteenth century. As a result the Chinese merchant class, certainly no less enterprising or numerous than the Japanese in 1850, never succeeded in making that alliance with the State which was so important in laying the foundations of industrial capitalism in Japan, and earlier in Europe." "Japan's Response to the West: The Contrast with China," *World Politics*, vol. IX, no. 1 (October 1956), p. 46.

5. Cited in Ssu-yu Teng and John K. Fairbank, *China's Response to the West* (Cambridge, Mass.: Harvard University Press, 1954), p. 163. The following citation from Liang Ch'i-ch'ao is taken from the same source, pp. 221–222. It might be noted in passing that to the Communists Liang is "the mortal enemy of democratic revolution in the last days of the Manchu Dynasty." Hu Sheng, *Imperialism and Chinese Politics* (Peking: Foreign Language Press, 1955), p. 220.

6. Sun Yat-sen, *San Min Chu I*, p. 214. The following material comes from the same source. In relation to the concept of political tutelage, see also his *The Cult of Dr. Sun*, trans. Wei Yung (Shanghai: The Independent Weekly, 1931). A useful exposition of Sun's views on democracy is contained in Paul Myron Anthony Linebarger, *The Political Doctrines of Sun Yat-sen* (Baltimore: The Johns Hopkins Press, 1937).

7. *Revolution in China* (London: The Cresset Press, 1952), p. 44. For his analysis of China's lack of the requisites for democracy, see pp. 25 ff.

8. Chiang's interest in a return to China's more ancient ways is manifest throughout his *China's Destiny* (New York: The Macmillan Company, 1947). For a somewhat extreme version of this theme see Mary C. Wright, "From Revolution to Restoration: the Transformation of Kuomintang Ideology," *The Far Eastern Quarterly*, vol. XIV, no 4 (August 1955), pp. 515–522.

9. *United States Relations with China*, U.S. Department of State Publication 3573, August 1949, pp. 568–570. C. P. Fitzgerald held that it was the fear of social revolution which inhibited all Kuomintang support for the guerrilla resistance, and that it was the failure of the government to carry the revolution through to the villages which was the cause of its downfall. *Revolution in China*, p. 81.

10. See Charles Issawi, "Economic and Social Foundations of Democracy in the Middle East," *International Affairs*, vol. XXXII, no. 1 (January 1956), pp. 27–42.

11. Noting that the region was exposed to much Western interference but never to outright colonial rule, Dankwart A. Rustow commented that "its indigenous ruling classes generally survived the Western onslaught." *Politics and Western Civilization in the Near East* (Princeton: Center of International Studies, Princeton University, 1956), p. 3.

12. George Lenczowski divided Middle Eastern states into three cate-

gories: patriarchal societies — Saudi Arabia, Yemen, and Afghanistan; modernized societies — Turkey and Israel; and the intermediate societies which embrace the rest. His summary estimate of this third category was that "Their body politic is diseased, their statecraft weak, and their politics turbulent." "Political Institutions," *Mid-East: World-Center*, ed. Ruth Nanda Anshen (New York: Harper & Brothers, 1956), pp. 118–172.

13. *Whither Islam*, ed. H. A. R. Gibb (London: V. Gollancz Ltd., 1932), p. 327. He added: "The somewhat erratic workings of the representative system in most Moslem countries do not detract from the significance of the principle. The theory of absolutism has been definitely discarded, and its place taken by the theory of national sovereignty." A useful corrective to this position is contained in the suggestion of Dankwart A. Rustow that since Western political institutions were often adopted in the Middle East as much for reasons of foreign policy and defense as of domestic need, the allegiance to particular political systems has been opportunistic. Thus democratic institutions were adopted when they were generally favored. "Kemal Ataturk in Turkey and Reza Shah in Iran consolidated their dictatorial rule at a time when dictatorships were the fashion throughout Europe"; etc. *Politics and Westernization in the Near East*, pp. 13–14.

14. "Parliamentary Regimes in the Middle East," *Middle Eastern Affairs*, vol. IV, no. 8–9 (August-September 1953), p. 257.

15. *The Arabs*, pp. 118–119.

16. Jean Vigneau, "The Ideology of the Egyptian Revolution," *The Middle East in Transition*, ed. Walter Z. Laqueur (New York: Praeger, 1958), p. 144. Albert Hourani discerned in the political life of Egypt and Syria a return to "something like the pattern which existed in Mamluk and Ottoman days before it was disturbed by the coming of the West." The new regimes "rest on a combination of army officers, officials who have mastered the technique of modern administration, and educated nationalists." "The Decline of the West in the Middle East," *International Affairs*, vol. XXIX, no 2 (April 1953), p. 180.

17. Cited by Charles Issawi, "Economic and Social Foundations of Democracy in the Middle East," *International Affairs*, vol. XXXII, no. 1 (January 1956), p. 27.

18. Gamal Abdel Nasser, "The Egyptian Revolution," *Foreign Affairs*, vol. XXXIII, no. 2 (January 1955), p. 208.

19. *Egypt's Liberation: The Philosophy of the Revolution* (Washington, D.C.: Public Affairs Press, 1955), pp. 70–71.

20. *The Economist*, vol. CLXXVI, no. 5845 (September 3, 1955), p. 779. For a somewhat more detailed assessment of the Thai situation, see my *Representative Government in Southeast Asia* (Cambridge, Mass.: Harvard University Press, 1955), pp. 159–166.

CHAPTER XV. THE EROSION OF DEMOCRACY IN THE NEW STATES

1. Cited by C. Northcote Parkinson, *The Evolution of Political Thought* (Boston: Houghton Mifflin Co., 1958), p. 253. For the succeeding

quotation, see A. C. Wilgus, ed., *South American Dictators* (Washington, D.C.: George Washington University Press, 1937), p. 24.

2. *The New York Times*, March 24, 1957. Mr. King acknowledged that Ghana had better roads, schools, harbor facilities, and a more highly developed industry, agriculture, and public revenue. John Gunther, acknowledging the advantages of enlightened colonialism, reported that most educated Africans pay lip service to Liberia because of its independence, but inwardly despise it because it is regarded as a betrayal of what modern Africans stand for. *Inside Africa*, p. 847. He added (p. 860) that it is a striking phenomenon that three of Africa's independent states — Ethiopia, Libya, and Liberia — should be the poorest and most backward on the continent, much poorer than most colonial areas.

3. "Democracy is the Middle East — Its State and Prospects," *Middle Eastern Affairs*, vol. VI, no. 4 (April 1955), p. 105.

4. *The Interplay of East and West* (New York: W. W. Norton & Co., 1957), p. 47. See also Herbert Lüthy, "The Passing of the European Order," *Encounter*, vol. IX, no. 5 (November 1957), p. 6.

5. George McT. Kahin, Guy J. Pauker, and Lucian W. Pye, "Comparative Politics of Non-Western Countries," *American Political Science Review*, vol. XLIX, no. 4 (December 1955), p. 1024.

6. Charles Burton Marshall, "Reflections on a Revolution in Pakistan," *Foreign Affairs*, vol. XXXVII, no. 2 (January 1959), p. 253.

7. See Seymour Martin Lipset, "Some Social Requisites of Democracy: Economic Development and Political Legitimacy," *American Political Science Review*, vol. LIII, no. 1 (March 1959), pp. 69–105.

8. Cited by Zeine N. Zeine, *Arab-Turkish Relations and the Emergence of Arab Nationalism* (Beirut: Khayat's, 1958), p. 91, n. 3.

9. O. Mannoni came to the conclusion that the majority of Madagascans, if left to themselves, would spontaneously recreate a feudal type of society: "They would lack the courage to face the terrors of a genuine liberation of the individual." *Prospero and Caliban: The Psychology of Colonization* (New York: Frederick A. Praeger, 1956), p. 65.

10. U Law Yone, "Burma's Socialist Democracy," *The Atlantic Monthly*, vol. CCI, no. 2 (February 1958), p. 158.

11. *Wanted: An Asian Policy* (New York: Alfred A. Knopf, 1955), p. 165.

12. *The Social Contract*, book II, chap. vi.

13. *Dawn*, Nov. 1, 1958. For the preceding citation from Sukarno, see Gerald S. Maryanov, *Decentralization in Indonesia as a Political Problem*, Interim Reports Series of the Modern Indonesia Project (Ithaca: Department of Far Eastern Studies, Cornell University, 1958), pp. 49–50.

14. See the letter of the Press Attaché of the Pakistan Embassy, Washington, in the *Washington Post*, Jan. 30, 1959. This letter also asserted the maintenance of the rule of law and of civil administration by the new government.

15. J. H. Price, cited in Hansard Society for Parliamentary Government, *What Are the Problems of Parliamentary Government in West Africa?* (London: Hansard Society, 1958), p. 48.

16. *The Birth of Pantjasila*, 3rd ed. (Djakarta: Republic of Indonesia, Ministry of Information, 1958), p. 27.

17. *Ghana*, p. xvi. It takes little reading between the lines in Richard Wright's *Black Power* (New York: Harper & Brothers, 1954), to sense the danger to democracy in Nkrumah's methods; and Wright's concluding open letter to Nkrumah explicitly advocated a disciplined militarization of African life from above as a bridge to span the gap between tribal and industrialized ways of life.

18. *The Gold Coast in Transition*, pp. 202, 294. Nkrumah's biographer, Bankole Timothy, asserted that, because of fear of possible political rivalry, Nkrumah "surrounded himself with timeservers, job-hunters and syco-phants; in other words, 'yes-men' who were out for personal favours." *Kwame Nkrumah*, p. 118. Timothy, who was later expelled from Ghana, maintained that "There is no doubt at all that Nkrumah's success has, to a large extent, been due to the co-operation of the unsophisticated masses; their gullibility, their hero-worship, and their capacity for following blindly." P. 172.

19. Henry L. Bretton, "Current Political Thought and Practice in Ghana," *American Political Science Review*, vol. LII, no 1 (March 1958), p. 52. Seeing Ghana as a new country of conflicting tribes without any cohesion and lacking all possibility of making a Western style of democracy work, Peregrine Worsthorne accused the British of making dictatorship inevitable there through the "monstrous folly" of imposing parliamentary government as a face-saving device to cover colonial retreat. "Trouble in the Air," *Encounter*, vol. XII, no. 5 (May 1959), pp. 3–13.

20. *Our Struggle* (Yaba: John Okwesa & Co., 1955), pp. 30, 56. See *West Africa*, no. 2045 (June 23, 1956), p. 413 for a brief "Portrait" of Chike Obi. An earlier and more moderate version of elitism, asserting the rightful claim of the articulate minority to rule, was put forward by another Nigerian, Obafemi Awolo, later premier of Western Nigeria, in his *Path to Nigerian Freedom* (London: Faber and Faber, Ltd., 1947), p. 63.

21. Cited by Thomas F. Brady, *The New York Times*, section 4, May 3, 1959. He has also stated: "The party exercises a dictatorship, it is the dictatorship of the people." *Afrique Nouvelle* (Dakar), April 10, 1959.

22. Conference paper no. F/413, p. 2. The conference was held under the auspices of the Congress for Cultural Freedom in association with University College, Ibadan,, Nigeria.

23. "Summary of Discussions," Ibadan Conference, paper no. F/415, p. 4.

24. *New York Times*, April 20, 1959.

25. Cited in *Ghana Today*, vol. II, no. 23 (Jan. 7, 1959), p. 4. Raymond Aron has remarked that the prime necessity is a working machinery of government. "Particularly in the new states what is first needed is not an opposition but a majority." *Manchester Guardian Weekly*, Oct. 23, 1958.

26. Guy J. Pauker, "Southeast Asia as a Problem Area in the Next Decade," *World Politics*, vol. XI, no. 3 (April 1959), pp. 339–340.

27. *The British in Asia* (London: Faber and Faber, Ltd., 1947), p. 131.

28. "Party of the Second Party," *Harper's Magazine*, vol. CCXIII, no. 1269 (February 1956), p. 32.

CHAPTER XVI. THE PRINCIPLE OF SELF-DETERMINATION

1. *The Public Papers of Woodrow Wilson*, ed. Ray Stannard Baker and William E. Dodd (New York and London: Harper and Brothers, 1925), I, 542.

2. It pleased the fancy of Sir W. Ivor Jennings to say that a professor of political science who was also President of the United States enunciated a ridiculous doctrine which was widely accepted as sensible: self-determination. "On the surface it seemed reasonable: let the people decide. It was in fact ridiculous because the people cannot decide until somebody decides who are the people." *The Approach to Self-Government*, p. 56.

3. Erno Wittmann, *Past and Future of the Right of National Self-Determination* (Amsterdam: Van Holkema and Warendorf, 1919), p. 53.

4. *Survey of British Commonwealth Affairs* (London, New York, Toronto: Oxford University Press, 1937), I, 500.

5. Chapter X of the Constitution lays it down that by a two-thirds vote of the State Council any State may pass a resolution in favor of secession. Thereupon the President of the Union shall order a plebiscite to ascertain the will of the people of the State concerned. See Josef Silverstein, "Politics in the Shan State: The Question of Secession from the Union of Burma," *Journal of Asian Studies*, vol. XVIII, no. 1 (November 1958), pp. 43–57.

6. This episode is briefly treated by Cobban, *National Self-Determination*, pp. 27–28, and more elaborately in the histories and documentary collections dealing with the drafting of the Covenant.

7. See F. van Langenhove, "Aspects Récents du Principe des Nationalités," *La Revue Générale Belge*, vol. LXXXVIII (November 1952), p. 11; D. B. Levin, "Foreign Policy of the U.S.S.R. and International Law," *U.S.S.R. Information Bulletin*, vol. VIII, no. 1 (January 14, 1948), p. 6.

8. *Documents of the United Nations Conference on International Organization* (London, New York: United Nations Information Organizations in cooperation with the Library of Congress, 1945), VI, 296, Doc. 343. The Committee's Rapporteur emphasized the necessity of securing "a free and genuine expression of the will of the people, which avoids cases of the alleged expression of the popular will, such as those used for their own ends by Germany and Italy in later years." P. 396, Doc. 885.

9. For a review of the concern of the United Nations with these problems, see Benjamin Rivlin, "Self-Determination and Dependent Areas," *International Conciliation*, no. 501 (January 1955).

10. For a summary of these actions and the texts of the resolutions, see Commission on Human Rights, *Report of the Eighth Session; Economic and Social Council, Official Records*, 14th Session, Supp. No. 4, U.N. Docs. E/2256, E/CN 4/669. A number of the key issues involved in this session of the Human Rights Commission are usefully spelled out in an

article by Charles Malik, "Human Rights in the United Nations," *United Nations Bulletin*, vol. XIII, no. 5 (September 1, 1952), pp. 248–253.

11. The citation from the Committee of Jurists appears in the *League of Nations Official Journal*, Special Supp. No. 3 (October 1920), p. 5; that from the Commission of Rapporteurs in *Report of the Commission of Rapporteurs*, April 16, 1921, League Council Doc. B.7. 21/68/106.

12. For Metternich, see *Nachgelassene Papiere* (Vienna: W. Braumueller, 1880–84), V, 315–316. Carl Sandburg gives the text of Lincoln's first Inaugural in *Abraham Lincoln, The War Years* (New York: Harcourt, Brace & Co., 1939), I, 132. Indicating the extent to which circumstances determine cases, a quite contrary view was expressed by Lincoln in 1848 in relation to the Mexican war. At this time he said: "Any people anywhere being inclined and having the power have the right to rise up and shake off the existing government, and form a new one which suits them better. This is a most valuable, a most sacred right — a right which we hope and believe is to liberate the world. Nor is this right confined to cases in which the whole people of an existing government may choose to exercise it. Any portion of such people that can may revolutionize and make their own so much of the territory as they inhabit." *The Speeches of Abraham Lincoln* (London, New York: The Chesterfield Society, 1908), p. 20.

13. *Report of the States Reorganization Commission*, p. 64.

14. Harry S. Truman, *Memoirs* (New York: Doubleday and Co., Inc., 1955), I, 237. For a cautiously worded statement of the American position, see the article by Deputy Under-Secretary of State Robert Murphy, "The Principle of Self-Determination in International Relations," *Department of State Bulletin*, vol. XXXIII, no. 857 (November 28, 1955), pp. 889–894. For a similar statement in relation to dependent areas, see a speech by Assistant Secretary of State Henry A. Byroade, "United States Policy and the Colonial Problem," Department of State Bulletin, vol. XXIX, no. 751 (November 16, 1953), pp. 655–660.

15. *Between Red and White* (London: Communist Party of Great Britain, 1922), p. 86.

16. A number of the key issues were explored by Clyde Eagleton, "Excesses of Self-Determination," *Foreign Affairs*, vol. XXXI, no. 14 (July 1953), pp. 592–604. See also Günter Decker, *Das Selbtsbestimmungsrecht der Nationen* (Göttingen: Verlag Otto Schwarz & Co., 1955).

17. See Rivlin, "Self-Determination and Dependent Areas," *International Conciliation*, no. 501 (January 1955), p. 221.

18. The Report is printed as Appendix H by George Antonius, *The Arab Awakening* (London: Hamish Hamilton, 1938).

19. One of the most uncompromising expressions of this position was made in the Security Council on May 31, 1956, when it was proposed that the Secretary General be asked to continue his good offices in the Palestine area and to seek a peace settlement on a mutually acceptable basis. The latter phrase brought from the Syrian representative, Ahmed el Shukairy, the bitter comment that the only basis acceptable to the Arabs would be the reversal of everything which had happened since the partition resolution on November 29, 1947. "A homeland is the sacred possession of its

people, its legitimate people; and the people, the legitimate people, are lord and master in their homeland, be they Jews, Moslems, or Christians without discrimination . . . . For our part, Palestine is part and parcel of the Arab homeland. The Arab world is not prepared to surrender one single atom of their right to this sacred territory — let alone subjugating them to the acceptance or refusal of Israel." *The New York Times*, June 1, 1956.

20. Alan Lennox-Boyd, Secretary of State for the Colonies, attributed the refusal to the fear of the leaders of the Greek Orthodox Church that democratic institutions would cost them their temporal power. *British Record* (Political and Economic Notes Issued by British Information Services), June 8, 1956, p. 3.

21. This position has been regularly reiterated by the British. See for example, the statement of the Secretary of State for Foreign Affairs in the House of Commons on July 19, 1956: "If it were to be accepted that people have a right to self-determination whenever they ask for it, it would make nonsense of organized international society. I have never heard the most virulent supporters of self-determination suggest that the Turkish Cypriots should have the right of self-determination." *Cyprus* (New York: British Information Services), publications no. T. 26, July 29, 1956, p. 3. The proposal that the island should be partitioned between Greek and Turkish Cypriots has, however, been seriously advanced on several occasions.

22. Cheddi Jagan, *Forbidden Freedom: The Story of British Guiana* (London: Lawrence and Wishart, 1954), p. 95. Jagan, of East Indian descent, was educated in Chicago.

23. *Constitutional Commission Report*, Cmd. 9274 (London: H.M.S.O., 1954), p. 68. The Commission also concluded that the difficulties arose not from the ignorance or impetuosity of the P.P.P. but from deliberate refusal to believe in the possibility of achieving self-government by peaceful means and a consequent determination to invite rather than avoid a crisis.

24. This point was well brought out by J. Pera, "Paternalisme et Nationalités: Réflexions sur la politique coloniale," *L'Année politique et économique*, vol. XXV, no. 108 (June-August 1952).

25. "Togoland," *International Conciliation*, no. 509 (September 1956), p. 5.

26. See Buell, *The Native Problem in Africa*, II, 361-362.

27. One French version, put forward by a former Minister of Overseas France, portrayed the entire Ewe case as being ingeniously fabricated by the British Colonial Office to secure the whole of Togoland for the Gold Coast. Mitterand, *Présence Française et Abandon*, pp. 203 ff.

28. The General Assembly in Resolution 742 (VIII) of 1953 indicated the desirability of ensuring "the freedom of the population of a Territory which has associated itself with the metropolitan country to modify at any time this status through the expression of their will by democratic means," thus lending sanction to a continuing right of revolution.

29. The final version of the statute is to be found in Decree No. 56-847 of August 24, 1956, *Journal officiel de la République française*, no. 198 (August 26, 1956). Although the new statute represented a distinctive

advance over the prior political status of French Togoland, it was still far from giving full internal self-government.

30. "Be in Harmony with the Will of God," a speech delivered by President Sukarno on August 17, 1954, and issued by the Indonesian Ministry of Information. The Indonesians have denied that self-determination is involved in the West Irian dispute "since the whole Indonesian nation, including naturally West Irian, already exercised the right of self-determination on 17 August 1945, when it threw off the chains of colonialism and proclaimed Indonesia free and independent." *Report on Indonesia*, vol. VIII, no. 3 (January-February 1957), p. 30.

31. U.N. Doc. A/C.3/SR.444 (1952).

CHAPTER XVII. SELF-DETERMINATION IN PLURAL SOCIETIES

1. *Netherlands India* (Cambridge: Cambridge University Press, 1939), p. 468.

2. *Swords into Ploughshares* (New York: Random House, 1956), pp. 137-138.

3. See *Definition and Classification of Minorities*, Memorandum submitted by the Secretary-General to the Sub-Commission on Prevention of Discrimination and Protection of Minorities, Commission on Human Rights, U.N. Doc. E/CN.4/Sub.2/85 (1949).

4. *Kenya's Opportunity*, p. 154.

5. Cited by Hewan Craig, *The Legislative Council of Trinidad and Tobago* (London: Faber and Faber, 1952), p. 19.

6. *An African Survey*, p. 445.

7. *Future Policy for Kenya* (New York: British Information Services), publication no. T.29, April 23, 1959.

8. Charles R. Nixon, "The Conflict of Nationalisms in South Africa," *World Politics*, vol. XI, no. 1 (October 1958), pp. 54-55.

9. "Race Relations in the Commonwealth," *International Affairs*, vol. XXVI, no. 3 (July 1950), p. 314.

10. Cited by Cobban, *National Self-Determination*, p. 62. See also René Capitant, "Nation et démocratie," *Esprit*, vol. XXIII, no. 224 (March 1955), pp. 373-374.

11. Cited by Richard Symonds, *The Making of Pakistan* (London: Faber and Faber, 1950), pp. 30-31. The following "two nations" citation is derived from the same source. Lord Dufferin, Viceroy from 1884 to 1888, spoke of India as being composed of a large number of distinct nationalities, and of the Moslems as "a nation of fifty millions." See the *Montagu-Chelmsford Report*, Cd. 9109 (London: H.M.S.O., 1918), p. 117.

12. For the text to the address presented by the Moslem deputation to Lord Minto, and the latter's reply, see B. R. Ambedkar, *Pakistan, or the Partition of India*, Appendix XII.

13. See *Speeches and Statements of Iqbal*, compiled by "Shamloo."

14. *Report of the Indian Statutory Commission*, Cmd. 3586 (London: H.M.S.O., 1930), I, 29. Wilfred Cantwell Smith adds that in the 1930's it was not only the Moslems who were asserting themselves but also a num-

ber of other minor Indian "nationalisms." *Modern Islam in India* (London: Victor Gollancz Ltd., 1946), p. 191.

15. F. K. Khan Durrani, *The Meaning of Pakistan*, pp. 96–97. In good nationalist fashion Durrani asserted that what happens in the India of the Hindus is no concern of the Moslems: "Muslims as a nation can, in the first place, be interested only in their own security and well-being." P. 132.

16. For the text of this resolution see Rajendra Prasad, *India Divided* (Bombay: Hind Kitabs, 1947), pp. 211–212.

17. Cited by A. R. Desai, *Social Background of Indian Nationalism*, p. 383.

18. See Jamil-Ud-Din Ahmad, *Some Recent Speeches and Writings of Mr. Jinnah* (Lahore: M. Ashraf, 1947), I, 155. Volume II of this work gives the text of the wartime exchange of letters between Rajagopalachari and Gandhi on one side and Jinnah on the other, which are very revealing as to basic positions and attitudes.

19. *The Economist*, vol. CLXXXI, no. 5909 (November 2, 1956), p. 432.

20. *South-East Asia Between Two Worlds* (London: Turnstile Press, 1955), p. 270.

21. Cmd. 9274 (London: H.M.S.O., 1954), p. 15.

22. See *Africa Today*, ed. C. Grove Haines, pp. 225–256.

23. F. Oladipo Onipede, "African Nationalism: A Critical Portrait," *Dissent*, vol. III, no. 3 (Summer 1956), p. 279.

24. *Sociologie des Brazzavilles Noires*, p. 160. See also Hodgkin, *Nationalism in Colonial Africa*, pp. 84–87. Although Hodgkin here indicated the importance of the tribal associations, he suggested elsewhere that the changes presently under way in West Africa were weakening the hold of "tribal nationalism" and emphasizing "the common interests of clerks, teachers, railwaymen, lorry drivers and market women." "Towards Self-Government in British West Africa," *The New West Africa*, ed. Basil Davidson (London: Allen & Unwin, 1953), p. 98.

25. Although opposition by the Western-educated elements to the chiefs was the general rule, not all the early nationalists took this position. For example, Dr. J. B. Danquah, later one of the principal political figures in the Gold Coast, wrote in 1927 in the preface to a West African Student's Union pamphlet that, "if West Africa is to sustain an intensive national consciousness in the larger Imperial programme, no effective progress can be achieved except through the aboriginal rulers, through whom alone concerted action against all obstacles obstructing Negro progress in West Africa can be carried out." Cited by Philip Garique, "The West African Students' Union," *Africa*, vol. XXIII, no 1 (January 1953), p. 57.

26. For the French territories Hubert Deschamps reported that democracy restored political importance to the chiefs: their influence increased as the suffrage expanded to embrace the peasants, whereas a restricted suffrage favored the urban *évolués*. *L'Eveil Politique Africain*, p. 99.

27. For a full-scale survey, see Coleman, *Nigeria: Background to Nationalism*. The tribal complexities of Nigeria are well indicated in the 1958 *Report of the Commission Appointed to Enquire into the Fears of Minorities and the Means of Allaying Them*, Cmnd. 505.

28. Introduction to Joan Wheare, *The Nigerian Legislative Council*, p. x.

29. *West African Pilot*, July 6 and 7, 1949. Azikiwe later formulated his national conceptions differently. In a speech in London in 1955 he contended that Nigerians must now embark upon the building of a solid Nigerian nationality, educating the people to realize that "Nigeria is no longer a mere geographical expression but a nation in the emergence. We must teach our people that a nation is not necessarily racial or tribal, but an historically constituted community of peoples based on community of interests with which are interwoven community of race, community of language, community of religion, geographic unity and common political aspirations." "Zik's Views on Nigerian Constitution," *Venture*, vol. VII, no. 7 (December 1955), p. 5.

30. See Lord Hailey, *Native Administration in the British African Territories* (London: H.M.S.O., 1951), III, 22; and Philip Garigue, "Changing Political Leadership in West Africa," *Africa*, vol. XXIV, no. 3 (July 1954), pp. 223–224.

31. See the Oduduwa Day special edition of the *Nigerian Tribune*, June 5, 1950.

32. See J. Gus Liebenow, Jr., "Responses to Planned Political Change in a Tanganyika Tribal Group," *The American Political Science Review*, vol. L, no. 2 (June 1956), p. 447.

33. *Report of the Commission of Inquiry into the Disturbances in the Southern Sudan During August, 1955* (Sudan: McCorquedale & Co. Ltd., 1956), p. 81.

CHAPTER XVIII. TRADITIONALISM AND COMMUNISM

1. Cited by Sir Verney Lovett, *A History of the Indian Nationalist Movement* (London: John Murray, 1921), p. 89.

2. Cited by Harold Cooper, "Political Preparedness for Self-government," *Annals of the American Academy of Political and Social Science*, vol. CCCVI (July 1956), p. 71.

3. *The New York Times*, April 8, 1956. Similar threats against the privileges of the English-educated followed the electoral victory in May 1959, of the People's Action party in Singapore.

4. W. F. Wertheim wrote that in Indonesia the new élite of intellectuals, near-intellectuals, and the rising merchant class was only a thin upper crust, and that "the peasantry will, before long, become a decisive factor in the balance of social power." *Indonesian Society in Transition* (The Hague, Bandung: W. van Hoeve Ltd., 1956), p. 164.

5. Simon Kuznets has rightly warned that such a spread may not in fact take place. "International Differences in Income Levels: Some Reflections on Their Causes," *Economic Development and Cultural Change*, vol. II, no 1 (April 1953), p. 25.

6. I am indebted for the following analysis to Nadav Safran, "Modern Egypt in Search of an Ideology" (Unpublished Harvard Ph.D. dissertation, 1958).

7. *The Taming of the Nations* (New York: Macmillan, 1952), pp. 68–69. A similar position is taken in relation to Southeast Asia by Tibor Mende, *South-East Asia Between Two Worlds* (London: Turnstile Press, 1955), p. 271.

8. See Maurice Zinkin, *Development for Free Asia*, chap. ix: "The Role of the Politician."

9. I have elaborated somewhat on this theme in "The Progress of Nationalism," *Nationalism and Progress in Free Asia*, ed. Philip Thayer (Baltimore: The Johns Hopkins Press, 1956), pp. 71–82.

10. The extensive excerpts from the speeches of Khrushchev and Bulganin in India, Burma, and Afghanistan printed in the *Current Digest of the Soviet Press*, vol. VII, nos. 47, 48, and 49, amply repay reading.

11. Adam B. Ulam, "The Historical Role of Marxism and the Soviet System," *World Politics*, vol. VIII, no. 1 (October 1955), p. 29. Note also the comment of John Plamenatz that "Bolshevism is the distorted Marxism of a backward society exposed to the impact of the West." *German Marxism and Russian Communism* (London, New York, Toronto: Longmans, Green & Co., 1954), p. 318.

12. *Colonial Policy and Practice* (Cambridge: Cambridge University Press, 1948), p. 442.

13. What Giorgio Borsa says of China and the Chinese intelligentsia obviously has wider applicability: "In Lenin's theory of imperialism they found a way out from the contradiction by which the pro-Western intelligentsia in Asia was always embarrassed: by making capitalism alone responsible for the degradation of colonial and semi-colonial countries, Leninism justified the acceptance of other aspects of Western civilization such as industrialism, technical and scientific progress, universal education, etc." "A Historical Perspective for Western Policy in Asia," *Confluence*, vol. IV, no. 4 (January 1956), p. 416. See also Bernard Lewis, "The Middle Eastern Reaction to Soviet Pressures," *Middle East Journal*, vol. X, no 2 (Spring 1956), p. 130.

14. *Communism* (New York: Henry Holt & Co., 1927), p. 250.

15. "The Communist Problem in East Asia — An Asian View," *Pacific Affairs*, vol. XXIV, no. 3 (September 1951), pp. 229–230. Raymond Aron concluded that Communism, no longer addressing itself to mature capitalisms but to the nations humiliated or enslaved by the West, "has become a kind of national-socialism." *Les Guerres en Chaine*, 11th ed. (Paris: Gallimard, 1951), p. 162.

16. *The New York Times*, September 1, 1954.

17. Taya Zinkin, "Indian Foreign Policy: An Interpretation of Attitudes," *World Politics*, vol. VII, no. 2 (January 1955), p. 183.

18. *Wanted: An Asian Policy*, p. 133. Guy Wint saw the Chinese Revolution as the most intransigent of the Asian replies to pressure from the West, providing the extreme nationalists of other countries with "the model for the root and branch emancipation which they have not themselves achieved." *The British in Asia*, p. 223.

19. Geoffrey Fairbairn, "Aspects of the Burmese Political Scene," *Pacific Affairs*, vol. XXIX, no. 2 (September 1956), p. 211. For a general estimate of future prospects, stressing the strong position of Communism,

see Zbigniew Brzezinski, "The Politics of Underdevelopment," *World Politics*, vol. IX, no. 1 (October 1956), pp. 55–75.

20. Cited in *West Africa*, no. 1932 (March 6, 1954), p. 199. The visit of Richard Wright, an American ex-Communist, to the Gold Coast brought him to the somewhat oddly slanted conclusion that he knew enough about Communism to know that this was not Communism, which "was, above all, ideological; and what I had seen was the quintessence of passion." *Black Power*, p. 91.

CHAPTER XIX. THE VIRTUES OF NATIONALISM

1. *A Study of History*, IV, 185 and 163.
2. *The New York Times*, February 5, 1957. François Mitterand denounced as absurd a tendency toward national independence in Algeria and French tropical Africa, since there are no examples of national entities in Africa's past, and in Europe powerful nations are finding it necessary to renounce some of their sovereignty. "Il y a donc beaucoup de vanité dans cette floraison de nationalismes retardataires, sectaires et bornés." "Paradoxes et Promesses de L'Union française," *La Nef*, vol. XII, cahier no. 9, nouvelle série (June 1955), pp. 228–229.
3. Contrasting the British with the earlier rulers of India who "passed over like clouds . . . a mere drift over her surface of life," Rabindranath Tagore concluded that "this time we had to deal, not with kings, not with human races, but with a nation — we, who are no nation ourselves." *Nationalism*, pp. 18–19.
4. "Indeed, the denial of nationality may be regarded as the hallmark of imperialism at a certain stage in relation to a subject people; and the time may yet come when a learned American thesis will be written, with abundant factual evidence, to prove the 'vulgar error' of British nationality." R. Palme Dutt, cited by Victor Purcell, *Malaya, Communist or Free?* (London: Victor Gollancz, Ltd., 1954), p. 143.
5. *Viet-Nam: Sociologie d'une Guerre* (Paris: Editions du Seuil, 1952), p. 153.
6. U Ba U, *My Burma: The Autobiography of a President* (New York: Taplinger Publishing Co., 1959), p. 37.
7. *The Discovery of India*, pp. 274–275.
8. *The New York Times*, November 22, 1956.
9. *The Suez Canal Problem*, U.S. Department of State publication no. 6392, October 1956, p. 28.
10. Mollie Panter-Downes, "Letter from London," December 1, 1956, p. 158.
11. *Moral Man and Immoral Society* (New York: Charles Schibner's Sons, 1932), pp. 48–49; for a general treatment of the issue, see ch. iv, "The Morality of Nations." Even in Nazism the altruistic elements bulk large for the individual. A Nazi leader is quoted as saying: "I could not ignore the nation to which I belong; it was there with all its failings and weaknesses. If I was guilty, if we were all guilty, then our guilt was based on love."

Ernst von Salomon, *Fragebogen* (New York: Doubleday & Co., 1955), p. 520.

12. Karl W. Deutsch and others working with him on the problem of the formation of political communities declared that they had "found not a single full-fledged modern social-service state that has successfully federated or otherwise merged with another." *Political Community and the North Atlantic Area* (Princeton, N.J.: Princeton University Press, 1957), p. 22.

13. See J. A. Hobson, *Imperialism: A Study*, 3rd ed. (London: George Allen & Unwin, Ltd., 1948), p. 11; Thomas G. Masaryk, *The New Europe* (London: Eyre & Spottiswoode, Ltd., 1918), p. 26; Sun Yat-sen, *San Min Chu I*, p. 89. For the Nkrumah remark, see Bankole Timothy, *Kwame Nkrumah*, p. 186. Erno Wittman held that "the French Revolution proclaimed the right of nations to self-determination as a means of securing eternal peace." *Past and Future of the Right of Self-Determination*, p. 83.

14. "Nationality," *History of Freedom and Other Essays*, p. 299.

15. Cited by F. Melian Stawell, *The Growth of International Thought* (New York: Henry Holt & Co., 1930), p. 149.

16. *The Discovery of India*, p. 425. The Moslem League adopted the same kind of position: the Moslems in India would cooperate with the Hindus if they were granted freedom and equality.

17. *Internationalism and Nationalism* (Peking: Foreign Languages Press, 1951), pp. 8, 40.

18. *Collected Works of V. I. Lenin*, vol. XX: *The Revolution of 1917* (London: Martin Lawrence, Ltd., 1929), book II, p. 29. "We demand the freedom of self-determination, *i. e.*, independence, *i. e.*, the freedom of separation for the oppressed nations, not because we dream of an economically atomised world, nor because we cherish the ideal of small states, but on the contrary because we are for large states and for a coming closer, even a fusion of nations, but on a truly democratic, truly internationalist basis, which is *unthinkable* without the freedom of separation." "The Revolutionary Proletariat and the Right of Nations to Self-Determination," *Collected Works*, vol. XVIII: *The Imperial War*, p. 373.

19. "The International Character of the October Revolution," *The October Revolution* (New York: International Publishers, 1934), p. 160. (Italics in the original.)

20. *The New York Times*, February 4, 1957. Later in the year Defense Minister V. K. Krishna Menon, warning the Security Council off from action in relation to Kashmir, not only repudiated the idea of a UN force operating there, but also declared: "We will not permit the UN to get away with the idea that our sovereignty is at the disposal of votes." *Indiagram* (Washington: Information Service of India), no. 36, (September 20, 1957), p. 4.

21. Speech in the Lok Sabha (House of the People), March 26, 1957, as reprinted by the Information Service of India, Washington, D.C., April 10, 1957.

22. *An International Economy* (New York: Harper & Brothers, 1956), p. 320.

CHAPTER XX. THE NEW NATIONS AND
THE INTERNATIONAL COMMUNITY

1. See Edward Hallett Carr, *The Twenty Years' Crisis, 1919–1939* (London: Macmillan & Co., 1940), p. 105.

2. *United Nations Review*, vol. III, no. 2 (August 1956), p. 43.

3. *Swords into Ploughshares* (New York: Random House, 1956), pp. 239–240.

4. Cited by Dorothy Borg, *American Policy and the Chinese Revolution: 1925–1928* (New York: The Macmillan Co., 1947), p. 229.

5. *Congressional Record*, 58th Congress, 3rd Session, p. 19.

6. Cited by W. D. Puleston, *Mahan* (New Haven: Yale University Press, 1939), p. 217.

7. *United Nations Review*, vol. I, no. 7 (January 1955), p. 76.

8. *The New Republic*, December 17, 1956, p. 10.

9. "Colonial Issues and Policies with Special Reference to Tropical Africa," *Annals of the American Academy of Social and Political Science*, vol. CCXCVIII, March 1955, p. 84.

10. See Maurice Duverger, "Aid Given by the Mother Country to Colonized Peoples: the Example of France," *Confluence*, vol. IV, no. 4 (January 1956), p. 422.

11. For the Secretary-General's original proposal, see *United Nations Review*, vol. III, no. 1 (July 1956), pp. 10–15. A later and somewhat more modest version was presented to the Economic and Social Council in the Secretary-General's memorandum of June 10, 1957, entitled *An International Administrative Service*, U.N. Doc. E/3107.

12. *The New York Times*, September 12, 1957.

13. *An International Economy* (New York: Harper & Brothers, 1956), p. 133. Contrasting the relative homogeneity of the British people with the heterogeneity of Asian and African peoples, Sir Ivor Jennings made the same point: "In Asia there is greater wealth, more spectacular and flamboyant, while at the other extreme are hundreds of millions living at a level which Western Europe has long since forgotten and North America never known." *The Approach to Self-Government*, p. 79.

14. *The Wealth of Nations*, p. 591.

Index

M/